Emerging Practices for Online Language Assessment, Exams, Evaluation, and Feedback

Asli Lidice Gokturk-Saglam
University of South Eastern Norway, Norway

Ece Sevgi-Sole
University of Milan, Italy

A volume in the Advances in Educational Technologies and Instructional Design (AETID) Book Series

Published in the United States of America by
IGI Global
Information Science Reference (an imprint of IGI Global)
701 E. Chocolate Avenue
Hershey PA, USA 17033
Tel: 717-533-8845
Fax: 717-533-8661
E-mail: cust@igi-global.com
Web site: http://www.igi-global.com

Copyright © 2023 by IGI Global. All rights reserved. No part of this publication may be reproduced, stored or distributed in any form or by any means, electronic or mechanical, including photocopying, without written permission from the publisher. Product or company names used in this set are for identification purposes only. Inclusion of the names of the products or companies does not indicate a claim of ownership by IGI Global of the trademark or registered trademark.
Library of Congress Cataloging-in-Publication Data

Names: Gokturk-Saglam, Asli Lidice, DATE- editor. | Sevgi-Sole, Ece, DATE- editor.
Title: Emerging practices for online language assessment, exams, evaluation, and feedback / edited by: Asli Lidice Gokturk-Saglam, and Ece Sevgi-Sole.
Description: Hershey, PA : Information Science Reference, [2023] | Includes bibliographical references and index. | Summary: "Emerging Practices for Online Language Assessment, Exams, Evaluation, and Feedback investigates the main challenges of online language assessment when migrating from an in-class to an online environment due to academic integrity, adaptation to the new testing environment, technical problems, and anxiety. Covering key topics such as parental involvement, selfassessment, and language learners, this premier reference source is ideal for administrators, policymakers, industry professionals, researchers, academicians, scholars, practitioners, instructors, and students"-- Provided by publisher.
Identifiers: LCCN 2023004842 (print) | LCCN 2023004843 (ebook) | ISBN 9781668462270 (hardcover) | ISBN 9781668462317 (paperback) | ISBN 9781668462287 (ebook)
Subjects: LCSH: Language and languages--Ability testing. | Language and languages--Examinations. | Language and languages--Web-based instruction.
Classification: LCC P53.4 .E64 2023 (print) | LCC P53.4 (ebook) | DDC 418.0076--dc23/eng/20230419
LC record available at https://lccn.loc.gov/2023004842
LC ebook record available at https://lccn.loc.gov/2023004843

This book is published in the IGI Global book series Advances in Educational Technologies and Instructional Design (AETID) (ISSN: 2326-8905; eISSN: 2326-8913)

British Cataloguing in Publication Data
A Cataloguing in Publication record for this book is available from the British Library.

All work contributed to this book is new, previously-unpublished material. The views expressed in this book are those of the authors, but not necessarily of the publisher.

For electronic access to this publication, please contact: eresources@igi-global.com.

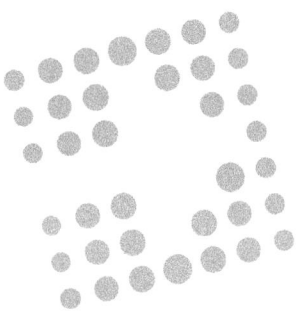

Advances in Educational Technologies and Instructional Design (AETID) Book Series

Lawrence A. Tomei
Robert Morris University, USA

ISSN:2326-8905
EISSN:2326-8913

Mission

Education has undergone, and continues to undergo, immense changes in the way it is enacted and distributed to both child and adult learners. In modern education, the traditional classroom learning experience has evolved to include technological resources and to provide online classroom opportunities to students of all ages regardless of their geographical locations. From distance education, Massive-Open-Online-Courses (MOOCs), and electronic tablets in the classroom, technology is now an integral part of learning and is also affecting the way educators communicate information to students.

The **Advances in Educational Technologies & Instructional Design (AETID) Book Series** explores new research and theories for facilitating learning and improving educational performance utilizing technological processes and resources. The series examines technologies that can be integrated into K-12 classrooms to improve skills and learning abilities in all subjects including STEM education and language learning. Additionally, it studies the emergence of fully online classrooms for young and adult learners alike, and the communication and accountability challenges that can arise. Trending topics that are covered include adaptive learning, game-based learning, virtual school environments, and social media effects. School administrators, educators, academicians, researchers, and students will find this series to be an excellent resource for the effective design and implementation of learning technologies in their classes.

Coverage

- K-12 Educational Technologies
- Classroom Response Systems
- Digital Divide in Education
- Collaboration Tools
- Adaptive Learning
- Instructional design
- Higher Education Technologies
- E-Learning
- Curriculum development
- Virtual School Environments

IGI Global is currently accepting manuscripts for publication within this series. To submit a proposal for a volume in this series, please contact our Acquisition Editors at Acquisitions@igi-global.com or visit: http://www.igi-global.com/publish/.

The Advances in Educational Technologies and Instructional Design (AETID) Book Series (ISSN 2326-8905) is published by IGI Global, 701 E. Chocolate Avenue, Hershey, PA 17033-1240, USA, www.igi-global.com. This series is composed of titles available for purchase individually; each title is edited to be contextually exclusive from any other title within the series. For pricing and ordering information please visit http://www.igi-global.com/book-series/advances-educational-technologies-instructional-design/73678. Postmaster: Send all address changes to above address. Copyright © 2023 IGI Global. All rights, including translation in other languages reserved by the publisher. No part of this series may be reproduced or used in any form or by any means – graphics, electronic, or mechanical, including photocopying, recording, taping, or information and retrieval systems – without written permission from the publisher, except for non commercial, educational use, including classroom teaching purposes. The views expressed in this series are those of the authors, but not necessarily of IGI Global.

Titles in this Series

For a list of additional titles in this series, please visit: www.igi-global.com/book-series

Cases on Effective Universal Design for Learning Implementation Across Schools
Frederic Fovet (Royal Roads University, Cnada)
Information Science Reference • © 2023 • 300pp • H/C (ISBN: 9781668447505) • US $215.00

Multifaceted Analysis of Sustainable Strategies and Tactics in Education
Theresa Dell Neimann (Oregon State University, USA) Lynne L. Hindman (Oregon State University, USA) Elena Shliakhovchuk (The Polytechnic University of Valencia, Spain) Marian Moore (Austin Community College, USA) and Jonathan J. Felix (RMIT University, Vitnam)
Information Science Reference • © 2023 • 300pp • H/C (ISBN: 9781668460351) • US $215.00

Fostering Diversity and Inclusion Through Curriculum Transformation
Cily Elizabeth Mamatle Tabane (University of South Africa, South Africa) Boitumelo Molebogeng Diale (University of Johannesburg, South Africa) Ailwei Solomon Mawela (University of South Africa, South Africa) and Thulani Vincent Zengele (University of South Africa, South Africa)
Information Science Reference • © 2023 • 315pp • H/C (ISBN: 9781668469958) • US $215.00

Handbook of Research on Implementing Inclusive Educational Models and Technologies for Equity and Diversity
Paula Escudeiro (ISEP, Polytechnic of Porto, Portugal & GILT, ATHENA European University, Portugal) Nuno Escudeiro (ISEP, Polytechnic of Porto, Portugal & GILT, ATHENA European University, Portugal) and Oscar Bernardes (ISEP, Polytechnic of Porto, Portugal & University of Aveiro, Portugal & GILT, ATHENA European University, Portugal)
Information Science Reference • © 2023 • 420pp • H/C (ISBN: 9798369304532) • US $270.00

Building Inclusive Education in K-12 Classrooms and Higher Education Theories and Principles
Kiyoji Koreeda (Toyo University, Japan) Masayoshi Tsuge (University of Tsukuba, Japan) Shigeru Ikuta (Otsuma Women's University, Japan) Elizabeth Minchin Dalton (Dalton Education Services International, USA) and Linda Plantin Ewe (Kristianstad University, Sweden)
Information Science Reference • © 2023 • 339pp • H/C (ISBN: 9781668473702) • US $215.00

Technology Management and Its Social Impact on Education
P.C. Lai (University of Malaya, Malaysia)
Information Science Reference • © 2023 • 310pp • H/C (ISBN: 9781668491034) • US $215.00

701 East Chocolate Avenue, Hershey, PA 17033, USA
Tel: 717-533-8845 x100 • Fax: 717-533-8661
E-Mail: cust@igi-global.com • www.igi-global.com

Editorial Advisory Board

Henrik Bohn, *University of South-Eastern Norway, Norway*
Thomas Wulstan Christiansen, *Università del Salento, Italy*
Slobodanka Dimova, *University of Copenhagen, Denmark*
Hossein Farhady, *Yeditepe University, Turkey*
Anna Mouti, *Aristotle University of Thessaloniki, Greece*
Aylin Unaldi, *University of Huddersfield, UK*
Antonios Ventouris, *Aristotle University of Thessaloniki, Greece*
Karin Vogt, *Heidelberg University of Education, Germany*

Table of Contents

Preface xiii

Acknowledgment xvi

Chapter 1
Trends and Challenges in Formative Assessment of Reading and Writing: Online EAP Contexts 1
    Inanc Karagoz, Bartin Universitesi, Turkey
    Imelda Bangun, Keiser University, USA

Chapter 2
University Language Examinations Ante, Interim, and Post COVID-19: Trapped in the Culture of Trust? 21
    Linda Nepivodova, Masaryk University, Czech Republic
    Simona Kalova, Masaryk University, Czech Republic

Chapter 3
Online Formative Assessment via the E-Portfolio: Attitudes of Greek and Russian EFL University Students 39
    Vicky Papachristou, CITY College, University of York Europe Campus, Greece
    Maria-Araxi Sachpazian, CITY College, University of York Europe Campus, Greece
    Olga Safonkina, National Research N.P. Ogarev State University, Russia

Chapter 4
The Impact of Online Feedback Practice on Pre-Service English Teachers During the Pandemic 64
    Bruna Lourenção Zocaratto, Federal Institute of Brasilia, Brazil
    Gladys Quevedo-Camargo, University of Brasilia, Brazil

Chapter 5
The Effectiveness of Dynamic Assessment on Improving Multilingual Students' Writing Skills in Distance Education 82
    Ifigeneia Karagkouni, University of Nicosia, Cyprus
    Thomais Rousoulioti, Aristotle University of Thessaloniki, Greece
    Dina Tsagari, Oslo Metropolitan University, Norway

Chapter 6
Learning Through Assessment in Anthrogogic Contexts: Wash-Forward 99
    Shree Deepa, University of Hyderabad, India
    Geetha Durairajan, English and Foreign Languages University, Hyderabad, India

Chapter 7
Providing Alternative Assessments Through Experiential Learning in an Online Language
Teacher Training Course 119
    Amy S. Burden, Center for Applied Linguistics, USA

Chapter 8
Participant Evaluation of an Online Course on Language Assessment Literacy 142
    Asli Lidice Gokturk Saglam, University of South Eastern Norway, Norway
    Ece Sevgi-Sole, University of Milan, Italy

Chapter 9
Digital Assessment Literacy: English Assessment Practice in Vietnam 162
    Thuy Thai, University of Huddersfield, UK
    Susan Sheehan, University of Huddersfield, UK
    Quynh Thi Ngoc Nguyen, University of Languages and International Studies, Vietnam
        National University, Hanoi, Vietnam
    Thao Thi Phuong Nguyen, University of Languages and International Studies, Vietnam
        National University, Hanoi, Vietnam
    Yen Thi Quynh Nguyen, University of Languages and International Studies, Vietnam
        National University, Hanoi, Vietnam
    Hien Thi Thu Tran, University of Languages and International Studies, Vietnam National
        University, Hanoi, Vietnam
    Chi Thi Nguyen, University of Languages and International Studies, Vietnam National
        University, Hanoi, Vietnam
    Hoa Quynh Nguyen, University of Languages and International Studies, Vietnam National
        University, Hanoi, Vietnam
    Sao Bui, University of Languages and International Studies, Vietnam National University,
        Hanoi, Vietnam

Chapter 10
"We Don't Know What We Don't Know": Classroom Assessment Literacy for Remote and Online
Contexts – Insights From an Inter-Country Comparative Study 184
    Toni Mäkipää, University of Helsinki, Finland
    Anna Soltyska, Ruhr-Universität Bochum, Germany

Compilation of References 209

Related References 239

About the Contributors 256

Index 261

Detailed Table of Contents

Preface xiii

Acknowledgment xvi

Chapter 1
Trends and Challenges in Formative Assessment of Reading and Writing: Online EAP Contexts 1
    Inanc Karagoz, Bartin Universitesi, Turkey
    Imelda Bangun, Keiser University, USA

The digital transformation of English for academic purposes (EAP) settings has gained momentum as a result of innovations in educational technology. Both face-to-face and remote instruction witnessed the use of various online tools to support language learning. Based on recent research findings, this chapter discusses specific ways online formative assessment could and should be used when engaging students in critical discussion of the reading content, checking their reading comprehension and vocabulary acquisition, facilitating the peer assessment process for writing, and providing teacher feedback. It is concluded with a critical discussion of the most pertinent challenges researchers and practitioners are likely to encounter, including, but not limited to, monitoring and managing peer interactions and ensuring progress-oriented peer feedback, and creating formative assessments that go beyond prompting learners to select an instructor-written choice statement in multiple-choice quizzes towards involving critical thinking.

Chapter 2
University Language Examinations Ante, Interim, and Post COVID-19: Trapped in the Culture of Trust? 21
    Linda Nepivodova, Masaryk University, Czech Republic
    Simona Kalova, Masaryk University, Czech Republic

This chapter draws attention to different modes of language exam administration in the context of tertiary education. Student perceptions of computer-based written language exams in supervised and unsupervised settings and also oral language exams taken face-to-face and distantly form the focus of this research study. Overall, it describes language testing procedures which currently take place at a Department of English and American studies in the Czech Republic and details the necessary changes that needed to be implemented in order for the language exams to be administered distantly due to COVID 19. It depicts the benefits and drawbacks of testing the students in different modes as viewed by students. The final part looks into the future and outlines pedagogical implications based on the research outcomes.

Chapter 3
Online Formative Assessment via the E-Portfolio: Attitudes of Greek and Russian EFL University Students.. 39
    Vicky Papachristou, CITY College, University of York Europe Campus, Greece
    Maria-Araxi Sachpazian, CITY College, University of York Europe Campus, Greece
    Olga Safonkina, National Research N.P. Ogarev State University, Russia

The study explores Greek and Russian EFL university students' attitudes towards the use of electronic portfolios as one of the most suitable forms of formative assessment to monitor the process and progress of foreign language learning for online language education. To that end, data were collected online via a questionnaire by 75 Greek and 115 Russian participants who have experienced studying English online during the pandemic and face-to-face. The results have shown that all students hold positive attitudes towards this type of assessment and are aware of its facilitative and beneficial role in enhancing self-learning which could lead to significantly better results. Based on the findings obtained, the authors will attempt to put forth some practical recommendations for English practitioners in teaching English online who seek educational support in this area.

Chapter 4
The Impact of Online Feedback Practice on Pre-Service English Teachers During the Pandemic...... 64
    Bruna Lourenção Zocaratto, Federal Institute of Brasilia, Brazil
    Gladys Quevedo-Camargo, University of Brasilia, Brazil

The purpose of this chapter is to examine the results of a study on the impact of online feedback practice on the learning and education of pre-service English teachers at a Federal Institute of Education, Science, and Technology. To this end, questionnaires were used, and focus groups were conducted at the beginning and end of two English classes of the same level, during a period of two months in 2021. Thematic analysis was employed to analyze and interpret the data. Results showed that participants recognized the importance of online feedback for their learning and professional development, identified the need for a balance between corrective and motivational types, looked at it beyond a simple procedure linked to errors and grades, and showed interest in conducting fair and ethical assessment practices, with the reproduction of peer assessment and the use of rubrics.

Chapter 5
The Effectiveness of Dynamic Assessment on Improving Multilingual Students' Writing Skills in Distance Education 82
    Ifigeneia Karagkouni, University of Nicosia, Cyprus
    Thomais Rousoulioti, Aristotle University of Thessaloniki, Greece
    Dina Tsagari, Oslo Metropolitan University, Norway

Research has shown that the implementation of dynamic assessment in the second/foreign language (L2) teaching affects students' learning potential and improvement. In this light, the aim of this chapter is to examine the effectiveness of the method of dynamic assessment on improving adult learners' writing skills in Greek as L2 during the Covid-19 pandemic. This research focuses on the effect of online feedback, mediation, and strategies adopted on improving text quality and the writing process in general. A four-week on-line teaching intervention focused on teaching and assessing writing was carried out. Findings based on quantitative analysis show that students improved their writing competence on content development, text organization, and grammar accuracy. Nonetheless, the limitations of this study indicate the need for further research on the implementation of dynamic assessment by distance.

Chapter 6
Learning Through Assessment in Anthrogogic Contexts: Wash-Forward 99
    Shree Deepa, University of Hyderabad, India
    Geetha Durairajan, English and Foreign Languages University, Hyderabad, India

This chapter charts the wash-forwards gained by the teacher authors who learnt through assessment in the process of teaching an online English language proficiency course that was offered to adult students in mainstream higher education classrooms. The whole course used scenario-based learning and assessment as its tapestry. Students were treated as equal partners; the learnings and the feed-forwards for further courses for the author-teachers were in the areas of time management; new group dynamics, the use of new technological tools as taught by students, the varied uses of plurilingual language use, and new ways of raising an awareness of the potentiality of language to be used in a constructive, neutral, or destructive manner. The students also benefited because they learnt to reflect on their own academic lives, to take responsibility for their academic decisions, and to be aware of their own language use. Though the primary context was the online teaching context during Covid-19, the implications are for regular offline and post-Covid classrooms.

Chapter 7
Providing Alternative Assessments Through Experiential Learning in an Online Language
Teacher Training Course 119
    Amy S. Burden, Center for Applied Linguistics, USA

In the form of a case study, the chapter focuses on the value of experiential learning and how it was adapted for the online learning environment during the pandemic. Employing Kolb's Experiential Learning Cycle, the project served as an alternative assessment that engaged in more democratic grading practices. The designed learning outcomes were for students to grow in their autonomous metacognitive reflections of their own grading and assessment practices through alternative assessments such as self and dynamic assessments. Additionally, they would employ multiple identities in the online classroom: teacher, student, and peer. Finally, through participation in the experiential learning project, they would demonstrate explicit knowledge of a variety of alternative assessments for language learning through co-constructed assessments, rubrics, and presentations. Data were collected through observation and document analysis and analyzed qualitatively. Results show growth in explicit knowledge of alternative assessments and confidence with alternative assessment design and grading.

Chapter 8
Participant Evaluation of an Online Course on Language Assessment Literacy 142
    Asli Lidice Gokturk Saglam, University of South Eastern Norway, Norway
    Ece Sevgi-Sole, University of Milan, Italy

This chapter reports on participant evaluations of an online professional development course on language assessment literacy (LAL) for practitioners interested in the field. With the introduction and widespread of online courses following the Covid era, the need to evaluate the effectiveness of the new modalities and platforms to deliver these courses as well as the online course content has become inevitable. To serve for this purpose, this chapter presents the analysis of data collected from a multinational online community of language teachers through the end-of-course questionnaire (n=13) and focused interviews (n=6). The results of the analysis suggested three main issues indicated by the course participants:

learning in an online community, course design, and course content. The chapter which discusses the emerging sub-themes has implications for teacher educators, researchers, and course designers interested in learning about the participant perspective towards an online course in a multicultural LAL context.

Chapter 9
Digital Assessment Literacy: English Assessment Practice in Vietnam 162
    Thuy Thai, University of Huddersfield, UK
    Susan Sheehan, University of Huddersfield, UK
    Quynh Thi Ngoc Nguyen, University of Languages and International Studies, Vietnam
        National University, Hanoi, Vietnam
    Thao Thi Phuong Nguyen, University of Languages and International Studies, Vietnam
        National University, Hanoi, Vietnam
    Yen Thi Quynh Nguyen, University of Languages and International Studies, Vietnam
        National University, Hanoi, Vietnam
    Hien Thi Thu Tran, University of Languages and International Studies, Vietnam National
        University, Hanoi, Vietnam
    Chi Thi Nguyen, University of Languages and International Studies, Vietnam National
        University, Hanoi, Vietnam
    Hoa Quynh Nguyen, University of Languages and International Studies, Vietnam National
        University, Hanoi, Vietnam
    Sao Bui, University of Languages and International Studies, Vietnam National University,
        Hanoi, Vietnam

This chapter reports on a project explored which classroom-based English language assessment practices, with a particular emphasis on digital assessments, in Vietnam. A mixed-method approach to data collection was adopted to understand the current assessment landscape. The methods include questionnaire (N = 2569) and teaching observations with follow-up interviews (N =7). The results of the project revealed what were behind teachers' choices of assessment tasks in their classroom, the use of assessment feedback and the challenges faced by the teachers in their practices in online environment. The project has extended an understanding of the current assessment landscape in Vietnam. Discussions on how the data has informed an online toolkit which will provide assessment and testing resources and recommendation for best practices will be presented as effective assessment can support and promote learning, and as Crusan et al. point out it is the students who lose out if assessment practices are poor.

Chapter 10
"We Don't Know What We Don't Know": Classroom Assessment Literacy for Remote and Online
Contexts – Insights From an Inter-Country Comparative Study 184
    Toni Mäkipää, University of Helsinki, Finland
    Anna Soltyska, Ruhr-Universität Bochum, Germany

This chapter studies post-pandemic assessment literacy and professional development related to assessment literacy for English teachers in Finland and Germany. The aim of the research is to determine the extent to which language instructors in both countries have been prepared for designing, performing, and evaluating assessment activities, particularly in remote teaching contexts. The study also explores available training options to enhance teachers' assessment literacy. The current study addresses teachers at all levels of education, including primary, secondary, tertiary, and vocational. Qualitative and quantitative data were collected through an online survey (N = 124) and structured video conference interviews (N = 27). The results indicate a significant gap in assessment literacy regarding online assessment (irrespective of the country of the participants, their age, or teaching experience). Furthermore, the results corroborate that there is ample demand for training in online assessment design and administration, suggesting the preferred modes and topics of such training.

Compilation of References 209

Related References 239

About the Contributors 256

Index 261

Preface

Within the last few years, educational practices have undergone a rapid technological transition following a sudden increase in the need for flexibility regarding accessibility to learning opportunities. Unsurprisingly, this change did not come free of challenges. However, it also gave birth to a brand-new era in digital learning and assessment in the field of education. The rise of online platforms and digital tools have inspired educators and researchers to search for effective methods and novel approaches to assess language proficiency in virtual environments (Chapelle & Voss, 2021; Tsiplakou & Tsagari, 2023; Wise 2019).

As it is widely known, any change brings about the need for adaptation. Inevitably, this sudden technological shift in educational and assessment practices during the early 2020s was first perceived by the educators and any concerned parties as a challenge. Nevertheless, this challenge rapidly turned into an approach towards teaching, learning, and assessment by setting a trend called *'adaptive assessment'*, which originally dates back to 1970s when Computerized Adaptive Testing (CAT) was first introduced (Wainer et al.,1990), where the phenomena of adaptation basically referred to the technology in test-taking through the use of computers as an alternative to the traditional pen-paper. Building up on the definitions offered by Wainer (1979) and Crossley & McNamara (2017) we suggest defining adaptive assessment in the context of language education as tailor-made assessment based on the needs of the learners and institutions, conditions and affordances, or a synthesis of all with an aim to provide accurate, informative, and constructive feedback on the language proficiency levels of the learners. The biggest challenges along the way towards adaptive assessment practices, on the other hand, have been reported to be technical considerations which involve infrastructural reliability, equality in accessibility, data protection and security, all leading to pedagogical considerations primarily related to validity. To address these challenges, collaboration among assessment experts, educators, researchers, and technological experts is eminently sought for.

This preface introduces a collection of emerging online practices in language assessment from a variety of instructional settings and countries. Together, we will embark on a journey where we will be witnessing how these challenges posed by the transition to technological assessment have been handled by the use of tailor-made methods within localized, specific contexts. The book is organized into 10 chapters. A brief description of each of the chapters follows.

In Chapter 1, Inanc Karagoz and Imelda Bangun provide an overview of discussions presented by various authors in terms of the digital transformation of English for Academic Purposes (EAP) settings. Chapter 1 also serves as a practical resource for teachers, providing them with guidance and insights on the available tools for assessment and how they can be effectively utilised. Its primary aim is to assist teachers in understanding and leveraging these tools to enhance the assessment process. Authors conclude by critically examining the significant challenges that practitioners are expected to face. These challenges encompass a range of issues, such as monitoring and effectively managing peer interactions, ensuring peer feedback is focused on progress, and designing formative assessments that encourage critical thinking. The authors contend that facilitating learner interactions with peers and offering opportunities for expanding their existing understanding through active engagement in assessment facilitates the process of learning and alleviates challenges encountered by learners .

Linda Nepivodova and Simona Kalova in Chapter 2, explore students' perceptions of various modes of language test administration that are used in higher education in the Czech Republic, including face-to-face oral and written examinations conducted under both supervised and unsupervised conditions. Chapter 2 presents an analysis of the advantages and disadvantages of employing different testing modes, modifications to online assessment practices from the viewpoint of students. Their research findings demonstrate instances where students violated academic integrity during unsupervised computer-based exams, with the data indicating that students openly admitted to such misconduct. The authors of this chapter also suggest certain pedagogical recommendations and implications that could be used in similar educational contexts.

In Chapter 3, building upon previous studies that examine the educational backgrounds of Greek and Russian students and their shared assessment practices, Olga Safonkina, Vicky Papachristou, and Maria-Araxi Sachpazian document the perspectives of Greek and Russian university students enrolled in English as a foreign language (EFL) programs regarding the use of electronic portfolios for formative assessment. Chapter 3 argues that students hold positive attitudes towards this type of assessment and are aware of its facilitative and beneficial role in enhancing self-learning which could lead to effective learning. One of the interesting findings of the study highlights that despite the differences in the English proficiency levels of the learners, attitudes towards e-portfolios remain consistently positive due to their prior experience with portfolios, which demonstrated the facilitative nature of e-portfolios in English language learning. Thus, authors draw attention to significance of language assessment literacy (LAL) and suggest that this form of formative assessment can be implemented at any English proficiency level, as long as teachers are adequately trained to utilize this alternative assessment tool.

In Chapter 4, Bruna Lourenção Zocaratto and Gladys Quevedo-Camargo report on the impact of online feedback on pre-service English teachers in Brazil. The authors indicate the importance of understanding the perceptions of the novice teachers about the facilitative effects of online feedback in the integration of such procedures into online course-designs. They further suggest that importance be paid to developing ethical policies.

Chapter 5 by Ifigeneia Karagkouni, Thomais Rousoulioti and Dina Tsagari examines how dynamic assessment functioned to improve adult learners' writing skills during the Covid-19 pandemic period in Greece. More specifically, the researchers analysed how students improved their competence in content development, text organisation, and grammatical accuracy through online platforms.

In Chapter 6, Shree Deepa and Geetha Durairajan report on the findings of an in-depth examination into the wash-forward effect on the teacher-authors as a result of their experience in the online assessment-design of an English language proficiency course in India. The teacher-authors report how this online course that was offered to adults facilitated the institution, students' learning, as well as teachers' professional development.

In Chapter 7, Amy Burden investigates how experiential learning was valued and adapted to fit into online learning environments in the United States of America during the pandemic. The author explains the novelty of the project by referring to the utilisation of "self-contained virtual exchange" in a fully

Preface

online course designed for pre-service language teachers through their engagement in all four stages of Kolb's Experiential Learning Cycle (1984).

We as editors also contributed to this book by reporting on participant evaluations of an online professional development course on Language Assessment Literacy following the aim of bringing further insight to online course designs in the relevant subject matter through the eyes of the course participants who were from diverse cultural backgrounds and institutional contexts.

In Chapter 9, Thuy Thai, Susan Sheehan, Quynh Thi Ngoc Nguyen, Thao Thi Phuong Nguyen, Yen Thi Quynh Nguyen, Hien Thi Tran, Chi Thi Nguyen, Hoa Quynh Nguyen, and Sao Thien Bui offer relevant empirical evidence of teachers' digital assessment knowledge and practices in Vietnam.

Last but not the least, Toni Mäkipää and Anna Soltyska in Chapter 10 report on the post-pandemic assessment-literacy needs of English teachers in Finland and Germany with an aim to identify the 'readiness' of the teachers to design, perform, and evaluate assessment tasks given specific attention to remote instructional contexts. The authors assert that their study sheds light on the professional needs of the teachers regarding assessment literacy in these two local contexts.

We hope you enjoy it!

Asli Lidice Gokturk-Saglam
University of South-Eastern Norway, Norway

Ece Sevgi-Sole
University of Milan, Italy

REFERENCES

Chapelle, C. A., & Voss, E. (2021). Introduction to validity argument in language testing and assessment. *Validity argument in language testing: Case studies of validation research*, 1-16.

Crossley, S. A., & McNamara, D. S. (Eds.). (2017). *Adaptive educational technologies for literacy instruction*. Routledge.

Kolb, D. A. (1984). *Experience as the source of learning and development. Upper Sadle River*. Prentice Hall.

Tsiplakou, S., & Tsagari, D. (2023). Language ideologies and washback effects in a high-stakes Greek language examination. *Research Papers in Language Teaching and Learning*, *13*(1), 64–92.

Wainer, H., Dorans, N. J., Green, B. F., Steinberg, L., Flaugher, R., Mislevy, R. J., & Thissen, D. (1990). Computerized adaptive testing. *PRiMER: Peer-Reviewed Reports in Medical Education Research*.

Wise, S. L. (2019). Controlling construct-irrelevant factors through computer-based testing: Disengagement, anxiety, & cheating. *Education Inquiry*, *10*(1), 21–33. doi:10.1080/20004508.2018.1490127

Acknowledgment

We would like to express our deepest gratitude to members of the editorial advisory board who contributed their time, expertise, and invaluable insights to the editing process of this book. Their dedication and meticulous attention to detail have significantly enhanced the quality and coherence of the chapters. We extend our heartfelt appreciation to each of them for their invaluable contributions. We would like to thank Aylin Unaldi, Karin Vogt, Slobodanka Dimova, Hossein Farhady, Anna Mouti, Henrik Bohn, Thomas Wulstan Christiansen, and Antonios Ventouris for providing valuable feedback that helped shape the content and structure of several chapters. Their insightful comments and constructive criticism were instrumental in refining the ideas and arguments presented in various chapters, improving the overall readability and clarity of the book.

We are also grateful to Nihada Delibegović, Amy Erenay, Merve Selcuk and Filiz Seremet Ogut for their invaluable contributions to the editing process. Their meticulous proofreading and attention to detail played a crucial role in enhancing the overall quality of the book. Their commitment to excellence and their ability to provide constructive feedback were truly commendable.

We would like to extend our thanks to all peer reviewers who contributed their time and expertise, even if not explicitly mentioned here. Your collective efforts and commitment to excellence have been instrumental in shaping this book and making it a valuable resource for readers.

Finally, we would like to express our gratitude to our families, colleagues, and friends who supported us throughout the process of editing and publishing this book. Their unwavering encouragement and understanding were invaluable during this endeavor.

Chapter 1
Trends and Challenges in Formative Assessment of Reading and Writing:
Online EAP Contexts

Inanc Karagoz
https://orcid.org/0000-0001-7350-7978
Bartin Universitesi, Turkey

Imelda Bangun
Keiser University, USA

ABSTRACT

The digital transformation of English for academic purposes (EAP) settings has gained momentum as a result of innovations in educational technology. Both face-to-face and remote instruction witnessed the use of various online tools to support language learning. Based on recent research findings, this chapter discusses specific ways online formative assessment could and should be used when engaging students in critical discussion of the reading content, checking their reading comprehension and vocabulary acquisition, facilitating the peer assessment process for writing, and providing teacher feedback. It is concluded with a critical discussion of the most pertinent challenges researchers and practitioners are likely to encounter, including, but not limited to, monitoring and managing peer interactions and ensuring progress-oriented peer feedback, and creating formative assessments that go beyond prompting learners to select an instructor-written choice statement in multiple-choice quizzes towards involving critical thinking.

DOI: 10.4018/978-1-6684-6227-0.ch001

INTRODUCTION

Even though online language learning and assessment practices existed prior to the emergence of COVID-19, it was not until the pandemic that most educators had to undertake the challenge of reshaping instructional tasks within an entirely online format for the first time. Many instructors have been in search of effective tools and methods that could not only simulate the communicative affordances of face-to-face learning but also enhance learners' language skills. Such an abrupt shift resulted in a need to rethink and transform language assessment to reflect the dynamics of online learning. Even after the recent return to face-to-face learning around the world, many online practices remained part of the instruction. Indeed, Huang et al. (2021) found that instructors had positive perceptions regarding the pedagogical, managerial, assessment, social, and developmental affordances of teaching through an online learning platform. They pointed out its benefits in recording student participation, managing group work, monitoring learners' progress, and facilitating student communication.

Assessment is a process of data collection through observation to provide feedback and enhance current performance (Brown, 1990). It is of critical importance that English for Academic Purposes (EAP) instructors understand the measurement process, either formatively or summatively, of how many learning objectives are achieved through scaffoldings and active involvement of the instructors and learners (Fernandes et al., 2012; Mubayrik, 2020). Formative assessment is designed to continuously observe students' achievement and progress during the learning process (Martin & Collins, 2011). On the contrary, summative assessment is designed to assess student achievement at the endpoint such as after completing a course (Trumbull & Lash, 2013).

Formative reading assessments in EAP contexts are critical for monitoring and facilitating learners' vocabulary acquisition and comprehension in English. In face-to-face settings, these assessments may often be in the form of comprehension quizzes, cloze exercises, and vocabulary quizzes. In online settings, formative assessment of reading involves the use of digital tools to evaluate learners' growth in terms of learning objectives for reading. Digital tools have become the medium for comprehension and vocabulary quizzes. New developments in accessing and processing information have enabled immediate and personalized feedback through such tools. Immediate and automated feedback can guide the instructor towards adjusting their teaching strategies and providing necessary interventions so that students are well-prepared for academic reading tasks in the future. In addition to online quizzes, interactive tools may allow the learners to organize the ideas in the reading texts and discuss their interpretations of them. The interactivity of the formative assessment process may foster collaboration among learners while engaging them with content analysis, critical thinking, and opinion exchange.

According to Graham et al. (2015), formative writing assessments improve the writing proficiency skills of the students by evaluating the impact of the feedback on the students' writing progress based on particular writing skills and strategies. They added that an effective formative assessment and its feedback are pertinent as it monitors students' progress and provides information that the students can use to improve their writing skills and guide teachers with their instruction. Li (2021) posited that formative writing assessments allow teachers to identify the effectiveness of their instruction and apply modifications as needed. When assessing students formatively within an e-learning environment teachers do not need to completely reinvent the traditional formative assessments. In fact, many online formative assessment tools would pair well with traditional formative assessments. Without going on board, teachers may embed short quizzes, polls, surveys, and games as part of online formative assessment to check for understanding before moving on to the next lesson.

Vygotsky (1978) defined the Zone of Proximal Development (ZPD) as "The distance between the actual development level as determined by independent problem solving and the level of potential development as determined through problem-solving under guidance or in collaboration with more capable peers" (p. 86). As such, it is argued that when continuously monitoring student achievements, the language teaching approach in the classroom should be guided by the learners' ZPD. In terms of online assessment in EAP contexts, the unique needs of EAP learners led the foci of practice to reading and writing skills. Formative assessment has a significant role in the growth of learners as it guides their progress in a low-stakes manner. In addition to receiving quick feedback on their learning, students could actively interact with each other to shape their understanding and output. These interactions could help them be in the ZPD.

Against this backdrop, it is necessary to review how reading and writing assessments were incorporated online so that EAP instructors could gain insights from research findings and equip themselves with methods and tools that their colleagues utilized. Therefore, this chapter aims to discuss current trends and tools with a survey of recent literature, address challenges, and offer pedagogical implications on online formative assessments of reading and writing skills in various EAP contexts.

ONLINE TOOLS FOR FORMATIVE READING ASSESSMENT

EAP instructors worldwide have employed several online tools to assess learners' vocabulary acquisition (e.g., Yarahmadzehi & Goodarzi, 2020) and reading comprehension (e.g., Tseng et al., 2015; Muravev 2022). There are many tools (e.g., Google Forms, Socrative, learning management system-based quiz tools, Quizizz, Quizlet, and Kahoot) to create online quizzes that could provide learners with immediate and automated feedback. Meanwhile, it is possible to incorporate peer interactions and critical thinking through social annotation tools (e.g. Hypothesis, A.nnotate, and Perusall), discussion boards, and digital concept mapping tools (e.g. Mindomo, MindMeister, and Miro). This section will discuss the impact and potential uses of these trending tools (see Table 1) for the formative assessment of reading skills.

Online Quizzes

Online quizzes consist of sets of question items published via online web-based or mobile channels. Possible question types include multiple-choice questions, true/false questions, and open-ended questions. In the context of EAP reading tasks, they can be used to assess learners' reading comprehension and vocabulary acquisition. The instant and automated feedback to multiple-choice and true/false questions makes them efficient tools for demonstrating learners' ongoing performance across various checkpoints throughout a reading task. Open-ended questions could encourage deeper engagement with the reading content by prompting the learners to form a response without providing them with any fixed choices and thus constitute an opportunity to connect writing skills with reading skills.

Kahoot is an online quiz platform that enables learners to use their smart devices as a clicker for a real-time quiz competition. While creating the assessment, the instructor has the ability to adjust the number of answer choices and the time limit. It is also possible to enhance the quiz items by attaching visuals. Learners gain points by responding to questions accurately and quickly. Its possibility to gamify quick formative assessments makes it applicable across many age groups and subject matter areas. In synchronous EAP settings, Kahoot may facilitate the assessment of academic vocabulary acquisition through sentence completion items with target words. Instant feedback on accuracy may indeed increase learners' vocabulary gain. In this vein, Naz et al. (2022) found that Pakistani undergraduate learners performed significantly better at vocabulary when the instructional activities included the use of Kahoot quizzes for six weeks as opposed to traditional instruction. Similarly, a significant impact of Kahoot use on vocabulary acquisition was found among Moroccan university students (Boulaid & Moubtassime, 2019) and Indonesian students (Pahamzah et al., 2022). Besides vocabulary benefits, Tao, and Zou (2021) reported an increase in Chinese learners' intrinsic and extrinsic motivation which correlated with their perceptions of Kahoot as a fun activity.

In addition to the popular quiz application Kahoot, other tools such as Socrative, Quizziz, and Google Forms have been used by language teachers to assess vocabulary learning. Pre-intermediate learners in an Iranian context learned the target words better when they received 10 sets of 20-item multiple-choice vocabulary quizzes through Socrative (Yarahmadzehi & Goodarzi, 2020). Instant feedback seemed to contribute to better performance. Furthermore, learners displayed a positive attitude toward using this tool. Quizziz, on the other hand, offers relatively more options to gamify the assessment process for EAP students. They could go beyond solely typing or clicking, and record videos of themselves. The option to request multimodal responses makes it possible to incorporate the assessment of learners' pronunciation performance in integrated contexts where learning objectives in the reading domain overlap with those in the speaking domain. Furthermore, the assessment could be assigned as individual homework if real-time competition with a limited time allowance is not suitable for learning goals.

Aside from vocabulary quizzes, instructors often design online comprehension assessments with multiple-choice items through tools such as Google Forms and Learning Management System (LMS)-powered quiz tools. With automated scoring, these assessments may quickly inform the instructor about learners' use of reading strategies practiced during class sessions and portray the need for further explicit instruction and exercise in the following sessions. Latimer and Chan (2022) investigated the eye movements of intermediate and advanced learners while taking an online multiple-choice comprehension test. They identified five processing levels during learners' online test performance: (1) creating text-level representation, (2) integrating information, (3) making inferences of the content, (4) evaluating own understanding or progress, and (5) establishing representation at levels of clauses and sentences. They encouraged test designers to identify the target reading processes for test takers and include questions promoting engagement in diverse processes. While comprehension quizzes could simply demonstrate learners' ability to conclude whether a given statement is true or false, it is crucial for instructors to design assessment items that activate complex comprehension processes to acquire rich data about learners' progress, shaping the next instructional activities.

Social Annotation Tasks

Social annotation tools are online applications that allow users to collaboratively annotate websites or documents without requiring them to send each other updated copies of the reading resource with added annotations. When users read the materials, they see other users' annotations on the margins in real-time. Examples of such tools include A.nnotate, Hypothes.is, Perusal, Hylighter, and eComma. Highlighting and commenting is the most common feature such tools offer. In collaborative and telecollaborative learning contexts, employing these tools could facilitate interaction among learners on the reading content as they share their perspectives and knowledge about specific portions of the reading materials. In other words, employing social annotation tasks could connect exact textual chunks from reading materials with learners' input during their shared meaning-making process. Implementing social annotation tools for formative assessment requires instructors' active involvement in the assessment and feedback since automation is not possible as of date. Nonetheless, the instructor's ability to monitor their interactions via these tools provides insights for any necessary intervention to achieve learning goals. Specifically, annotation prompts could function as instruments to collect data on learners' abilities to point out key components such as hooks, main ideas, and supporting evidence in reading materials. Furthermore, they could lead to a demonstration of critical thinking through conversations among learners on their opinions on the reading content. Both familiarity with text structure and engagement with its content could support reading comprehension.

Tseng et al. (2015) examined Taiwanese learners' use of A.nnotate and its impact on their reading comprehension. They found that the frequency of marking vocabulary, adding Chinese explanations, marking information, and summarizing paragraphs resulted in different levels of surface-based, text-based, and situation-based comprehension. Therefore, teachers may guide students into engaging in a specific type of annotation to achieve reading comprehension at different levels in accordance with the learning objectives. Such guidance could enable teachers to involve learners' annotations as part of the criterion-referenced formative assessment.

Collaborative reading in English through annotations reduced Taiwanese high school students' reading anxiety significantly, particularly when the instructor took part in supporting their interactions (Chen et al., 2021). It is possible to argue that higher education EAP contexts could also benefit from well-structured annotation prompts by maintaining a low-anxiety environment for formative assessment. To illustrate, Liu and Lan (2016) explored the use of Google Docs for collaborative reading at the tertiary level and reported an insignificant but slightly lower level of test anxiety among the participants in the experimental group. Social annotation tasks have the potential to be progress-oriented low-stake assessment instruments that allow learners to benefit from the more knowledgeable others in their groups and advance in their zone of proximal development.

Employing social annotation tools for formative assessment has the potential to demonstrate learners' skills in various ways. For instance, creating annotation prompts asking learners to identify a list of items in the text could show whether or not they could determine the signal words suggesting a sequence. However, it is worth noting that such data would mostly be limited to their collective performance with little information on their individual performance. This is because learners could simply imitate each other's highlights as they highlight words or phrases while working in groups. In other words, highlighting prompts in social annotation tasks may mainly inform the instructor about group performance. It is necessary to consider some strategies for monitoring progress at the individual level. In that regard, going beyond highlighting prompts toward asking learners to talk about the reading content could encourage them to not only engage in deeper thinking but also demonstrate their individual understanding of the reading text.

Discussion Boards

Discussion boards are digital platforms for posting and responding to messages. Their use is not limited to educational settings; however, they commonly facilitate asynchronous communication among learners. Most LMSes such as Canvas accommodate online discussion boards making it possible to manage learners' interactions through deadlines that show up in user calendars and the built-in word processing tools allowing users to quote others, adjust the font to convey emphasis, and attach multimedia content in their posts. Concerning L2 reading instruction, discussion boards may facilitate online scaffolding with learners' active involvement. Learners' input in these boards may demonstrate their current understanding and their ability to interpret the reading text while suggesting any gaps that need to be addressed. Furthermore, since discussion boards connect reading and writing skills, formative assessment via this practice could refer to the learning objectives in both domains. The instructor could prompt learners to respond to the reading material by summarizing or analyzing the author's argument. Discussion questions could also lead learners to form evidence-based arguments regarding the reading content. The instructor could create a rubric showcasing the characteristics of discussion entries and manually assess learners' posts. The feedback could be communicated through such rubrics. Learners could also provide peer feedback on each other's posts which not only supports their awareness of the learning objectives but also centralizes learners' roles in taking ownership of their learning.

Similar to social annotation tasks, online discussion boards have the potential to yield the affordances of collaborative reading. Sociocultural theory (Vygotsky, 1978) posits that learners may benefit from their interactions with more knowledgeable others who could be their peers or instructors. Online discussion boards could constitute the stage for such interactions to occur. Additionally, the call for learners' explanations and inferences could generate more in-depth processing of the reading material in comparison to multiple-choice tests and gamified quizzes with fixed answers that are readily presented to the learners. In online discussion boards, learners could express their points of views, elaborate on their peers' contributions, express disagreements with their peers' opinions, or provide additional evidence on a given issue. Engaging the learners in critical thinking through discussion prompts could improve their comprehension and grasp of the key concepts in the reading materials. However, learners may need explicit guidance without which the quality of their discussion posts may remain sub-par. Reading exemplar posts shared by the instructor may show them the assessment criteria in action and evoke insights into the depth of thinking they could employ (To & Carless, 2016). In certain cases where the discussion prompts require the learners to resort to additional reading resources independently, they would practice their research strategies which is a pertinent skill for academic reading. With proper guidance, learners' attempts at synthesizing the knowledge they gained from various resources could enhance their textual production (Zhao & Hirvela, 2015). Therefore, their participation in the discussions could enrich their learning experience by leading them to think deeply across multiple reading sources (Nor et al., 2010) and integrating learning objectives from the writing domain in the process.

In addition to its potential for evoking higher-order thinking, employing discussion boards as an assessment instrument may have a positive impact on learners' motivation (Rovai, 2003). Peer feedback, in particular, could lead to positive attitudes regarding participation in discussion boards (Ekahitanond, 2014, Son, 2002) by raising awareness about the learning goals and how they relate to their language needs in academic contexts (Mohammadi et al., 2018). Smith (2008) examined the use of concepts from Newman et al.'s (1995) critical thinking model for peer assessment of online discussion boards in an undergraduate setting. The assessment criteria addressed the relevance, importance, novelty, outside knowledge, ambiguities, linking, justification, critical assessment, practical utility, and width of understanding of peers' contributions. Despite the ambiguities in learners' perceptions of some of these qualities, this model was deemed to be suitable for peer assessment (Smith, 2008). Since the reading objectives for academic purposes in L2 overlaps with many of these aspects, peer assessment incorporating these criteria may improve both the quality of the posts by reaching the objectives at the application level and raising their awareness at the analysis level.

Instructors' involvement in monitoring the discussions is crucial with regard to attaining the benefits of discussion boards as formative assessment tools. Before initiating the discussion tasks, it is necessary to assign deadlines to online discussion procedures to ensure that learners post their initial posts and their responses to peer posts in a timely manner. Moreover, it is important to design mechanisms for peer interactions that promote not only acknowledgment but also critique and improvement of each other's contributions. These mechanisms may be sustained by providing the learners with assessment rubrics that have specific references to a variety of learner interactions including summarizing the reading content, offering alternative perspectives to the issues at hand, expanding on peers' arguments by introducing more supporting evidence from additional research, expressing disagreement by pointing out conflicting data, and analyzing the structure of the argument in the reading text.

Digital Concept Mapping

Digital concept maps are tools for organizing and visually representing ideas and their relationship with other ideas and concepts. They commonly contain a central concept or idea that is connected with surrounding ideas through lines and arrows. Concept maps are useful for analytically organizing the reading content in succinct chunks showcasing their role in the overall reading material. In the formative assessment sense, they could show whether learners could associate concepts or events with each other. Moreover, they could assess the learners' ability to identify cause-and-effect relationships, determine hierarchies, and demonstrate chronological order. In online learning environments, digital concept mapping tools (e.g. MindMup, Mindomo, Miro, and MindMeister) may enable the learners to reconsider the way they organized the events and concepts (Schanze & Grüß-Niehaus, 2008, as cited in Krabbe, 2014) by easily moving them around, deleting them, and adding further spots to the map. Learners could also identify the gaps in their understanding and seek help for additional information or clarification. The instructors could implement self-assessment and peer-feedback processes to support their comprehension and analysis of the reading material. They can also provide the learners with feedback as they monitor learners' performances.

The format of concept mapping tasks determines the extent to which learners demonstrate their knowledge. Ruiz-Primo (2000) points out that concept mapping tasks differ in terms of directedness. The tasks could vary in directedness from high to low depending on the input given as part of the mapping task. While high-directed concept mapping tasks present the learners with a list of concepts, relation words, and linking lines, low-directed ones provide them with only a list of concepts or nothing at all. The variation of directedness makes its use as a formative assessment tool possible for informing the instructor on the use of differing levels of skills. It could simply measure the accuracy of learners' understanding through high-directed tasks with map structure and components. Low-directed tasks, on the other hand, encourage a deeper level of thinking by expecting the learner to identify the concepts from the reading and relate them to each other. Scoring, too, could be automated or based on a comparison to a reference map depending on the features of the mapping tool and the directedness of the task (Krabbe, 2014).

Some digital concept mapping tools (e.g., LucidSpark, MindMeister, and Miro) allow collaboration among users while specifically showing the contribution of each learner when users click on or move their cursors over the components of the shared digital concept maps. Such a response mode promotes opportunities for reconsidering and strengthening the understanding of the reading text and its components. Since reading practice in EAP settings often involves analysis of the text structure, digital concept mapping tasks may be helpful in visually organizing the input and reviewing it as an exemplary model for the target genre in academic writing.

Table 1 summarizes how the digital tools given as examples in this section could function during the formative assessment of certain reading skills. It shows which reading skills could be assessed, what kind of learner interactions are possible, and the essential characteristics of the assessment procedure.

Table 1. Online Tools for Formative Assessment of Reading

Reading Skills to Assess	Assessment Instruments	Tools	Mode of Interaction	Characteristics of Assessment
Understanding the meaning of target words Using the target words in appropriate contexts Spelling the target words correctly	Vocabulary Quizzes	Quizlet Quizizz Kahoot Google Forms Socrative LMS-Based Quizzes	Matching Choosing Writing	Instructor-created Automated and instant grading Feedback limited to accuracy Some of these tools make the assessment competitive
Identifying the main idea and supporting details Identifying the relationship between ideas based on transition words	Social Annotation Prompts Digital Concept Mapping	Hypothes.is Perusal Miro MindMeister	Highlighting Labeling Commenting Writing Connecting	Feasible for small group collaboration Monitoring learners' performance in real-time Scoring is not-automated
Locating information in the text Interpreting the relationships between ideas	Multiple-Choice Comprehension Quizzes	Google Forms LMS-Based Quizzes	Choosing	Automated and instant grading Feedback limited to accuracy
Understanding the main idea Understanding the supporting details Making inferences Summarizing paragraphs	Discussion Prompts Social Annotation Prompts	LMS Discussion Board Perusal Hypothes.is	Writing Responding to peers	Learner-centered Criterion-referenced No fixed answers Encourages deep level of engagement with the text

ONLINE TOOLS FOR FORMATIVE WRITING ASSESSMENT

Due mainly to its ubiquity, the use of technology in formative assessment has become a popular feature in academic writing classes among adult English learners (Du & Zhou, 2019; Mohamadi, 2018; Mohamadi Zenouzagh, 2019). Technology has been utilized not only for teaching critical thinking and writing skills but also for assessing students writing performance formatively (Mohamadi, 2018). Mohamadi (2018) investigated the effectiveness of e-portfolio writing, e-writing forum, and online electronic writing summative assessment in improving university students' learning and scores. Based on the pre-and post-test result, her findings showed that the students improved their learning performance during the learning process and when they completed the summative assessment (i.e., IELTS). Mohamadi Zenouzagh (2019) conducted another study to find out the effectiveness of e-collaborative discussion forums, e-portfolio writing, e-writing forum, and online electronic writing summative assessment in improving students' learning and competencies among adult learners attending a vocational institution in Iran. She concluded that the interventions helped the students improve their learning and competencies through online effective feedback. Mubayrik (2020) additionally identified several online formative assessment tools being employed in the higher education contexts in her systematic literature review. The e-learning tools include online peer feedback, e-portfolios, Plickers App, Blogosphere, e-Portfolio, and e-writing forum. The studies were conducted among adult English learners within various higher education settings. She concluded that the employment of online writing formative assessment is appropriate in higher education contexts as it promotes a student-centered approach and ample opportunities for instructors and students to improve language instruction and the learning process. The findings from these different studies showed that similar online formative assessment tools were utilized, and they were effective in helping instructors achieve their learning objectives.

Web-Enhanced Collaborative Peer Feedback

Web-enhanced collaborative peer feedback is a type of feedback provided by peers through web-based resources after completing. Storch (2013) defined collaborative writing as a writing interaction and negotiation among students to produce a passage where they share various tasks. In recent years, the student-centered approach guided by the ZPD theoretical has emerged as the purpose of this approach is to distinguish the interest of the students to work collaboratively and independently in completing academic writing assignments (Elboshi, 2021). In this context, the ZPD guided the instruction due to the pertinence of providing learning opportunities from more capable peers through collaboration. Peer feedback either without or enhanced with technology use has been implemented in the language learning process. Through peer feedback, students are encouraged to use their critical thinking skills by identifying the typographical errors based on prompts and strengths and weaknesses of the content of the writing while improving their writing skills. When technology is unavailable, students give written feedback in notebooks or papers in class. A web-enhanced learning environment provides a greater chance for students to provide and read comments not restricted to times and physical classrooms (Bangun, et al., 2023).

With transforming knowledge from reading into academic writing, much research shows that opportunities for students to revise their written work are also essential to improving writing skills (Beach & Friedrich, 2006; Carifio et al., 200). Many studies confirm that the integration of peer feedback with academic coursework can facilitate student learning because it engages students and fosters active and collaborative learning (Li et al., 2010; Li et al., 2012). Zeng and Takatsu (2009) confirmed that peer feedback using online tools allows students to assist in proofreading and editing each other's writings while having collaborative dialogues. As a result, students were engaged when working with instructors and peers in online environments, and the interaction accrued had a positive effect on student collaboration and engagement. Peer feedback is beneficial to both the receivers and providers because it allows students to develop their critical thinking skills by evaluating writings objectively according to the prompts and rubric from the instructors. Increasingly, innovative second/foreign language (L2) instructors seek to employ computer-assisted language learning to motivate students and provide authentic learning experiences.

Li (2021) summarized the technologies employed to represent web-enhanced collaborative peer feedback including Google Docs, Padlet, PBWorks, Wikidot, Fandom, Etherpad, Manubot, and Edmodo. Google Docs is commonly used to share information and write collaboratively online. Similarly, Padlet can be used for collaboration and to share content through virtual bulletin boards. PBWorks and Wikidot are similar in terms of the ability to host an online classroom to share information and collaborate. Fandom is another online hosting tool where users get to share the same interests in popular culture. Etherpad and Manubot support collaborative writing and editing on a free and open-source platform. Edmodo, similar to other web-enhanced tools, supports collaborative writing and video communication; however, it is a learning management system commonly used in the K-12 context.

Automated Writing Assessment Tools

Digital tools are online tools being utilized to monitor and assess students' progress formatively. The feedback received through these digital tools is given automatically to the students. The accuracy of automated writing evaluation (AWE) as a digital tool to assess students' writing performance has been disposed of by previous scholars (i.e., Zhang, 2020; Ranalli et al., 2017; Wang, 2020). They stated that research comparing the consistency between AWE and human feedback has not been studied sufficiently and observed in the long term. AWE has not been able to provide feedback to the writers at a deeper level, particularly in providing feedback at a micro level. Wang (2020) posited that the AWE system detects errors automatically at a surface level (i.e., grammar, syntax, and mechanics) which can be beneficial to reduce typographical errors and improve writing accuracy. It is argued that the AWE system provides vague feedback; however, in the academic writing process, it is important that deeper-level feedback is involved.

Although some studies have provided compelling evidence that AWE has some drawbacks, some studies have also suggested that AWE has positive impacts. Chapell et al., 2015 stated that the AWE system provides effective feedback that can be utilized to improve linguistics skills and writing strategies through error identification and general feedback for each student. Several studies (i.e., Hyland, 2019; Link et al., 2014; Wang et al., 2013) find that AWE increases students' motivation as this system helps them correct their mistakes, enhanced their metacognition, and allowed learners autonomy. Additionally, their studies showed that instructors believed AWE tools were effective in employing writing mechanical feedback to the users which allows the instructors to focus on content and organization instead of grammar syntax and mechanics.

The representative automated writing evaluation tools that can be employed within EAP contexts include Grammarly, PaperRater, WriteToLearn, Criterion, and Pigai (Li, 2021). Li elaborated that in general, the purposes of these AWE tools are to build writing skills and develop reading comprehension. For instance, Grammarly claims that its software detects mechanical errors better than a word processor. The Hemmingway App focuses on the use of adverbs and passive voice to increase readability. PaperRater, additionally, evaluates the writing mechanics and plagiarism by comparing a paper with other papers at the same proficiency level. Like PaperRate, WriteToLearn is a web-based tool that helps students not only improve their reading comprehension but also writing skills through automated feedback and scoring parameters. Li further explains that Criterion is an online writing evaluation service that claims to assist students with planning, writing, and editing their essays and Pigai provides an automatic scoring system based on corpora and cloud computing programs to help teachers score efficiently and help students improve syntax.

Digital Writing Platforms

Digital writing platforms are online platforms that can be integrated into a writing course where students are assigned to publish their writings where they can receive feedback from peers or the public. The role of digital tools to facilitate writing assessment in EAP classrooms may empower educators and learners due to their pedagogical values. Bangun et al. (2019) indicated that the use of digital tools has become an essential part of the academic writing process. In their paper, they further discussed digital storytelling as one digital writing practice that has become paramount in improving writing skills. Technology supported the language learning experience due to the implementation of digital storytelling in enhancing critical thinking, linguistics, and digital skills.

The effect of implementing digital tools in writing assessments (e.g., vlog, blog, and social media) has been investigated by numerous studies (Hung, 2011; Wagener, 2006). Wagnener (2006) found that the use of video-based activities not only improves public speaking skills but also engages the students and promotes independent learning while improving writing skills. While the outcome of this project was a video blog, the students had plenty of opportunities to plan, organize, write, and edit their scripts. He concluded that through vlogs the students showed improvement in vocabulary use and lexical richness. Amir et al. (2011) posited digital writing practices such as blogs or podcasts provide interaction among students that make the learning process more personalized and dynamic. They added that blogging helps students improve their linguistic knowledge through writing. In addition, blogging can help increase student collaboration through writing.

The employment of vlogs, web blogs, and social media in EAP writing courses improves the learning process where the students and teachers interact in a meaningful way. The implementation of vlogging, using social media, and practicing digital storytelling includes the use of YouTube, Vimeo, Facebook, Instagram, TikTok, DailyMotion, and Twitch. The implementation of blogging as a digital practice could be facilitated by the tools Wix, WordPress, Weebly, Medium, Ghost, Blogger, and Tumblr.

Quiz-Style Online Feedback

Quiz-style online feedback in relation to formative assessment is a teaching approach that employs apps that allow teachers to create quizzes with multiple choices or true/false formats while providing feedback automatically. Online quiz style with automated feedback where the students are engaged through game-based learning has become an innovation in language learning pedagogical. Giessen (2015) indicated that game-based learning is effective in assessing student learning, fostering critical thinking skills where students are encouraged to identify the right answer based on the new knowledge, they have learned, increasing metacognitive skills, and improving all academic skills. Game-based learning includes both in-person and virtual games such as in-person literacy games, scavenger hunts, and online quiz-style games. This section particularly discusses online quiz-style games to assess mechanic elements in academic writing. Burzynski Bullard and Anderson (2014) conducted a quasi-experimental design to determine the effectiveness of online quiz-style game-based learning in improving students' mastery and retention of basic grammar in writing. They find that game-based learning has positive impacts in enhancing students' grammar skills.

Aside from receiving immediate feedback, the online quiz style allows instructors to streamline formative assessments in the classroom and check students' understanding. The results of the quiz also help instructors determine if certain concepts need to be further reviewed (Winstone & Carless, 2020). When this language learning pedagogical is implemented, students are the center of the learning process, they are engaged, and they are given the opportunity to increase their problem-solving skills. In his study, Omar (2017), stated that technology-based assessment tools such as Kahoot! increases motivation, self-esteem, metacognition, and self-regulation among the students. This conclusion was supported by Wang and Tahir's (2020) literature review on the use of Kahoot! for learning within the U.S. context. After reviewing 93 studies, they concluded that Kahoot! had a positive impact on the students, increased learning performance, and decreased anxiety.

In-class quizzes such as fill in blanks and multiple choices assessments using pencil and paper are still applicable; however, when considering in-class formative assessments, instructors have moved to use online quizzes styles such as Kahoot, Quizziz, Web-based games, Google Slides, Jeopardy! Quizlet, Menti, and Socrative. These technology-based tools allow creativity in giving formative assessments and engagement among students and instructors.

This section elaborates on different online tools that can be integrated when employing formative writing assessments. The different tools presented above are used to help monitor students' progress and inform teachers of the effectiveness of their instruction. The following (Table 2) is the summary of the online formative assessment instruments and components for academic writing skills:

Table 2. Online Tools for Formative Assessment of Writing

Writing Skills to Assess	Assessment Instruments	Tools	Mode of Interaction	Characteristics of Assessment
Planning, organizing, writing, and editing texts based on prompts	Essay writing Research papers Web-enhanced collaborative peer feedback	Google Docs, Padlet, PBWorks, Wikidot, Fandom, Etherpad, Manubot, and Edmodo.	Writing collaboratively with peer and instructor feedback Writing individually with peer and instructor feedback	Instructors provide the prompts Limited feedback from peers confirmed by the instructors The use of target language in providing feedback Not restricted to times and physical classrooms Scoring is not automated
Implementing proper syntax with fluency Distinguishing and implementing proper mechanics (spelling and grammar)	Automated writing feedback	Grammarly, Hemingway App, PaperRater, WriteToLearn, Criterion, and Pigai	Writing sentences or passages individually with automated writing feedback	Automated and instant grading feedback with limited accuracy
Planning, organizing, writing, and editing script or writing contents based on prompts	Digital writing prompts and feedback	Vlog and Digital Storytelling: YouTube, Vimeo, Facebook Instagram, TikTok DailyMotion, Twitch Blog: Wix, WordPress, Weebly, Medium, Ghost, Blogger, Tumblr	Individual or small group project Writing collaboratively with peer and instructor feedback Writing individually with peer and instructor feedback	Instructors provide the prompts Not restricted to times and physical classrooms Project-based learning Scoring is not automated
Implementing proper syntax with fluency Using transitions and implementing formal tone and style Distinguishing and implementing proper mechanics (spelling and grammar)	Quiz-style online feedback	Blooket, Kahoot, Quizziz, Web-based, Google Slides, Jeopardy!, Quizlet, Menti Socrative	Writing sentences individually with automated writing feedback Writing mechanics, organization, and transition	Automated and instant grading Feedback Feedback accuracy based on the instructors' entries

CHALLENGES AND PEDAGOGICAL CONSIDERATIONS

The novelty of employing online tools for formative assessment may excite practitioners to incorporate them into their teaching of EAP. However, access to these tools, distractions over competitiveness, domination of discussion by a few students, finding it difficult to share something new, limited digital literacy, and low level of language proficiency may impede learners' participation and performance in the assessment tasks. It is important to understand these challenges so that they can be mitigated through guidance and assessment strategies.

Infrastructural issues and access to mobile devices pose a challenge to ensuring opportunities for equal participation of all students. In remote learning contexts at the tertiary level, EAP classes may have an international student population from different parts of the world which complicates the access to online assessment instruments. Certain countries are known to prohibit tools (Ferracane & Lee-Makiyama, 2017) like Google Forms and such a ban makes it impossible or challenging for some learners to participate in the assessment. In addition, slow internet connection speeds may interrupt or perhaps prevent some learners' real-time collaboration and participation in gamified competition tasks like Kahoot quizzes. Instructors should consider potential issues with access, especially if there are learners attending the class remotely from other countries.

Employing real-time quiz competitions during class sessions may result in benefits in terms of motivation (Tao & Zou, 2021) and vocabulary learning (Boulaid & Moubtassime, 2019, Naz et al., 2022; Pahamzah et al., 2022; Yarahmadzehi & Goodarzi, 2020); however, Göksün and Gürsoy (2019) reported that learners found it distractive to look at the main screen while responding on their mobile devices. Their study did not find a significant impact of using Quizziz in learning activities on learners' academic achievement and engagement. Nonetheless, entertainment was one of the emerging themes in their study. In summary, these conflicting findings by Göksün and Gürsoy (2019) call attention to considering class dynamics when choosing a formative assessment design in order to prevent distractions due to dual visual input sources and potential rivalry that may overpower the learning objectives. It is also worth noting that multiple-choice questions in these quizzes may not yield comprehensive data about learners' use of cognitive strategies.

Collaborative reading through social annotation tasks facilitates learners' efforts to deconstruct the reading text by marking main ideas and supporting details (Lo et al., 2013). It requires learners' active participation in locating information and sharing their interpretations of it. Even though their interactions are valuable opportunities for receiving the support of the more knowledgeable others, sometimes annotations get repetitive or scarce. Learners find it difficult to post something original as their peers already pointed out what they wanted to share (Thoms & Poole, 2017). In the context of earlier counterparts of discussion boards, Mason, and Lockwood (1994) suggested that the abundance of posts might overwhelm the students and poses a risk for misunderstandings. Furthermore, the discussions might be dominated by a few students. Instructor guidance via collaboration prompts that share their own perspective on the reading content by addressing specific aspects explicitly addressed in the assessment may remedy the situation. Limiting the collaboration teams to a small number of students would be another strategy for avoiding anxiety over making distinct contributions.

In terms of online formative assessment in writing, the types of assessments have been considered pertinent for a technology-enhanced environment. The types of assessments affect the students' interaction and collaboration more than the technology itself (Lee, 2010). Storch (2013) agreed that when giving writing assessments, the tasks themselves must employ opportunities for students to collaborate than simply cooperate. Although some studies have provided compelling evidence that peer and instructor feedback have positive impacts (Lyu & Lai, 2022; Ma, 2020; Tseng & Yeh, 2019), some studies have also reported the drawbacks associated with peer and expert review (Allaei & Connor, 1990; Hanrahan & Isaacs, 2001). Studies conducted by Allaei and Connor (1990) and Hanrahan and Isaacs (2001) maintained that it might be challenging for a student and a reviewer with considerably different linguistic abilities to sustain continuous and successful interactions while providing feedback if the L2 learners lack mutual understanding. These researchers pointed out another obstacle underscoring that less proficient learners may not be able to provide useful and relevant feedback for their more competent peers. To overcome this obstacle, the instructors may employ scaffoldings and differentiate their prompts to meet the needs of the learners.

Another challenge faced by instructors and students when utilizing AWE in formative writing assessment is the students must use their critical thinking skills to accept or reject the AWE and limited linguistics knowledge to either accept or reject the automatic feedback due to a lack of ability to evaluate complex sentences or not knowing the context presented in the writing (Wang 2020). Therefore, the instructors must recommend the best AWE tools to be implemented in the classroom. Oftentimes, the instructor might also have to review the feedback from the AWE tools for accuracy. Further challenges in employing online writing formative assessment such as vlogging, blogging, or digital storytelling are the instructors themselves must have advanced digital literacy skills to teach the students how to publish the writings or projects in various digital forms (Amir et al., 2011; Wagener, 2006). The major challenges reported by the students when engaging in online style quizzes are related to technical difficulties such as unreliable internet connections, the stress of not being able to answer correctly in a limited time, and afraid of losing and being embarrassed (Wang & Tahir, 2020).

CONCLUSION

The main conclusion in giving formative reading and writing assessments within a technology-based environment is that this language learning pedagogy has a positive impact in not only effectively providing feedback to the students but also increasing their linguistics skills. This feedback either from instructors, peers, or technology generated regarding global or local issues, content, organization, and reading comprehension has helped learners improve their academic writing skills and reading comprehension. While the use of technology in formative assessment has positive impacts, learners face some challenges due to lack of accuracy, limited linguistics knowledge, limited digital literacy skills, and technical difficulties.

Similar to cameras, each online assessment instrument captures pictures with different qualities; some simply show whether certain objects exist within the frame with the click of a button while others expect the accurate or thoughtful employment of light, focus, and the layout of objects to produce an intricate image. Utilizing most of the novel tools for assessing learning has many affordances (i.e., automated instant feedback, facilitating collaboration and communication, engaging learners in critical thinking). Instructors' concerns to ensure the timeliness of teacher feedback may promote the dominant use of online quizzes with automated scoring in comparison to other tools that would require more resources to interpret students' performances. Yet assessment instruments should vary across the course span to fit the learning objectives appropriately. Attention should be paid to the dynamics of the learning environment and the nature of the desired learning path. These considerations would assist the instructor in choosing and designing formative assessments that could provide the necessary data to efficiently support learners' growth. They also inform future assessment practices by addressing current shortcomings that instructional technology could overcome and the opportunities they offer. Lastly, providing opportunities for learners' interactions with more knowledgeable others and allowing room for building on their current understanding with assessments that involve multiple stages of collaboration along a timespan would support learners' growth in the zone of proximal development.

REFERENCES

Allaei, S. K., & Connor, U. (1990). Using performative assessment instruments with ESL student writers. In L. Hamp-Lyons (Ed.), *Assessing second language writing in academic contexts* (pp. 227–240). Ablex.

Amir, Z., Ismail, K., & Hussin, S. (2011). Blogs in language learning: Maximizing students' collaborative writing. *Procedia: Social and Behavioral Sciences*, *18*, 537–543. doi:10.1016/j.sbspro.2011.05.079

Bangun, I., Li, Z., & Mannion, P. (2019). Future teacher educators in critical evaluation of educational technology through collaborative digital storytelling projects. In K. Graziano (Ed.), Proceedings of Society for Information Technology & Teacher Education International Conference (pp. 595-600). Las Vegas, NV, United States: Association for the Advancement of Computing in Education (AACE). Retrieved from https://www.learntechlib.org/primary/p/207702/

Bangun, I., Mannion, P., & Li, Z. (2023). EAP writing with peer and instructor e-feedback: A qualitative study. Manuscript submitted for publication.

Beach, R., & Friedrich, T. (2006). Response to writing. In C. A. MacArthur, S. Graham, & J. Fitzgerald (Eds.), *Handbook of writing research* (pp. 222–234).

Bin Mubayrik, H. F. (2020). New Trends in Formative-Summative Evaluations for Adult Education. *SAGE Open*, *10*(3). doi:10.1177/2158244020941006

Boulaid, F., & Moubtassime, M. (2019). Investigating the role of Kahoot in the enhancement of English vocabulary among Moroccan university students : English department as a case study. *International Journal of Innovation and Applied Studies*, *27*(3), 797–808.

Brown, D. H. (1990). *Language assessment: Principles and classroom practices*. Longman.

Burzynski Bullard, S. B., & Anderson, N. (2014). "I'll take commas for $200": An instructional intervention using games to help students master grammar skills. *Journalism & Mass Communication Educator*, *69*(1), 5–16. doi:10.1177/1077695813518778

Carifio, J., Jackson, I., & Dagostino, L.James Carifio, Ina Jackson, Lorrain. (2001). Effects of diagnostic and prescriptive comments on the revising behaviors of community college students. *Community College Journal of Research and Practice*, *25*(2), 109–122. doi:10.1080/10668920150218498

Chapelle, C. A., Cotos, E., & Lee, J. (2015). Validity arguments for diagnostic assessment using automated writing evaluation. *Language Testing*, *32*(3), 385–405. doi:10.1177/0265532214565386

Chen, C.-M., Wang, J.-Y., Chen, Y.-T., & Wu, J.-H. (2016). Forecasting reading anxiety for promoting English-language reading performance based on reading annotation behavior. *Interactive Learning Environments*, *24*(4), 681–705. doi:10.1080/10494820.2014.917107

Du, W. Y., & Zhou, C. Y. (2019). Web-based scaffolding teaching of EAP reading and writing. *Creative Education*, *10*(8), 1863–1872. doi:10.4236/ce.2019.108134

Ekahitanond, V. (2014). Promoting university students' critical thinking skills through peer feedback activity in an online discussion forum. *The Alberta Journal of Educational Research*, *59*(2), 247–265. doi:10.11575/ajer.v59i2.55617

Elboshi, A. (2021). Web-enhanced peer feedback in ESL writing classrooms: A literature review. *English Language Teaching*, *14*(4), 66–76. doi:10.5539/elt.v14n4p66

Fernandes, S., Flores, M. A., & Lima, R. M. (2010). Students' views of assessment in project-led engineering education: Findings from a case study in Portugal. *Assessment & Evaluation in Higher Education*, *37*(2), 163–178. htps:// doi:10.1080/02602938.2010.515015

Ferracane, M. F., & Lee-Makiyama, H. (2017). *China's technology protectionism and its non-negotiable rationales*. European Centre for International Political Economy. https://euagenda.eu/upload/publications/untitled-96376-ea.pd f

Giessen, H. W. (2015). Serious games effects: An overview. *Procedia: Social and Behavioral Sciences*, *174*, 2240–2244. doi:10.1016/j.sbspro.2015.01.881

Göksün, D. O., & Gürsoy, G. (2019). Comparing success and engagement in gamified learning experiences via Kahoot and Quizizz. *Computers & Education*, *135*, 15–29. doi:10.1016/j.compedu.2019.02.015

Graham, S., Hebert, M., & Harris, K. R. (2015). Formative assessment and writing: A meta-analysis. *The Elementary School Journal*, *115*(4), 523–547. doi:10.1086/681947

Hanrahan, S., & Isaacs, G. (2001). Assessing self-and peer-assessment: The students' view. *Higher Education Research & Development*, *20*(1), 53–66. doi:10.1080/07294360123776

Hung, S. T. (2011). Pedagogical applications of vlogs: An investigation into ESP learners' perceptions. *British Journal of Educational Technology*, *42*(5), 736–746. doi:10.1111/j.1467-8535.2010.01086.x

Hyland, K. (2019). *Second language writing* (2nd ed.). Cambridge University Press.

Krabbe, H. (2014). Digital concept mapping for formative assessment. In: D. Ifenthaler, R. & Hanewald. (Eds) Digital knowledge maps in education (pp. 275–297). Springer. doi:10.1007/978-1-4614-3178-7_15

Latimer, N., & Chan, S. (2022). Eye-tracking L2 students taking online multiple-choice reading tests: Benefits and challenges. *International Journal of TESOL Studies*, *4*(1), 83–104. doi:10.46451/ijts.2022.01.07

Lee, L. (2010). Exploring wiki-mediated collaborative writing: A case study in an elementary Spanish course. *CALICO Journal*, *27*(2), 260–276. doi:10.11139/cj.27.2.260-276

Li, L., Liu, X., & Zhou, Y. (2012). Give and take: A re-analysis of assessor and assessee's roles in technology-facilitated peer assessment. *British Journal of Educational Technology*, *43*(3), 376–384. doi:10.1111/j.1467-8535.2011.01180.x

Li, M. (2021). Computer-mediated teacher feedback. In *Researching and Teaching Second Language Writing in the Digital Age*. Palgrave Macmillan. doi:10.1007/978-3-030-87710-1_3

Lin, W.-C., & Yang, S.-C. (2011). Exploring students' perceptions of integrating Wiki technology and peer feedback into English writing courses. *English Teaching*, *10*(2), 88–103.

Link, S., Dursun, A., Karakaya, K., & Hegelheimer, V. (2014). Towards Better ESL Practices for Implementing Automated Writing Evaluation. *CALICO Journal*, *31*(3), 323–344. doi:10.11139/cj.31.3.323-344

Liu, S. H.-J., & Lan, Y.-J. (2016). Social constructivist approach to web-based EFL learning: Collaboration, motivation, and perception on the use of Google Docs. *Journal of Educational Technology & Society*, *19*(1), 171–186.

Lo, J.-J., Yeh, S.-W., & Sung, C.-S. (2013). Learning paragraph structure with online annotations: An interactive approach to enhancing EFL reading comprehension. *System*, *41*(2), 413–427. doi:10.1016/j.system.2013.03.003

Lyu, B., & Lai, C. (2022). Learners' engagement on a social networking platform: An ecological analysis. *Language Learning & Technology*, *26*(1), 1–22.

Ma, Q. (2020). Examining the role of inter-group peer online feedback on wiki writing in an EAP context. *Computer Assisted Language Learning*, *33*(3), 197–216. doi:10.1080/09588221.2018.1556703

Mak, B., & Coniam, D. (2008). Using wikis to enhance and develop writing skills among secondary school students in Hong Kong. *System*, *36*(3), 437–455. doi:10.1016/j.system.2008.02.004

Martin, J., & Collins, R. (2011). Formative and summative evaluation in the assessment of adult learning. In V. C. X. Wang (Ed.), *Assessing and evaluating adult learning in career and technical education* (pp. 127–142). IGI Global. doi:10.4018/978-1-61520-745-9.ch008

Mason, R., & Lockwood, F. (1994). *Using communications media in open and flexible learning*. Routledge.

Mohamadi, Z. (2018). Comparative effect of online summative and formative assessment on EFL student writing ability. *Studies in Educational Evaluation*, *59*, 29–40. https://doi-org.sdl.idm.oclc.org/10.1016/j.stueduc.2018.02.003. doi:10.1016/j.stueduc.2018.02.003

Mohamadi Zenouzagh, Z. (2019). The effect of online summative and formative teacher assessment on teacher competences. *Asia Pacific Education Review*, *20*(3), 343–359. doi:10.100712564-018-9566-1

Mohammadi, M., Jabbari, A., & Fazilatfar, A. (2018). The Impact of the Asynchronous Online Discussion Forum on the Iranian EFL Students' Writing Ability and Attitudes. *Applied Research on English Language*, *7*(4), 457–486. doi:10.22108/are.2018.112792.1351

Muravev, Y. (2022). Improving second language acquisition by extensive and analytical reading in a digital environment. *Journal of College Reading and Learning*, 1–17. doi:10.1080/10790195.2022.2084798

Naz, R., Nusrat, A., Tariq, S., Farooqi, R., & Ashraf, F. (2022). Mobile assisted vocabulary learning (M learning): A quantitative study targeting ESL Pakistani learners. *Webology*, *19*(3), 1342–1364.

Newman, D. R., Webb, B., & Cochrane, C. (1995). A content analysis method to measure critical thinking in face to face and computer supported group learning. *Interpersonal Computing and Technology, 3*(2), 56–77.

Nor, N. F. M., Razak, N. A., & Aziz, J. (2010). E-learning: Analysis of online discussion forums in promoting knowledge construction through collaborative learning. *WSEAS Transactions on Communications, 9*(1), 53–62.

Omar, N. N. (2017). The Effectiveness of Kahoot Application Towards Students' Good Feedback Practice. *The International Journal of Social Sciences (Islamabad), 3*(2), 2551–2562.

Pahamzah, J., Syafrizal, S., & Nurbaeti, N. (2022). The effects of EFL course enriched with Kahoot on students' vocabulary mastery and reading comprehension skills. *The Journal of Language and Linguistic Studies, 18*(1), 643–652. doi:10.3316/informit.400435517746294

Ranalli, J., Link, S., & Chukharev-Hudilainen, E. (2017). Automated writing evaluation for formative assessment of second language writing: Investigating the accuracy and usefulness of feedback as part of argument-based validation. *Educational Psychology, 37*(1), 8–25. doi:10.1080/01443410.2015.1136407

Rovai, A. P. (2003). Strategies for grading online discussions: Effects on discussions and classroom community in Internet-based university courses. *Journal of Computing in Higher Education, 15*(1), 89–107. doi:10.1007/BF02940854

Ruiz-Primo, M. (2000). On the use of concept maps as an assessment tool in science: What we have learned so far. *Revista Electrónica de Investigación Educativa, 2*(1), 29–52.

Smith, H. (2008). Assessing student contributions to online discussion boards. *Practitioner Research in Higher Education, 2*(1), 22–28.

Son, J.-B. (2002). Online Discussion in a CALL Course for Distance Language Teachers. *CALICO Journal, 20*(1), 127–144. https://www.jstor.org/stable/24149612. doi:10.1558/cj.v20i1.127-144

Storch, N. (2013). *Collaborative writing in L2 classrooms*. Multilingual Matters. doi:10.21832/9781847699954

Tao, Y., & Zou, B. (2021). Students' perceptions of the use of Kahoot! in English as a foreign language classroom learning context. *Computer Assisted Language Learning, 0*, 1–20. doi:10.1080/09588221.2021.2011323

Thoms, J. J., & Poole, F. (2017). Investigating linguistic, literary, and social affordances of L2 collaborative reading. *Language Learning & Technology, 21*(1), 139–156. 10125/44615

To, J., & Carless, D. (2016). Making productive use of exemplars: Peer discussion and teacher guidance for positive transfer of strategies. *Journal of Further and Higher Education, 40*(6), 746–764. doi:10.1080/0309877X.2015.1014317

Trumbull, E., & Lash, A. (2013). *Understanding Formative Assessment: Insights from Learning Theory and Measurement Theory*. Wested. https://www.wested.org/online_pubs/resource1307.pdf

Tseng, S.-S., & Yeh, H.-C. (2019). The impact of video and written feedback on student preferences of English speaking practice. *Language Learning & Technology, 23*(2), 145–158.

Tseng, S.-S., Yeh, H.-C., & Yang, S. (2015). Promoting different reading comprehension levels through online annotations. *Computer Assisted Language Learning*, *28*(1), 41–57. doi:10.1080/09588221.2014.927366

Vygotsky, L. S. (1978). *Mind in society: The development of higher psychological processes* (M. Cole, Ed. & Trans.). Harvard University Press.

Wagener, D. (2006). Promoting independent learning skills. *Computer Assisted Language Learning*, *19*(4-5), 279–286. doi:10.1080/09588220601043180

Wang, A. I., & Tahir, R. (2020). The effect of using Kahoot! for learning – A literature review. *Computers & Education*, *149*, 183818. doi:10.1016/j.compedu.2020.103818

Wang, Y. J., Shang, H. F., & Briody, P. (2013). Exploring the impact of using automated writing evaluation in English as a foreign language university students' writing. *Computer Assisted Language Learning*, *26*(3), 234–257. doi:10.1080/09588221.2012.655300

Wang, Z. (2020). Computer-assisted EFL writing and evaluations based on artificial intelligence: A case from a college reading and writing course. *Library Hi Tech*, *40*(1), 80–97. doi:10.1108/LHT-05-2020-0113

Winstone, N., & Carless, D. (2020). *Designing effective feedback processes in higher education: A learning-focused approach*. Routledge.

Yarahmadzehi, N., & Goodarzi, M. (2020). Investigating the role of formative mobile based assessment in vocabulary learning of pre-intermediate EFL learners in comparison with paper based assessment. *Turkish Online Journal of Distance Education*, *21*(1), 181–196. doi:10.17718/tojde.690390

Zeng, G., & Takatsuka, S. (2009). Text-based peer-peer collaborative dialogue in a computer-mediated learning environment in the EFL context. *System*, *37*(3), 434–446. doi:10.1016/j.system.2009.01.003

Zhang, Z. V. (2020). Engaging with automated writing evaluation (AWE) feedback on L2 writing: Student perceptions and revisions. *Assessing Writing*, *43*, 100439. doi:10.1016/j.asw.2019.100439

Zhao, R., & Hirvela, A. (2015). Undergraduate ESL students' engagement in academic reading and writing in learning to write a synthesis paper. *Reading in a Foreign Language*, *27*(2), 219–241.

ADDITIONAL READING

Chen, C.-M., Chen, L.-C., & Horng, W.-J. (2021). A collaborative reading annotation system with formative assessment and feedback mechanisms to promote digital reading performance. *Interactive Learning Environments*, *29*(5), 848–865. doi:10.1080/10494820.2019.1636091

Grier, D., Lindt, S. F., & Miller, S. C. (2021). Formative assessment with game-based technology. [IJTES]. *International Journal of Technology in Education and Science*, *5*(2), 193–202. doi:10.46328/ijtes.97

Guo, Q., Feng, R., & Hua, Y. (2022). How effectively can EFL students use automated written corrective feedback (AWCF) in research writing? *Computer Assisted Language Learning*, *35*(9), 2312–2331. doi:10.1080/09588221.2021.1879161

Lv, X., Ren, W., & Xie, Y. (2021). The effects of online feedback on ESL/EFL writing: A meta-analysis. *The Asia-Pacific Education Researcher*, *30*(6), 643–653. doi:10.100740299-021-00594-6

Prendes-Espinosa, M. P., Gutiérrez-Porlan, I., & García-Tudela, P. A. (2021). Collaborative work in higher education: tools and strategies to implement the e-assessment. In R. Babo, N. Dey, & A. S. Ashour (Eds.), *Workgroups eAssessment: Planning, Implementing and Analysing Frameworks*. Springer. doi:10.1007/978-981-15-9908-8_3

Yeganehpour, P., & Zarfsaz, E. (2021). The impact of positive peer feedback on second language writing accuracy. *Turkish Studies*, *16*(1), 409–426. doi:10.7827/TurkishStudies.47713

KEY TERMS AND DEFINITIONS

Automated Writing Evaluation (AWE): An online digital tool employed in an academic writing task to automatically provide mostly mechanical error feedback.

Digital Storytelling: A project-based assignment within a technology environment where the students are assigned to write a short script and present their project digitally.

English for Academic Purposes (EAP): Reading, writing, speaking, and listening skills in the English language are necessary for attending academic programs and participating in academic interactions.

Formative Assessment: Collecting information about learners' ongoing performance during instruction so that further tasks could be designed in a way that enhances learners' current performance levels towards learning objectives.

Interaction: Communicative activity among learners with little or no teacher involvement.

More Knowledgeable Other: Vygotskian perspective considers these peers or instructors as individuals who can support a learner thanks to having a more comprehensive level of understanding concepts or employing certain skills with more experience.

Social Annotation: Learner groups' behavior of annotating reading texts in a collaborative manner, usually through online annotation tools.

Telecollaboration: A process where the students collaborate to complete academic writing assignments using digital tools to write collaboratively and provide feedback to each other based on prompts from the instructor.

Zone of Proximal Development: A term coined by Vygotsky referring to the difference between what learners could achieve independently and what they could achieve with guidance from more knowledgeable individuals.

Chapter 2
University Language Examinations Ante, Interim, and Post COVID-19:
Trapped in the Culture of Trust?

Linda Nepivodova
Masaryk University, Czech Republic

Simona Kalova
Masaryk University, Czech Republic

ABSTRACT

This chapter draws attention to different modes of language exam administration in the context of tertiary education. Student perceptions of computer-based written language exams in supervised and unsupervised settings and also oral language exams taken face-to-face and distantly form the focus of this research study. Overall, it describes language testing procedures which currently take place at a Department of English and American studies in the Czech Republic and details the necessary changes that needed to be implemented in order for the language exams to be administered distantly due to COVID 19. It depicts the benefits and drawbacks of testing the students in different modes as viewed by students. The final part looks into the future and outlines pedagogical implications based on the research outcomes.

INTRODUCTION

Learning, teaching, and assessing have been moving away from traditional classrooms into the online environment rather unobtrusively and haphazardly over the past 20 years. In 2020, COVID-19 brought about an urgent need to instantly transform all face-to-face methods into online formats and thus accelerated the whole transformation process outside the realm of imagination. As a direct consequence of the COVID-19 restrictions worldwide, online instruction and assessment have been on the increase in most educational institutions, especially tertiary. In an attempt to evaluate the impact of the pandemic on

DOI: 10.4018/978-1-6684-6227-0.ch002

tertiary education, a growing number of studies have investigated the challenges this new situation has posed to teachers and students alike. These explore a variety of topics, from learner academic integrity (Munoz & Mackay, 2019; Holden, Norris & Kuhlmeier, 2021) to student perceptions of onsite and online learning and examining (Elsalem & al, 2021; Graf, Rasmussen and Ruge, 2021; Jaap et al., 2021; Galetić & Herceg, 2022). The latter area, especially student perceptions of language exams conducted online, remains relatively understudied and will therefore be the main focus of this chapter.

The aim of this study is to critically evaluate language testing practices utilized at a Department of English and American Studies in the Czech Republic from the student point of view. The main objective of the mixed method research study is to investigate students' perceptions concerning different modes of language test administration, face-to-face oral and written examination in supervised conditions in the pre-COVID era and online distant examining in unsupervised conditions. Under supervised conditions, test-takers had no access to the internet other than the Moodle-based exam and two invigilators provided instructions and assistance and eliminated any attempts at cheating. In unsupervised conditions, tests were taken remotely from home, with cameras switched off. The research questions addressed in this study concern students' overall preferences regarding the two modes of exam administration and their attitudes towards academic integrity when taking exams. The last research question seeks some recommendations for the testing practices currently taking place at the department. The chapter will report the findings of a questionnaire study with 91 research participants, all current students at one of the biggest departments of English and American Studies in the Czech Republic, where the researchers both work as teachers and test developers.

Language exams at the department consist of two components, written and oral. All exams are developed at the department. For the written component, solely computer-based written exams had been used since 2003 yet always under supervised conditions. When the COVID 19 pandemic broke out, the department was well-prepared to administer the written language exams online. Given the general university policy, which encouraged trust and advised against taking strict security measures in those difficult times not to add stress for the students, the use of web camera supervision or any kind of distant monitoring during exam sittings was decided against. However, there was a noticeable discrepancy in scores between supervised and unsupervised exam sittings. Statistical analysis was carried out and the results showed significant improvement in student scores when taking the written exam unsupervised. This gave rise to questions related to the academic integrity of students and possible cheating.

As far as the oral component is concerned, before COVID-19, face-to-face examining was used. In this proficiency exam, students' speaking abilities were tested. Since 2020, distant oral examining online through Zoom has been used. The format was slightly adapted to fit the online environment better but even when face-to-face examining became a possibility again, some of the oral proficiency exams at the department remained online.

In this chapter, student perceptions of written and oral language exams administered online in supervised and unsupervised conditions will be explored and differences between the two modes of administration, if any, will be identified. Challenges to academic integrity will also be addressed and students' preferences and recommendations for improvement will be discussed.

Literature Review

With the growing popularity of computer-based testing over the last 20 years, a great deal of research has explored to what extent test-takers' behaviour and performance are affected by the online environment in which examinations are administered in unsupervised conditions (Carstairs & Myors, 2009; Hollister & Berenson, 2009; Ladyshewsky, 2015; Marks & Cronjé, 2008; Prince, Fulton & Garsombke, 2009; Underwood, 2006). This question has become increasingly important since even pre-COVID research-based evidence indicated growing tendencies of "undergraduate students to exhibit dishonest behavior on graded assignments" (Fask, Englander & Wang, 2014, p.110). In addition to research into academic integrity, other important topics have emerged in the post-Covid era, namely changes affecting instruction and assessment in an online as opposed to onsite environment, especially in higher education, and how students and teachers perceive online classes and exams. In this review of the literature, published research into student preferences regarding different modes of exam administration, academic integrity in online versus onsite exams and recommendations for the improvement of exam administration will be presented.

Data from several studies exploring student attitudes to online versus onsite examining suggest that most respondents perceive a variety of aspects of examining online, both positive and negative. A survey conducted by Galetić and Herceg (2022) analyzed responses from 276 university students, out of which 52% perceived online exams as worse in comparison to onsite exams, and 57% would choose onsite exams if given the choice. Similarly, the results of a large-scale cross-sectional study investigating student attitudes to distant online exams carried out in 2021 by Elsalem et al. indicate participants´ preference for onsite exams. This was reported by two thirds of the 730 participants. Students´ suggestions of how online exams can be improved were also explored. Increased stress levels, more time and effort in preparation and high levels of academic dishonesty in online exams were reported as problematic. The respondents suggested that exams should be modified in order to eliminate cheating, different sets of questions and questions examining higher cognitive skills should be adopted.

Unlike the two studies detailed above, student experience with remote online exams was perceived as positive overall by 447 participants of an online survey conducted in 2021 by Jaap et al. The results suggest that very few technical or practical problems occurred overall and mixed results in test anxiety were observed, where some experienced higher stress levels, while others reported lower stress levels. Despite their overall positive attitudes to online exams, most participants also expressed preferences for onsite exams. The performance in the exams was higher in the remote-administered exam in one of the two groups, n=236, and equivalent in the other, n=211. The authors conclude that unsupervised remote online exams are a legitimate alternative to onsite exams.

Similarly, a large-scale study on the comparison of oral exams administered online and onsite and teachers´ and students' perceptions of the two conducted in Denmark (Graf, Rasmussen and Ruge, 2021) brought mixed results. The authors reported "overall satisfaction with online oral examinations on the part of both students and examiners" but also "conflicting experiences with online oral examinations" (p. 1) where some dissatisfaction was reported by teachers and students alike. These differences were highly individual. Students found it "stressful to have the responsibility for the proper functioning of the technology" (p. 15) and the internet connection also played a role. One third of the students reported higher levels of nervousness when taking oral exams online, but the majority found the experience satisfactory and wished for online oral exams in the future, a view also shared by some of the teachers.

A much larger body of research was concerned with academic integrity. The findings related to the impact of unsupervised online testing on cheating were not always conclusive and the reported results were often contradictory. Data from some of the studies suggest that methods adopted by students when cheating do not seem to be influenced in online testing environments when unsupervised (Hollister & Berenson, 2009; Ladyshewsky, 2015), while others assert that unsupervised online testing might produce new ways of cheating (Underwood, 2006) and suggest that online examinations in such conditions should be avoided (Carstairs & Myors, 2009).

Hollister & Berenson (2009) adopted an experimental design with a randomized selection of participants. The subjects of their study were 214 students, randomly divided into two fully comparable groups of 107; Group 1 took the test in supervised classroom conditions and Group 2 online in unsupervised conditions. The study aimed to identify differences, if any, in the overall performance in exams by using statistical methods. No statistically significant overall differences in performance were revealed between the groups. Contrary to expectations, these results indicate no measurable influence of an unsupervised exam environment on test takers' performance. Similarly, Ladyshewsky (2015) conducted a large-scale research study with 250 participants. They took a test in supervised conditions and an online unsupervised test. The aim was to determine to what extent unsupervised testing encourages cheating at exams. The results confirm previous research studies (Hollister & Berenson, 2009) indicating that no statistically significant differences between the two modes of test administration were identified and suggest that students who intend to engage in dishonest behaviour do so no matter which of the two modes is adopted.

A surprising result was published by Fask, Englander and Wang (2014). They used an experimental design to find out how the performance of 44 students changed when taking exams in supervised and unsupervised conditions. Students tested in a supervised environment outperformed students tested online; this result was statistically significant (pp.106-109). In accord with the previously reported findings (Hollister & Berenson, 2009), it seems that while unsupervised exam conditions might lead to an increased tendency to cheat at exams, it might also have adverse effects on students' performance for reasons unrelated to dishonest behaviour. This might be caused by a variety of factors, from more frequent distractions when taking tests in other than classroom environments to potential problems with technology and internet connectivity. The major flaw appears to be the impossibility for test-takers to ask the invigilator for clarifications of any kind, a fact that might have a significant negative impact on the test results (Fask, Englander and Wang, 2014). In view of this statistically significant finding confirming the negative effect of an online testing environment on exam scores, it can be argued that this adverse factor mitigates the possibly positive effect cheating has on the overall exam scores.

A different result was reported by Prince, Fulton and Garsombke (2009) who analysed the test scores of 76 students who took tests both in supervised and unsupervised environments. It was reported that all participants scored significantly lower on supervised exams, 79% on average, versus unsupervised exams, in which they scored considerably higher, 87% on average. The results of this study clearly indicate that online test-taking in unsupervised conditions is compromised, and it is therefore advisable to prefer supervised exams which produce more reliable exam scores.

In a thorough review of research into why students engage in cheating in post-secondary education, Holden, Norris, and Kuhlmeier (2021) identify four major factors affecting academic integrity: "individual factors, institutional factors, medium-related factors, and assessment-specific factors" (p. 2). The authors confirm that while it is a commonly accepted belief that cheating online is more frequent than in the classroom, comparative studies examining cheating in class and online are not numerous, and the existing ones often produce contradictory results. Four of the eight studies reviewed by Holden et al. reported increased levels of cheating in the online environment, two indicated similar levels of cheating in both online and classroom environments, and two suggested that more cheating occurred in the classroom environment (Holden et al., 2021). The paper has confirmed claims made by other authors (e.g., Hollister & Berenson, 2009; Fask, Englander & Wang, 2014; Ladyshewsky, 2015) that more research is required in this area as with online environments being increasingly adopted in education, questions related to academic dishonesty cannot be ignored.

In summary, it should be noted that "irrespective of which side of the argument is correct, no testing method can conclusively eliminate all cheating" (Munoz & Mackay, 2019, p. 6). This does not mean that efforts should not be made to provide teachers and test administrators with clear research-based evidence on how such dishonesty could be minimised. Given the often contradictory results of the studies reviewed, it seems that further research into student perceptions of online versus onsite exams, as well as a more detailed account of academic integrity is in order. With a few exceptions, most of the studies presented here were conducted in areas other than language teaching. This chapter therefore focuses on language exams and attempts to explore how learners perceive taking language exams online and onsite, academic integrity and what suggestions for exam improvement they might offer.

Context of the Study

The language testing practices that are used at the department will now be described in more detail in order to better understand the context of this research study. Computer-based testing has been used at the department since 2003. Initially, existing pencil and paper exams were digitised and began to be administered online in supervised settings. Later, new written tests and exams were developed specifically for the online environment, and it was felt necessary to compare the two modes of test administration (pencil and paper and computer-based) as there were some discrepancies in individual student test results and their overall performance. A longitudinal study looking into the comparability of pencil and paper and computer-based tests in supervised conditions took place at the department from 2011-2016. The results from the final stages of research (2015-16) showed that students were more used to the computer-based format of testing, their results from the two modes were comparable and no statistically significant differences in the student scores across the modes were found (Nepivodova, 2023).

Written Component

The written component is a computer-administered Moodle-based proficiency exam. It is compulsory for all students at the department and aims to test their overall proficiency level irrespective of any course or material studied. It tests their reading comprehension, use of English and listening comprehension and makes use of test types such as multiple choice, open cloze, gapped sentences, word formation and sentence transformation. The exam takes 90 minutes with approximately 30 minutes for each domain tested. Without this exam, students cannot continue their studies and must repeat the year, so it can be expected that their motivation to succeed is high. This exam is first marked automatically by computer and then all written-in answers are manually checked by the examiners to make sure that all correct answers are accepted. Test items are also analysed after each run of testing and malfunctioning distractors and questions are replaced to ensure that the exams produce valid and reliable results.

Changes in the Written Component During the Pandemic

Despite the fact that all our written exams were already computerized and administered through Moodle, which is the platform used at the department, certain measures still had to be taken to fit the newly established requirement of the exams to be administered distantly and in unsupervised conditions.

Various technical and organisational issues had to be addressed; for example, more technical support was needed, the time limit was reconsidered and subsequently shortened, but overall, the process was smooth and obstacle-free.

Oral Component

The oral exam, which must be taken by all students at the department, tests students' ability to communicate effectively with the interlocutor and a speaking partner in a variety of contexts, addressing a range of topics. There are two examiners, an interlocutor, who asks questions and presents visual and written prompts, and an assessor, who focuses on the candidates´ performance and assesses their oral proficiency according to the pre-set criteria. The exam is taken by pairs of candidates or groups of three in case of an odd number of candidates, consists of three parts, and lasts for approximately 15 minutes (22 minutes if taken by a group of three).

The format and content of the original face-to-face exam is the following. Each of the three parts focuses on a different type of interaction. Part 1, in which general interactional language is tested, is between the individual candidate and the interlocutor and the candidates answer questions related to their free time, interests, studies, plans, etc. (4 minutes). Part 2 is an individual long turn based on picture prompts (approx. 5 minutes) and Part 3 is a collaborative task based on visual prompts again, followed by some more follow-up questions (5 minutes). The examiners assess the candidates according to criteria which were modelled on C1 Advanced, one of Cambridge English Qualifications exams. The criteria are grammar, vocabulary, discourse management, pronunciation, and interactive communication and each is assessed on a 5-point scale. The minimum passing score is 16.25 points, out of 25 points.

Changes in the Oral Exam During the Pandemic

Originally, this spoken exam was always conducted face-to-face but with the onset of the COVID-19 world pandemic in 2019, this was no longer possible. The researchers reacted to the situation promptly, adapting the format of the exam and shifting it from the onsite environment online. The oral exam was administered via Zoom and both the students and examiners had their cameras on. After a long and fruitful discussion of the team of experienced examiners, it was decided to implement two major changes in the format of the exam. First, the number of parts of the exam was reduced from three to two, and second, visual stimuli were abandoned. The reason for this change was primarily technical difficulties in sharing the visuals in adequate quality with the candidates.

Part 1 remains very similar to the original exam; candidates answer general questions regarding their interests, free time, etc. and interact mainly with the interlocutor. This part now takes about 6 minutes. In Part 2 candidates are asked to discuss a set of questions on a more complex topic together and engage in a discussion. This part also takes about 6 minutes. Some additional questions can be asked individually afterwards only if needed, e.g., if one of the candidates did not contribute enough. The assessment criteria and procedures remain unchanged.

Methods

The main objective of the mixed method research design introduced below is to map out and critically evaluate the testing practices which take place at a Department of English and American Studies in the

Czech Republic, and which have been heavily influenced by the COVID 19 pandemic. The student point of view forms the focus of this study.

The following research questions have been devised based on the research objectives:

Research Questions:
1. What are the students' preferences regarding the different modes of test administration?
2. Do students admit any violations of academic integrity during unsupervised computer-based test sittings?
3. Do students offer any recommendations or possible improvements to the testing practices at the department in general? If yes, what are they?

The participants were sampled on the basis of convenience sampling; in this case, these were all students studying at the Department of English and American Studies who were registered for a proficiency exam in the autumn semester of 2022 (n=91). This sampling method ensured that these students have experienced both the written component (i.e., the written proficiency exam) and the oral component (i.e., the oral proficiency exam) in different modes.

Research Instrument

In order to answer the research questions addressed in this study, a questionnaire regarding the different modes of testing was administered to the students and its results will be analysed and discussed. The questionnaire was anonymous, and the students agreed to participate in the research by signing informed consent before accessing the questionnaire administered in Google Forms online. They were informed that the data provided would be confidential and their answers would only serve the purposes of research leading to possible improvements in the overall testing practices at the department. The main purpose of the questionnaire was for the students to comment on the existing past and present testing and assessment practices that they have experienced, express their preferences, and suggest possible improvements.

The researchers' assumption is that students will prefer taking unsupervised proficiency exams as they will find them less stressful and more comfortable. As for the oral exams, some technical difficulties related to unstable connections, problems with sound, etc. might also be mentioned with reference to the online administration of the oral exams.

The questionnaire devised by the researchers was first used in a study looking into the possible differences between pencil and paper and computer-based language proficiency exams (Nepivodova, 2007). It was based on three previously validated instruments, namely an instrument used in the Program for International Student Assessment (PISA) investigating computer familiarity, Knezek and Christensen's Computer Attitude Questionnaire (1997) with the last instrument being the Computer Familiarity Questionnaire devised by Weir et al. (2007). The questionnaire was then updated and revised in accordance with Noyes and Garland's (2008) claim against using, for example, computer attitude scales devised in the 1990s because of possible changes in the construct. Questions on computer usage were thus mostly eliminated since the students work with computers on a daily basis, yet a number of questions related to the specifics of taking written and oral exams online have been added. Most of these came from the qualitative data collected during a longitudinal study in which the questionnaire was also piloted and analysed (Nepivodova, 2023). While there are various validated questionnaires regarding computer familiarity in general, none of those is directly linked to language assessment. In this day and age, using technology for educational purposes is more than common, especially in our university context; however, students still lack experience in being tested online and their first experience with high-stakes computer-based language testing often comes only when they start studying at the department. Furthermore, being tested in class and at home also poses a lot of questions and that is why the researchers felt the need to devise and then modify their own research instrument.

The questionnaire contains 26 questions. Eighteen questions are of a closed response format with either alternative answers (n=6) or a Likert scale (n=12) asking the students to express their opinions on a 7-point scale with agree/disagree as the extreme points. The 7-point scale was chosen in accordance with Finstad, who claims that "seven-point Likert items have been shown to be more accurate, easier to use, and a better reflection of a respondent's true evaluation" (2010, p.109). Eight questions are open-ended questions asking the students to fill some information based on their experience in a non-restrictive way. These fall under the category of qualitative data (Creswell, 2014). Table 1 below presents the items that are designed to elicit data for the following indices.

Table 1. Questionnaire indices

Index	Specification	Questions
Perceived ability	General	Q2, Q19, Q20, Q22, Q23
	Experience	Q3, Q4
	Responding	Q10, Q11, Q12, Q13
Preference	General	Q1, Q5, Q6, Q21
	Comfort	Q7, Q8, Q9
	Stress	Q14
Opinion	Integrity	Q15, Q16, Q17, Q18
	Recommendations	Q24, Q25, Q26

Given the limited scope, this study addressed the indices of preference and opinion only. The closed response item questions were analyzed by quantifying the responses provided. The analysis of the open-ended questions representing the qualitative data in this study was approached from the realistic as opposed to the narrative perspective (Silverman, 2006). A close link between the statements made and the original source of data is strictly observed, hence, for example, the students are quoted directly without linguistic alterations of their answers as recommended by Švaříček et al. (2007). Given the students' high level of English and the fact that the whole degree programme is taught in English, the questionnaire was in English and so were the students' answers. The analysis of the qualitative data consisted of three phases of coding, namely open, which Dörnyei (2007) considers to be "the first level of conceptual analysis of the data", axial, which aims to make links between categories, and selective, which pinpoints the core categories to be focused on (pp.260-261). The coding was carried out in Microsoft Excel and categories were developed and given mostly descriptive codes. The coding procedure was doublechecked by the researchers themselves and some minor inter-researcher discrepancies in coding were eliminated.

Results

Tables 2 and 3 below summarize the questionnaire results of the closed questions under scrutiny based on the frequency of data but are by no means exhaustive. The qualitative data is presented below the tables to further clarify some of the students' answers.

Table 2. Index: Preference regarding online versus onsite modes of exam administration

Specification	%	Responses
General	58.3% 50.6%	prefer online exams to f2f ones (Q1) would benefit from some training in computer-based test taking strategies. (Q21)
Comfort	53.9% 88%	feel comfortable taking oral computer-based language exams (Q7) feel comfortable taking the written computer-based language exams (Q8)
Stress	84.7%	find unsupervised computer-based exams less stressful (Q14)

As Table 2 demonstrates, 84.7% agree that unsupervised computer-based exams are less stressful, but only 58.3% claim they prefer the online format to f2f in general and 50.6% feel that some training in computer-based test taking strategies would help them perform better. There is a noticeable difference between the written and oral computer-based exams. While 88% of students feel comfortable taking the computer-based written language exams, the percentage drops to 53.9 when asked about the comfort perceived in the oral computer-based language exams (Q7). This lower percentage was confirmed by student answers to Q5 (see Figure 1 below, in which 1 stands for strongly disagree and 7 for strongly agree), which asked whether if given the choice, the students would like the Oral Practical English exam to be administered online and 50.6% expressed various degrees of disagreement, 9.9% remained neutral while only 39.6% expressed various degrees of agreement.

Figure 1. Index: Preference regarding the mode of oral exam administration

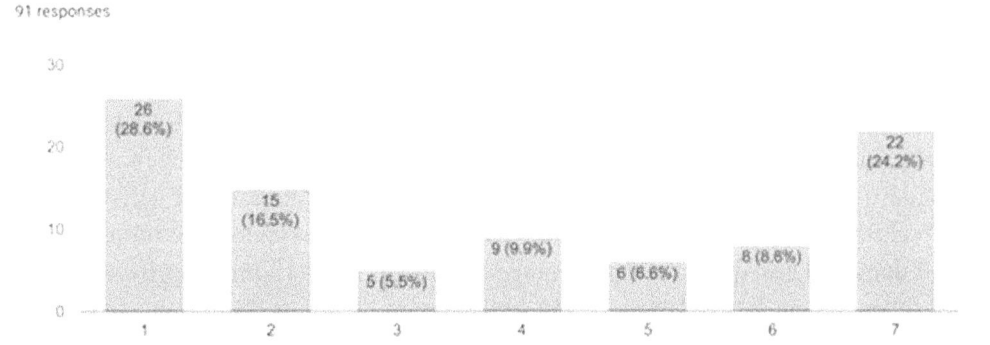

If given the choice, I would like the ORAL Practical English Exam to be administered online.
91 responses

- 1: 26 (28.6%)
- 2: 15 (16.5%)
- 3: 5 (5.5%)
- 4: 9 (9.9%)
- 5: 6 (6.6%)
- 6: 8 (8.8%)
- 7: 22 (24.2%)

This question was followed by an open-ended question 6, in which the students expressed the reasons for their preferences. It is interesting to note that without being forced to give their reasons, all 91 students (100%) provided their responses to this open-ended question. The respondents felt very strongly about their choice and supported it with a variety of complex arguments. In comparison, for question 26, in which respondents were asked to provide suggestions how testing at the department could be improved, only 40% replied.

Those in favour of the f2f format of the oral exam most often claimed that the f2f oral exam was more natural and genuine (Students 4, 5, 27, 36, 39, 43, 49, 54, 59, 63, 64, 67, 74, 75, 76, 84, 87, 92). For example, Student 27 believes that "face to face exams is a bit more natural, especially those oral ones, when the verbal and nonverbal communication is key" or as Student 54 puts it: "I think that the oral exam would be better in person because the conversation could feel more natural and would be easier to interact". Some students believe that f2f format improves their performance, e.g. "I prefer presential exams because it allows me to use my personality while speaking and thus improving my overall impression." (Student 76). Student 9 comments on the examiner judgment in relation to f2f exams: "I believe in-person exams allow the examiners to better judge whether the student is simply nervous or is lacking the required skill/knowledge."

Not having to worry about technical issues was yet another advantage of the f2f format as Student 26 summarizes by saying: "Technical issues, not directly speaking to the examiner, feeling of disconnect, microphone issues, latency of the call and so on." Technical issues were often mentioned in connection to stress and feelings of anxiety (Students 7, 14, 18, 32, 55, 58, 91). For example, Student 91 notes that "in a face-to-face exam [they] don't need to be stressed about [their] laptop sabotaging [them]". There were a few students stating that the online mode makes them more nervous in general as e.g., Student 22 testifies: "I just prefer face-to-face interaction to videochat, not only for exams. I am usually more nervous in an online setting."

When looking at the answers on the other end of the continuum, a recurrent reason for an online oral exam being a good option was the convenience of taking exams from home and not having to commute to the department (Students 11, 14, 16, 53, 56, 57, 61, 63, 71, 58, 83). This goes hand in hand with time management and saving time as claimed by Students 12, 72 and 78. Not having to commute was also often directly linked to feeling comfortable at home as e.g., Student 13 expressed: "Online is better because I do not have to commute, I can just pet my rabbit and turn on camera and do my exam in my own peaceful environment." A comfortable environment was a frequently mentioned advantage, as is evidenced by Students 3, 24, 30, 51, 57, 60, 65, 77, 86.

Finally, Reduced stress, which once again can be connected to feelings of comfort, was actually the most frequently mentioned advantage of taking the oral exam online (Students 1, 2, 6, 25, 31, 37, 42, 45, 56, 73, 79, 80, 81, 82) as e.g. Student 1 noted: "Since I am a very shy person, I would very much appreciate more online based exams. It would reduce my anxiety and stress a lot". Interestingly, there were some rare voices that complained about the online mode not being stressful enough. For example, Student 38 believes that "...it's very important for students to feel the pressure of surroundings and situation..." and feels that the online mode "...would decrease the value and relevance of the oral exam part".

As Table 3 demonstrates, quite a low percentage of students (6.6%) admit they have cheated during a supervised written computer-based exam (Q15) while almost a half (48.4%) admit some misconduct on their part during an unsupervised written computer-based exam (Q17). An open-ended question (Q18) asking about the reason for cheating followed. Out of the 48.4% of students who admitted they have cheated, 70% of these students (n=31) supplied their reasons, too. Student 35 briefly yet aptly summarized some of the reasons by saying: "stress, anxiety, time pressure". Another student claimed that it "made [them] feel more secure in [their] answers to double check" (Student 53). Student 21 provided a longer explanation for their behaviour by saying: "This was mostly because of spelling because I find it a bit difficult to write properly while writing on my computer. It is better to write stuff by hand in the case of spelling." Student 41 was quite straightforward when claiming "not to get an A or anything, just to make sure I pass. No other reason." Among the most frequent reasons for cheating during unsupervised exams mentioned by the students were the following: checking answers to make sure they are correct (e.g. Students 3, 17, 22, 27, 34, 42, 43, 53, 55, 74), not knowing the answers (e.g. Students 30, 48, 49, 51, 57, 58, 69) or admitting they have not studied enough (e.g. Students 7, 59), fear of failing (e.g. Students 12, 22, 24, 41, 61), panic and stress (e.g. Students 8, 35, 46) often mentioned in connection with time pressure (e.g. Students 35, 46).

Table 3. Index: Opinion towards student integrity and recommendations for improvement

Specification	%	Responses
Integrity	6.6%	admit they have cheated during a supervised written computer-based test/exam (Q15)
	48.4%	admit they have cheated during an unsupervised written computer-based test/exam (Q17)
Recommendations	40%	provide recommendations for possible improvement (Q26)

Recommendations for Improvement

The last question in the questionnaire (Question 26), in which respondents were asked to provide comments and suggestions on how the overall language testing process at the department could be improved, was only answered by 33 students.

The most often mentioned problem, which eight respondents had, was with different aspects of time limits at written exams (Students 17, 47, 48, 53, 56, 58, 80, 86). Some of them felt very strongly about it, saying that "The most significant factor, however, is time" (Student 80). More time would be felt as beneficial, as Student 56 suggested "I think adding at least 20 more minutes to the exam time would not do much harm.", and in addition to this, the area requiring a more generous time limit was specified by Student 86, who demanded "a longer time limit, especially for the reading and listening part". More careful consideration of time limit imposed on individual questions depending on the level of difficulty was also suggested: "Time limits for some questions are still an issue sometimes, way too short for questions that need a bit more time or way too long for short and/or trivial questions." (Student 17). In one of the comments, the reduced time limit, which was imposed in unsupervised distant testing in order to reduce the chances of cheating, was mentioned: "Shrinking the time limit was very stressful for me as my reading speed is pretty slow. It felt demotivating and not objective, but I understand why you had to do it" (Student 47). This was also mentioned by Student 80, who was aware of why it was inevitable at unsupervised exams but suggested students were given more time at f2f exams in supervised conditions: "The time limitation does not benefit in any way, and there is no reason for doing that, especially when it´s face to face. I know some people cheated when this was online, maybe that´s the reason why."

Another frequently addressed area, mentioned by seven respondents (Students 3, 20, 21, 54, 63, 68, 75), was the demand for more practice before the exams. This could be in the form of mock tests: "It would be nice if there were some mock tests for the written English exam" (Student 63), or more language courses provided by the department, either a course directly aimed at improving test-strategies: "I would always welcome a tutored course preceding such an important exam" as proposed by Student 68, but also general language courses: "I wish for more classes that would work actively with students' language skills like vocabulary, fluency, grammar, teaching English. Making us take language exams without providing sufficient amount of language classes seems hypocrite" (Student 20).

Concerning the written proficiency exams, some students pointed out that the format of some of the test items, especially when testing reading comprehension, was problematic for them (Students 6, 22, 45, 56, 65, 78, 80). Some found the organization of the text confusing: "I do not remember exactly which test it was, but I remember one exercise was really confusing, there were sentences and we were supposed to fill in the gaps but the text was weirdly sectioned" (Student 22). It seems that at times, the reason for this was the mode of administration, as Student 80 quite clearly stated: "the possibility of taking the exam on the paper would do wonders, at least for me. Especially for the reading part, I wouldn´t have to constantly scroll up and down and could underline the important info". Also, identifying incorrect sentences was regarded as challenging by some, "I think trying to evaluate whether a sentence is written correctly or not is just impossible for a non-native speaker, especially if the mistakes are not completely obvious" and suggested tasks in which sentences are rewritten instead "I think it would be more beneficial if the questions would ask to write a sentence using a word or checking if a specific word is used correctly in a sentence. Or adding questions with the goal of rewriting an original sentence using a given word" (Student 56). Some students also expressed their positive attitudes to open-ended questions, which were, in their view, beneficial especially in tests that encourage critical thinking (Students 45, 78), while others felt open questions in language tests when rephrasing is required were too stressful when computer-marked without manual correction by the teacher (Student 6).

Some students were questioning the relevance of taking language exams. One of the respondents suggested somewhat dramatically, but paradoxically in rather inaccurate language that: "I would strongly recommend to consider whether are the exams necessary -- I see the oral exam as sensible and meaningful but the written one... anyone can have luck to guess correctly the phrase or collocation..." (Student 65). Student 16 pointed out that since they already passed international exams, there was no need for other language exams to be taken at the department: "Because I already have a certificate and it just takes extra time which is needed for focus on other exams. And I practice my English daily, so I think the exam is redundant."

DISCUSSION AND CONCLUSION

In this part, the quantitative and qualitative questionnaire results will be brought together, summarized, and interpreted in order to answer the research questions.

In response to the first research question, which asked about the student preferences regarding the different modes of administration, the findings report that students seem to be perfectly comfortable when taking computer-based written tests, while noticeably less so when taking the oral exam on computers. Percentage-wise, more students prefer the f2f oral exam mode to the online mode. Students find the onsite oral exam more natural and appreciate that they do not have to deal with any technical issues that might have an impact on their performances. Some of them claim they are more nervous overall when the exam is administered online and their stress is often linked to fear of the technology giving up on them. The results related to online oral exams, especially the problems caused by technology reported and increased levels of nervousness felt by some students, are consistent with those of Graf, Rasmussen and Ruge (2021).

There are clear supporters of the online mode too and the main reasons for this as stated by the students are reduced stress, not having to commute and comfortable environments. In the student answers, reduced stress is quite often linked to if not actually attributed to students being able to take the exam in the comfort of their own homes. Since the 'stress' theme is frequently present on both sides of the Likert scale, it would be interesting to match the questionnaire answers to the individual student results and see whether this is somehow reflected in their scores. Unfortunately, this was not possible as the questionnaire was anonymous but is potentially an area of further research.

Not surprisingly, a great majority of students feels less stressed when taking unsupervised computer-based written exams and this would certainly be the ideal format for them. However, since they themselves admit certain violations of academic integrity during such exams as will be further commented on below, this does not seem to be a viable mode of test administration as far as the reliability of student results is concerned.

In response to the second research question, which is concerned with student violations of academic integrity during unsupervised computer-based test sittings, the findings show that students admit such misconduct. This came as a surprise to the researchers as although they had a feeling that some misconduct was taking place during the unsupervised test sittings, they did not expect the students to actually admit that. In contrast to their assumptions, more than half of the students admitted they had cheated in some way when not being monitored as opposed to only about 6% of students admitting some form of misconduct during supervised test sittings. The most recurring reasons for such behaviour during unsupervised test administration mentioned by the students were checking answers and not knowing answers. Fear of failing, stress and panic also played a part. This result agrees with some previously published research, as reported by Holden (2021). Further research could shed some light on how the student scores correlate with student answers to the questionnaire questions on academic integrity. In order to be able to work with the results and pair them up, the questionnaires would have to be signed and the question is whether students would speak so openly and honestly about their misconduct.

In response to the third research question, the students offered some recommendations or possible improvements to the testing practices at the department, a variety of different tendencies can be observed in the answers which were analysed. One of the most frequent comments was related to the time limit applied at written language exams. This was unanimously felt as being too tight and a longer time limit was required, especially since, according to some respondents, the time limit was at times too long for simple questions and too short for the demanding ones. This remark, however, does not seem to be justified since an overall time limit is imposed on the test and how much time test-takers spend on answering the individual questions, as well as the order in which they answer is entirely up to them. In fact, when tests are administered, students are always encouraged to start with the questions they regard as easy and leave the most challenging ones for later, according to their personal preferences. Another reported problem was the lack of focused practice before the exams, either in courses or mock tests. It has to be noted that a language course aimed at improving both general and academic language is only taught in the first year at the department, while in the higher years, students are expected to improve their language skills by self-study and exposure to authentic language, either at the department or outside of it. Another recurrent topic was the format of the test tasks, and mode of administration, especially in reading comprehension tests, for which pencil and paper format was suggested as a more student-friendly one, a claim supported by earlier research (Nepivodova, 2023). The most radical opinion expressed in this part of the survey was the relevance of language exams in philological programmes altogether, which was questioned by some. This claim, however, was sometimes undermined by the inaccuracy in the language the respondents used when expressing their views.

Pedagogical Implications

Based on the research outcomes, some pedagogical implications were formulated. The findings suggest that students do not perceive computer-based written exams as more challenging than onsite ones, but they should be supervised to avoid breaches of academic integrity. They further indicate that students would benefit from exam practice materials and mock tests and an optional course helping them to prepare for the language exams. Regarding oral exams, students should be given a choice in the format – there is a need to make sure the results are equivalent; further research is needed in this area. The results also support the idea that feedback on oral exams would be beneficial – if not personalized, then at least comments on some general problematic areas, common mistakes, etc. provided after each test sitting. The findings also have implications for the recognition of international certificates and organization of exams at the department. Students should take fewer language exams throughout their BA studies – they now take a proficiency language exam three times during their bachelor studies – this decision should be revisited and the number of exams reduced to 2 maximum (i.e. a C1-level exam after year 1 and a C2-level at the end of their studies).

Research Limitations

The current study is not without limitations. First, its scope was to analyse student perceptions of exams only. It would be interesting to see to what extent the examiners agree and what other possible challenges or advantages of the two exam modes they might perceive. Second, the research was conducted at one department only and expanding it to other English language departments in the Czech Republic or even abroad might provide interesting comparisons. Third, exploring how some of the findings emerging from the analysis are supported by exam results in the pre-COVID and COVID eras would offer a more complex picture of the area under scrutiny. Notwithstanding its limitations, the current study offers some valuable insights into student perceptions of written and oral exams applicable in testing.

Suggestions for Future Research

Some of the findings identified in this study could be supported by further research. This should focus on analysing both written and oral exam results in post-COVID times to see whether they correspond to the years prior to the Covid year (2020). This would give us a more complex picture of the differences between the two modes of language testing procedures, and support or contradict the reported violations of academic integrity.

Also, gathering qualitative data from the examiners regarding the two modes of oral exam administration would shed some more light on the process of examining and could elicit their attitudes to examining onsite as opposed to online, which could then provide possible explanations for some of the student preferences.

Some of the open-ended questions in the questionnaire yielded interesting results and their detailed analysis would be beneficial. It could explore how frequently students practice before taking exams and what strategies they adopt; this information could be applied when language courses are prepared in the future.

Conclusion

This chapter aimed to describe and analyse past and present language testing practices at a Department of English and American Studies in the Czech Republic as viewed by students, and based on the results offers some suggestions and teaching implications for the future that could be applicable in different contexts.

To highlight and summarize some of the main findings: Students feel generally comfortable taking computer-based written exams and their stress levels decrease even more when such exam is unsupervised. Very different attitudes of students were identified when it comes to oral exams administered online as opposed to onsite. The communication feeling unnatural and increased stress levels due to possible failure of technology were the most often voiced caveats of the online mode while convenience and reduced levels of stress when taking the exam in the comfort of students' homes were seen as the benefits of the online mode. Academic integrity is significantly more at risk in unsupervised exam sittings as the questionnaire data analysis testifies. Students' main reasons for cheating are their urge to check some answers, not knowing the answer at all or fear of failure.

A few rather singular findings are worth mentioning. Surprisingly, some students doubt the relevance of language exams altogether. In relation to computer-administered exams, pencil and paper form was suggested a few times as a viable option, especially when testing reading comprehension. It also came as a surprise that some students welcome certain levels of stress as being a desirable condition for producing better results at exams.

For a variety of reasons, computer-based testing and oral examining online will inevitably remain viable options in language assessment even in the post-COVID era. Based on the analysis of the results, advantages and caveats of computer-based testing and oral examining online have been outlined and some pedagogical implications for making the process as smooth as possible have been formulated. The researchers hope that teachers and test administrators find the study carried out to be relevant and the conclusions arrived at useful and helpful in their everyday practice.

REFERENCES

Brown, J. D. (2005). *Testing in language programs: A comprehensive guide to English language assessment*. Prentice Hall Regents.

Carstairs, J., & Myors, B. (2009). Internet testing: A natural experiment reveals test score inflation on a high-stakes, unsupervised cognitive test. *Computers in Human Behavior*, *25*(3), 738–742. https://www.sciencedirect.com/science/article/pii/S0747563209000260. doi:10.1016/j.chb.2009.01.011

Creswell, J. W. (2014). *Research design: Qualitative, quantitative, and mixed methods approaches* (4th ed.). Sage.

Dörnyei, Z. (2007). *Research methods in applied linguistics: Quantitative, qualitative, and mixed methodologies*. Oxford University Press.

Elsalem, L., Al-Azzam, N., Jum'ah, A. A., & Obeidat, N. (2021). Remote E-exams during Covid-19 pandemic: A cross-sectional study of students' preferences and academic dishonesty in faculties of medical sciences. *Annals of Medicine and Surgery (London)*, *62*, 326–333. doi:10.1016/j.amsu.2021.01.054 PMID:33520225

Farhady, H. (1982). Measures of language proficiency from the learner's perspective. *TESOL Quarterly*, *16*(1), 43. doi:10.2307/3586562

Fask, A., Englander, F., & Wang, Z. (2014). Do Online Exams Facilitate Cheating? An Experiment Designed to Separate Possible Cheating from the Effect of the Online Test Taking Environment. *Journal of Academic Ethics*, *12*(2), 101–112. https://www.researchgate.net/publication/272018789. doi:10.100710805-014-9207-1

Finstad, K. (2010). Response interpolation and scale sensitivity: Evidence against 5-point scales. *Journal of Usability Studies*, *5*(3), 104–110.

Galetić, F., & Herceg, T. (2022). Student Preferences for Online and Onsite Learning and Exams - How Credible at the Grades Obtained in Online Exams? *FEB Zagreb International Odyssey Conference on Economics, 4*(1), 198-211.https://www.researchgate.net/publication/366067341

Graf, S. T., Rasmussen, F., & Ruge, D. (2021). *Online oral examinations during Covid-19. A survey study at University College level.* Tidsskriftet Læring og Medier (LOM), Nr. 24 2021ISSN: 1903-248X. https://tidsskrift.dk/lom/article/view/125805/174782

Grijalva, T., Nowell, C., & Kerkvliet, J. (2006). Academic Honesty and Online Courses. Coll. *Student J.*, *40*(1), 180–185.

Hartle, S. (2022). University student perceptions of English language study changes: Reactions to remote emergency teaching during the COVID-19 emergency. *Language Learning in Higher Education*, *12*(2), 429–451. doi:10.1515/cercles-2022-2056

Holden, O. L., Norris, M. E., & Kuhlmeier, V. A. (2021). Academic Integrity in Online Assessment: A Research Review. *Front. Educ., 14 July 2021 Sec. Frontiers in Education*, *6*, 639814. Advance online publication. doi:10.3389/feduc.2021.639814

Holden, O. L., Norris, M. E., & Kuhlmeier, V. A. (2021). Academic Integrity in Online Assessment: A Research Review. *Frontiers in Education, 6 - 2021*, NA. https://doi.org/https://doi.org/10.3389/feduc.2021.639814

Hollister, K. K., & Berenson, M. L. (2009). Proctored versus Unsupervised Online Exams: Studying the Impact of Exam Environment on Student Performance. *Decision Sciences Journal of Innovative Education, 7*(1). https://www.learntechlib.org/p/157703

Hughes, A. (2003). Testing for Language Teachers. (2nd or 3rd edition). Cambridge: CUP.

Jaap, A., Dewar, A., Duncan, C., Fairhurst, K., Hope, D., & Kluth, D. (2021). Effect of remote online exam delivery on student experience and performance in applied knowledge tests. *BMC Medical Education*, *21*(1), 86. doi:10.118612909-021-02521-1 PMID:33530962

Jansem, A. (2021). The Feasibility of Foreign Language Online Instruction During the Covid-19 Pandemic: A Qualitative Case Study of Instructors' and Students' Reflections. *International Education Studies*, *14*(4), 93–101. https://doi.org/doi. doi:10.5539/ies.v14n4p93

Khan, Z., & Balasubramanian, S. (2012). Students Go Click, Flick and Cheat… e-Cheating, Technologies, and More. *Journal of Academic and Business Ethics*, *6*, 1–26.

King, D. L., & Case, C. J. (2014). E-cheating: Incidence and Trends Among College Students. *Issues in Information Systems*, *15*(I), 20–27.

Knezek, G., Christensen, R., & Rice, D. (1997). Changes in Teacher Attitudes During Information Technology Training. In J. Willis, J. Price, S. McNeil, B. Robin & D. Willis (Eds.), *Proceedings of SITE 1997--Society for Information Technology & Teacher Education International Conference* (pp. 763-766). Waynesville, NC USA: Association for the Advancement of Computing in Education (AACE). https://www.learntechlib.org/primary/p/47182

Ladyshewsky, R. K. (2015). Post-graduate student performance in 'supervised in-class' vs. 'unsupervised online' multiple choice tests: Implications for cheating and test security. *Assessment & Evaluation in Higher Education*, *40*(7), 883–897. doi:10.1080/02602938.2014.956683

Lanier, M. M. (2006). Academic Integrity and Distance Learning. *Journal of Criminal Justice Education*, *17*(2), 244–261. doi:10.1080/10511250600866166

Marks, A. M., & Cronjé, J. C. (2008). Randomised Items in computer-based tests: Russian roulette in assessment? *International Forum of Educational Technology and Society*. *11* (4), 41–50. https://digitalknowledge.cput.ac.za/handle/11189/3519

Munoz, A., & Mackay, J. (2019). An online testing design choice typology towards cheating threat minimisation. *Journal of University Teaching & Learning Practice*, *16*(3), 54–70. doi:10.53761/1.16.3.5

Nepivodova, L. (2007) *On Communicative Language Ability, Validity and Different Modes of Administration (The analysis of the second-year Practical English Examination)*. [Unpublished MA dissertation, Masaryk University, Brno].

Nepivodova, Linda. (2023) *Computer or Paper? Comparison of two modes of test administration*. Brno: Masarykova univerzita. Cizí jazyky a jejich didaktiky: teorie, empirie, praxe.

Noyes, J. M., & Garland, K. J. (2008). Computer-vs. paper-based tasks: Are they equivalent? *Ergonomics*, *51*(9), 1352–1375. doi:10.1080/00140130802170387 PMID:18802819

Prince, D. J., Fulton, R. A., & Garsombke, T. W. (2009). Comparisons Of Proctored Versus Non-Proctored Testing Strategies In Graduate Distance Education Curriculum. [TLC]. *Journal of College Teaching and Learning*, *6*(7). doi:10.19030/tlc.v6i7.1125

Radosavlevikj, N. (2021). Students´ Attitudes and Preferences to Online Teaching During the Pandemic COVID -19 Period. *Yearbook - Faculty of Philology*, *12*(17), 103-115. https://eds.s.ebscohost.com

Silverman, D. (2006). *Interpreting qualitative data: Methods for analyzing talk, text and interaction.* Sage Publications.

Stuber-McEwen, D., Wiseley, P., & Hoggatt, S. (2009). Point, Click, and Cheat: Frequency and Type of Academic Dishonesty in the Virtual Classroom. *Online Journal of Distance Learning Administration, 12*(3), 1.

Suvorov, R., & Hegelheimer, V. (2014). *Computer-assisted language testing. The 167 companion to language assessment.* Wiley. http://onlinelibrary.wiley.com/doi/10.1002/9781118411360.wbcla083/full

Švaříček, R., & Šeďová, K. (2007). Kvalitativní výzkum v pedagogických vědách. *Portal (Baltimore, Md.).*

Underwood, J. (2006). Digital Technologies and Dishonesty in Examinations and Tests. *Review, Qualifications and Curriculum Authority, 10*(5). https://www.researchgate.net/publication/253936339

Varble, D. (2014). Reducing Cheating Opportunities in Online Test. *Atlantic Marketing J., 3*(3), 131–149.

Weir, C., O'Sullivan, B., Yan, J., & Bax, S. (2007). Does the computer make a difference? Reaction of candidates to a computer-based versus a traditional handwritten form of the IELTS writing component: Effects and impact. *IELTS Research Report., 7*(6), 1–37.

KEY TERMS AND DEFINITIONS

Academic Misconduct: Also known as academic dishonesty, a breach of academic integrity, behaviour that goes against honesty and trust, e.g. cheating.

Academic Integrity: Behaving in an honest, responsible, and fair way during one's studies and academic work.

Computer-based Test: A test, which is administered through the use of a computer as opposed to a pencil and paper test, which is written by hand.

Proficiency Exam: An exam which measures the overall level of student ability, e.g. how proficient they are in a particular language.

Supervised Setting: An exam condition, during which the students are proctored by invigilators or test administrators.

Unsupervised Setting: An exam condition, during which the students are not monitored, e.g. when they sit tests in the comfort of their homes.

Chapter 3
Online Formative Assessment via the E-Portfolio:
Attitudes of Greek and Russian EFL University Students

Vicky Papachristou
https://orcid.org/0000-0001-5067-6330
CITY College, University of York Europe Campus, Greece

Maria-Araxi Sachpazian
CITY College, University of York Europe Campus, Greece

Olga Safonkina
https://orcid.org/0000-0002-5802-1897
National Research N.P. Ogarev State University, Russia

ABSTRACT

The study explores Greek and Russian EFL university students' attitudes towards the use of electronic portfolios as one of the most suitable forms of formative assessment to monitor the process and progress of foreign language learning for online language education. To that end, data were collected online via a questionnaire by 75 Greek and 115 Russian participants who have experienced studying English online during the pandemic and face-to-face. The results have shown that all students hold positive attitudes towards this type of assessment and are aware of its facilitative and beneficial role in enhancing self-learning which could lead to significantly better results. Based on the findings obtained, the authors will attempt to put forth some practical recommendations for English practitioners in teaching English online who seek educational support in this area.

DOI: 10.4018/978-1-6684-6227-0.ch003

INTRODUCTION

Due to the COVID-19 pandemic, emergency remote teaching (ERT) has been quickly and suddenly adopted by educational institutions all over the world, which has significantly boosted the use of online assessment (Hodges et al., 2020). Research has shown that this type of assessment provides a number of advantages to teachers and students including adaptability, systematic and ongoing support, interaction and the opportunity for quick and direct feedback (Gikandi, et al., 2011; Topuz et al., 2022). But it also comes with difficulties, such as worries about cheating, validity and reliability of assessment tasks, technical difficulties, and accessibility for students with disabilities, among other things (Radu et al., 2020; School Education Gateway, 2020).

Unfortunately, the urgency to employ ERT as the mainstream mode of teaching in all levels of education globally, did not mean that both teachers and learners were well prepared or even aware how online instruction and online assessment could have been implemented (European Commission, 2020; Ikeda, 2020). Regarding the contexts of the current research, neither the Greek nor the Russian states were prepared for a shift from face-to-face teaching and traditional assessment to emergency online instruction and assessment, as several vital issues emerged ranging from improper digital infrastructure, limited availability of digital educational material to students' and teachers' lack of digital literacy (Markova 2020; Nenyuk 2021; Nikolopoulou et al., 2019; Perifanou et al., 2022; Tzifopoulos 2020).

As a result of the implementation of ERT, formative assessment has become significant in teaching several subjects, including English as a Foreign Language (EFL), as it fosters deep and meaningful learning along with critical 21st century skills (Baleni, 2015). Formative assessment in ERT can take many different forms, such as peer-to-peer evaluations, online quizzes and online discussions, via several online tools and platforms. Previous research has established that this mode of assessment can be considerably beneficial in giving students ongoing feedback to assist their learning, helping learners track their progress, enabling them to identify areas where more support may be required and helping them overcome any emerging difficulties (Abduh, 2021; Gikandi, et al., 2011).

Therefore, drawing from prior research concerning the Greek and Russian educational backgrounds and the similarities they share in terms of assessment, the focal point of this research is to explore Greek and Russian EFL university students' attitudes towards online formative assessment through e-portfolios and whether they are aware of the supportive and facilitative role of e-portfolios in enhancing English language learning. That also takes the authors to the attempt to explore if tertiary level students are aware of the connections between e-portfolios as a tool of formative assessment and the development of self-monitoring and self-learning, as according to previous research, learners do not seem to know or realize this connection during language learning (Baleni, 2015).

Literature Review

It is an undeniable fact that the use of ICT has reshaped and redefined the educational sector as "interactive, learner-centered, open and flexible environment of online learning" (Jabeen & Thomas, 2015, p. 1). The outbreak of COVID-19 pandemic and the abrupt shift from face-to-face teaching and learning to remote classes, was according to Abduh (2021) "a transformative experiment" (p. 3), mainly because teachers and students were asked to take this giant leap, with little or no preparation, while at the same time they were left with no other option but online teaching (Abduh, 2021). This was the first time in the history of education that digital (remote or web-based) teaching became the norm and was not merely an optional mode via which education could be delivered. In fact, researchers proposed a specific term coined for this type of instruction, called Emergency Remote Teaching (ERT) (Hodges et al., 2020). This notion is based on the assumption that ERT has a temporary nature due to crisis circumstances and refers to fully remote teaching solutions that both teachers and learners have to deal with. If these crisis conditions do not apply, then these classes would be planned and delivered in a face-to-face mode or as a part of blended teaching. Therefore, the main goal of ERT is not to try to establish "a robust educational ecosystem", but to build up a temporary access and teaching support that could be reliable enough for temporary measures (Hodges et al., 2020).

Turning to the issue of assessment, and particularly online assessment, which is the focal point of discussion in this chapter, there is no doubt regarding its central role in the educational process. The pandemic had a profound and an inevitable impact on it, as it limited the assessment options available to educators to online ones only (Abduh, 2021). As it is stated in ERT research, "one of the main challenges higher educational institutions encounter amid the recent COVID-19 crisis is transferring assessment approaches […] to the online ERT approach" (Allehaiby & Al-Bahlani, 2021, p. 3). Therefore, teachers had not only to rethink and adapt their teaching principles and strategies to match the digital environment, but also to adjust assessment (whether summative or formative) to the online setting to achieve and enhance effective learning.

It is clear in the existing literature that summative assessment has a role to play in recording the students' performance for administrative reasons as well as to ensure their progress to the next level of study, but it is formative assessment (or assessment for learning) which shapes the students' learning as it is an on-going process, more qualitative and not necessarily concerned with grades (Baleni, 2015). Hence, its focus is on providing feedback in the form of descriptive comments instead of a numeric representation of the students' performance, monitoring learning and giving students multiple attempts to accomplish a task, since the goal is learning and not simply scoring (Abduh, 2021). Referring to the role that formative assessment plays in the context of ERT, researchers seem to concur that this type of assessment is more suitable as it provides meaningful interaction between teachers and students "... while the assessment is being conducted" (Allehaiby & Al-Bahlani, 2021, p. 11). This claim is in agreement with current ongoing research addressing the changes in classroom assessment practices during emergency remote teaching, as in the case of COVID-19 pandemic, and reinforces the proposition that formative assessment is a more widely preferred one and "...the most common strategy" chosen by teachers of English (Panadero et al., 2022, p. 22). Unfortunately, despite its pivotal role in fostering learning, formative assessment continues to receive little attention, especially in online tertiary education, which is the context of the current research, rendering summative assessment via tests and exams as the most prevailing mode (Pachler et al., 2010).

One of the tools of formative assessment that has been widely used for teaching and learning on all levels of education is portfolio. A number of instructors have implemented it as a tool to compile collections of student work for specific objectives such as assessment, ability documentation, or employability (Ciesielkiewicz, 2019). The portfolio has been defined and described in several ways in the literature. Hung (2012) claims that portfolios are collections of students' artifacts that serve as a record of their growth throughout time and "range from writing samples, reading logs, reflections and peers' comments to teacher's feedback" (p. 22). Griva and Kofou (2017) define portfolios as a "continuous cumulative record of language development and a holistic view of student learning and work that demonstrates achievement or improvement" (p. 29), highlighting the critical function of the portfolio in measuring accomplishment of learning objectives. Generally, a portfolio that focuses on enhancing learning is based on a constructivist model that allows students to have as many fresh learning starts as possible, receive constructive feedback from peers and teachers, reflect on their work and revise what has been learnt and practiced (Barett & Carney, 2005).

With the adoption and extensive use of ICT in classrooms, paper-based portfolios began to evolve into electronic portfolios (e-portfolios) which made them more accessible and portable compared to the traditional ones. The distinctive feature of an e-portfolio is that of being digital, which is reflected in most definitions provided by scholars, as "an e-portfolio is described as a selective and structured collection of information, gathered for specific purposes, showing/evidencing one's accomplishments and growth which are stored digitally and managed by appropriate software, developed by using appropriate multimedia and customarily with in a web environment and retrieved from a website, or delivered by CD-ROM" (Challis, 2005, p. 3). This "digitized" nature and format of the e-portfolio has not changed since it has been articulated in the definitions provided by Lorenzo and Ittelson (2005) and Gray (2008) who along with Barett and Carney (2005) underline that an e-portfolio is a dynamic, constantly evolving, diverse, reflective, and authentic tool that offers evidence of the learners' learning, voice, critical and reflective thinking.

Both paper-based and e-portfolios can be used as tools for formative assessment as well as self-assessment, therefore they share basic characteristics. Firstly, they are *authentic, reflective, and motivational*, as students take ownership of their learning by reflecting and assessing on their learning strategies and skills in order to improve them, hence they become autonomous. Secondly, they are *controllable* as students can amend the content of the portfolios based on their reflections. A third characteristic is that portfolios are *communicative* and *interactive* because students can communicate, interact, and get feedback from their peers and teachers to enhance their learning. Also, portfolios are *dynamic*; the more the learners reflect, self-assess, organize, and modify the content of tasks, the more diverse the portfolio becomes. Moreover, portfolios are highly *personalized* since each student forms his/her own portfolio that mirrors his/her individual learning goals, competencies, growth, and achievements over time. Another interesting feature of portfolios is that they are *integrative*, as they connect students' lives and academic outcomes. Finally, they are *multi-purposed* and *multi-sourced*, since portfolios can be used to provide information and evaluations to students regarding their learning, to teachers about learners' performance and to institutions in relation to education programmes (Griva & Kofou, 2017; Yastibas & Yastibas, 2015, pp. 5-6).

All the aforementioned features render portfolios/e-portfolios as an alternative and diverse assessment tool in second/foreign language teaching and learning. Evidence from research asserts that they promote collaborative learning, can help students monitor their progress, receive peer and teacher's feedback based on which they can reflect and self-assess their learning processes and skills, personalize their learning, report their experiences authentically, improve themselves and generally become more active and autonomous agents of their own learning (Cummins & Davesne, 2009; Babaee & Tikoduadua, 2013). In short, portfolios/e-portfolios are in line with the tenets of learner-centered approaches which focus on the process of learning, thus they serve as a formative assessment tool (Aghazadeh & Soleimani, 2020; Griva & Kofou, 2017; Muin & Hafidah, 2020; Yastibas & Yastibas, 2015). It is precisely of these benefits that prior literature has documented the popularity of this digital tool in second/foreign language learning as well as the effectiveness and usefulness of implementing portfolios/e-portfolios to improve EFL students' language competence, skills and subject-specific learning in elementary, secondary and higher education (Alexiou & Paraskeva, 2010; Baturay & Daloğlu, 2010; Bolliger & Shepherd, 2010; Demirel & Duman, 2015; Farahian & Avarzamani, 2018; Hung, 2012; Song, 2021; Vasileiou et al, 2023;

Wang & Jeffrey, 2017). Adding to that, several studies have reported that students hold positive attitudes towards the use of portfolio/e-portfolio assessment contrary to traditional paper-based ones as the former promotes more meaningful and deeper learning along with 21st century skills (Aghazadeh & Soleimani, 2020; Hsieh, Lee & Chen, 2015; Namaziandost et al., 2020; Syafei et al., 2021). What is more, the existing literature suggests that via the use of e-portfolios, students can visualize the connection and benefits between what they are taught, their learning and future employability (Aghazadeh & Soleimani, 2020; Ciesielkiewicz, 2019; Hsieh et al., 2015; Hung, 2012; Syzdykova et al., 2021).

Therefore, the current study sets out to address and explore Greek and Russian EFL university students' attitudes towards the use of e-portfolios in enhancing English language learning online. Based on this research objective, we will try to further understand if tertiary level students, who have experienced ERT and online formative assessment via e-portfolios, are aware of the connections between e-portfolios as an assessment tool and the development of self-monitoring and self-learning.

METHODOLOGY

Participants

One of the objectives of the current study is to explore Greek and Russian EFL undergraduate university students' attitudes towards the implementation of e-portfolios as an assessment tool. Before profiling the participants, it is necessary to provide critical information about the two educational systems. Beginning with the Greek educational system, it places a high priority on teaching foreign languages, especially English. As a result, English is "the default foreign language adopted by the state for students" for all levels of education (Sifakis & Sougari, 2005, p. 471). More specifically, Greek primary schools began teaching foreign languages in 1987, but until English became a required subject in the curriculum in 1991, there were few other languages other than English that were offered by schools. The teaching of the English language expanded to the last four grades of primary education in 2003, and in 2016 it is taught from the first grade of elementary school implementing more communicative approaches and teaching techniques (Anastasiadou, 2015; Mattheoudakis & Alexiou, 2009; Greek Ministry of Education and Religious Affairs, 2016). Even more recently, English language instruction was introduced in the kindergarten by the Greek Ministry of Education and Religious Affairs (2021) aiming at promoting, boosting, cultivating, and strengthening learners' multicultural awareness and adaptability from a very young age. Despite these developments in the Greek EFL context, in public schools English is typically taught by a non-native speaker, the contact hours are few and most importantly classrooms are frequently large and mixed-ability ones (Angouri et al., 2010). As a result, this render "language provision at state institutions [...] to be rather devalued" (Angouri et al., 2010, p.192), which has led to the emergence of a thriving private sector of foreign language instruction, also called "shadow education" (Tsiplakides, 2018). This sector serves the great majority of students, that is about 80%, offers more contact hours, extremely intensive exam-focused courses with rigid testing and traditional assessment and gives the chance to students to take standardized proficiency exams towards obtaining a language certificate (Angouri et al., 2010; Mattheoudakis & Alexiou, 2009). Therefore, it can be undoubtedly inferred that the status of the English language appears to be quite prestigious in the Greek educational system and the Greek society in general, since Greeks hold the opinion that learning a foreign language is essential for them to be able to communicate with others outside of their home country, have more career prospects, and ultimately have a higher socioeconomic level (Mattheoudakis & Alexiou, 2009).

Regarding the Russian education system and the place of English language teaching in it, evidence suggests that it has been quite turbulent and with considerable fluctuations historically speaking. Despite this status, teaching modern languages, and especially English, is a mandatory part of the curriculum of both secondary and higher education in the Russian education system (Ter-Misanova, 2005). Focusing particularly on the teaching of the English language in Russia, some decades ago it was mostly characterized by the meticulous and in-depth study of grammar and vocabulary, accompanied by respective tasks, which were hardly aligned with the students' needs. Recently there has been a shift to employing more communicative techniques and strategies in teaching English, adopting a sociocultural approach in which practicing speaking, listening and writing are of equal importance to reading, in an attempt to address and boost the skills students need in a more globalized, competitive and demanding world (Ter-Misanova, 2005). Regarding the more technical aspects of the education system, secondary school students start studying English in their second grade and continue till university. Since 2009 the acceptance to Russian Universities has been based on the results of Unified National Tests (EGE) including the test in the English language. Being a norm-referenced test, which usually consists of traditional and stiff testing techniques, the level of complexity of the test is up to B2, as it is stated in the specification of the Unified National State Exam in English (Solnyshkina et al., 2014). Still, despite the aforementioned developments in the education system and state schools, private language schools propagate, establishing a strong private sector which offers more targeted teaching of English (Ter-Misanova, 2005).

Following the background on the education systems of the two countries, overall, 75 Greek and 115 Russian second-year students and onwards were recruited online via emails. The specific selection was opted as optimal since these students had experienced both face-to-face and online classes of English (as part of ERT) in their home countries, and hence traditional and online assessment, given the outbreak of COVID-19 pandemic; as such, a direct comparison between the two modes can be made. Of them all, 58 Greek and 66 Russian students' responses were analyzed for the current study as these were the ones that knew what an e-portfolio is and had previously used it. This selection was determined through the questionnaire which included the definition of the e-portfolio, and based on this, students were requested to indicate whether they have prior experience with it or not to be eligible to continue with filling in the questionnaire (see App. 1). Moreover, these two student populations were chosen as their contexts share other common characteristics too. For example, both Greek and Russian students are taught English as a foreign language (FL) from a young age till university, both contexts tend to be student-centered and employ communicative approaches to teaching English and both countries have a thriving private sector that offers extra classes in English. Furthermore, the respondents from both countries came from various scientific fields, whereas just over half the sample was female. Regarding the participants' age, Greek students ranged from 18 to 45 years old and Russian ones from 18 to 29 years old. As per their level of competence in English, most Greek participants reported having a C2 level, which was based on evidence from their language certificates. On the other hand, most Russian respondents identified themselves as having a B2 level based on the Unified National State Exam in English. Finally, given that the participants were contacted online, they came from different places around Greece and Russia, therefore there were no geographical limitations.

Research Instrument

Considering the above aim, the use of a quantitative research method and an online questionnaire was deemed as the most appropriate tool to collect data. According to Dörnyei (2007) "quantitative inquiry is systematic, rigorous, focused and tightly controlled" (p. 34) and the use of the questionnaire to yield quantitative results is most applied in social sciences, especially in studying people's attitudes (Dörnyei, 2007; Dörnyei & Taguchi, 2010). The appeal of online questionnaires stems from the fact that they are easy to use, fast, flexible and cost effective as they are distributed via social media and/or emails. Also, they can reach a wide and diverse audience as there are no geographical limitations, thus collecting data from a large pool of people. Moreover, respondents can answer the questionnaire anywhere, anytime and at their own pace, hence increasing the response rates. Finally, such data collection can be processed and analyzed relatively fast using computer software programs, such as SPSS (Ball, 2019; Dörnyei, 2007; Dörnyei & Taguchi, 2010; Lefever et al., 2007; Sue & Ritter, 2012).

Regarding the content of the questionnaire, it was adopted and adapted on the basis of previously designed ones and similar topics to the one of the current projects (Aghazadeh & Soleimani, 2020; Song, 2021). More specifically, it was divided into two parts and took approximately 8 minutes for the respondents to complete. The first part included demographic information to profile the participants while the second one consisted of statements addressing the students' attitudes towards the use of e-portfolio-based assessment. All statements were of a Likert scale type ranging from strongly disagree (1) to strongly agree (5), as this is "a scale and technique for attitude measurement" (Göb, McCollin & Ramalhoto, 2007, p. 604). The choice of this scaling technique lies in the fact that it is a straightforward, adaptable, and trustworthy tool to explore the attitudes of a specific target group (Dörnyei & Taguchi, 2010). Pertaining to the five-grade scale, Dörnyei and Taguchi (2010) further support that this is the most prevalent number, as response options beyond five or six could lead to incorrect or unreliable answers due to the respondents' difficulty in discerning between different degrees of agreement or disagreement.

It is critical to highlight that the present research has obtained ethical approval by CITY College, University of York Europe Campus's Ethics Review Committee. Following, prior to commencing data collection through the online questionnaire, each participant was informed via an information sheet about the scope and objectives of the study and was given a consent form; only after agreeing and assigning the form, could the participant proceed with filling in the questionnaire.

Data Analysis

Data management and analysis were performed using SPSS software (version 27). As such, to describe general trends and the variability of the scores, descriptive statistics, including frequencies and percentages, were used to analyze the quantitative data that was retrieved from the questionnaire (Dörnyei, 2007). Also, a composite index was created which included all the questions regarding attitudes aiming at finding the mean value and determining whether the attitudes are positive, neutral or negative. Furthermore, Pearson correlation coefficient tests were employed, which reveal whether there is a statistically significant relationship between any two variables and show "the strength and direction of their relationship or association with each other" (Dörnyei, 2007, p. 223). Finally, One-Way ANOVAS and multiple regression analyses were run to compare the means of the Greek and Russian students' attitudes in an attempt to observe any differences as well as examine simultaneously the relation of more than one parameter (i.e., age, gender, country, etc.) with the dependent variable (i.e., attitudes) (Darren & Mallery, 2020).

FINDINGS

Descriptive Statistics

This section reports the frequencies and percentages to observe the general trends and variability in the scores of the quantitative data collected. The first set of questions aimed to explore the demographics of the sample, while the second part of the questions set out to investigate the participants' attitudes towards the use of e-portfolios as an assessment tool while learning English at a university level.

The first set of questions addressed the demographics of both populations. More specifically, descriptive analyses have revealed an uneven ratio between male and female respondents as most of them were female ones in both countries; that is in the Greek data 61.3% (46/75) were female students while 38.7 (29/75) were male ones and in the Russian data 84.3% (97/115) were female participants whereas 15.7% (18/115) were male ones. Regarding the age distribution, the mean frequency value for the Greek students is M=23 years old and for the Russian ones is M=20.5 years old, which correspond to their years of studies, that is mainly the second and third year. Moreover, these students were found to study various subjects, with Humanities/Social Sciences and English Philology/Studies/Linguistics receiving the highest percentages in both countries, namely 48% and 17,3% for the Greek data and 12,2% and 80% for the Russian data respectively. When the participants were asked about the tools they have used during online teaching, 30.7% of the Greek students reported the use of Kahoot, 13.3% the use of Moodle and 12% the use of Quizlet. In a relatively similar vein, 83.5% of the Russian students reported that they mostly used Quizlet, while Padlet and Kahoot were popular choices as well, reaching 60.9% and 50.5% respectively. If we now turn to the results regarding the participants' level of English proficiency, a comparison of the two populations revealed interesting, yet expected differences. Figures 1 and 2 present an overview of the students' results and as can be seen from the pie charts below, 56% of the Greek students reported to have a C2 level of English, 25% a C1 level and only a minority of 17% a B2 level. On the contrary, 17% of the Russian students indicated that they have a B1 level of English, 44% a B2 level, 28% a C1 level and only 3% a C2 level. As discussed in the literature review, this difference can be accounted for on the basis that the two countries have different regulations and policies regarding English language exams and respective certificates of competency.

Another interesting finding is related to students' experience with the electronic portfolio and whether they are familiar with this type of assessment. It is apparent from Figures 3 and 4 below that most of both Greek and Russian students do have some experience with this mode of assessment. In particular, 77.3% (58/75) of the Greek students answered positively to this question, while 22.7% (17/75) gave a negative reply. In a similar vein, 57,4% (66/115) of the Russian students provided a positive answer whereas 42.6% (49/115) replied negatively. It is worth pointing out that the students' field of study did not seem to affect their answers regarding experience with e-portfolio, as even some students of English Philology/Studies/Linguistics who are trained to be teachers, appeared to reply negatively to this question.

Figure 1. Greek students' level of proficiency in English

Greek students' level of English

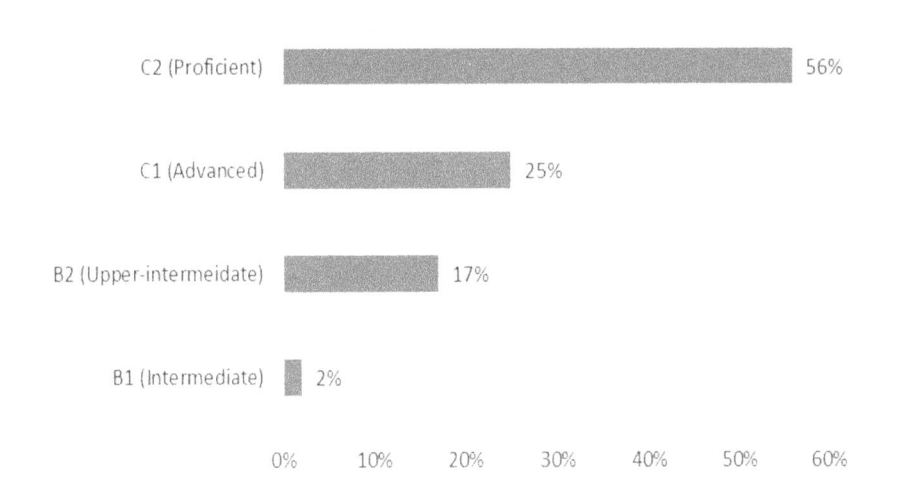

- C2 (Proficient): 56%
- C1 (Advanced): 25%
- B2 (Upper-intermeidate): 17%
- B1 (Intermediate): 2%

Figure 2. Russian students' level of proficiency in English

Russian students' level of English

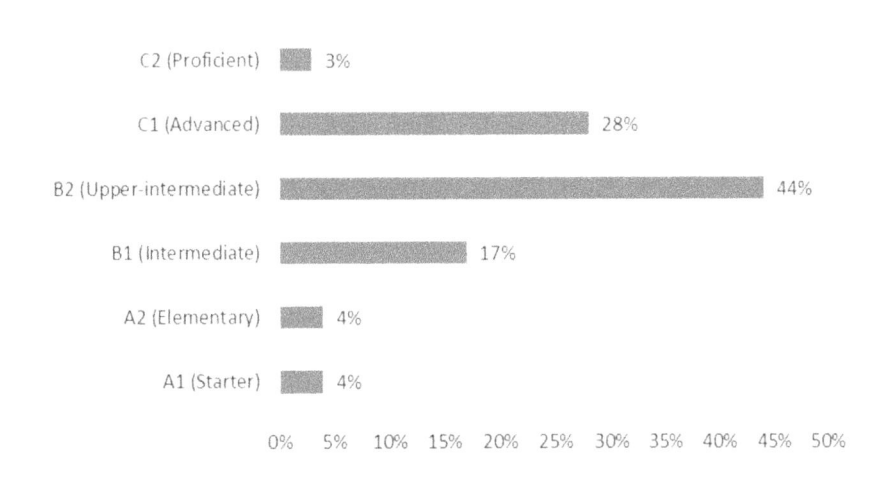

- C2 (Proficient): 3%
- C1 (Advanced): 28%
- B2 (Upper-intermediate): 44%
- B1 (Intermediate): 17%
- A2 (Elementary): 4%
- A1 (Starter): 4%

The second set of questions aimed to explore the students' attitudes towards the use of e-portfolio as a formative assessment tool while learning English and attempted to investigate if their attitudes are positive, neutral, or negative and if they are aware of the connections between e-portfolios and the development of self-monitoring and self-regulation. It is important to highlight that only those who answered positively to having an experience with e-portfolios continued with filling in the rest of the questionnaire, which resulted in having 58 Greek and 66 Russian respondents out of the original sample. To that end, descriptive analyses were conducted for all Likert scale questions and their mean score values were calculated to show the students' central tendency. The results have shown that all mean values for all questions were close to four (4 = "agree" option) for both student populations which could mean that students tend to have positive attitudes towards the use of e-portfolio as a formative assessment tool while learning English. In order to corroborate this finding, two composite indexes for attitudes were created which included all the questions exploring attitudes (questions 8-28), excluding question 25 that has a negative phrasing. These analyses confirmed the above finding and provided further evidence of the students' positive attitudes, which are depicted in the histograms below. As it is shown in Figures 5 and 6, the mean value of the Greek composite index is M = 3.77 and for the Russian one is M = 3.70.

Figure 3. Greek students' responses regarding experience with e-portfolios during online learning

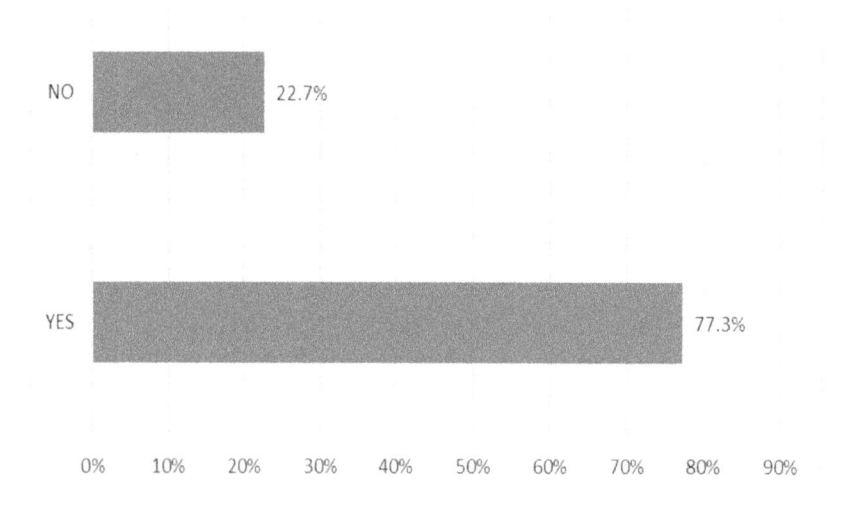

Figure 4. Russian students' responses regarding experience with e-portfolios during online learning

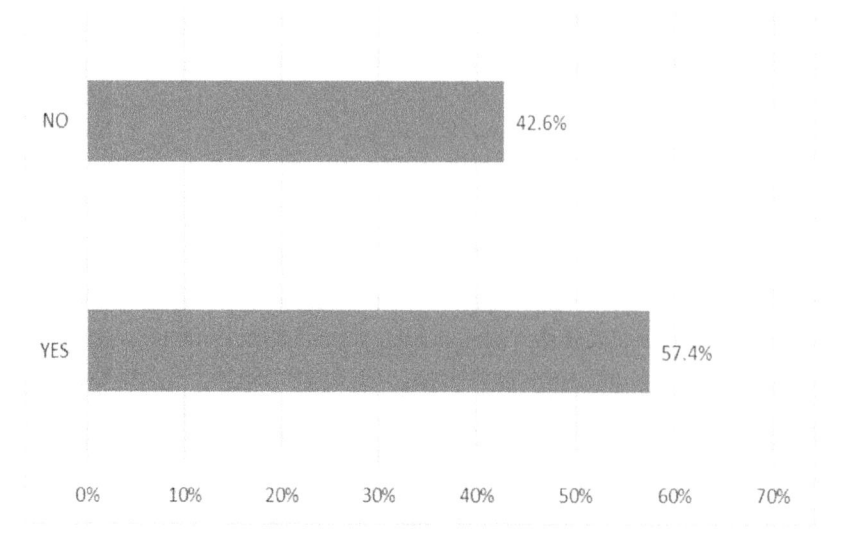

Figure 5. Composite index for Greek students' attitudes towards e-portfolios

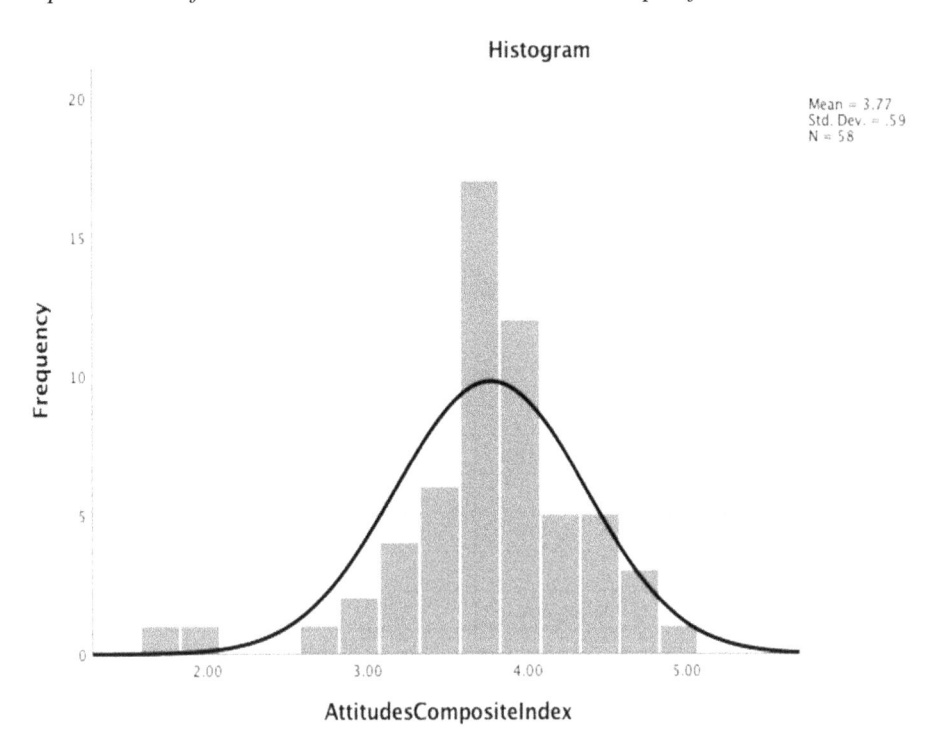

Figure 6. Composite index for Russian students' attitudes towards e-portfolios

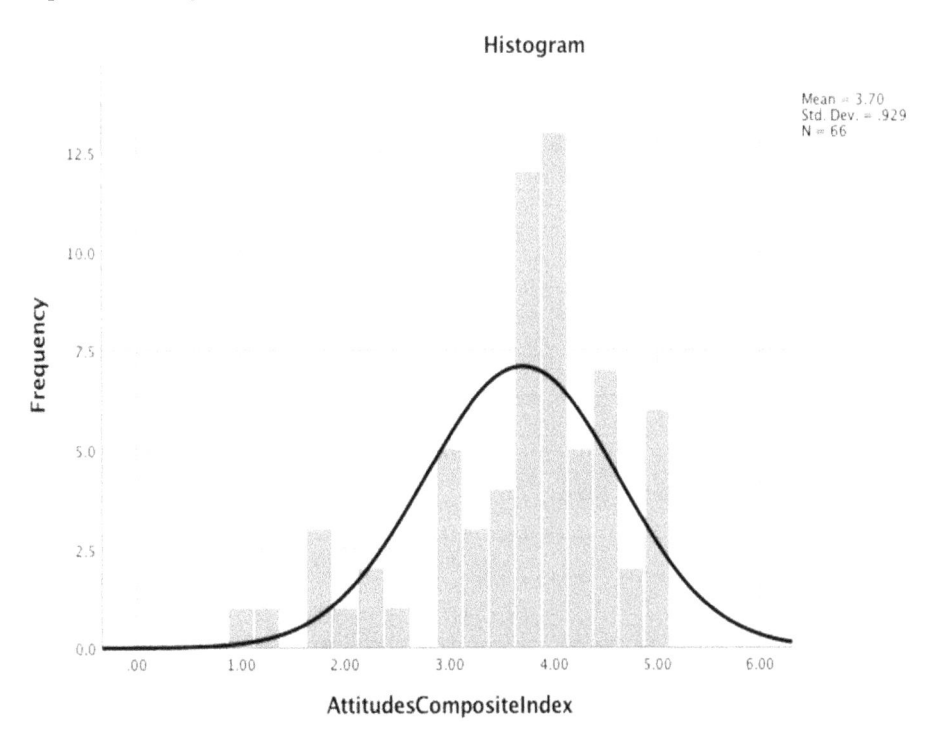

Regarding both student populations' awareness of the connection between e-portfolio assessment and self-monitoring and self-learning, it seems that students generally tend to be aware of the effectiveness of having this type of assessment while learning English in terms of their performance and development and appear to be positively disposed towards it. In fact, the overall responses to the questions addressing this issue were positive as it is shown in Table 1 and Table 2, as both Greek and Russian students mostly agree/strongly agree with the statements below.

Table 1. Greek students' responses regarding awareness of the connection between e-portfolio assessment and self-monitoring and self-learning

Statements	Strongly Disagree	Disagree	Neither Agree Nor Disagree	Agree	Strongly agree
E-portfolios help find out my strengths and weaknesses in English	1.6%	4.8%	30.6%	46.8%	16.1%
E-portfolios help reflect on my learning process	1.6%	0%	22.6%	50%	25.8%
E-portfolios help evaluate my learning	3.2%	6.5%	19.4%	46.8%	24.2%
E-portfolios help organize and arrange learning	3.2%	4.8%	17.7%	58.1%	16.1%
E-portfolios are a good tool to show how learning is taking place	1.6%	4.8%	25.8%	56.5%	11.3%
E-portfolios represent learning results	1.6%	8.1%	32.3%	37.1%	21%
E-portfolios provide a multi-dimensional perspective about learning and assessment	1.6%	3.2%	19.4%	53.2%	22.6%
E-portfolios provide a good sample to assess my performance	0%	3.2%	27.4%	51.6%	17.7%
E-portfolios record evidence of learning	3.2%	4.8%	27.4%	43.5%	21%
E-portfolios help me with personal development	3.2%	9.7%	29%	46.8%	11.3%
E-portfolios lead to more professional development	1.6%	4.8%	22.6%	58.1%	12.9%

Table 2. Russian students' responses regarding awareness of the connection between e-portfolio assessment and self-monitoring and self-learning

Statements	Strongly Disagree	Disagree	Neither Agree Nor Disagree	Agree	Strongly agree
E-portfolios help find out my strengths and weaknesses in English	7,6%	1,5%	24,2%	37,9%	28,8%
E-portfolios help reflect on my learning process	6,1%	9,1%	15,2%	39,4%	30,3%
E-portfolios help evaluate my learning	7,6%	6,1%	16,7%	37,9%	31,8%
E-portfolios help organize and arrange learning	7,6%	6,1%	16,7%	34,8%	34,8%
E-portfolios are a good tool to show how learning is taking place	4,5%	3,0%	24,2%	42,4%	25,8%
E-portfolios represent learning results	7,6%	6,1%	19,7%	33,3%	33,3%
E-portfolios provide a multi-dimensional perspective about learning and assessment	1,5%	7,6%	31,8%	37,9%	21,2%
E-portfolios provide a good sample to assess my performance	4,5%	6,1%	22,7%	39,4%	27,3%
E-portfolios record evidence of learning	4,5%	9,1%	18,2%	34,8%	33,3%
E-portfolios help me with personal development	7,6%	10,6%	19,7%	34,8%	27,3%
E-portfolios lead to more professional development	6,1%	3%	28,8%	36,4%	25,8%

Online Formative Assessment via the E-Portfolio

Interesting findings have also emerged in relation to the students' attitudes towards the use of online tools, traditional pen-and-paper assessment, and e-portfolio assessment, as shown in Table 3 and Table 4.

Table 3. Greek students' responses towards the use of online tools, traditional pen-and-paper assessment, and e-portfolio assessment

Statements	Strongly Disagree	Disagree	Neither Agree Nor Disagree	Agree	Strongly agree
E-portfolios offer more helpful feedback than traditional pen-and-paper assignments	1.6%	14.5%	27.4%	37.1%	19.4%
E-portfolios are better than the traditional pen-and-paper exams	4.8%	8.1%	25.8%	30.6%	30.6%
I prefer assessment through e-portfolios than traditional assessment	4.8%	9.7%	40.3%	27.4%	17.7%
I think online tools are not useful in my learning	25.8%	38.7%	6.5%	14.5%	14.5%
I think online tools are useful in my learning	3.2%	4.8%	8.1%	50%	33.9%
Using online tools improves my effectiveness in learning	4.8%	4.8%	19.4%	50%	21%

Table 4. Russian students' responses towards the use of online tools, traditional pen-and-paper assessment, and e-portfolio assessment

Statements	Strongly Disagree	Disagree	Neither Agree Nor Disagree	Agree	Strongly agree
E-portfolios offer more helpful feedback than traditional pen-and-paper assignments	4.5%	13.6%	31.9%	30.3%	19.7%
E-portfolios are better than the traditional pen-and-paper exams	7.6%	12.1%	30.3%	28.8%	21.2%
I prefer assessment through e-portfolios than traditional assessment	3%	16.7%	34.9%	33.3%	12.1%
I think online tools are not useful in my learning	30.3%	24.2%	19.7%	15.2%	10.6%
I think online tools are useful in my learning	7.6%	4.5%	19.7%	30.3%	37.9%
Using online tools improves my effectiveness in learning	7.6%	7.6%	25.8%	33.2%	25.8%

Both student populations seem to acknowledge the usefulness and effectiveness of the online tools in facilitating their learning, as the great majority of the participants have responded positively to these questions. What seems to be particularly thought-provoking pertains to the students' attitudes towards their preference for assessment via the traditional exams and e-portfolios. Observing the data above it seems that the participants are relatively split in half, as some of them are more positive towards assessment through e-portfolios, while others are neutral lingering between traditional and e-portfolio types of assessment. This result may be explained by the fact that the former mode of assessment is deeply rooted in the educational background of both Greek and Russian students, in spite of the recent developments documented in the two education systems and the attempt to modernize teaching and assessment techniques.

Statistical Analyses

To reveal whether there is a statistically significant relationship between any two variables, individual Pearson correlation coefficient tests were employed (Dörnyei, 2007, p. 223). Regarding the Greek data, no significant differences were found between gender, level of English and individual questions on attitudes, hence it can be claimed that there is no influence of these two variables on Greek students' attitudes. Moreover, only trace amounts of the variable of years of undergraduate studies were detected in the correlation tests between this variable and individual questions on attitudes, yet this cannot constitute robust evidence of the effect of this variable on the participants' attitudes. On the contrary, strong correlations were observed between age and each question on attitudes, as several statistically significant differences emerged; yet, these were negative Pearson correlations, which means that the younger students held more positive attitudes than the older ones towards the use of e-portfolio as a formative assessment tool while learning English. This finding was further confirmed when the composite index for attitudes was correlated with age, as there was a statistically significant difference of a p-value of 0.004 and negative Pearson coefficient -.371.

Turning now to the Russian data, a lot of similar results have been obtained. In particular, participants' attitudes appeared to be unaffected by gender, age and years of undergraduate studies as no individual significant correlations were reported. In contrast, important positive correlations were revealed between the students' level of English and each question on attitudes, suggesting that the higher the level of English competence the students have, the more positive attitudes they hold towards the use of e-portfolio as a formative assessment tool while learning English. Once again, this result was supported further as the Pearson correlation coefficient between the composite index of attitudes and level of studies was found to be .278 with a corresponding p-value of 0.024.

Apart from individual analyses, comparisons between the two data sets were realized to capture significant differences between the two groups of students. To that end, One-Way ANOVAS were carried out to compare the means of the attitudes between Greek and Russian students, genders, and levels of English. The results did not show any significant differences in the mean values of the attitudes between the two countries, genders, or the different levels of competency in English, therefore the participants' attitudes are not affected by these variables. In order to solidify any of the aforementioned results, multiple regression analysis was conducted as this estimation analysis allows the simultaneous examination of the relation and effect of more than one parameter on the dependent variable, in this case the impact of age, gender, country, level of English and years of studies on students' attitudes towards the use of e-portfolio as a type of assessment in learning English. The results of the regression indicated that the model explained 5.8% of the variance and that the model was not a significant predictor of attitudes, $F(5,11) = 1.45$, $p = .211$, hence it seems that there is no overall relation between the examined variables and the students' positive attitudes.

Taken together, these results suggest that both Greek and Russian undergraduate EFL university students tend to hold positive attitudes towards the use of e-portfolio as a type of formative assessment in learning English. Moreover, they seem to be aware of its usefulness and facilitative role in learning English more actively and effectively, along with enhancing self-monitoring and regulating their own learning. While individually each student population's attitudes appear to be affected by one variable, that is age for Greek participants and level of English for Russian ones, yet, when the two samples are compared, overall, these positive attitudes do not seem to be affected by any of the variables examined in this study.

DISCUSSION

The primary objective of the current study was to explore the Greek and Russian EFL university students' attitudes towards the use of e-portfolio as a type of formative assessment while learning English. In reviewing the literature, prior studies have documented the efficacy and usefulness of using portfolios/e-portfolios to facilitate and enhance EFL students' language proficiency, skills and subject-specific learning in both higher education and elementary/secondary levels (Alexiou & Paraskeva, 2010; Demirel & Duman, 2015; Farahian & Avarzamani, 2018; Hung, 2012; Song, 2021). Additionally, a number of studies have found that students are positively disposed towards e-portfolio assessments compared to more traditional paper-based ones, because the former encourages deeper and more meaningful learning (Aghazadeh & Soleimani, 2020; Hsieh et al., 2015; Namaziandost et al., 2020; Syafei et al., 2021). Consistent with the literature, the results of the present study revealed that both Greek and Russian participants have positive attitudes towards the implementation of e-portfolio assessment in learning English as a foreign language. Regarding the Greek respondents, the most influential variable in shaping their positive attitudes was age, as the younger students were more positive towards the use of the e-portfolio as an assessment tool. This may be partly justified by the fact that these younger learners have experienced the new developments in the teaching of English in the Greek education system, as some of them had some prior experience with the use of portfolios and some more communicative teaching techniques. When it comes to the Russian students, the level of English proficiency seems to be the most prominent variable affecting attitudes, as the higher level the learners obtain, the more positive they are towards the use of e-portfolio assessment. This is a relatively expected outcome since all students in Russia need to take the Unified National State Exam in English to enter university which is up to B2 level. As explained earlier, this is a strict and high-stake type of assessment, so any students who wish to pursue English competency beyond that level, will have to attend more classes and can be exposed to different and more alternative types of assessment and ways of teaching. What is interesting is that, despite the differences of the respondents' level of English proficiency, this did not seem to play a role in shaping their attitudes towards the use of e-portfolio assessment when the two populations were compared. This finding may suggest that firstly, the students' attitudes are genuinely positive as their previous experience with portfolios has shown them how facilitative they can be in learning English, and secondly, this mode of formative assessment could be used at any level of English, providing that primarily the teachers are trained to apply such an alternative tool of assessment.

Also, the authors attempted to investigate if EFL tertiary level students are aware of the connections between e-portfolios and the development of self-monitoring and self-learning. Previous research has suggested that learners do not know or do not realize the above connection (Baleni, 2015); however, the results of the present study have provided evidence that the students are well aware that e-portfolios can serve as an assessment tool in teaching and learning. E-portfolios can help them monitor their progress, receive teacher's feedback based on which they can reflect and self-assess their learning processes and skills, personalize their learning, report their experiences authentically, improve themselves and generally become more active and autonomous agents of their own learning. These findings further support the idea that e-portfolios and the accompanying feedback can help learners identify their weaknesses (e.g. inability to speak freely, inability to paraphrase, limited range of structures) and strengths (e.g. rich context, well-researched topic, an attempt to involve the audience in the presentation) which also evaluate some of the 21st century skills, such as digital literacy and ability to communicate among others (Aghazadeh & Soleimani, 2020; Griva & Kofou, 2017; Muin & Hafidah, 2020; Yastibas & Yastibas, 2015).

Despite the aforementioned positive findings regarding students' attitudes towards the implementation of e-portfolios as an assessment tool in learning English, certain concerns and limitations should be pinpointed which emerged during the course of this study. An important concern is related to the lack of some students' experience with e-portfolios as a type of assessment. Even though in the current study this proportion was not a large one, still it cannot be disregarded as it is directly connected with the educational mentality and context of the countries. As it has been stated elsewhere, despite the fact that the education systems in Greece and Russia have started to become relatively more student-centered, still Greece has a robust private foreign language education industry that caters to the majority of students, provides incredibly intensive exam-focused courses that begin at a young age and focus considerably on traditional pen-and-paper assessment (Angouri et al., 2010). Regarding Russia's educational context, despite its recent developments, a lingering traditional approach to Russian education shows that changing traditional assessment practices tends to be a complicated task as it means changing the prevailing teaching culture (Bolotov et al., 2013). What is more, student populations come from two specific countries, which could limit the generalizability of the findings, since learners who are educated in more progressive education systems, may yield somewhat different responses and hence a different outcome. Following this, another limitation that should be acknowledged is the unequal sample size between the two countries. Given that this is not an easily controllable variable and could possibly affect some of the results, still the present study offers some useful information on the topic in question. Also, the fact that only students' attitudes are explored, shows one side of the coin, as we do not delve into English teachers' attitudes on the issue of using e-portfolios as a tool for formative assessment. Notwithstanding these limitations, the insights gained from this study may be of assistance to teachers of English, help them reconsider their teaching methodology and suggest an alternative way of assessing students' skills and knowledge both online and face-to-face.

Based on the results obtained by the questionnaire, the authors could put forth some practical recommendations for using e-portfolio as a tool to establish systematic formative assessment. These suggestions can be employed by teachers of English during face-to-face, blended, or online teaching, including ERT. Since any educational process is highly dependent on continuous training and professional development, educators who are open to change are more likely to experience higher levels of satisfaction towards online education and adopt a more innovative and learner-centered teaching mindset.

To begin with, the issue of feedback provided to the students as part of their online formative assessment is especially important as it motivates them to reflect on their strengths and weaknesses, rather than simply glance at their score. The feedback received is infinitely more useful and valid if the task is developed in steps and stages and students receive feedback every step of the way, thus being able to incorporate the feedback into every next stage of the task. An e-portfolio seems to be exactly of this type of the task which can be developed in steps providing the students with the possibility to obtain and apply the feedback. This process implies that formative assessment is related to the development of self-regulated learning, which is more productive and a necessary element of life-long learning (Aghazadeh & Soleimani, 2020; Griva & Kofou, 2017; Muin & Hafidah, 2020).

Another area to consider for the recommendations is that online learning and more importantly ERT requires new or reconceptualized educational tools to be introduced into the learning environment. That renders the use of technology being a focal point in the classroom requiring students to cultivate new learning skills and competencies (ElSaheli-Elhage, 2021). As these emerging practices for online language assessment are the new reality, it lies within the teachers to get further educated and trained, incorporate such teaching approaches and tools into their online teaching process and foster inclusive and sustainable learning environments (Gratz & Looney, 2020). The current data seem to suggest that both Greek and Russian students do not see online formative assessment as a second best in comparison with traditional pen-and-paper assessment and are mindful about the tools which can be used during online learning.

If we view the existence of digital teaching and learning as a possibility and reality, and not as a limited-range option, we should find best practices that can ensure high standards and guarantee that students can take part in online assessment which adequately and effectively replicates assessment in the physical classroom (Baleni, 2015). It is also important that the online assessment methods to be used allow learners to create meaningful bonds, collaborate and interact with the community of learners and focus on more than simply recalling information. Last but not least, it is necessary for that learning to be transferable, which means that the knowledge tested, and the skills evaluated are what learners will need in their professional settings (Baleni, 2015). In other words, part of the online assessment best practices should be the avoidance of merely acquiring and recalling of knowledge and focus more on the promotion of assessment types that engage learners with "sociocognitive processes" that are necessary for their social and professional life (Gikandi et al., 2011, p. 2334).

Despite the undoubtful advantages of e-portfolio-based assessment, it should be acknowledged that such a tool requires both teachers and students to master additional technical skills and receive specific training which can be rather time consuming. Also, all stakeholders and parties involved should be convinced of this type of assessment to be included in the programme and curriculum, which can be a challenging process (Griva & Kofou, 2017). Therefore, future research could be firstly directed towards exploring teachers' attitudes and perceptions towards the use of e-portfolio assessment in teaching English. This is of pivotal importance as these insights can possibly help trainers identify teachers' weaknesses, gaps and needs and develop programmes that will train teachers on how to implement formative assessment via e-portfolios. A further study could be the actualization of using this kind of assessment in the classroom and assess its effectiveness in facilitating and enhancing students' competence and performance in the English language.

CONCLUSION

The literature review, data analysis, discussion of the findings and other issues presented above highlight that if online teaching is to be considered as a mainstream option and a step into the future, then it is necessary to find reliable tools for teaching and learning. These tools should also form part of a framework of online formative assessment that can connect the use of ICT for the delivery of the content of assessment, allow room for feedback and feedforward during the stages of the assessment and inspire students to adopt the active process of learning and not the score. The need for such a tool might well be faced with the active and principled use of electronic portfolios for assessment purposes, especially for assessing students' achievements while learning English as a foreign language. Most importantly, e-portfolios allow teachers to track and monitor students' progress over a period of time, both in a traditional face-to-face instructional environment and under ERT conditions, and promote vital 21st century skills, such as self-assessment and self-control skills.

ACKNOWLEDGMENT

This research received no specific grant from any funding agency in the public, commercial, or not-for-profit sectors.

REFERENCES

Abduh, M. (2021). Full-time online assessment during COVID-19 lockdown: EFL teachers' perceptions. *Asian EFL Journal Research Articles*, *28*(01), 26–46.

Aghazadeh, Z., & Soleimani, M. (2020). The effect of e-portfolio on EFL learners' writing accuracy, fluency and complexity. *The Reading Matrix: An International Online Journal*, *20*(2), 182–199.

Alexiou, A., & Paraskeva, F. (2010). Enhancing self-regulated learning skills through the implementation of an e-portfolio tool. *Procedia: Social and Behavioral Sciences*, *2*(2), 3048–3054. doi:10.1016/j.sbspro.2010.03.463

Allehaiby, W. H., & Al-Bahlani, S. (2021). Applying Assessment Principles during Emergency Remote Teaching: Challenges and Considerations. *Arab World English Journal*, *12*(4), 3–18. doi:10.24093/awej/vol12no4.1

Anastasiadou, A. (2015). EFL Curriculum Design: The Case of the Greek State School Reality in the Last Two Decades (1997-2014). *International Journal of Applied Linguistics and English Literature*, *4*(2), 112–119.

Angouri, J., Mattheoudakis, M., & Zigrika, M. (2010). Then how will they get 'the much-wanted paper'? A multifaceted study of English as a foreign language in. Greece. In A. Psaltou-Joycey & M. Mattheoudakis (Eds.), *Advances in Research on Language Acquisition and Teaching: Selected Papers* (pp. 179–194). Greek Applied Linguistics Association.

Babaee, M., & Tikoduadua, M. (2013). E-portfolios: A New Trend in Formative Writing Assessment [IJMEF]. *International Journal of Modern Education Forum*, *2*(2), 49–56.

Baleni, Z. G. (2015). Online formative assessment in higher education: Its pros and cons. *Electronic Journal of e-Learning*, *13*, 228–236.

Ball, H. L. (2019). Conducting Online Surveys. *Journal of Human Lactation*, *35*(3), 413–417. doi:10.1177/0890334419848734 PMID:31084575

Barrett, H., & Carney, J. (2005). Conflicting paradigms and competing purposes in electronic portfolio development. *Educational Assessment*. https://electronicportfolios.org/portfolios/LEAJournal-BarrettCarney.pdf

Baturay, M. H., & Daloğlu, A. (2010). E-portfolio assessment in an online English language course. *Computer Assisted Language Learning*, *23*(5), 413–128. doi:10.1080/09588221.2010.520671

Bolliger, D. U., & Shepherd, C. E. (2010). Student perceptions of ePortfolio integration in online courses. *Distance Education*, *31*(3), 295–314. doi:10.1080/01587919.2010.513955

Bolotov, V., Kovaleva, G., Pinskaya, M., & Valdman, I. (2013). *Developing the Enabling Context for Student Assessment in Russia. T*he International Bank for Reconstruction and Development. https://documents1.worldbank.org/curated/en/673371468336535823/pdf/Developing-the-enabling-context-for-student-assessment-in-Russia.pdf

Challis, D. (2005). Towards the mature ePortfolio: Some implications for higher education. *Canadian Journal of Learning and Technology*, *31*(3). https://www.learntechlib.org/p/43166/. doi:10.21432/T2MS41

Ciesielkiewicz, M. (2019). The use of e-portfolio in higher education: From the students' perspective. *Issues in Educational Research*, *29*(3), 649–667.

Cummins, P. W., & Davesne, C. (2009). Using electronic portfolios for second language assessment. *Modern Language Journal*, *93*, 848–867. doi:10.1111/j.1540-4781.2009.00977.x

Darren, G., & Mallery, P. (2020). *IBM SPSS Statistics 26 Step by Step. A Simple Guide and Reference* (7th ed.). Routledge.

Demirel, M., & Duman, H. (2015). The use of portfolio in English Language Teaching and its effects on achievement and attitude. *Procedia: Social and Behavioral Sciences*, *191*, 2634–2640. doi:10.1016/j.sbspro.2015.04.598

Dörnyei, Z. (2007). *Research Methods in Applied Linguistics: Quantitative, Qualitative and Mixed Methodologies*. Oxford University Press.

Dörnyei, Z., & Taguchi, T. (2010). *Questionnaires in Second Language Acquisition: Construction, Administration and Processing* (2nd ed.). Routledge.

ElSaheli-Elhage, R. (2021). Access to students and parents and levels of preparedness of educators during the COVID-19 emergency transition to e-learning. *International Journal on Studies in Education*, *3*(2), 61–69. doi:10.46328/ijonse.35

European Commission (2020). *Digital Education Action Plan 2021-2027. Resetting education and training for the digital age*. COM (2020) 624.

Farahian, M., & Avarzamani, F. (2018). The impact of portfolio on EFL learners' metacognition and writing performance. *Cogent Education*, *5*(1), 1–21. doi:10.1080/2331186X.2018.1450918

Gikandi, J. W., Morrow, D., & Davis, N. E. (2011). Online formative assessment in higher education: A review of the literature. *Computers & Education*, *57*(4), 2333–2351. doi:10.1016/j.compedu.2011.06.004

Göb, R., Mccollin, C., & Ramalhoto, M. F. (2007). Ordinal methodology in the analysis of Likert scales. *Quality & Quantity*, *41*(5), 601–626. doi:10.100711135-007-9089-z

Gratz, E., & Looney, L. (2020). Faculty resistance to change: An examination of motivators and barriers to teaching online in higher education. *International Journal of Online Pedagogy and Course Design*, *10*(1), 1–14. doi:10.4018/IJOPCD.2020010101

Gray, L. (2008). Effective practice with e-portfolios. *JISC*, 5-40.

Greek Ministry of Education and Religious Affairs. (2016). *Teaching of English in the first grade of elementary school*. https://www.aftodioikisi.gr/mediafiles/2016/05/%CE%91%CE%93%CE%93%CE%9B%CE%99%CE%9A%CE%91-%CE%99%CE%9D%CE%A3%CE%A4%CE%99%CE%A4%CE%9F%CE%A5%CE%A4%CE%9F.pdf

Greek Ministry of Education and Religious Affairs. (2021). *Circular: English in Kindergarten*. Minestry of Education. https://www.minedu.gov.gr/ypapegan/ypour-apof/50174-23-09-21-egkyklios-agglika-sta-nipiagogeia-2

Griva, E., & Kofou, I. (2017). *Alternative assessment in Language learning: challenges and practices*. Kyriakidis Editions.

Hodges, Ch., Moore, S., Lockee, B., Trust, T., & Bond, A. (2020). The Difference Between Emergency Remote Teaching and Online Learning. *EDUCAUSE Review,* https://er.educause.edu/articles/2020/3/the-difference-between-emergency-remote-teaching-and-online-learning

Hsieh, P.-H., Lee, C.-I., & Chen, W.-F. (2015). Students' perspectives on e-portfolio development and implementation: A case study in Taiwanese higher education. *Australasian Journal of Educational Technology*, *31*(5), 641–656. doi:10.14742/ajet.1605

Hung, S. T. A. (2012). A washback study on e-portfolio in an English as a Foreign Language teacher preparation program. *Computer Assisted Language Learning*, *25*(1), 21–36. doi:10.1080/09588221.2010.551756

Ikeda, M. (2020). *Were schools equipped to teach – and were students ready to learn – remotely? PISA in Focus, No. 108*. OECD Publishing., doi:10.1787/4bcd7938-

Jabeen, S. S., & Thomas, A. J. (2015). *Effectiveness of Online Language Learning. Proceedings of the World Congress on Engineering and Computer Science (WCECS 2015)*, San Francisco, USA.

Lefever, S., Dal, M., & Matthíasdóttir, A. (2007). Online data collection in academic research: Advantages and limitations. *British Journal of Educational Technology*, *38*(4), 574–582. doi:10.1111/j.1467-8535.2006.00638.x

Lorenzo, G. & Ittelson, J. (2005). An overview of e-portfolios. *Educause Learning Initiative*, 1-27.

Markova, Y. S. (2020). About the consequences and problems in the higher education system during the pandemic. *Scientific interdisciplinary research, 5*, 226-229. https://cyberleninka.ru/article/n/o-posledstviyah-i-problemah-v-sisteme-vysshego-obrazovaniya-vo-vremya-pandemii

Mattheoudakis, M., & Alexiou, T. (2009). Early Foreign Language Instruction in Greece: Socioeconomic Factors and Their Effect on Young Learners' Language Development. In M. Nikolov (Ed.), *The Age Factor and Early Language Learning* (pp. 227–252). http://rcel.enl.uoa.gr/docsforpeap/Mattheoudakis%20and%20Alexiou.pdf doi:10.1515/9783110218282.227

Muin, C. F., & Hafidah, H. (2020). Students' perceptions on the use of e-portfolio for learning assessment: A case study. *ELITE Journal*, *3*(1), 13–20.

Namaziandost, E., Alekasir, S., Sawalmeh, M. H. M., & Miftah, M. Z. (2020). Investigating the Iranian EFL learners' attitudes towards the implementation of e-portfolios in English learning and assessment. *Cogent Education, 7*(1), 1–32. doi:10.1080/2331186X.2020.1856764

Nenyuk, E. A. (2021). The first results of distance learning: the evolution of opinions. *The world of science, culture, education, 3*(88), 221-223. https://cyberleninka.ru/article/n/pervye-itogi-distantsionnogo-obucheniya-evolyutsiya-mneniy

Nikolopoulou, K., Akriotou, D., & Gialamas, V. (2019). Early Reading Skills in English as a Foreign Language via ICT in Greece: Early Childhood Student Teachers' Perceptions. *Early Childhood Education Journal, 47*(5), 597–606. doi:10.100710643-019-00950-8

Pachler, N., Daly, C., Mor, Y., & Mellar, H. (2010). Formative e-assessment: Practitioner cases. *Computers & Education, 54*(3), 715–721. doi:10.1016/j.compedu.2009.09.032

Panadero, E., Fraile, J., Pinedo, L., Rodríguez-Hernández, C., & Díez, F. (2022). Changes in classroom assessment practices during emergency remote teaching due to COVID-19. *Assessment in Education: Principles, Policy & Practice, 29*(3), 361–382. doi:10.1080/0969594X.2022.2067123

Perifanou, M., Economides, A. A., & Tzafilkou, K. (2022). Greek teachers' difficulties & opportunities in emergency distance teaching. *E-Learning and Digital Media, 19*(4), 361–379. doi:10.1177/20427530221092854

Radu, M. C., Schnakovszky, C., Herghelegiu, E., Ciubotariu, V. A., & Cristea, I. (2020). The impact of the COVID-19 pandemic on the quality of educational process: A student survey. *International Journal of Environmental Research and Public Health, 17*(21), 1–15. doi:10.3390/ijerph17217770 PMID:33114192

School Education Gateway. (2020) *Survey on online and distance learning – Results*. School Education Gateway. https://www.schooleducationgateway.eu/en/pub/viewpoints/surveys/survey-on-online-teaching.htm

Sifakis, N. C., & Sougari, A.-M. (2005). Pronunciation issues in EIL pedagogy in the periphery: A survey of Greek state schoolteachers' beliefs. *TESOL Quarterly, 39*(3), 467–488. doi:10.2307/3588490

Solnyshkina, M. I., Harkova, E. V., & Kiselnikov, A. S. (2014). Unified (Russian) State Exam in English: Reading Comprehension Tasks. *English Language Teaching, 7*(12), 1–11. doi:10.5539/elt.v7n12p1

Song, B. K. (2021). E-portfolio implementation: Examining learners' perception of usefulness, self-directed learning process and value of learning. *Australasian Journal of Educational Technology, 37*(1), 68–81.

Sue, V. M., & Ritter, L. A. (2012). *Conducting Online Surveys* (2nd ed.). SAGE Publications, Inc. doi:10.4135/9781506335186

Syafei, M., Mujiyanto, J., Yuliasri, I., & Pratama, H. (2021). Students' perception of the application of portfolio assessment during the COVID-19 pandemic. *Academic International Conference on Literacy and Novelty*, pp. 61–70). KnE Social Sciences. doi 10.18502/kss.v5i7.9320

Syzdykova, Z., Koblandin, K., Mikhaylova, N., & Akinina, O. (2021). Assessment of e-portfolio in higher education. *International Journal of Emerging Technologies in Learning, 16*(2), 120–134. doi:10.3991/ijet.v16i02.18819

Ter-Misanova, S. G. (2005). Traditions and innovations: English language teaching in Russia. *World Englishes*, *24*(4), 445–454. doi:10.1111/j.0883-2919.2005.00427.x

Topuz, A. C., Saka, E., & Faruk Fatsa, Ö. (2022). Emerging trends of online assessment systems in the emergency remote teaching period. *Smart Learning Environments*, *9*(17), 1–21. doi:10.118640561-022-00199-6

Tsiplakides, I. (2018). Shadow Education and Social Class Inequalities in Secondary Education in Greece: The Case of Teaching English as a Foreign Language. [online]. *The International Journal of Social Education*, *7*(1), 71–93. doi:10.17583/rise.2018.2987

Tzifopoulos, M. (2020). In the shadow of Coronavirus: Distance education and digital literacy skills in Greece. *International Journal of Social Science and Technology*, *5*(2), 1–14.

Vasileiou, S., Papadima-Sophocleous, S., & Giannikas, C. N. (2023). Technologies in Second Language Formative Assessment: As Systematic Review. *Research Papers in Language Teaching and Learning*, *13*(1), 50–63.

Wang, P., & Jeffrey, R. (2017). Listening to learners: An investigation into college students' attitudes towards the adoption of e-portfolios in English assessment and learning. *British Journal of Educational Technology*, *48*(6), 1451–1463. doi:10.1111/bjet.12513

Yastibas, A. E., & Yastibas, G. C. (2015). The use of e-portfolio-based assessment to develop students' self-regulated learning in English language teaching. *Procedia: Social and Behavioral Sciences*, *176*, 3–13. doi:10.1016/j.sbspro.2015.01.437

KEY TERMS AND DEFINITIONS

Alternative Assessment: Non-traditional exam-based assessment.
Attitudes: Someone's beliefs or opinions.
Digital Classroom: Classrooms that improves student learning by utilizing computers, tablets, the internet, and instructional software.
E-Portfolio: A user-assembled and managed collection of digital evidence that is typically found online.
Foreign Language: Any language that is not the state language, is taught at school for a limited amount of time by a non-native speaker and is not used for daily communication.
Formative Assessment: The process of gathering specific data that may be used to alter education and student learning as it happens.
Emergency Remote Teaching: A temporary shift from face-to-face instruction to online teaching due to extenuating circumstances, such as a pandemic
Self-Learning: The process through which students understand how they learn and evaluate their knowledge.

APPENDIX

Student Questionnaire

Adopted from Aghazadeh & Soleimani, 2020; Song, 2021

"Employing e-portfolio for building an effective system of online formative assessment: Greek and Russian EFL university students' attitudes."

In order to participate in this study, you need to be a native speaker of Greek, be a second-, third-, fourth-, fifth- or sixth-year undergraduate university student at a university in Greece and have attended English classes at university during your studies.

Part I

Please complete the following personal information

1. What is your gender?
   - Male
   - Female
   - Other
2. What is your age?
3. Please select your level of English
   - A1 (Starter)
   - A2 (Elementary)
   - B1 (Intermediate)
   - B2 (Upper-intermediate)
   - C1 (Advanced)
   - C2 (Proficient)
4. Please select your year of undergraduate studies
   - Second
   - Third
   - Fourth
   - Fifth
   - Sixth
   - Other (please specify) ……………
5. Choose your field of studies
   - English Philology/Studies/Linguistics
   - Humanities and social sciences (Anthropology, Archaeology, History, Linguistics and Languages, Philosophy, Religion, Arts, Economics, Geography, Psychology, Political Science and Sociology)
   - Natural sciences (Biology, Chemistry, Earth sciences, Physics, Space sciences)
   - Formal sciences (Computer science, Mathematics, Systems science)

- Professions and applied sciences (Agriculture, Business, Education, Engineering and technology, Environmental studies and forestry, Family and consumer science, Journalism, media studies and communication, Law, Library and museum studies, Medicine, Military sciences, Public administration, Social work and Transportation)
- Other (please specify) ……………………..

6. Choose the tools you have used during online learning (choose the one you have used more)
    - Kahoot
    - Padlet
    - Socrative
    - Quizlet
    - Moodle
    - Edmondo
    - Facebook
    - Twitter
    - Other (please specify)……..

7. Definition of e-portfolio: "An e-portfolio is described as a selective and structured collection of information, gathered for specific purposes, showing one's accomplishments and growth which are stored digitally and managed by appropriate software".

Based on the above definition, indicate if you have experience with e-portfolios during online learning.
- Yes
- No

If you have answered "No" to the above question, please do not proceed with the questionnaire.

Part II

For each of the statements below choose the number 1-5 that best characterises how you feel about the statement, where 1= Strongly Disagree, 2= Disagree 3. Neither Agree Nor Disagree 4= Agree 5= Strongly Agree.

	1 Strongly Disagree	2 Disagree	3 Neither Agree Nor Disagree	4 Agree	5 Strongly Agree
8. E-portfolios increase willingness to learn English more actively					
9. E-portfolios increase classmates' cooperative learning and mutual growth in English					
10. E-portfolios help find out my strengths and weaknesses in English					
11. E-portfolios help reflect on my learning process					
12. E-portfolios help evaluate my learning					
13. E-portfolios help organize and arrange learning					
14. E-portfolios are a good tool to show how learning is taking place					
15. E-portfolios represent learning results					
16. E-portfolios increase teacher-student interaction					

Online Formative Assessment via the E-Portfolio

	1 Strongly Disagree	2 Disagree	3 Neither Agree Nor Disagree	4 Agree	5 Strongly Agree
17. E-portfolios provide a multi-dimensional perspective about learning and assessment					
18. E-portfolios provide a good sample to assess my performance					
19. E-portfolios provide a good source to save and store my work					
20. E-portfolios record evidence of learning					
21. E-portfolios help me with personal development					
22. E-portfolios offer more helpful feedback than traditional pen-and-paper assignments					
23. E-portfolios are better than the traditional pen-and-paper exams					
24. E-portfolios lead to more professional development					
25. I think online tools are not useful in my learning					
26. I prefer assessment through e-portfolios than traditional assessment					
27. Using online tools improves my effectiveness in learning					
28. I think online tools are useful in my learning					

Chapter 4
The Impact of Online Feedback Practice on Pre-Service English Teachers During the Pandemic

Bruna Lourenção Zocaratto
Federal Institute of Brasilia, Brazil

Gladys Quevedo-Camargo
University of Brasilia, Brazil

ABSTRACT

The purpose of this chapter is to examine the results of a study on the impact of online feedback practice on the learning and education of pre-service English teachers at a Federal Institute of Education, Science, and Technology. To this end, questionnaires were used, and focus groups were conducted at the beginning and end of two English classes of the same level, during a period of two months in 2021. Thematic analysis was employed to analyze and interpret the data. Results showed that participants recognized the importance of online feedback for their learning and professional development, identified the need for a balance between corrective and motivational types, looked at it beyond a simple procedure linked to errors and grades, and showed interest in conducting fair and ethical assessment practices, with the reproduction of peer assessment and the use of rubrics.

INTRODUCTION

The global emergency caused by the new corona virus from 2020 to 2022 had a significant impact on education and led to the need to find new ways and models of teaching, learning, and assessment to enable the continuity of educational activities, now with digital means of communication and interaction. In this context, according to Zocaratto and Quevedo-Camargo (2022), the use of feedback is fundamental for the success of teaching and learning, as it drives improvement and supports the continuous progress of both processes. Feedback has considerable potential to promote interaction in virtual environments and provides accurate information about the conditions under which learning is taking place and the

DOI: 10.4018/978-1-6684-6227-0.ch004

degree of success of the pedagogical work being done. However, it is important to emphasize that the use of feedback must be carefully evaluated to ensure that it is effective and constructive for students and does not hurt their self-esteem or discourage their engagement in learning.

For prospective teachers, the feedback they receive from professors for instance during activities to enhance their professional development is of utmost importance as such input significantly influences their thoughts and behaviors in certain educational situations (Yang et al., 2021). The training tasks they experience gradually improve their performance through continuous guidance, which is certainly the case with online feedback in teacher education programs (Prilop et al., 2021a). In online learning environments, expert feedback plays a crucial role in shaping the professional vision of classroom management for pre-service teachers. Therefore, it is essential to develop and refine their online feedback literacy, critical thinking, and reflective skills as they serve as a valuable source of feedback in their future practice. By improving their online feedback experience, prospective English teachers can benefit from enhanced professional learning (Yang et al., 2021).

Nonetheless, Fluminhan et al. (2013) show that although feedback is considered an important communication resource, it is still neglected for a variety of reasons, such as lack of time and knowledge or the inability to use it regularly, consistently, and appropriately, leading pre-service teachers to refrain from practicing it. In addition, the authors point out that there is little research addressing this issue to "explore the opportunities for monitoring, instruction, and correction offered by this important pedagogical tool" (Fluminhan et al., 2013, p. 721).

In light of such considerations and the sparse identification of research examining feedback practices in the context of teacher education in virtual environments (Koşar, 2021; Mahapatra, 2021; Zocaratto & Quevedo-Camargo, 2022), this study aims to understand the contribution of the use of feedback in the development of English teachers' learning in initial education and in the construction of their perceptions about this practice in the pandemic context. As a result, the following specific aims were formulated: to explore English teachers' perceptions of feedback; to identify possible effects of feedback practice on participants' learning; and to determine to what extent experiences with feedback practice contributed to the construction of new perspectives in online feedback.

Due to the emergency remote teaching during COVID-19 pandemic, the pedagogical work in the subject investigated, named English 6, was conducted through synchronous one-hour meetings once a week on Google Meet and asynchronous activities on online platforms such as Google Classroom, Padlet, and Flipgrid. The instructor frequently provided constructive feedback on these assignments, ensuring that students received timely support for their learning. This approach allowed for a flexible and dynamic learning environment that met the needs of the students and the circumstances presented by the pandemic.

For written tasks, the instructor corrected them, provided feedback in the form of written comments, and gave participants the opportunity to redo the assignments to encourage reflection on and learning from mistakes. The oral tasks followed a similar process, but the instructor's response was recorded since immediate feedback was not possible. This also served to provide students with specific guidance on how to improve their oral communication and performance, while fostering active listening skills and building rapport between students and instructor. Additionally, for activities that required students to provide feedback to their peers, there was prior preparation through an explanatory video and time to clarify what a rubric is and how to use it (Brookhart, 2013). Students had the opportunity to complete this activity twice: once to assess a written assignment and once to assess an oral task. Both of them had been created beforehand by their classmates.

In the following sections, the authors of this study present the theoretical framework that served as the basis for the entire study. Then, the methodological path to collect and analyse the data and the limitations or challenges encountered during the research process are described. This section is followed by the analysis of all the information gathered, supported by the use of tables that help the reader to better understand the results of the study. Finally, the authors likely drew conclusions based on their findings.

ONLINE FEEDBACK AND IMPLICATIONS FOR TEACHER EDUCATION

Formative assessment and feedback are essential components of teaching and play a crucial role in the learning process, supporting interpretations with the goal of facilitating student learning and teacher instructional practice without the mere intent of grading and classifying (Barram, 2017). This type of assessment is an important tool that helps teachers identify learners' strengths and weaknesses and adjust teaching strategies accordingly. Through the use of formative assessment, teachers can provide learners with ongoing feedback that allows them to identify areas that need improvement and focus on specific learning goals. In addition, this feedback can help learners feel more confident in their progress and encourage them to take an active role in their learning.

Likewise, Jones and Gerzon (2020) argue that formative assessment involves the use of evidence to guide learning. However, they acknowledge that this process is not as simple as it may seem. To use formative assessment effectively, teachers must have a clear understanding of the intended learning outcomes, and, according to the authors, it involves attention to emergent and unfolding aspects of learning as students speak, produce, and write. As a result, teachers can help learners understand their learning progress and manage their expectations, which will help them develop the skills and mindsets required to learn how to learn and, we should add, learn how to give feedback properly – a critical skill that can help pre-service teachers succeed in their academic and professional endeavors.

Taking the discussion above into account as well as the specifics of the pandemic context in education, particularly with regard to teacher education through remote teaching, it has been possible to identify an emerging and extraordinary need for readjustment of pedagogical practices and new ways of thinking about and delivering assessment and feedback mediated by digital technologies; what was once a choice has now become a necessity. Providing feedback, however, is not an easy task, which underscores the need to address it in teacher education (Jeffs et al., 2021). For prospective teachers to be able to use it appropriately and plausibly, they must first understand what, why, when, and how to assess. In this way, they will be better able to do the same with feedback: what kind of information to offer, for what purpose, at what time, and in what way(s).

In a study carried out by Odo's (2022), for instance, the researcher investigated the effects of using videos with online feedback to promote self-reflection among English language teachers in training. Each participant was required to make and upload a 20-minute recording based on a submitted lesson plan. The professor then analyzed the recordings and provided feedback. Some main benefits of watching videos with feedback, according to the prospective language teachers, were: the ability to see their teaching practices more objectively as well as to observe aspects and parts of the planning that they had not paid attention to before and that they began to see more clearly with more detailed feedback; and the ability to review the microteaching they had recorded and watch it as many times as needed so that nothing went unnoticed, which would not happen if the feedback were given in person.

Another interesting study was conducted by Koşar (2021), whose aim was to analyze the progress of a prospective English teacher in giving feedback during online instruction. At the end of each of the participant's observed virtual lessons, he interviewed her remotely, by telephone, and asked her about the choices she had or had not made in developing her pedagogical work. In this way, the participant had the opportunity to respond, argue, and justify her decisions, thus leading her to engage in a process of reflection on her actions. However, the researcher's questioning regarding the participant's non-use of a particular style of feedback in their online practice is another intriguing finding. The participant said that she had no knowledge of it and stressed that after the researcher had explained and exemplified it, she would undoubtedly utilize it in future practices. The participant added that she believed the courses she had completed up to that point had not adequately prepared future teachers to provide feedback to their students. These findings demonstrate the significance of assessing and understanding feedback as well as one's practical experience in teacher preparation courses.

Zocaratto and Quevedo-Camargo (2022) point out that teachers' limited and instinctive knowledge of feedback prevents them from aligning their perceptions with classroom actions, creating gaps and weaknesses and leading to arbitrary, superficial, and unclear decisions. On the contrary, by reflecting on their teaching practices through formative feedback, pre-service or in-service teachers can engage more actively, reflect on what happened, on how and why, and what they could have done differently to achieve the teaching and learning goals established.

Therefore, it becomes increasingly clear that acknowledging feedback as an important pedagogical resource to trigger the construction of continuous learning through virtual interactions is a first and necessary step towards (re)defining initial education teachers' perceptions of this procedure. It is thus essential that they are given opportunities to experience this mechanism of formative assessment in an online context (Fluminhan et al., 2013; Prilop et al., 2021a, 2021b; Yang et al., 2021; Zocaratto & Quevedo-Camargo, 2022).

TYPES AND POSSIBILITIES OF ONLINE FEEDBACK

The importance of thinking carefully about what kind of feedback should be given and how it should be delivered has been a concern for many researchers for some time. Schwartz and White (2000), for example, identify two types of feedback: summative and formative. The former tests the student to assign a grade, while the latter gradually leads to changes in a student's behavior to enhance learning, aimed at keeping students motivated and preventing them from feeling isolated.

Paiva (2003) similarly distinguishes between two types of feedback: evaluative feedback, which provides information about the student's or teacher's academic performance, and interactional feedback, which focuses on capturing responses to the student's or teacher's interactive behavior. In the former, the teacher assesses the performance of a student or group, and the student requests feedback in a pedagogical activity, evaluates the course, the teacher him/herself, and assesses another student. The latter, on the other hand, includes the use and exchange of messages related to content, pedagogical processes, technical tips, behavioral instructions, and responses between teacher-student or student-student.

Cardoso (2011) states that the types of feedback can vary depending on purpose, direction, timing, and source. The first aspect varies according to the type of information/target, which is categorized as recognition, motivational/interactional, technological, and informational/evaluative, as well as the degree of complexity of its content. Feedback that contains longer and more complicated messages is considered complex, whereas feedback that contains clearer and more objective messages are considered non-complex. As for the direction, the feedback can be individual or addressed to the whole group and can be asynchronous or synchronous, which characterizes the timing of its implementation. Finally, as for the source, it can be done by the teacher, the computer (automatic feedback) or by the students.

Canals et al. (2020) indicate that there are two types of feedback in online contexts that are directly related to when they are given: a more immediate one, resulting from established synchronous interactions and instant reactions, and a delayed one, where there is a temporal difference between the student's performance and the teacher's feedback. In the first case, synchronous computer-mediated communication can be done through applications such as Skype, WhatsApp, and especially Zoom for real-time teaching, which has become more widespread due to the pandemic. The authors emphasize that online feedback in this type of communication can be "text-based (or text chat), audio-based, video-based, or multimodal (a combination of text, audio, or video)" (p. 183). They also point out that it may be difficult for teachers in distance learning scenarios to provide immediate or synchronous feedback due to scheduling conflicts between them and their students. Therefore, delayed or asynchronous feedback might be a more viable choice. In this case, written reports or voice/video recordings can be used, for example.

In this study, the author responsible for the instructions provided both formative and summative feedback (Schwartz and White, 2000; Paiva, 2003) with the aim of enhancing the learning development of the study participants, while at the same time having to award the grades required by the assessment system. The use of interactional/motivational feedback (Paiva, 2003; Cardoso, 2011) was employed to establish productive interactions with these students through email exchanges. The focus was on understanding their difficulties and the reasons why some activities were not completed. Feedback was also given in the form of messages of varying lengths, depending on the quality of the work produced by the participants and the instructor's need for comments. Feedback was mostly given individually, as a significant proportion of the assigned tasks were asynchronous (Cardoso, 2011), resulting in delayed rather than immediate feedback (Canals et al., 2020). The latter was more common in the weekly synchronous sessions. Platforms or media used for feedback included written rubrics, written and verbal interactions on Google Meet, private messages on Google Classroom, comments on Google Docs and Google Forms, and audio recordings on Flipgrid.

As Mahapatra (2021) noted, the need for online change and innovative practices intensified with the pandemic and took an even more remarkable trajectory as every stakeholder involved in teaching, learning, and assessment had to move to online platforms to proceed by means of virtual pedagogical work. In this regard, it is interesting to observe that formative online feedback in language teaching and learning has occurred over time in a variety of ways: written, audio, video, mobile devices, social media, Google platforms, or WhatsApp (Mahapatra, 2021). According to the author, this process becomes versatile, accessible, and useful, increasing the possibility of creating a virtual environment that generates confidence and motivation in both teachers and learners when implemented in a timely and immediate manner.

Overall, Mahapatra (2021) also acknowledges that the usability and value of online formative assessment tools can play a critical role, but also points to the use of relevant strategies in the process of feedback in a virtual context, such as online peer assessment. This process can enable learners to reflect on their learning, as the feedback they receive from their peers can impact it positively (Mahapatra, 2021). Likewise, it can be stated that such reflection also impacts on the training of future teacher assessors. As Prilop et al. (2021b) point out, education research indicates that receiving feedback from teachers, mentors, or supervisors can significantly improve teachers' professional competence, and the same is true when given by peers. They suggest that training and improving the quality of peer feedback in teacher education can lead (prospective) teachers to engage more meaningfully with formative assessment practice. All these experiences provided to teachers in initial education become even more consistent when we integrate the use of rubrics to make the assessment process more transparent, ethical, and truly aimed at improving student learning. According to Brookhart (2013, p. 4), "a coherent set of criteria for students' work that includes descriptions of levels of performance quality on the criteria" helps to provide clarity about what state learning is in and what aspects require attention so that it can continually evolve.

Regardless of the type of feedback, the emphasis should always be on creating the necessary conditions for the student to make positive changes in his or her learning situation. This directly or indirectly affects their motivation and interest in learning and influences the processes of interaction and communication with others involved in educational work. It is important to provide constructive feedback that not only identifies areas for improvement, but also offers support and resources to help the student overcome the challenges they face. In this way, an environment can be created that fosters motivation to learn and encourages students to take an active role in their education. Ultimately, it is the teacher's responsibility to ensure that their feedback is not only informative, but also serves as a catalyst for positive change and growth in their students.

METHODOLOGY

This research was qualitative in nature and draws on the principles of action research, which, according to Tripp (2005), is a term for methodologies that aim to make educational interventions in a continuous and progressive way, through strategies "for developing teachers and researchers to use their research to improve their teaching and thus their students' learning" (p. 445). The whole process has some main cyclical steps, starting from the identification of a problem and followed by planning improvement in practice, implementing what was previously planned, monitoring, and describing the effects of this action, and evaluating the results observed. In this sense, our study took into consideration the following research problem: what is the impact of using online feedback to improve the learning of English teachers, and to what extent does the experience of this practice contribute to building broader and more reflective perceptions of this mechanism in the pandemic context?

Site of Study

The research context was an English as a Foreign Language teachers' education course in Brazil, specifically, with students enrolled in a subject entitled "English 6", corresponding to pre-intermediate level or to A2-B1 levels of the Common European Framework of Reference for Languages – CEFR (Council of Europe, 2010). This course, as outlined in its syllabus, does not focus on assessment and feedback, but rather aims to cover the four language skills. Yet, this does not prevent the professor from addressing these topics and allowing students to engage with them.

The research was carried out in the second semester of 2021 from October to December. The classes as well as this study were conducted with Google Classroom, through synchronous meetings on Google Meet once a week, and asynchronous assignments were posted weekly.

Participants

The first author of this chapter was responsible for teaching both groups, including planning, developing, and grading the pedagogical activities and conducting all phases of the action research as part of her postdoctoral period. The second author was responsible for supervising the entire study and effectively advised the first author on the development of the theoretical framework, data collection, data analysis, and conclusion. She also validated the questions developed for the questionnaires and focus groups and reviewed them. All decisions were discussed and made together.

The undergraduate students who participated in the study were all young adults. Some of them were already working in regular schools as teacher assistants or in private English schools as teachers, so they had a wealth of experience to share. Those who were not working had already completed at least a year-long supervised internship, meaning that they had some experience in school. Since this research was conducted in an undergraduate course at a Higher Education Institute in Brazil, it is crucial to highlight that these students do not normally use English at home but use it in their studies or at workplace. All these participants were in the sixth semester of the course, and within a year and a half, they will be graduating.

Due to the impact of the pandemic on the educational context, some necessary measures had to be considered for the development of this research. One of them concerns the fact that student attendance at synchronous sessions was not compulsory, as their presence was counted based on the completion of the proposed activities. Therefore, a very extensive awareness-raising process was carried out with the students to emphasize the importance of their participation in this investigation. Thus, a total of 33 students participated and had their responses analyzed. In order to evaluate the real impact of the feedback given and experienced, the researchers only considered as valid participants those who were involved in the first and last application of at least one of the two methodological tools used.

It should also be noted that all measures were taken to ensure research ethics.

Methodological tools

The need to take measures to socially distance researchers from the spread of the Coronavirus led to changes in online and remote methodological procedures being introduced during the pandemic. As a result, they were forced to rethink many traditional face-to-face data collecting techniques while maintaining the ongoing process of investigative activities (Saberi, 2020). Due to this scenario, the following instruments, and methodological procedures: questionnaires, on Google Forms, and focus groups, on Google Meet.

The former was considered because it can reach a large number of people, even if dispersed over a wide geographical area, and enables people to respond at their most convenient time (Gil, 2021). For these reasons, it was recognized as a useful tool given the research objectives and the pandemic context in which the investigation was developed. The initial questionnaire was applied on October 4th, 2021, during the first week of classes. It was composed of open and closed-ended questions divided into two sections: 1-) Feedback & Learning as a Student; and 2-) Feedback & Teacher Education. The final questionnaire, in turn, was applied on December 2nd, during the last week of classes, and it had the same structure as the first one, mainly because the purpose was to observe in the students' responses the extent to which the online feedback experience in English 6 contributed to their learning and training as assessors. Therefore, the number and names of the sections were identical. The students had two weeks to answer both questionnaires.

The other methodological procedure was the focus group (Gatti, 2005), which was used twice with the same purpose of the two questionnaires: to conduct one at the beginning of this investigation and one at the end to examine the impact of practice with the use of online feedback on learning and training teachers as future assessors. In this study, the focus group technique provided a valuable moment to allow participants to interact more flexibly about their understanding of online assessment and feedback, as well as their experiences in emergency remote teaching.

The undergraduates had the opportunity to elaborate on their responses, and researchers were able to obtain more in-depth data by asking questions, which aided in enriching the data collected. Both focus groups were conducted via the Google Meet platform and were recorded with the consent of all participants. The questions were designed to elicit (1) perceptions of online feedback, (2) whether the interaction facilitated by feedback contributed to participants' interest in learning, (3) how online feedback contributed to errors in revision, learning and grade improvement among participants, (4) to what extent the experience of receiving feedback from their instructor contributed to their training as future assessors, (5) whether the experience of peer assessment brought contributions to their process of education as assessors, and (6) the potential replication of online feedback in future practices considering what they had previously experienced. It is worth noting that the questions in the first questionnaire referred to their experience in other subjects, while the enquiries in the second one were about their experience in English 6.

In this investigation, a total of six undergraduate students from Class A and seven from Class B participated in the first and final focus groups. In terms of the time length, a range of 90 to 110 minutes was established for the application of the techniques (Morgan, 2019). Before the focus groups began, some essential rules had to be established, such as mutual respect when listening, clarity that there was no right or wrong answer, and the need to be as honest as possible. Therefore, participants were instructed to speak up using the Google Classroom feature "hand raise" icon and to find a quiet place so as not to disrupt each other's understanding; however, in some cases, there were problems with the microphone, the camera or slow connection. As an alternative, the moderator, the first author of this chapter, asked for interaction via chat in exceptional cases.

Digital Tools for Online Assessment

Due to the pandemic, measures were required to enable English 6 teaching and this research to be conducted remotely in 2021, such as the use of:

- Google Classroom for: organizing all pedagogical activities related to the subject, posting the questionnaires, notifications, including the focus groups, and links to access websites while doing the activities; establishing communication and interaction between the teacher and the students and among the students themselves through written messages; and sending written feedback or links to access oral feedback on the activities conducted;
- Google Docs for: elaborating activities for students to complete individually, in pairs or in groups; entering corrections and drafting comments that helped students reflect on and learn from mistakes through the ability to redo all written activities; and using rubrics to assess peer activities
- Google Forms to access questionnaires or topic activities;

- Padlet to encourage interaction between students and the opportunity to assess peer's written paragraphs;
- Flipgrid to: a) enable oral production and asynchronous oral interaction in online learning environments; b) access the teacher's oral feedback for the topic through the use of rubrics; and c) assess a colleague's oral production through the use of rubrics as well.

Data Analysis Process

The analysis and interpretation of the information gathered by means of the questionnaires and focus groups were conducted by using thematic analysis (Braun and Clarke, 2006). Two main dimensions were highlighted in relation to the impact of the use of online feedback before and after the implementation of the action research: 1-) online feedback and the learning process of pre-service English teachers; and 2-) online feedback and the process of education of pre-service English teachers. Therefore, the identified thematic units were analyzed and interpreted within the corresponding dimensions, with the following themes listed in the first one: a catalyst for teaching and learning, interest and motivation, and types and purposes. In the second dimension, the main theme was: assessor and deliberate practices.

GENERAL OVERVIEW

Before conducting a more in-depth analysis of the identified thematic units, some general information that may have directly or indirectly influenced the responses analyzed is provided in the next section. The responses are shown in Table 1 below.

In general, responses from different classes were quite similar, possibly reflecting a common culture of online feedback practice in the same course. These data also indicate that it is important for educators to be aware of the potential downsides of a feedback culture and to actively promote a culture of constructive criticism and open dialogue in which pre-service teachers are encouraged to receive and provide feedback on the assessment process itself as well as on the work of their peers.

ONLINE FEEDBACK AND THE LEARNING PROCESS OF PRE-SERVICE ENGLISH TEACHERS

This section and the following themes aim to answer the first and second specific objectives pointed out in the introduction.

Catalyst of Teaching and Learning

Initially, the participants were asked the following questions in the first questionnaire and focus group, respectively: "what do you understand by online feedback?" and "what is online feedback?". Based on the responses, the construction of more general or evasive perceptions were observed as illustrated in a student comment: "I think it has to do with returning something to someone". (Student B)

Table 1. Responses to close-ended questions in the questionnaires[1]

Questions	Majority of responses			
	Class A		Class B	
	Initial	Final	Initial	Final
How often have you received feedback on the activities?	Sometimes	Always	Sometimes	Always
When was the feedback offered?	From 15 days to a month	Within a max of 15 days	From 15 days to a month	Within a max of 15 days
What were the most common forms of online feedback sent?	Written	Written	Written	Written
What was the content of the most frequently sent online feedback?	Asking for correction or reformulation of an answer	Encouraging students to participate in activities.	Guidance when the student feels confused	Individual or group encouragement for the student to think about a particular issue or doubt and try to resolve it
What was the most commonly given type of feedback?	Formative and summative	Formative and summative	Formative and summative	Formative and summative
What were the most common experiences with online feedback within an evaluative dimension?	Teacher assesses the student / group	Teacher assesses the student / group Student assesses a peer	Teacher assesses the student / group	Teacher assesses the student / group Student assesses a peer
What were the most common experiences with online feedback within an interactive dimension?	Teacher assesses the interaction	Teacher encourages the student's participation and remain in the group	Teacher assesses the interaction	Teacher encourages the student's participation and remain in the group

Source: Authors' own elaboration

At the end of the semester, when d the same questions were asked, it was identified that the participants, based on their experience in English 6, were able to make consistent statements and recognize the importance of online feedback both to improve learning and support teaching work. They could identify the existence of a hitherto limited perspective change and adopt one in which virtual feedback is understood as a valuable formative mechanism of assessment that goes beyond the simple return to those involved in the processes of teaching and learning, thus understanding feedback as a necessary practice given the pandemic context in which they were inserted, as the following excerpt show.

In the past, my view of feedback was limited to issues of assessment and delivering information about how useful something, or somebody's work is. However, that has changed somewhat because I have come to understand that it goes beyond that. Feedback can help especially in the construction of knowledge from what is done with it, whether it is the student's feedback or the teacher's feedback, because both should always be able to learn from each other. (Student B)

Another group of undergraduates, in the initial stages of using the methodological instruments, showed a more sophisticated perception of feedback, taking it as an action whose goal is to present a benefit to students' learning and teaching practice. Comparing with the answers they gave a priori, the experiences they had in English 6 seemed to have been enough to broaden and deepen their perception of this assessment procedure, as the following excerpt show:

In the initial questionnaire, I had focused feedback on the positive and/or improving aspects of a person's action or behavior, but through experience in English 6, I was able to see the social and learning benefits that feedback provides for both student and teacher/assessor, such as correcting mistakes, approaching and improving the teacher-student relationship, motivation, and the like. (Student D)

Based on such comments, it can be stated that as a result of the use of online feedback in the development of pedagogical work, in general, the undergraduates in this study began to reinforce their role in promoting improvements in learning and also in teaching, favoring the identification of errors and the search for their understanding, recognizing their responsibility for their own learning, adopting a more autonomous attitude and, consequently, promoting more conscious learning.

One of the possible reasons for these research findings lies in the strategies used during the classes to give feedback, which went far beyond a superficial assessment, such as "you did a good job," "very good," "you need to improve." Instead, the feedback given to students on written activities was always aimed at pointing out what was good and what needed improvement so that they had clarity about what was necessary to be done to progress. Another common practice was to ask in each synchronous meeting what they thought of the pedagogical activities, the quality of the feedback given, what the professor could do differently to meet their expectations or help them improve their learning. Students were then listened to, and instructional practices were modified as much as possible to align their expectations with what was being applied. In general, they felt that decisions were made in a transparent, fair, and ethical manner.

However, it is important to clarify that, especially at the beginning of the study, comments were made, and evaluative feedback was registered only in the activity file itself. When it was returned to the students, they would normally read the following message: "check some things that need attention and revision in your activity. Please let me know if you are interested in revising." In this way, the professor found that teacher-student interaction through written feedback was not effective because students did not generally look back at the corrected file to know what needed to be done and ended up not revising the exercise. Thus, to make the feedback more effective, a summary of what the student should pay attention to was included in the message privately sent to the student through Google Classroom. This reinforced responses provided, increased the participants' engagement with the feedback process, and made the experience with this procedure more meaningful, as well as positively influenced the way they understood and responded to it.

In the final focus group, when asked "based on your experiences with online feedback in English 6, what is your perception of this mechanism for formative assessment?" and "did the way the feedback was given help you understand your mistakes and learn from them?", a participant said, for example:

I feel that it was more in-depth feedback because, now during the pandemic, we are a bit lost in terms of instructions and what we have to do [...] in this subject, I felt that the feedback was more thorough, like "you made a mistake here", "try doing it again" or "try rewriting this part, it's not very good." Then, we would go back and rewrite it, and it would be returned to us. I felt that it was much more in-depth, and I really liked that. (Student C)

Based on the data, the researchers found that the experience with online formative feedback contributed to students' use of the information they received primarily for learning and not necessarily for improving their grades, so this assessment process really fulfilled its function. This may have happened because the professor always pointed out the strengths and weaknesses of each student's written or oral production when giving feedback, and this procedure was not always accompanied by grades in a way that students could focus on the necessary changes in their learning. When the feedback was graded, they were aware that if they repeated the activity according to the professor's comments, they could change the grade if progress was evident.

Interest and Motivation

In developing the pedagogical activities in English 6, the professor consistently sought interaction with her students through written or oral feedback on assignments, emails, and WhatsApp messages, with the help of the class representative, to inquire, for instance, why a particular activity was not completed, whether the student was doing well or not, and if the student needed help. This interactive connection with the students contributed to some extent to their motivation and interest in their learning process. In the final questionnaire and focus group, when asked: "how important did you find the use of online feedback in English 6? Why?" and "did the interaction with the teacher through feedback contribute to your interest in learning the subject?", a participant's response was:

During the semester I felt that the teacher cared about whether I did the assignments or not by correcting them and giving feedback. I felt support from her as if I was not alone in my learning process. With the pandemic, being alone became a routine, but the feedback made me feel closer to her. I didn't get a return just with numbers that quantified my performance. (Student K)

Based on these statements, it is possible to state that feedback in the online context is not only a resource of fundamental importance but can also be considered one of the most expected or even anticipated assessment practices. This occurs because, when used properly and with quality, students may perceive their teacher as more present, closer, and feel more confident when they receive a response from them with pedagogical guidelines. Moreover, the use of formative assessment can motivate them and arouse their interest in their learning development when their possible doubts are addressed and answered. The cold and impersonal online environment, also provoked by the pandemic context, gives way to a friendlier and more collaborative one.

Types and Purposes

In this study, it was interesting to observe that before applying the action research, undergraduates had virtually no reference to the types and purposes of feedback in their previous experiences in the online context. After conducting it, it was possible to see that they recognized, for example, the importance of interactive/motivational feedback for their own learning, as seen below:

Feedback in the form of messages such as "try to do [the activity]", "I will extend the deadline," and also the possibility of dialogue between student and teacher stimulated me to revise or redo the activity:

I saw it as a stimulus, a motivation for me to try to go beyond what I was already doing, to get out of my comfort zone a little bit. (Student H)

It is important to clarify that participants also acknowledged the significance of corrective (or summative, evaluative) feedback as a source of information about their learning. For example:

If it was corrective, it encouraged me to do the next oral and written activities more carefully and attentively. [If it was motivational feedback] it made me feel that the results of my efforts and studies were worthwhile. (Student O)

A comment from another participant also shows a clearer perception of how feedback can be given in different ways."I see it as something indispensable in the teaching-learning process. Whether it's shorter, general feedback or personalized feedback, it's absolutely essential to achieving learning goals". (Student H)

This statement indicates the participant was able to recognize that, regardless of the type of feedback given, it is still a powerful tool. According to Quevedo-Camargo (2021), this assessment process contributes in a very positive way to improving students' performance in assessment tasks, and, if used correctly, allows them to examine the results, reflect on the information obtained and use it to monitor their progress and learning. Therefore, when using online feedback, one should not lose sight of the commitment to building assertive and fruitful communication that allows for learner interaction and integration into their own learning.

ONLINE FEEDBACK AND THE PROCESS OF EDUCATION OF PRE-SERVICE ENGLISH TEACHERS

The purpose of this section is to answer the third specific objective stated in the introduction.

Assessor and Deliberate Practice

In this study, the participants went through two peer assessment experiences, a written and an oral one of activities created by peers in units studied before. In the first case, a previously developed activity on Padlet was used as a reference in which all students completed a written production and interacted with each other to create an informational board in fast fashion. To conduct the peer assessment activity, they were provided with a video recorded by the professor explaining its purpose, what a rubric is, and how to complete it. Then, each student was assigned a colleague's post on this platform based on which they had to identify strengths and weaknesses and suggest improvements based on the criteria. Once the assessment was completed, the professor analyzed the quality of the work and provided feedback on aspects that could be improved, and then, the completed rubric was shared with the person whose written work had been assessed. The second time, an oral activity that students had created on Flipgrid in the previous unit was used. The professor provided participants with another rubric composed of different criteria for assessing oral skills, and they had to follow the same steps as in the first activity. Again, at the end of the peer assessment, the professor analyzed the relevance of the feedback and made comments and corrections. After that, the rubric was shared with the student whose oral production was assessed.

This experience was very valuable in developing the participants' assessment skills. It provided them with the opportunity to think and reflect critically and to learn from their peers by giving and receiving feedback. As a result, some participants made interesting observations about the process of assessing a classmate, and based on that, the authors were able to observe the power of this tool for learning and assessment processes, which requires high level of engagement and commitment from all participants, as well as clear guidelines and criteria for assessment.

Activities that rely on the use of peer assessment and rubrics add authenticity to the teaching and learning process and also contribute to greater individual engagement by using the student as a protagonist. It's a great exercise to assess others because students are used to just being assessed. (Student G)

These statements show that feedback, represented by peer assessment and the use of rubrics, is undoubtedly a mechanism of fundamental importance in the online context, especially in language teacher education courses. The participants' comments evidenced that they recognized the importance of feedback and affirmed their intention to incorporate it in their pedagogical work in the classroom, as lived experiences provided more clarity about the assessment practice. This was also confirmed, when students were asked "Did the experience with feedback in English 6 contribute to your initial training as an assessor?", as seen below:

My experience with online feedback has shown me the importance of good time management, organization, and flexibility when providing feedback to students. It helped 200%, you know, I think it turned me inside out. (Student N)

It should also be highlighted that through the use of online feedback, students were generally able to engage in critical reflection. They became aware of its importance to the full implementation of their teaching practice and not only recognized what they should assess, but also established ethical, fair, and transparent criteria to evaluate their students with quality. Thus, they became to some extent conscious assessors with reflective practices – another thematic unit identified in this study that can be confirmed with the following statement.

I have been constantly thinking about the role of feedback, not only in the summative sense, but also in terms of the bridges it can build between the student and the teacher, and especially how important it is in determining the path that both the student and the teacher take. (Student J)

As Villas Boas (2014) highlights, to assess is to learn, because as one assesses, one learns, and as one learns, one assesses. With feedback, it could be no different: When you practice, you learn, and when you learn, you practice. In order to inform future pedagogical work, formative assessment practices, of which feedback is a part, must be given high priority as teachers learn to assess in their training.

CONCLUSION

The problematization of the data presented revealed that, as a result of their participation in the development of this study, the undergraduates were able to deepen or broaden their perceptions of the importance of online feedback both for their learning process and their training as future language teachers as assessors. Their statements became more detailed and assertive, relating this assessment process directly to the educational context rather than in a more general way. Their experiences fostered the perception that they needed to change their attitudes about their learning in an online environment, feel more responsible for it, and take a more autonomous stance in their quest for improvement and continued progress. Thus, participants were able to recognize the need for online feedback practice with a focus on achieving learning goals, i.e., they understood that there is no way to separate the act of assessment from the teaching and learning processes; otherwise, the very purpose of education, which is to learn, would hardly be achieved.

In addition, by identifying the relevance of feedback to their academic training, participants saw its benefits for both online and face-to-face courses and recognized its positive impact when used properly and in accordance with the assessment situation, i.e., how to give it and how best to do it. Their experiences revealed ways and opportunities to take a careful look at ethical and fair practices of classroom assessment, the impact this mechanism can have on the student and the assessor, and the possibility of strengthening the pedagogical interaction between all those involved when conducting activities in a virtual context. Recognizing feedback as an important pedagogical resource to trigger the building of learning in a continuous way through online interactions is a first and necessary step to (re)shape initial teacher education perceptions of this process. Therefore, it is essential that future teachers are given opportunities to experience this learning strategy of assessment in an online context.

Based on the proposed objectives and the results, possible contributions of online feedback to participant learning and education are observed: 1- identification of strengths and weaknesses: feedback can help students identify areas in which they excel and areas that need improvement; 2- encouraging self-reflection: when students received feedback, they were encouraged to reflect on their own learning and find ways to improve. This helped them become more self-aware and self-directed learner; 3- promoting growth mindset: feedback encouraged students to adopt a growth mindset, where they could see their skills as malleable and develop them through effort and practice; 4- increasing motivation: effective feedback increased students' motivation to learn and improved by giving them a sense of accomplishment and recognition for their efforts; 5- improving learning: feedback helped students achieve better learning outcomes by giving them guidance on how to improve their work and deepen their understanding of the subject; and 6- challenging, engaging, and relevant feedback experiences provided them with practical language assessment skills and knowledge that were essential to their future roles as assessors and led them to develop a sense of ownership over their future students' learning.

REFERENCES

Barram, K. (2017). *How to Use Formative Feedback to Help Students Achieve Better Marks in Summative Assesment.* The University of Manchester. https://www.elearning.fse.manchester.ac.uk

Braun, V., & Clarke, V. (2006). Using thematic analysis in psychology. *Qualitative Research in Psychology, 3*(2), 77–101. doi:10.1191/1478088706qp063oa

Brookhart, S. (2013). *How to create and use rubrics for formative assessment and grading.* Association for Supervision and Curriculum Development.

Canals, L., Granena, G., Yilmaz, Y., & Malkicka, A. (2020). Second language learners' and teachers' perceptions of delayed immediate corrective feedback in an asynchronous online setting: An exploratory study. *TESL Canada Journal, 37*(2), 181–209. doi:10.18806/tesl.v37i2.1336

Cardoso, A. C. S. (2011). Feedback em contextos de ensino-aprendizagem on-line. *Linguagens e Diálogos, 2*(2), 17–34.

Council of Europe. (2010). *Common European Framework of Reference for Languages: learning, teaching, assessment.* Council of Europe Publishing. www.coe.int/lang-CEFR

Fluminhan, C. S. L., Arana, A. S. A., & Fluminhan, A. (2013). A importância do feedback como ferramenta pedagógica na educação a distância. *Colloquium Humanarum, 10*(Especial), 721-728.

Gil, A. C. (2021). *Métodos e técnicas de pesquisa social* (7th ed.). Atlas.

Jeffs, C., Nelson, N., Grant, K. A., Nowell, L., Paris, B., & Viceer, N. (2021). Feedback for teaching development: Moving from a fixed to growth mindset. *Professional Development in Education, 47*, 1–14. doi:10.1080/19415257.2021.1876149

Jones, B., & Gerzon, N. (2020). *The power of evidence use in formative assessment.* WestED. https://csaa.wested.org/

Koşar, G. (2021). The progress a pre-service English language teacher made in her feedback giving practices in distance teaching practicum. *Journal of English Teaching, 7*(3), 366–381.

Mahapatra, S. K. (2021). Online formative assessment and feedback practices of ESL teachers in India, Bangladesh and Nepal: A Multiple Case Study. *The Asia-Pacific Education Researcher, 30*(6), 519–530. doi:10.100740299-021-00603-8

Morgan, D. (2019). *Basic and Advanced Focus Groups.* SAGE Publications. doi:10.4135/9781071814307

Odo, D. M. (2022). An action research investigation of the impact of using online feedback videos to promote self-reflection on the microteaching of pre-service EFL teachers. *Systemic Practice and Action Research, 35*(3), 327–343. doi:10.100711213-021-09575-8 PMID:34248347

Paiva, V. L. M. de O. (2003). Feedback em ambiente virtual. In V. Leffa (Ed.), *Interação na aprendizagem das línguas* (pp. 219–254). Educat.

Prilop, C. N., Weber, K. E., & Kleinknecht, M. (2021a). The role of expert feedback in the development of pre-service teachers' professional vision of classroom management in an online blended learning environment. *Teaching and Teacher Education, 99*, 103276. doi:10.1016/j.tate.2020.103276

Prilop, C. N., Weber, K. E., Prins, F. J., & Kleinknecht, M. (2021). Connecting feedback to self-efficacy: Receiving and providing peer feedback in teacher education. *Studies in Educational Evaluation, 70*, 101062. doi:10.1016/j.stueduc.2021.101062

Quevedo-Camargo, G. (2021). *Avaliação online: um guia para professores*. Letraria.

Saberi, P. (2020). Research in the time of coronavirus: Continuing ongoing studies in the midst of the COVID-19 pandemic. *AIDS and Behavior, 24*(8), 2232–2235. doi:10.100710461-020-02868-4 PMID:32303924

Schwartz, F., & White, K. (2000). Making sense of it all: giving and getting on-line course feedback. In K. W. White & B. H. Weight (Eds.), *The on-line teaching guide* (pp. 167–182). Allyn & Bacon.

Tripp, D. (2005). Pesquisa-ação: Uma introdução metodológica. *Educação e Pesquisa, 31*(3), 443–466. doi:10.1590/S1517-97022005000300009

Villas Boas, B. M. F. (2014). Avaliação para aprendizagem na formação de professores. *Cadernos de Educação, 26*, 57–77.

Yang, M., Mak, P., & Yuan, R. (2021). Feedback experience of online learning during the COVID-19 pandemic: Voices from pre-service English language teachers. *The Asia-Pacific Education Researcher, 30*(6), 611–620. doi:10.100740299-021-00618-1

Zocaratto, B. L., & Quevedo-Camargo, G. (2022). Feedback on-line na formação inicial de professores de línguas: Estado da arte. *Estudos Em Avaliação Educacional, 33*, e09532. doi:10.18222/eae.v33.9532

ADDITIONAL READING

Havnes, A., Smith, K., Dysthe, O., & Ludvigsen, K. (2012). Formative assessment and feedback: Making learning visible. *Studies in Educational Evaluation, 28*(1), 21–27. doi:10.1016/j.stueduc.2012.04.001

Irons, A. (2008). *Enhancing learning through formative assessment and feedback* (1st ed.). Taylor & Francis Group.

Tan, K. (2013). A Framework for assessment for learning: Implications for feedback practices within and beyond the gap. *International Scholarly Research Notices, 2013*, 640609.

William, D. (2016, April 1). The secret of effective feedback. *Ascd*. https://www.ascd.org/el/articles/the-secret-of-effective-feedback

KEY TERMS AND DEFINITIONS

Assessment: A process of gathering information about a learner's knowledge, language skills, improvements, and weaknesses in a variety of ways.

Assessment Literacy: The necessary knowledge and skills to plan, design, implement, and evaluate assessment practices with ethics.

Evaluation: A means by which information is gathered to analyse the decisions made and practices implemented in the classroom from a broader perspective.

Feedback: Information or expressions of opinion given about a student's performance or something he has produced that can tell him how successful he has been.

Formative Assessment: A process that focuses on overcoming difficulties and weaknesses and developing a student's learning in a continuous way.

Remote Teaching: Teaching that takes place in an online format where there is no in-person interaction between the learner and the teacher.

Virtual Context: Any online environment where the teaching and learning processes can take place through synchronous or asynchronous meetings.

ENDNOTE

[1] The answers to the open-ended questions with be analysed in the next sections of this chapter.

Chapter 5
The Effectiveness of Dynamic Assessment on Improving Multilingual Students' Writing Skills in Distance Education

Ifigeneia Karagkouni
University of Nicosia, Cyprus

Thomais Rousoulioti
Aristotle University of Thessaloniki, Greece

Dina Tsagari
Oslo Metropolitan University, Norway

ABSTRACT

Research has shown that the implementation of dynamic assessment in the second/foreign language (L2) teaching affects students' learning potential and improvement. In this light, the aim of this chapter is to examine the effectiveness of the method of dynamic assessment on improving adult learners' writing skills in Greek as L2 during the Covid-19 pandemic. This research focuses on the effect of online feedback, mediation, and strategies adopted on improving text quality and the writing process in general. A four-week on-line teaching intervention focused on teaching and assessing writing was carried out. Findings based on quantitative analysis show that students improved their writing competence on content development, text organization, and grammar accuracy. Nonetheless, the limitations of this study indicate the need for further research on the implementation of dynamic assessment by distance.

DOI: 10.4018/978-1-6684-6227-0.ch005

INTRODUCTION

Due to the COVID-19 pandemic, during the spring of 2020 many institutions implemented remote instruction to deliver synchronous distance learning (Serhan, 2020). The abrupt shift to e-learning and teaching shocked the majority of the language education community who had to familiarize themselves with online tools overnight (Giannikas, 2020). The pandemic highlighted the crucial role of technology in language education. However, most of the times the successful integration of technology and digital tools depends mainly on teachers' knowledge and digital literacy.

On the other hand, writing is a complex activity in which L2 learners have to put into action their lexical, syntactical and spelling skills in a very coherent way. Apart from these, writing also requires not only mental analysis, but sociolinguistic competence as well (Sapkota, 2012). According to Raimes (1983), producing a piece of writing entails purpose, grammar, syntax, word choice, content, mechanics, organization and an audience, to compose a "clear, fluent and effective communication of ideas" (p.6). From the above, it emerges that writing process and assessment should be regarded as a dynamic social experience (Xiaoxiao & Yan, 2010), which became much more difficult to be implemented in distance education during the COVID-19 pandemic.

The assessment of writing is even more demanding. Most L2 teachers and raters pay attention to the written text and mainly to the grammatical and syntactic forms. As Ur (1996) claims, the assessment of writing must first focus on the message transmission to the predetermined receiver and assess the communicative competence of the sender. Therefore, a substantial part of the assessment of writing is the assessment of the content, organization, coherence and style of the written text. Additionally, assessment is not always the goal in itself. On the contrary, assessment is equivalent to providing feedback which motivates and rewards students.

In this procedure mediation is significant. Mediation can be determined according to an individual's responsiveness to particular kinds of support (e.g., hints, feedback, reminders) (Poehner & Wang, 2021) which are important for the future development of a student. According to Leontjev (2016, p. 144) "no assessment can provide a full picture of learners' development without incorporating their potential for development".

The aforementioned approach seems to attune to the Dynamic Assessment (DA), an alternative method of assessment, as the teacher/mediator attempts to acquaint his/her students with strategies and a course of action which involves brainstorming, a first draft, feedback, revises, a second draft and feedback again. This dynamic interaction demonstrates to learners how to use L2 and go beyond their difficulties in similar and more challenging activities (Lantolf & Poehner, 2004). Additionally, the mediation stage plays an important role in assessing writing as it is an ongoing process in which the teacher investigates problems, provides directions, and enables students to maximize their potential at the same time (Anam et al., 2023).

In this context it was decided to implement DA during COVID-19 pandemic. The aim of the research was to improve students' writing ability in the context of Greek as a second language learning (GSL) with the support of DA. The implementation of face-to-face DA method was not feasible in conventional classrooms due to the abrupt closure of schools during the first phase of the pandemic. Thus, an alternative form of Dynamic Assessment was attempted which is described in this paper emphasizing on the implementation of dynamic assessment by distance.

BACKGROUND OF THE STUDY

This section discusses the concept of 'dynamic assessment' followed by preliminary assumptions based on literature regarding the advantages and disadvantages of DA and the role of mediation and feedback.

Dynamic Assessment

DA is an alternative process which aims to define, not only the learners' current level in L2, but also to support them to move a step forward as well as to collect important information about planning the future curriculum based on learners' needs (Pyrtsiou & Rousoulioti, 2022). Roots of DA can be found in Vygotsky's theory of Zone of Proximal Development (ZPD) (Poehner, 2008). Vygotsky (1978) defined ZPD as "the distance between the actual development level...and the level of potential development" (p.86) meaning that when a student receives suitable guidance by a more capable person, such as the teacher or a more skillful classmate, it is more likely to solve a problem or achieve a task. In short, ZPD is the transitional stage between the goals a student can reach on his own and those which are outside the limits of his potential and can be achieved only by guidance. Upon student's potential, that can be achieved by his/her teacher support. As Poehner (2008, p.24) states "cognitive abilities of a student can only be fully understood by actively promoting their development".

The implementation of DA in L2 classroom settings refers to either a "cake" or a "sandwich" approach (Fulcher, 2013). The "sandwich" approach involves a three-stage process that includes a pre-test, a mediation and a post-test procedure. While every stage of this process has a different goal, all three stages aim for the same purpose: to help learners overcome their present development level and achieve a higher goal. Specifically, the pre-test stage showcases what learners are capable of doing in L2 as a result of their previous knowledge, whereas the post-test measures mediation's efficacy. At the mediation stage, the mediator, which is usually the teacher, uses mediation strategies, such as implicit hints and questions, and interacts with each learner in specific but challenging learning contexts. If the learner recursively fails to give the right answer to a question, then this is given by the teacher/mediator.

DA focuses on defining or redefining students' learning potential and enhancing their skills with the contribution of the teacher/mediator. In this respect, it is of great importance the creation of an interactive learning environment that promotes the emergence of this potential based on students' ZPD (Mehrabany & Bagheri, 2017).

Advantages and Disadvantages of DA

In comparison to Conventional Assessment (CA), DA provides important information about students' performance (Pyrtsiou & Rousoulioti, 2022). On the other hand, time and cost are the main concerns of teachers/researchers, when it comes to the implementation of DA method. The reliability and the validity of the method which is closely related with teachers' previous experience are also issues that affect the success of each alternative assessment method (Rousoulioti, 2015). However, the key elements for the effective implementation of DA are mediation and feedback.

Mediation

In the context of mediation, modification comes through experiences and elaboration of self-control and mental analysis (Lidz, 1997). Time and place that intervention occurs count for little. Teacher's intervention is characterized by quality, while he/she detects not only learners' difficulties in an initial test but imparts strategies for the future too (Kozulin & Garb, 2002). Interaction is not also pre-defined and there can be changes in intervention's structure and substance, although it is always lifelike and communicative (Grigorenko και Sternberg, 1998) and furthermore, according to the teacher's guiding instructions (Abbasian, 2016).

Feedback

A great part of mediation process is feedback. Within the framework of writing assessment, feedback may take the form of explicit or implicit, positive or negative comments (Hyland & Hyland, 2006). In supplying explicit feedback, mediator informs students directly about their written text errors. Feedback is also linked to metalinguistic awareness (Hendrickson, 1978). In the form of implicit feedback, mediator doesn't correct learners' errors directly, but implements strategies (rephrasing, leading questions, expressions, clues, hints, and silence) to restore the accuracy of learners' answers (Tootkaboni & Khatib, 2014). Implicit feedback can also be provided by noticing the problem without highlighting clearly the mistake itself (Ellis, 2009). One point of view is that implicit feedback is associated with long-lasting results in learning (Bitchener & Storch, 2016) as it redounds to language acquisition (Ioannou & Tsagari, 2022) as much as explicit does and both contribute to self-control on use of the target language (Lantolf & Thorne, 2006).

DYNAMIC ASSESSMENT IN L2

Results of several studies suggested that the implementation of dynamic assessment in the L2 teaching contributes to the development of students' learning potential and improvement on writing (Babamoradi et al., 2018; Heidari, 2020; Rahmani et al., 2020; Shabani, 2018). Miao & Mian (2013) implemented DA on teaching writing. In particular, they studied whether coherence, lexical or grammatical accuracy in writing has been improved in an experimental group after their teacher's intervention. For that matter, they compared the results that arose from the *sandwich intervention* with similar papers of the control group that it did not participate in the mediation process. Statistical analysis of student performance between the two groups showed the positive impact of mediation in writing.

Ghahremani & Azarizad (2013) incorporated into DA the elements of intentionality, reciprocity, and transcendence (Feuerstein, 1988) to determine the efficiency of interactions. A three-week mediation stage followed the *sandwich approach* to achieve the aim in the field of content, structure and revision improvement. Positive results have emerged by comparing learners' pre and post-tests, which indicated the contribution of DA on writing enhancement and, mainly, in terms of organization and cohesion.

Sadek (2015) combined a number of strategies used equally in the implementation of interventionist and interactionist approach by generating a hybrid DA (HDA) model for establishing its impact. The stages of the intervention were like *sandwich's approach* (pre-test, mediation, post-test), however the mediation stage included self-assessment and revision on the teacher's contribution and the use also of strategies (elicitation, clarification, correction, indication, hinting, direct question etc.). According to the researcher, the significance of the HDA model lies in its implementation flexibility which allows students to become aware of their language weaknesses and the ways to overcome them.

Mauludin & Ardianti (2017) formed two group of students (a control and an experimental group) to collate DA to CA and their results in summary teaching and writing ability. An intervention carried out into three sessions based on *sandwich approach*. Research findings underlined the advantages of DA in terms of learning outcomes in comparison to those of CA. Similarly, Farrokh & Rahmani (2017) concluded that mediation given to an experimental group added some problem insight and improvement to syntactical and lexical level in the learners' ZPD.

Aljaafreh and Lantolf's (1994) Research

There is a great number of research in foreign literature that study the effectiveness of DA and feedback on L2 learning. On the contrary, there no such studies on teaching Greek as L2. The present paper attempted firstly to review the relevant research at international level with an ultimate objective to investigate the efficacy of DA and mediation feedback on improving writing with emphasis on the regulatory scale of Aljaafreh and Lantolf. Aljaafreh and Lantolf's (1994) research, and particularly, the dialogical process, the focus on writing and the small group of the three participants, is fully in line with this research and has a great impact on it.

In Aljaafreh & Lantolf's (1994) research, three female students participated in an eight-week study that consisted of a six one-hour weekly advanced level ESL reading and writing session in an American University. The objective of the mediation was to provide students with gradual feedback focused on grammar (articles, prepositions, modal verbs and verb tense) and encourage them to act autonomously in the revision of the written essays (Lantolf et al., 2017). When two students were facing the same language problem, the revision process individualized in order the teacher to meet each student's needs separately (Poehner & Lantolf, 2005). The researchers observed that interaction helps to identify learners' ZPD, the knowledge of which is essential in providing input, so learners can intake it and progressively turn it into an output (Aljaafreh & Lantolf, 1994). More precisely, Aljaafreh & Lantolf (1994) created a regulatory scale between 0-12 (see Table 1) made to adjust to learners' ZPD. On this scale, the starting point for feedback is zero (0) help to the students, while full support to them is point twelve (12). In the

Table 1. Regulatory scale: Implicit to explicit feedback (Aljaafreh & Lantolf, 1994, p. 471)

Scale Items
0. Tutor asks the learner to read, find and correct errors independently.
1. Construction of a "collaborative frame" prompted by the presence of the tutor.
2. Tutor or learner reads the sentence that contains the error.
3. Tutor indicates that something may be wrong in a segment (sentence, clause, line).
4. Tutor rejects unsuccessful attempts at recognizing the error.
5. Tutor narrows down the location of the error, but does not identify the error.
6. Tutor indicates the nature of the error, but does not identify the error.
7. Tutor identifies the error.
8. Tutor rejects learner's unsuccessful attempts at correcting the error.
9. Tutor provides clues to help the learner arrive at the correct form.
10. Tutor provides the correct form.
11. Tutor provides some explanation for use of the correct form.
12. Tutor provides examples of the correct pattern.

beginning, teacher's assistance is implicit but if a student faces difficulties in identifying and correcting her errors, then teacher's assistance is explicit.

Aljaafreh & Lantolf (1994) did not prefabricate their regulatory scale to provide feedback, but they formed it through the tutor-learner's one-on-one interactions during their research. In this manner, they provided interaction examples and confirmed that learning and ZPD's development is not a foreseeable process, basically what Vygotsky (1987) thought about the development in ZPD as "revolutionary". In addition, the most important throughout this process was the type of the mediation given that was first implicit and then explicit (Poehner & Lantolf, 2005). As Tavakoli & Alhossaini (2014) claim, Aljaafreh & Lantolf (1994) also did not develop their scale in the frame of DA and their aim was to reconstruct learner's ZPD through a dialectical co-operation and by understanding problems in L2. However, Poehner & Lantolf (2005) argue that DA is based on Vygotsky's ZPD (Figure 1) and as much it provides relevant insights into the DA process.

Figure 1. Vygotsky's zone of proximal development

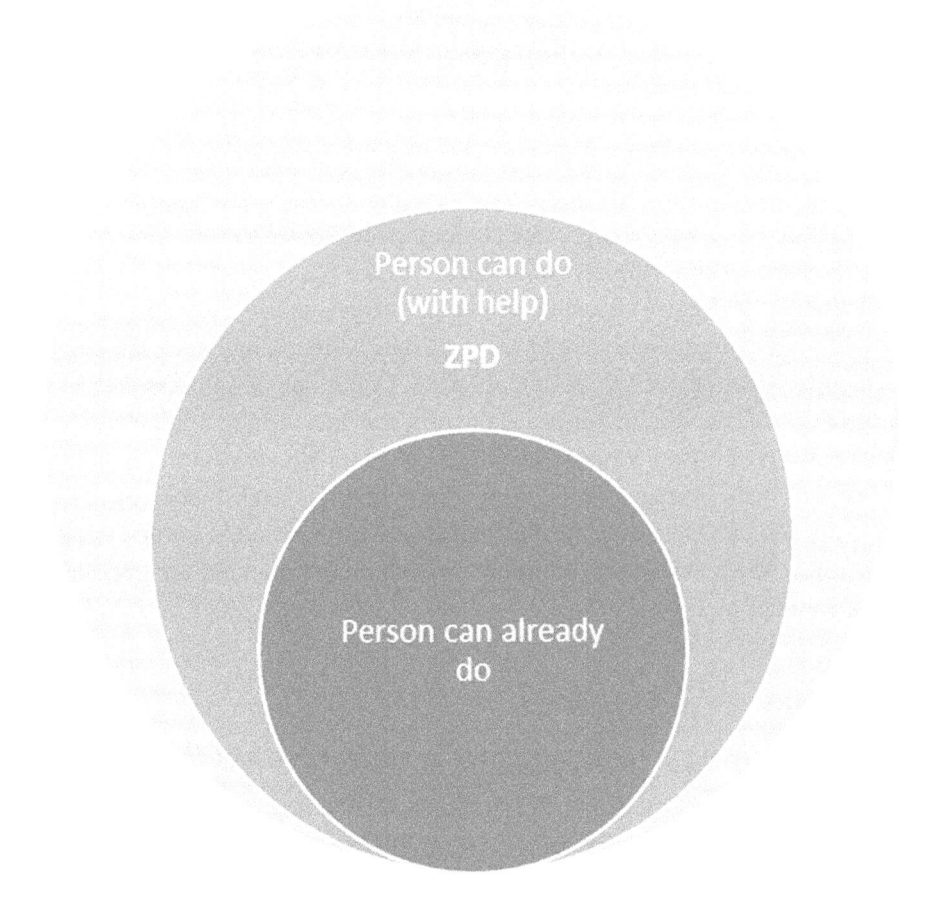

METHOD

The absence of relative studies in the field of Greek literature composes the main research question of this study:

Can DA improve students' writing ability in the context of Greek as a second language (GSL) learning?

Namely, this research intends to:

1) Assess two students' writing ability because of their previous knowledge.
2) Implement mediation strategies and feedback to strengthen students' writing skill in GSL.
3) Evaluate the effectiveness of mediation strategies and feedback implemented in teaching GSL writing.

It is worth mentioning that the present research acknowledges the fact that the method of DA has restrictions. According to Fulcher (2013, p. 75) "mediation is not possible with large classes". In addition, no generalization of the current research results is attempted, but instead, an effort is made to improve teaching and assessment practices in a specific case, individualized and contextualized each time.

Participants

For this research a four-week case study was carried out in the Association of Greek-Russian Friendship, Letters and Culture of Trikala, Greece, where lessons of Greek and Russian as L2 were usually delivered via zoom once a week for ninety minutes during the first period of the pandemic Covid-19. The participants in the study were two Russian women, 35-40 years old, native speakers of Russian who lived permanently in Greece for more than 10 years and they were taking Greek language course. Both had a bachelor's degree, and both were part-time workers. One of the researchers was a teacher of GSL in the Association of Greek-Russian Friendship at the time the intervention implemented. Both research participants lived in Greece for many years and held a B2 level certificate of attainment in Greek proving good knowledge of the Greek language. They were continuing to take GSL courses in the Association. They continued to attend GSL courses to further improve their knowledge of the Greek language (see Table 2). Some of their weaknesses in written texts was the reason behind their teacher's decision to implement a DA intervention.

Table 2. Research participants' demographics

Gender	Age	Nationality	Years of residence in Greece	Education	Employment	Certification of attainment in Greek
Female (Participant A)	38	Ukrainian	15	Ba Pedagogy	Part time	Level B2
Female (Participant B)	40	Russian	12	Ba Mathematics	Part time	Level B2

Procedure

The research was conducted in three stages. The whole procedure included the stages of 1) the pre-test, 2) the mediation, and 3) the post-test. Two writing tests of similar difficulties and requirements were designed to collect data, a pre and a post-test that implemented before and after the mediation process. The tests sent to the students as attached documents via e-mail and back to the teacher from the students with the same procedure. The regulatory scale of Aljaafreh & Lantolf (1994) implemented as a mediation feedback strategy between the pre- and the post-tests designed to assess students' ability in writing essays. The pre- and post-test writing procedure lasted almost fifty minutes. Time delimitation for the test completion was decided according to the findings of research that highlight the forty five to fifty minutes as the right time required to complete writing tests (Zhang, 2010· Miao & Mian, 2013).

In both the pre-test and the post-test, the topic of the written text was about *Traveling* according to the homonymous topic in the Common European Framework for Languages (2001). This topic also selected based on the view of Ghahremani & Azarizad (2013) that the writing theme should be realistic and interesting. More specifically, in the pre-test the learners were asked to write an essay about their town arguing why it is worth a visit, while in the post-test the purpose was to describe a place that they had already visited describing their impressions from the trip. It was considered that the pre-test would provide information about learners' ZPD and current level of knowledge and the post-test would show changes in their performance after the mediation sessions.

Data Collection and Analysis

Pre- and post-test texts, as well as Zoom video recordings were used for data collection, analysis and drawing conclusions. The whole mediation procedure took place, as already mentioned, via the Zoom platform. During the COVID-19 pandemic, many institutions, universities, and schools used Zoom to deliver remote learning to their students. This specific platform provides a series of features and possibilities to organize online meetings with quality video and audio, screen sharing and recording (Serhan, 2020). Due to the reasons mentioned above, Zoom was chosen as the main tool of technology to carry out and record the mediation process, collect information to create a written repository of the dialogues and, consequently, observe the teacher-learner's interactions. On the other hand, as texts consist qualitative data, specific assessment criteria concluded by the Centre for the Greek language and reported in Table 3[1] have been used for the assessment of the written texts by the teacher.

RESULTS

Text analysis of the pre-tests showed that students' writings contained spelling, lexical and grammatical mistakes, so the mediation procedure focused on these points, but also attention has been paid in communicating writing strategies such as planning and grouping ideas about a topic. The Regulatory Scale of Aljaafreh & Lantolf (1994) implemented in a twenty long minute time intervention. It should be noted that, as in the original mediation of Aljaafreh & Lantolf (1994), the teacher did not predesign a list of specific hints and questions, but she was based on the interactions between her and the students. Firstly, the teacher asked from each student to read her essay to identify if were any mistakes in it. The students recognized some mistakes in their essays, especially in spelling, while they failed to identify grammati-

Table 3. Holistic scoring scale for B2 level), centre for the Greek language (2013)

Score Range	Description
1-4	There is no connection between the content and the requested theme. The number of words in the text is significantly less. Poor understanding of the differences among the text types and styles. The written text is not well organized. Sentences and phrases are broken down unruly. There is no adherence and comprehensibility. The vocabulary of the text is very poor, while there are many mistakes and repeats. A lot of errors in form and syntax make the message transmission impossible. Several spelling mistakes. There are a few or not at all stress marks. The text is written in capital letters.
5-8	There is a vague connection between the content and the topic. No essential opposing views are presented. Therefore, the text has lexical gaps. A significant but unsuccessful effort is made to achieve the requested text type and style. Organization and coherence are not effective. Vocabulary is poor and often repeated, wrong or unsuitable. There are many morphosyntactic errors. Spelling mistakes make the text difficult to understand. Punctuation and stress marks remain problematic.
9-12	The topic center is not clear and the content development is limited or even insufficient but supportable. The text seems extensive but remains deficient to the number of words. The appropriateness of the text style is limited to topics of familiar text styles. Despite the lack of coherence, the organization is conspicuous. Effort is made in the creation of paragraphs, but not always successfully. Vocabulary choice is almost accurate, but limited and repeated. At the same time, an attempt is made to adopt a repertoire of phrases but it is "noticeably" unsuccessful. Despite the effort being made for the adoption of complex language structures, the morphosyntactic errors are many and not negligible, but most of them are not quite serious. However, in combination with spelling and stress mark errors may affect the understanding of the text.
13-16	The main concept is clear enough, but some aspects are not quite developed and as a result, the content fails to highlight all sides of the topic. For the most part, the text responds to the requested genre. It is relatively well organized with several textual markers. Appropriate style is used on several points. Relating to the use of vocabulary, that is adequate but not excellent, with a reasonable degree of accuracy, while the lexical errors are few. The use of appropriate morphosyntactic structures is effective, but not always accurate. There are a few, not quite serious, spelling as well as punctuation and stress mark mistakes.
17-20	The topic center is clear, and the arguments related to the subject are fully developed. The text is excellently organized, and the use of connective and coherence mechanisms is successful. Outstanding sequence of meanings. Text style choices are the most appropriate. Exceptional use of the vocabulary which is appropriate for the specific language level. The morphosyntactic structures are correct and cover the full range of the taught phenomena. There are no spelling mistakes. Excellent stress marking and punctuation.

cal errors. For each error the students couldn't recognize, the teacher provided hints and prompts that being made gradually increasingly specific. It is considered that hints and prompts promote the features of awareness and control (Ritonga et al., 2022). At the end, either the students found out their mistakes and correct them or the teacher provided them with the correct form with a number of examples on the whiteboard. The following is an example of the interaction between the teacher and one of the students during the online mediation process:

Teacher (T.): *Υπάρχει κάποιο πρόβλημα στην πρόταση;*
/ Is there anything wrong in the sentence? /
Student (S.): *Δεν βλέπω κάτι.*
/ I don't see anything wrong. /
T: *Οκ, υπάρχει όμως ένα πρόβλημα στο πρώτο μέρος της πρότασης.*
/ Ok, but there is a problem in the first part of the sentence. /
S: *...εσείς θα απολαύσετε μοναδική θέα του θεσσαλικού κάμπου;* /
/ ...will you enjoy unique view of Thessaly flatland? /
T: *Δεν είναι αυτό το πρόβλημα, αλλά μέσα σε αυτήν την φράση υπάρχει λάθος.*
/ This is not the problem, but in this phrase, there is a mistake. /

S: *Δεν μπορώ να καταλάβω.*
 / I can't understand. /

T: *Το λάθος έχει σχέση με το άρθρο. Θυμάσαι πότε χρησιμοποιούμε άρθρο;*
 / The mistake has to do with the articles. Do you remember when we need to use the articles? /

S: *Α, ναι. Κατάλαβα. Θέλει "θα απολαύσετε* **τη** *μοναδική θέα του θεσσαλικού κάμπου". Πάντα μπερδεύομαι με αυτό.*
 / Ah, yes. I understood. It should be made "you will enjoy **the** unique view of the Thessaly flatland". I'm always getting confused with that. /

T: *Όταν αναφερόμαστε σε κάτι συγκεκριμένο χρησιμοποιούμε το οριστικό άρθρο.*
 /When we write about something specific, we use the definite article. /

S: *Ναι, θυμάμαι.*
 / Yes, I remember. /

Following the above dialogue, several examples for the use of the definite articles were given to the student. This example selected in purpose to show that even though students are most of the time aware of the rules, they are not able to implement them in writing. The students that participated in the mediation process are both speakers of Russian as a first language. In Russian language, unlike the Greek, there are no articles. Because of this, it is very difficult for Russian students to identify when to use them. Sometimes, in their effort to use the articles correctly they overgeneralize the rule using it where is not the case.

In the above dialogue it appears that the student knew about the rule but could not recognize the problem in the sentence. It is not certain that, after the mediation process, the student would be able to use the articles correctly in every case. Anywise, this was not the aim from the beginning. The aim was to help the student overcome a stage that shapes her interlanguage and ZPD to a higher level of development, approaching the correct use of the target language.

These kinds of interactions repeated in the three following mediation sessions, like the first one. The students were asked again to read the essays they have produced and try to revise their content, first on their own and then with their teacher's help who supported them with strategies. In the beginning of each session, the teacher remained neutral to students' mistaken responses checking whether the students transferred the writing strategies they have learnt in previous sessions to face new challenges or not.

The results arose from the post-tests showed that students' writings were extended in number of words (see Tables 4 and 5 in comparison) and decreased in grammatical errors (see Charts 1 and 2). Furthermore, general improvement observed on the level of connection between the content and the requested topic, as well as on content organization and the use of arguments. Finally, at the post-test it became apparent that for both students increased the number of words and the number of sentences in their texts with the exception of the number of paragraphs who were the same for both of them.

Table 4. Pre-tests' data

	Participant A	Participant B
Number of words	189	336
Number of sentences	17	44
Number of paragraphs	7	10

Table 5. Post-tests' data

	Participant A	Participant B
Number of words	283	465
Number of sentences	37	58
Number of paragraphs	7	10

The spelling mistakes were mainly of stress marking, while morphosyntactic errors were observed in the usage of the voices of the verbs (e.g., *George was discovered the route* instead of *George discovered the route*), verb tense (e.g., *Recently I take a trip* instead *of Recently I took a trip*) and lack of articles (e.g., *There are a lot of the bridges at the village* instead of *There are a lot of bridges at the village*), when needed. In both pre-tests there were syntactic mistakes concerning the right usage of articles and nouns (*a big cities* instead of *a big city*) and the verb and the subject matching (*The traditional pie taste amazing* instead of *The traditional pie tastes amazing*) (Chart 1). In the text of Student A was also noticed lack of prepositions (e.g. *It will fill you up beautiful pictures* instead of *It will fill you up with beautiful pictures*).

Figure 2. Typology and number of errors of the pre-tests

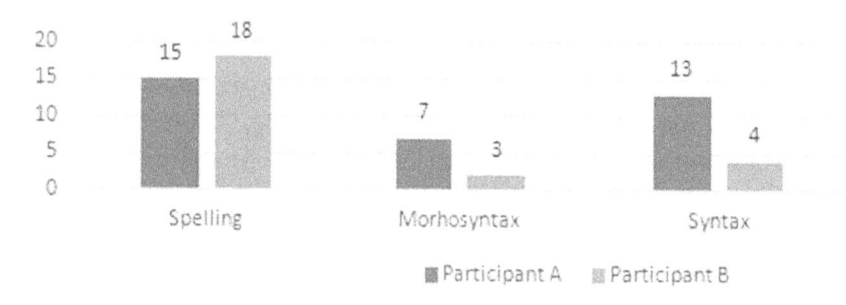

In general, the typology of errors in the post-tests (Chart 2) was the same with that observed in the pre-tests but their number halved. Most of the errors noticed in the following categories: a) spelling mistakes, b) morphosyntactic errors: morpheme formation with emphasis on inflectional morphemes, use of appropriate verb tense, lack of articles and c) syntactic: article and noun matching, noun case and syntax matching, person of the verb and noun case matching .

Figure 3. Typology and number of errors of the post-tests

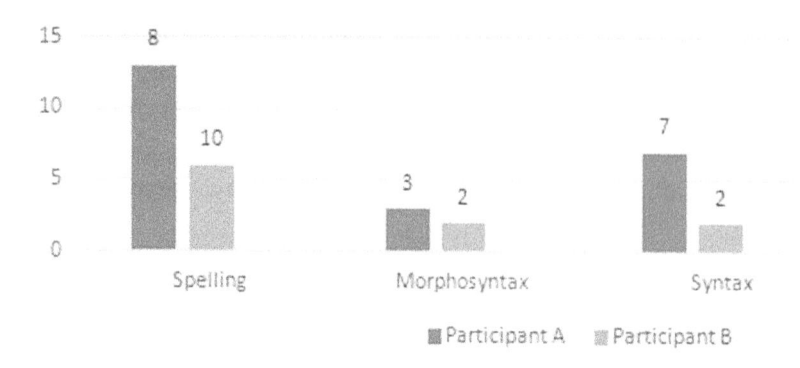

Discussion

This research has been conducted to investigate the efficacy of DA implemented by distance on improving writing ability of adult students of Greek as a L2. Results of several studies show that the implementation of DA in the L2 teaching supports the development of students' learning potential and improvement on writing (Babamoradi et al., 2018; Heidari, 2020; Rahmani et al., 2020; Shabani, 2018). Several studies presented in this paper are based on an interventionist DA approach (the Sandwich format) (Aljaafreh & Lantolf, 1994; Ghahremani & Azarizad, 2013; Miao & Mian, 2013; Sadek, 2015; Farrokh & Rahmani, 2017; Mauludin & Ardianti, 2017). In this research Aljaafreh and Lantolf's (1994) research methodology was adopted because of the dialogical process, the focus on writing and the small group of the participants that are fully in line with this research and have a great impact on it. Like Aljaafreh and Lantolf's research (1994), the mediational strategies developed in this research followed the abstract-concrete (implicit-explicit) principle.

The pre-test showed that the students had no control over spelling and grammar, even in words and morphosyntactic and syntactic phenomena they had already taught. Regarding the choice of vocabulary, there was no control either. For example, in some cases the students preferred to write a word whose sound exist also in their first language, instead of seeking the proper word in L2 or a synonym. This students' practice, found also in Farrokh & Rahmani research (2017), caused further spelling, semantic and lexical mistakes.

Moreover, in terms of substance it was found that the students were producing texts by writing down their thoughts without first doing a writing plan and grouping their thoughts into paragraphs. During the intervention sessions the students practiced in writing by creating plans and learning vocabulary related to the topic *Traveling*. Out of the total writing strategies (planning, vocabulary activation, control, and self-assessment) indicated to the students, planning seems to have had a stronger effect on them as both created plans before the final writing production. Their papers were also improved in appearance and content organization. No particularly significant improvement of the students' essays in vocabulary range, although grammar errors were reduced to about 50%.

It was apparent, by the post-tests analysis, that Aljaafreh & Lantolf's (1994) Regulatory Scale had a positive influence on the students becoming aware of their writing practices. The implementation of the aforementioned scale during the mediation procedure helped students not only to overcome some kinds of grammatical errors that they made in their essays, but through the interaction that took place, a lot of students' misconceptions were identified, analyzed and explained. Into pre-tests there were spelling mistakes in words which were also in the post-tests, but in smaller numbers. It is considered that the reduction of errors in spelling and grammar detected to the post-tests of the students is a result of the Regulatory Scale adopted. From another perspective, since the grammar mistakes were of a particular type and thus more limited, it was much easier to get them under control.

Based on the research findings, it is difficult to discover or estimate with certainty if the students participated in this research were at the same stage of ZPD. However, this is quite possible as their performance converge. It must be made clear though that some students may need a different kind of help based on their ZPD stage (Aljaafreh & Lantolf, 1994).

To summarize the study's results, providing feedback involves students in the assessment process, enabling them to realize that the difficulties they face in grammar accuracy, a conclusion also found in other studies (Aljaafreh & Lantolf, 1994· Sadek, 2015· Farrokh & Rahmani, 2017). At the same time, inclusion of writing strategies in mediation feedback provides students with internalization techniques that can be used in their future attempts, finding in accordance with Ghahremani & Azarizad (2013) and Sadek (2015).

Consequently, the facilitative intervention of dynamic assessment helped students to perform the writing process in a systematic way. In addition, the pedagogical implications drawn from this study are that DA-based teaching activities will lead to better writings of students (Etemadi & Abbasian, 2023)

There could be no absolute level of assurance that intervention's efficacy is attributed to the type of the scale implemented or the chosen strategies or even to third factors. The strategies adopted in this mediation context may not carry out similar results in future studies. The limitations of this study are elaborated further below.

CONCLUSION

The findings put forward by this study which investigated the use and effectiveness of DA method, and in particular, of mediation via videoconferencing, are particularly encouraging for L2 teachers who are called upon daily to cope with challenges in terms of teaching and assessment in distance education. However, listing the limitations seems to be necessary. It is a well-known fact that the dual role of the teacher/ researcher may affect her/his value judgments so that to excuse some students' mistakes as language slips. Similarly, it was not possible to exclude this fact from the present research. The conclusions of a small scale research like this could not be generalizable, but only to increase GSL teachers' interest to examine their students' learning potential implementing alternative methods of teaching and assessment. The intervention was short-term. Therefore, it cannot be determined whether the positive findings could be related to students' long-term performance.

A proposal for future research is the assumption that long-term online mediation sessions result in gradually better performances. A further proposal on this is the use of online mediation strategies into texts of different types, topics, subjects, and degree of difficulty according to the learning objectives. To conclude, this study is expected to give impetus to teachers of GSL to intergrade DA method on teaching writing by distance and conduct corresponding research to gain further knowledge on the questions raised on this issue and on their assessment literacy in general (Vogt et. al., 2020)

REFERENCES

Abbasian, M. (2016). Dynamic Assessment: Review of Literature. *International Journal of Modern Language Teaching and Learning*, *1*(3), 116–120.

Aljaafreh, A., & Lantolf, J. P. (1994). Negative feedback as regulation and second language learning in the zone of proximal development. *Modern Language Journal*, *78*(4), 465–483. doi:10.1111/j.1540-4781.1994.tb02064.x

Anam, S., Akhiriyah, S., & Iswati, H. D. (2023). Advances in Social Science, Education and Humanity Research: Looking into the Role of Dynamic Assessment in English Grammar Mastery of Indonesian EFL Learners. *Paper presented at the Unima International Conference on Social Sciences and Humanity 2022*. Atlantic Press. https://www.atlantis-press.com/proceedings/unicssh-22/125984028

Babamoradi, P., Nasiri, M., & Mohammadi, E. (2018). Learners' attitudes toward using dynamic assessment in teaching and assessing IELTS writing task one. *International Journal of Language Testing*, *8*(1), 1–11.

Bitchener, J., & Storch, N. (2016). Written Corrective [*Development*. Multilingual Matters.]. *Feedback*, L2.

Center for the Greek Language. (2013). *Common European Framework of Reference for Languages: Learning, Teaching, Assessment. Assessment criteria*. Greek trans. Centre for the Greek Language. https://www.greeklanguage.gr/certification/node/112.html

Chamot, A. U. (2005). Language learning strategy instruction: Current issues and research. [Cambridge University Press.]. *Annual Review of Applied Linguistics*, *25*, 112–130. doi:10.1017/S0267190505000061

Council of Europe. (2001). *Common European Framework of Reference for Languages: Learning, teaching, assessment*. Cambridge University Press.

Ellis, R. (2009). Corrective Feedback and Teacher Development. *Journal of Linguistics and Language Teaching*, *1*(1), 3–18.

Etemadi, S. H., & Abbasian, G.-R. (2023). Dynamic assessment and EFL learners' writing journey: Focus on DA modalities and writing revision types. *Teaching English Language, 17*(1), 53-79. https://www.teljournal.org/article_162923.html

Farrokh, P., & Rahmani, A. (2017). Dynamic assessment of writing ability in transcendence tasks based on Vygotskian perspective. *Asian-Pacific Journal of Second and Foreign Language Education*, *2*(10), 1–23. doi:10.118640862-017-0033-z

Feuerstein, R., Rand, Y., & Rynders, J. E. (1988). *Don't Accept Me as I Am. Helping Retarded Performers Excel*. Plenum. doi:10.1007/978-1-4899-6128-0

Fulcher, G. (2013). *Practical Language Testing*. Routledge. doi:10.4324/980203767399

Ghahremani, D., & Azarizad, R. (2013). The Effect of Dynamic Assessment on EFL Process Writing: Content and Organization. *International Research Journal of Applied and Basic Sciences*, *4*, 874–878.

Giannikas, C. (2020). Facebook in tertiary education: The impact of social media in e-learning. *Journal of University Teaching & Learning Practice*, *17*(1), 3. https://eric.ed.gov/?id=EJ1247596. doi:10.53761/1.17.1.3

Grigorenko, E., & Sternberg, J. R. (1998). Dynamic Testing. *Psychological Bulletin*, *124*(1), 75–111. doi:10.1037/0033-2909.124.1.75

Heidari, K. (2020). Critical thinking and EFL learners' performance on textually-explicit, textually-implicit, and script-based reading items. *Thinking Skills and Creativity*, *37*, 100703. doi:10.1016/j.tsc.2020.100703

Hendrickson, M. J. (1978). Error Correction in Foreign Language Teaching: Recent Theory, Research, and Practice. *Modern Language Journal*, *62*(8), 387–398.

Hyland, F., & Hyland, K. (2006). *Feedback in second language writing: Contexts and issues*. Cambridge University Press. doi:10.1017/CBO9781139524742

Ioannou, S., & Tsagari, D. (2022). Effects of Recasts, Metalinguistic Feedback, and Students' Proficiency on the Acquisition of Greek Perfective Past Tense. *Languages (Basel, Switzerland)*, *7*(1), 40. doi:10.3390/languages7010040

Kozulin, A., & Garb, E. (2002). Dynamic assessment of EFL text comprehension of at-risk students. *School Psychology International*, *23*(1), 112–127. doi:10.1177/0143034302023001733

Lantolf, J. P., Kurtz, L., & Kisselev, O. (2017). Understanding the revolutionary character of L2 development in the ZPD: Why levels of mediation matter. *Journal of Applied Linguistics*, *3*(2), 153–171. https://journal.equinoxpub.com/LST/article/view/608

Lantolf, J. P., & Poehner, M. E. (2004). Dynamic assessment of L2 development: Bringing the past into the future. *Journal of Applied Linguistics*, *1*(2), 49–72. doi:10.1558/japl.1.1.49.55872

Lantolf, J. P., & Thorne, S. (2006). *Sociocultural Theory and the Genesis of Second Language Development*. Oxford University Press.

Leontjev, D. (2016). Dynamic assessment of word derivational knowledge: Tracing the development of a learner. *Eesti Rakenduslingvistika Ühingu aastaraamat Estonian Papers in Applied Linguistics*, *12*, 141-160. https://www.researchgate.net/publication/303320043_Dynamic_assessment_of_word_derivational_knowledge_Tracing_the_development_of_a_learner

Lidz, S. C. (1997). Dynamic Assessment Approaches. In D. P. Flanagan, J. L. Genshaft, & P. L. Harrison (Eds.), *Contemporary Approaches to Assessment of Intelligence* (pp. 285–293). The Guilford Press.

Mauludin, L. A., & Ardianti, T. M. (2017). The Role of Dynamic Assessment in EFL Writing Class. *METATHESIS: Journal of English Language, Literature, and Teaching*, *1*(2), 82–93.

Mehrabany, Z., & Bagheri, M. (2017). Which one is superior; The cake approach or the sandwich approach? The effect of dynamic assessment on EFL undergraduates' vocabulary knowledge. [IJLLALW]. *International Journal of Language Learning and Applied Linguistics World*, *15*(2), 1–13.

Miao, T., & Mian, L. (2013). Dynamic Assessment in ESL Writing Classroom. *International Conference on Education Technology and Management Science*, (Icetms), 676–679. https://download.atlantis-press.com/proceedings/icetms-13/6996

Mu, C., & Carrington, S. (2007). An Investigation of Three Chinese Students' English Writing Strategies. *TESL-EJ: The Electronic Journal for English as a Second Language*, *11*(1), 1–23.

Poehner, M., & Wang, Z. (2021). Dynamic Assessment and second language development. *Language Teaching*, *54*(4), 472–490. doi:10.1017/S0261444820000555

Poehner, M. E. (2008). *Dynamic Assessment: A Vygotskian Approach to Understanding and Promoting L2 Development. Educational Linguistics*. Springer. https://link.springer.com/book/10.1007/978-0-387-75775-9

Pyrtsiou, F., & Rousoulioti, T. (2022). *Perceptions and Attitudes towards Assessment: Focusing on the Use of Portfolios in Formal and Informal Secondary Education in Greece*. Research Gate. https://www.researchgate.net/publication/362903598_Pyrtsiou_F_Rousoulioti_T_2022Perceptions_and_Attitudes_towards_Assessment_Focusing_on_the_Use_of_Portfolios_in_Formal_and_Informal_Secondary_Education_in_Greece_In_IPapadopolous_S_Chiper_Eds_Internati

Rahmani, A., Rashtchi, M., & Yazdanimoghadam, M. (2020). Interactionist and interventionist dynamic assessment approaches to teaching argumentative writing: Do complexity, accuracy, and fluency develop? *Journal of English Language Pedagogy and Practice*, *13*(27), 100–128. doi:10.30495/jal.2021.680912

Raimes, A. (1983). *Techniques in Teaching Writing*. Oxford University Press.

Ritonga, M., Farhangi, F., Ajanil, B., & Ayman, F. K. (2022). Interventionist vs. interactionist models of dynamic assessment (DA) in the EFL classroom: Impacts on speaking accuracy and fluency (SAF), foreign language classroom anxiety (FLCA), and foreign language learning motivation (FLLM). *Language Testing in Asia*, *12*(1), 43. doi:10.118640468-022-00195-0

Rousoulioti, T. (2015). Alternative assessment. In Th. Roussoulioti & V. Panagiotidou (Eds.), *Curricula Models for the teaching of Greek as a second/foreign language*. Zitis publication. https://www.researchgate.net/publication/340771917_Enallaktike_axiologese

Rousoulioti, Th., & Karagkouni, I. (2019). The assessment of writing: The present and the future. Kathedra: Vol. 4. *1. Department of Byzantine and Modern Greek Literature*. Lomonosov University. http://kathedra-ens.ru/hellenika/teukhi/.

Sadek, N. (2015). Dynamic Assessment (DA): Promoting Writing Proficiency through Assessment. *International Journal of Bilingual & Multilingual Teachers of English*, *2*(2), 59–70. doi:10.12785/ijbmte/030201

Sapkota, A. (2012). Developing Students' Writing Skill through Peer and Teacher Correction: An Action Research. *Journal of NELTA*, *17*(1-2), 70–82. doi:10.3126/nelta.v17i1-2.8094

Serhan, D. (2020). Transitioning from face-to-face to remote learning: Students' attitudes and perceptions of using Zoom during Covid-19 pandemic. [IJTES]. *International Journal of Technology in Education and Science*, *4*(4), 335–342. https://ijtes.net/index.php/ijtes/article/view/148. doi:10.46328/ijtes.v4i4.148

Shabani, K. (2018). Group dynamic assessment of L2 learners' writing abilities. *Iranian Journal of Language Teaching Research*, *6*(1), 129–149. doi:10.30466/ijltr.2018.20494

Sun, Y., Wang, T.-H., & Wang, L.-F. (2021). Implementation of Web-Based Dynamic Assessments as Sustainable Educational Technique for Enhancing Reading Strategies in English Class during the COVID-19 Pandemic. *Sustainability (Basel)*, *13*(11), 5842. doi:10.3390u13115842

Tavakoli, M., & Nezakat-Alhossaini, M. (2014). Implementation of corrective feedback in an English as a foreign language classroom through dynamic assessment. *Journal of Language and Linguistic Studies*, *10*(1), 211–232.

Tootkaboni, A. A., & Khatib, M. (2014). The Efficiency of Various Kinds of Error Feedback on Improving Writing Accuracy of EFL Learners. *Bellaterra Journal of Teaching & Learning Language & Literature*, *7*(3), 30–46. doi:10.5565/rev/jtl3.529

Ur, P. (1996). *A Course in Language Teaching: Practice and theory*. Cambridge University Press.

Vogt, K., Tsagari, D., & Spanoudis, G. (2020). What Do Teachers Think They Want? A Comparative Study of In-Service Language Teachers' Beliefs on LAL Training Needs. *Language Assessment Quarterly*, *17*(4), 386–409. doi:10.1080/15434303.2020.1781128

Vygotsky, L. (1978). *Mind in society: The development of higher psychological processes* (M. Cole, V. John-Steiner, S. Scribner, & E. Souberman, Eds.). Harvard University Press.

Vygotsky, L. S. (1987). The Collected Works of L. S. Vygotsky. Volume 1. Problems of General Psychology. Including the Volume Thinking and Speech. R. W. Rieber and A. S. Carton (Eds). Plenum.

Xiaoxiao, L., & Yan, L. (2010). A Case Study of Dynamic Assessment in EFL Process Writing. *Chinese Journal of Applied Linguistis (Bimonthly)*, *33*(1), 24–40.

Zhang, Y. H. (2010). Constructing Dynamic Assessment Mode in College English Writing Class. *Journal of PLA University of Foreign Languages*, *1*, 46–50.

ENDNOTE

[1] Unofficial translation in English by the authors of the present paper.

Chapter 6
Learning Through Assessment in Anthrogogic Contexts:
Wash–Forward

Shree Deepa
University of Hyderabad, India

Geetha Durairajan
English and Foreign Languages University, Hyderabad, India

ABSTRACT

This chapter charts the wash-forwards gained by the teacher authors who learnt through assessment in the process of teaching an online English language proficiency course that was offered to adult students in mainstream higher education classrooms. The whole course used scenario-based learning and assessment as its tapestry. Students were treated as equal partners; the learnings and the feed-forwards for further courses for the author-teachers were in the areas of time management; new group dynamics, the use of new technological tools as taught by students, the varied uses of plurilingual language use, and new ways of raising an awareness of the potentiality of language to be used in a constructive, neutral, or destructive manner. The students also benefited because they learnt to reflect on their own academic lives, to take responsibility for their academic decisions, and to be aware of their own language use. Though the primary context was the online teaching context during Covid-19, the implications are for regular offline and post-Covid classrooms.

INTRODUCTION

This chapter is a self-reflective (Roy & Uekusa, 2020) narrative that relies on "mining our own lives, our own experiences" (Rothman, 2007, p. 12) as we turn our everyday teaching experiences into research data and use them as topics of analysis (Francis & Hester, 2012; Rothman, 2007). This includes the strategies used by the two teacher authors to keep the students cognitively engaged during an adult mainstream (not distance mode), online undergraduate-level proficiency course in English. The deliberate focus is

DOI: 10.4018/978-1-6684-6227-0.ch006

on how we (both teachers and students) learnt through the varied strategic assessment practices that were intricately woven into the course. These include the modified use of scenario-based assessment (Purpura, 2021) for formative evaluation, the use of Parkinson's Law (Gutierrez & Kouvelis, 1991; Olleras et al., 2022; Parkinson, 1957) as a means to tap and enable higher-order language skills, modifications in the nature and type of group work done in class, the use of other languages in the English classroom as an asset, and the need to go beyond proficiency to raise awareness of how language has the potential to be used constructively, neutrally or destructively by all human beings.

The chapter focuses on teacher learnings primarily, but where evidence is available, also touches on students' learnings. These learnings (both by teachers and students) are reflective and post-experiential; rooted in grounded theory (Cresswell, 2002; Glaser & Strauss, 1967) they are an encapsulation of theorization from practice and structured in such a way that a separate literature review section is not feasible. Detailed theoretical postulations and critiques are therefore presented along with the discussion of the teachers' learning outcomes. This integration is due to the novel nature of the topic and the analytically unique treatment of the area that is exploratory in its direction, and implicatory in its conclusion based as it is in situational analysis (Clarke, 2007). Some terms that have been dormant in the literature are discussed as terminological clarifications for ease of comprehension, along with some of the major perspectival arguments that informed and shaped the course, assuming common knowledge of terms used in testing as a discipline. Some terms that are section specific are elaborated upon in the relevant sections. A brief discussion on the background to the main timeline, that is COVID-19, is also presented to situate the study and foreground the context adequately. The major areas of learning include discussions on time-management issues, the equal partnership of teachers and students in learning, group dynamics, the use of technological tools in real-time, the plurilingual reality of the Indian subcontinent, its implications in the classroom and language potentiality; these are elaborated to lead to a logical conclusion.

A few new terms that are used throughout the chapter, or that need clarification can be presented here initially and discussed in detail later where required to enhance the discussion: this revisiting is not a redundancy but is primarily for emphasis. The term 'anthrogogy' (Deepa, n.d., 2022a, 2022b, 2022c, 2022d; Trott, 1991) is one of the newest terms re-entering the realm of education; in this context, it is applied to mainstream higher education classrooms such as undergraduate classrooms in India where the students are 18+years of biological age and have registered for a degree in regular classrooms and not through the distance mode. The term though it has origins in 'andragogy' (Knowles, 1968) is not used in that sense but as a separate approach to language testing in this chapter. Anthrogogy "refers to teaching adults (all genders) and has its own set of principles of teaching and testing where the emphasis is on living a life of a cohabitant alongside other beings peacefully on planet earth." (Deepa, 2022c, p.165).

The term 'wash-forward' is originally attributed to van Lier (1989) and was later developed by Gordon, (2020) who used it as a testing term to describe "existing perceptions and/or practices that may influence how a test construct is operationalised" (p. 40). In this chapter, the term is used to indicate the learnings of the teachers that taught a course which have the possibility in some cases, and actual realisations in others to constructively feed forward into other courses as generic learnings and not necessarily be clasped only to testing as wash back does. The term wash-back is not used here because the focus is not on a single test but on the generic perspective itself that could feed forward into future courses: as such, wash-forward needs to be perceived as influencing not only students and teachers on one particular course, either as a consequence or influence of test use, but as a wash forward into further courses leading to professional development. This is one of the reasons why instead of using the term learning-oriented assessment (Turner & Purpura, 2016) which includes assessment of, for and as learning (Black & William, 1998) the term 'learning through assessment' has been used by us. For Woodward (1998) assessment as learning refers to "a true union of assessment and learning" (p. 421) while for Biggs (1999) it was 'constructive alignment' but for us, it refers to the learnings of both teachers and students through the process of the assessments that were a part of the anthrogogic course and not directly applied to students' learnings as is the oft practice. This term, learning through assessment accommodates the inclusion of a professional wash-forward within its purview which is the crux of this chapter. Other terms like Parkinson's Law, the concept that was used to enable better time management by students, language potentiality, and the use of the first/dominant/more enabled language as an asset in plurilingual contexts are critically elaborated in the relevant sections.

BACKGROUND

Covid-19 jolted many of our classroom procedures, teaching and testing practices in India and catapulted us into many unknown, uncharted territories. In a very significant yet natural manner, we teachers have had to go where no teacher had gone before and find solutions for problems never encountered earlier. The sudden shift from offline, face-to-face classes to online teaching and testing practices was a testing time for teachers, many of whom are technologically challenged like the two of us. With everything locked up under lockdowns, it forced both teachers and students into eerie solitude-filled rooms; both groups were expected to 'talk' to cameras and 'perform' for one another in the name of classes, excluding the trials with a variety of social media/communication platforms like WhatsApp groups, like Google classrooms, Learnex, Zoom, google meet etc. The teachers' frustrations rose when their students became a letter or an icon on the screen, a mere digital presence, with the video switched off during live classes to ensure network bandwidth because of connectivity issues. The teacher talking to or attempting to interact with what seemed like an empty audience hall had to cope with the 'physical absence' or rather 'muted' (pun intended) presence of the students. This was complicated by the administrative reality of most Universities in India deciding that 'attendance will not be marked as compulsory' because many students have connectivity issues and cannot be penalised for such technological failures. It is a ground reality that in many parts of India, power outages are widespread, routers do not work, and during monsoon times, even when there is power, network or connectivity is a problem to contend with.

At a personal level, a massive problem for the two of us, as teachers, was that 'teaching to a camera' was a 'first of its kind experience' to cope with; the two of us are teachers who rely on body language and gestures as an interactive feedback mechanism in our classes. With body language being conspicuously absent in online classes we had to find working solutions to get some kind of 'feedback' from students. Emergency strategies had to be developed to ensure that students' presence in the classroom if it could be called that, was not a mere digital icon on the screen with no proof or evidence that the same student was mentally, cognitively, or even physically present. With connectivity problems, whether real or otherwise, students would switch off video, mute their microphones and 'pretend' to listen with an occasional 'yes ma'am' or a 'no ma'am'. This meant that it was also necessary to find ways of organising online group work to take away monotony and enthuse students to participate; without this, the two of us felt that the online classes would get reduced to the drone of a bee, or at best, the mechanical doing of language exercises and tasks. Neither students nor teachers had a clue about how to handle such online classes; the solution that the two of us came up with was to find innovative ways of making attendance and participation 'academically' necessary, even if the administrative requirement was waived: this was to use assessment as a learning tool in the classroom, to go beyond formative or summative testing and make it a part of the teaching-learning loop. To do this, we attempted to ensure that nearly every class included some kind of incidental or deliberate assessment with students and the teacher learning from these classroom experiences as a wash-forward (Gordon, 2020; Van Lier, 1989).

The well-known practice of washback (Alderson & Wall, 1993; Cheng, 2005) would have only fed into classes which would feed into the test that follows; the assessment practices which were adapted by us were conceptualised in such a manner that they would initially feed into further classes and later also into future courses as "adaptive implementation" (Gordon, 2020, p. 41); this was done with the hope that they would enable a modification or adaptation of the innovation in such a way that it becomes "more easily assimilated into user practices and values" (Roberts-Gray & Gray, 1983, p. 216).

Profile of Teacher-Authors and Students

The teacher-authors had done their education at a time when computers were not introduced into classrooms and saw them being introduced slowly and their profile details will be narrated alternately as a deliberate move as it impacts the way the chapter is ideated. The primary author (SD) bought her first computer, an assembled desktop which ran on Windows, only in 2003, when she was twenty-nine years old with great financial difficulty. Even though she had been trained in the DOS platform in the 1990s, that did not help her negotiate Windows. She did pick up a sparse set of computer skills in her teaching experiences at the school level. However, she calls herself and identifies herself as a paper-pencil-pen person.

The second author (GD) was already forty years old in 1996 when she bought her first computer, an assembled desktop which worked on Windows 3.1. Both the teacher-authors are limited in their technology skills, and the primary author calls herself 'technologically disabled' with difficulty handling the ever-changing 'applications' or rather apps with their ever-elusive three-dots and drop-down menus. SD also considers herself a camera-shy person and becomes extremely conscious in front of a camera. GD feels even more disabled, though not camera shy: with many difficulties, only two years ago, she has learnt to go beyond using reviews and comments in MS word to work with google docs. She has not taught courses online and has never experienced what a breakaway room is and how it functions in an online course.

SD has nearly 25 years of experience in teaching English language proficiency courses, including school teaching experience, and has also taught a few content courses in the area of English language studies/education, and has supervised dissertations in the same area at a central university. GD now retired from active service, by contrast, has more than 30 years of experience in teaching courses primarily on testing and evaluation and in the field of second language education in multilingual contexts at the university level. She has supervised dissertations in the areas of ELE and testing. SD was initially stumped with the notion of an online English language proficiency course, consulted with GD on the teaching and testing practices and drew on her vast experience in the field of testing, assessment, and evaluation. Through this close consultative process, which was needed to handle the sudden onset of online classes, the two teacher-authors learnt about online assessment practices, technological tools, and many other related administrative and academic issues. SD almost always ensures that her courses in higher education classes are anthrogogic in their orientation and 'not pedagogic' (Knowles, 1968). Over her thirty years of teaching at the University level, GD has attempted to be anthrogogic in her teaching and assessment practices, initially, for the first ten years or so, without the awareness of either the terminology or the characteristics but later with growing awareness and over the past five years as a deliberate choice.

The students, all adults, kept deliberately anonymous for ethical reasons, were registered for their integrated master's degree in technology. In India, this implies that these students have completed their higher secondary level of education somewhat akin to the K 12 level. This is a part of slightly specialised schooling where students select four major subjects/areas to study and one or more of them becomes the focus of study at the college level. These integrated Masters students, where the course includes 3 years of under-graduation plus 2 years of post-graduation, were admitted through a national entrance test into a multidisciplinary central university in South India. For ethical reasons the name of the university is deliberately withheld. In these integrated programmes, English is a compulsory course that is taught for two semesters. The first-semester English course is the one discussed in this chapter. It was offered entirely online during the covid-19 lockdown in India, and the course was taught for four months as a four-credit course, translating into 46 hours of teaching. The platform used was Learnx, the in-house learning platform and integrated Zoom was the video conferencing interface/platform with the facility of breakaway rooms that could be used for smaller group discussions. There were about 42 students, with gender not considered as a variable. A WhatsApp group was also formed to keep the communication channels open and accessible with the awareness that net connectivity could be a problem for many students. This group of students was technology savvy as some were 'coders' and ethical hackers, while others had already handled big data. They were proficient in using editing and paraphrasing tools such as Grammarly, Turnitin, quillbot or spinbot. An initial writing assignment provided evidence that while some had a few accuracy problems with English, most did not have any linguistic system-based issues; thus, the focus was on enabling the higher-order academic skills of analysing, applying, evaluating, and creating.

METHOD

This chapter will be a self-reflective narrative that will focus on some of the testing practices and assessment strategies that were used by SD during the proficiency course at the graduate level, a part of the integrated master's program that was planned, liaised together with GD, capitalising on her expertise in educational evaluation that led to a different level of team teaching and testing. The attempt made will be to identify the strategies adopted by the two of us, one the primary teacher of the course and the other an online informal, friendly consultant, to ensure that the classes did not remain a series of boring lectures on how to write reports or make presentations, as is the norm in some proficiency courses, accompanied by postings of grammar and vocabulary exercises/tasks along with some texts for reading and listening, and tasks for writing and speaking which students merely had to finish and submit. The discussion will revolve around practices we identified and used under the given extenuating circumstances in the context of ongoing, formative, and summative assessment so that these practices would bias towards the best for all students (Swain, 1985).

The primary focus for both of us in this course was to verify and ensure that the participation of the students was cognitive and not merely a digital "iconic" one (Deepa, 2022c, p. 169) while also ensuring that genuine learning was taking place, with language ability and use being enabled and empowered. The attempt was also to ensure that the virtual presence of the students should not be reduced to a digital one on a technology device but be made experiential, without a struggle for corporeality (Willatt & Flores,

2022) and through constant cognitive engagement. The strategies that we used included ensuring an anthrogogic (Deepa, n.d., 2022a, 2022b, 2022c; Trott, 1991) course perspective, the use of scenario-based learning for skill integration, and a shift in focus from mere skill-based language proficiency enabling, to language use and awareness raising about the potentiality that language has to be used in a constructive, neutral or destructive manner (Deepa, 2022d). Scenario-based assessment (Purpura, 2021) which has been used in the literature mainly for summative evaluation, was used by us not only for formative assessment wherever possible but also as the basis of tasks when required. This was done to challenge the students and, at a base level, ensure that downloading and copy-pasting answers from the internet was not possible.

The concept of 'learning through assessment' in this chapter is applied primarily as a professional wash-forward for the two teachers who have learnt through their forays into the kind of teaching that had to be enmeshed with evaluation and assessment in an online English language proficiency course that was taught during the covid-19 lockdown. As an incidental outcome, wherever relevant and significant, the learnings by the students through their assessment are also briefly touched upon. The whole course was rooted in the Freirian perspective of education as conscientization and awareness raising (Freire, 1970/ 2005). This implied that the proficiency course could not be reduced to the use of mere texts for listening and reading comprehension, with a range of appropriate questions, followed by sessions on writing and speaking with a few grammar and vocabulary-focused classes thrown in. For such typical proficiency-oriented classes, assessment of, for and as learning (ARG, 2002; Black & William, 1998) may have been sufficient. Every 'text with questions' could have been presented as a 'test' or an 'assignment', but as assessors, in a purely online course, the authors/teachers would be clueless as to whether each one of them was being answered by the student or someone else. The solution was to go not only beyond the three types of assessment but also beyond learning-oriented assessment, which brought in feedback into the loop but largely attempted to encompass and bring under one umbrella assessment, for, of and as learning (Carless, 2006, 2007). Summative, formative, peer and self-assessment was not sufficient; there was the need to explore the possibility of *learning through assessment* (Driscoll, Bryant & National Research Council, 1998; Gibbs, 1995; Lubbe et al., 2021). This approach has been practised in content-based learning but not in the context of language enabling/empowerment.

In this chapter, and on the course, learning through assessment implied that every single assessment task was primarily for language learning, development and use and that the certification purpose was a secondary one. These learning-through-assessment tasks were our online alternative to the worksheets that would have been used in face-to-face classes. These tasks also provided us with wash-forward ideas to be used in future courses, both online and offline.

The Nature of the Course Discussed

The course in discussion was a compulsory English language proficiency course that focussed on the integrated development of the skills of reading, writing, listening and speaking, where grammar and vocabulary were treated as an inseparable part of the language itself. It was anthrogogic in its approach: the students were expected to learn to write academic essays, reports, and emails, read and respond to various texts which served as inputs for the essays and reports. Furthermore, they were expected to make presentations to an audience on one or more topics after carrying out some research that could include conducting surveys/interviews and the analysis and interpretation of data thus collected. Whenever needed, online materials/links were provided on the topics. This meant that students were expected to read in their chosen fields with reasonable comprehension, infer and go meta on the links made across texts, in order to write academic essays, reports, and emails, and make presentations with a reasonably good academic vocabulary of 3000 words or more. Since these were technology students, many integrations of web tools were anticipated and encouraged.

A range of classroom tasks was given to the students in the synchronous classes. The same was posted on the Learnx and WhatsApp platforms to enable students to access them in case they had a connectivity issue or were absent for some reason. The discussions on the assigned work were encouraged to be carried out synchronously. At the same time, I hovered over their breakaway chat rooms to get an insider view of what discussions were happening, while being available for clarification in the main chat room. I also encouraged out-of-timetable hours of discussion, planning and execution of the assignments over WhatsApp whenever needed.[1] This was done to value and respect the working hour patterns of different individuals while keeping the discussion and communication channels open. Since the course was entirely online, a range of assignments was given that were used for formative assessment, with a partially modified process portfolio form of assessment, drafts of essays alone, not actual notes and planning, along with a product portfolio -three best self-chosen assignments for evaluation (Durairajan, 2015). This was followed by a summative end-of-term evaluation, including a term paper as an open-source 48-hour examination. The formative versus summative score ratio was 50:50 for this course. The course followed a modified version of the scenario-based approach of teaching and testing as it was found to be the most suited to the anthrogogic context and to chart the participation of the students in an online platform; it also helped us to maintain connectivity across the classes that were timetabled every week (Banerjee, 2018; Deane et al., 2019; Purpura, 2021). Scenario-based enabling, as we would prefer to describe it, can be traced to its earlier versions, sometimes referred to as 'case-based' (Jackson, 2003), problem-based learning (Spencer & Jordan, 1999) or as 'appreciative inquiry' which has been understood as a learner centered approach where positivity and an appreciative mode is given primary emphasis in handling various issues at hand, particularly when working with adults (Cooperrider et al., 2008) and even task based language teaching, TBLT, (Prabhu, 2021). For us, scenarios, as Errington (2005, p. 10) elucidates, "provide an ideal platform for students to experience deep level learning tasks and attain higher order cognitive skills (decision-making and critical analysis)" and also echo with Smith et al. (2018), who state that our "students increasingly want to know that the theories and concepts they are being taught have real-world applications" (p. 155).

Errington (2005, 2011) develops this understanding of using and harnessing scenarios, as a possible motivation to optimise the learning experiences for the students and teaching experiences for us in the anthrogogic context of the knowledge co-creation paradigm. To ensure such co-creation, we harvested from multilingual reality, Parkinson's law, the modified use of a discourse completion questionnaire, technological tool availability and its free usage echoing authentic adult contexts and explored as many of these as possible, within the context of scenarios. These scenarios were not just textual materials but were also on-the-spot issues that needed urgent interventions and solutions. Thus, 'scenarios' for us is an all-inclusive adult response to any problem that might need our intervention, just like in the real time adult world. The responses to such scenarios, in the adult world, is not just a binary of fight or flight but a comfortable cline with 'handling the scenario' in between the binary that is rarely spoken about or studied in language sciences. Managing or handling the issue at hand as described/encountered in the close-to-life scenario was perceived by us as the first step in conflict resolution before the resultant fight or flight response kicks in. This handling or management is often related to language choices whenever and wherever it is used. We were not comfortable with the term 'problem-solving' because it assumes that there are only binary responses or that there is a clear-cut predetermined solution to the problem. Solutions lie in democratic and civil consensus and are as varied as the cultures of the world and are not absolute.

Scenario-based testing has been largely used thus far in the literature only in the context of online computer-aided evaluation (Purpura, 2021). To keep the cognitive connectivity of the students active, a scenario-based teaching and testing approach was used wherein scenarios or a couple of common themes were sustained for a few synchronous class hours, with backup work on the WhatsApp group in the asynchronous mode. My initial experiences in the course taught me that it was difficult to sustain the interests of students if standalone tasks were given because they were not serious in doing them; those who were absent also lost out on the opportunity of learning. The two of us had a few discussions to explore the possibility of using scenario-based teaching/assessment as an alternative to paper-pen classroom interaction; we decided that there was no harm in exploring the idea as both of us were new to teaching a bunch of icons on a laptop camera and we were eager to explore the possibilities it could offer. We learnt that such tasks are welcomed by anthrogogic students and plan to explore, develop, and use the approach as a wash-forward in our professional lives.

LEARNING THROUGH ANTHROGOGIC ASSESSMENT

In the rest of this chapter, we will attempt to articulate in some detail two levels of learning through assessment that we experienced and vehemently attempted to use as a wash-forward. The primary focus will be on the learning through assessment by the teacher-authors, but the learning spinoffs, where relevant, by the students will also be included so that it can be duplicated by other interested teachers. Our learnings were in a range of domains with reference to our decisions regarding both our teaching and testing practices with a wash-forward into teaching on further courses in other semesters. Time management was one of them; when we brought in a discussion on Parkinson's law to help them manage their own assignment timelines better, we learnt that they could handle timekeeping excellently.

Learning about the nature of group dynamics in adult classrooms was a valuable second; students teaching us about technological tools available for use featured as a third, with the potentiality of plurilinguality providing another massive learning point. The spinoff learnings of the students were that they learnt about their own time management skills or the lack of it, learnt about their own personalities, and learnt to solve not only their own but also our technological problems. Most importantly, they learnt that language is a powerful tool which can make or break a person, and therefore started to realise, activate, and use language potentiality- the use of humane constructive language choices (Deepa, 2022d) in an anthrogogic context.

The term anthrogogy implies that students must take responsibility for their academic lives and keep to their timelines for task/assessment completion in mainstream higher education courses and classrooms, both offline and online. This perspective hitherto unexplored was used on this course to guide and direct the classroom experiences where the teacher and the students are equal partners in the learning-teaching loop. Students above the biological and sociological age of eighteen or older are defined as adults with true-to-life adult responsibilities, including time management, particularly in the areas of keeping to assignment deadlines. If they need extensions beyond the stipulated deadlines, they should be able and willing to provide justifiable reasons well before the submission date, and not end up with a Peter Pan syndrome (Deepa, 2022c; Kiley, 1983), who are frozen as children in adult bodies. To facilitate such

Learning Through Assessment in Anthrogogic Contexts

awareness, without a pedagogy-oriented lecture/chiding Parkinson's law was introduced as a discussion/presentation topic.

Time-Management Issues and Anthrogogic Classrooms-Parkinson's Law

A few earlier courses both offline and online had taught us that very often, students do not take their assignment deadlines seriously; threats, cajoles and negotiations had not yielded any desirable results. These students were procrastinating helplessly and therefore Parkinson's law (Gutierrez & Kouvelis, 1991; Olleras et al., 2022; Parkinson, 1957) which discusses how many of us work only at the last minute to meet deadlines was used as the basis for finding a solution. This area was chosen for two reasons: first, students were finding it difficult to stick to deadlines and were prone to procrastination because they were finding it difficult to 'take responsibility for their own learning' (Deepa, 2022c). Secondly, we decided to use the concept as the basis for a group presentation, where the students would be able to not only learn about it, but also apply it to their own academic lives, be able to turn around on their own assessment deadlines, or the non-keeping of them, and write an individual report on their own findings. This ensured that we did not have to chide or scold about non-submissions: also, students could not do a 'copy-paste' assignment submission, for responses could not be lifted off the world-wide-web.

It produced the desired results as the students detected through assessing themselves, their own reasons for their procrastination tendency and learnt to minimize it. This was because, in order to do the assignment students had to research, understand, apply and analyse their own contexts. As participant A put it,

We could not copy from the internet as it was not found in the form to be copy-pasted. At the same time, we also 'had no option but to apply to the described contexts and use our awareness while we learnt about the Parkinson's law and applied to our own problems of procrastinations'(sic).[2]

This was a deliberate move taken by me for I had to ensure that the students learn through assessment and not become clever users of artificial intelligence tools such as Quillbot. If a mundane topic such as 'pollution', 'student election' or 'politics and students' was given it would have been very easy for the students to select a 'good' essay from the internet and pass it through a paraphrasing tool such as Quillbot and easily circumvent a similarity index checker such as Turnitin. In order to address this issue as a response to a real-time scenario of procrastination, a creative common licenced video from NAS daily (https://youtu.be/NDi3_vN3wa0) based on 'Parkinson's law' (Gutierrez & Kouvelis, 1991; Parkinson, 1957) was introduced. This video discussed the importance of keeping to time frames and schedules and its origins were traced to Parkinson's law. The students had to watch the video, read up a lot more on it from the internet or YouTube and later apply the law to their own assessment contexts and procrastination issues. As an assignment they were required to work initially individually while analysing their own relationships with deadlines of various academic assignments, introspect in pairs, groups or individually, as per their choice, while applying the law to their own formative assessment contexts and finally make a presentation to the whole class, followed by a written report. Some students went beyond introspection and even carried out a small survey of their own and other classmates' submission deadlines and reported their findings. Work-in-progress presentation reports were graded as formative scores and this scenario of time management was an under-weave tapestry thread theme throughout the semester that also led the students to volunteer to handle time management issues related to technology.

By the end of the semester, as Student B stated, many of them "learned the values of time and how important it is to schedule", "avoid falling into the trap of procrastination", "respect time of others", "make time my friend", and "avoid the snooze button of life." Student C remarked that his procrastination "took a U-turn" as a "lesson for life was learnt through this assignment." The social media site WhatsApp was also exploited to enable comfortable communication between the teacher and students on this and other topics. Its affordance for such academic purposes was a good learning point: students were able to use informal language and explain why they needed extra time, asynchronously, probably because of the 'socialness' of the site itself.

Through this task, we learnt that neither stringent scolding, lecturing, chiding nor punishment worked on the procrastination of students. In contrast, a single assignment based on their real-time problems with time management such as Parkinson's law, did it all: they learnt the value of timely responses to deadlines and procrastination became a thing of the past. The students also appreciated and valued the whole exercise and I found that the students were far better at keeping their deadlines: they also offered to help me keep time and offered reminder services to the whole student group. A huge learning for me has been that I now begin every one of my courses using Parkinson's law: on this course, my frustration levels with non-submissions came down to a large extent, as did my stress and tension levels. Three other courses that I have taught later yielded similar positive results as a professional wash -forward.

Teachers and Students as Equal Partners in the Anthrogogic Classroom

The course followed an anthrogogic perspective where the students were required to take responsibility for their own learning with the teacher playing the role of a consultant or a mentor rather than a 'sage-on-the-stage'; this meant that while respecting students' choices as adults, they ought to be treated with respect by the teacher as the other adult in the classroom. This perspective of teaching-learning experiences was based on mutual respect and the pooling in of different strengths, personal preferences, abilities, cultural bases and the knowledges that all adults bring into the classroom to create a pleasant, respect-filled crucible of language use from these different places of origin and varied backgrounds.

We learnt from this course that although students miss assignment deadlines, they are also excellent timekeepers and peer-influencers: they were meticulous executives of time for all the tasks that required handling of time. I had asked them to take care of this because in an online class, I could not technologically handle time, as would be shown on a digital clock in one tiny corner of the screen, and stay focussed on classroom interactions. A comfortable confession to this effect, of admission and acknowledgement of 'technological disabilities', led to the students volunteering to help me whenever I was in technological distress.

This learning I was able to carry into every other classroom as a wash-forward and have now made it common practice that students would be in charge of time; I realised that they anyway do this routinely as adults in their daily lives, such as being in the railway station on time to board a train or meeting someone on time. As Student A put it, "yes ma'am, we plan and land up at a movie theatre or a doctor's office on time", while Student C added to it by stating, "some of us are swimmers, and timing is crucial" and continued with a very reassuring "you don't worry ma'am, we know how to use a timer, we will also activate a bell sound when time is up". Student D summed it up when he said: "ma'am, we will even be your reminder service and remind our classmates and send them timely and before time reminders for submission of assignments, you be *bindass!* (Hindi word meaning 'take it easy')" *(italics and translation ours)*. The role of the anthrogogic teacher who fostered learning through the integration of mutual strengths, including handling time-related issues, also facilitated us teachers to learn about a different kind of group dynamics that now washes-forward to nearly every other teaching-learning context.

Group Dynamics Followed in the Anthrogogic Classroom

In line with anthrogogic teaching and testing practices, the choice of individual/ pair/ group work needs to be left to the students. We are of the firm belief that it is not ethical or appropriate to force random grouping systems on adult students who may have their own work pattern preferences and in order to respect that choice, the students were permitted to either work in groups with peer members selected based on comfort levels, or in pairs or as individuals. The philosophy applied was to offer the flexibility to the students to work at their comfort levels and with the group dynamics that suited them best so that high level productivity could be achieved. This helped me to stay away from complaints about 'members' who were seen as 'misfits' into the group dynamics of the working group/pair while respecting the students' intro/extrovert nature and choice of working partners. This was corroborated through my observations when assignments were given to the students, to be done in groups, during and outside contact hours. I had discreetly noticed that some of them had already formed their own comfortable groups, some students preferred one partner for they wanted to work as a pair, while others were comfortable working alone. I therefore decided to value this and asked them to form their own groups. Of the 42 students in the class, 4 students stated that they wanted to work alone, while 4 others said that they wanted to work in pairs. The remaining students preferred to work in groups: there were 4 groups with 6 members, 1 group with 7 members, and 1 group with only 3 members.

Both of us in our previous courses had worked with the classroom practices of creating groups of four, five or six depending on the number of students and the nature of work, with group members being mandated by us as teachers. We had also worked with random heterogeneous groups, the standard, count off from 1 to 4, 5, or 6, followed by the 'all the 1's get into one group please' or a deliberate informed by prior teacher knowledge homogeneous type of grouping. What I discovered, through my observation of the work done in the breakaway rooms, was that these adult students knew what kind of work they wanted to do, and whom to do it with. The incidental learning through these observations was that the freedom to choose their own group members or to work alone led to good productivity.

A quick self-reflection/introspection made us realise that compulsory group work stems from pedagogic assumptions about the nature of learning as being nurtured by others, where the genesis of language acquisition, particularly when it is a second or foreign language, is perceived as primarily sociocultural (Lantolf & Thorne, 2006). Our adult students are language users, not learners. More importantly, we did not want to fall into the trap of cooperative group work where some could remain passive members but aimed for collaborative work with outcomes (Paulus, 2005), which however were to be student and not teacher decided: the tasks were not pedagogic-oriented problem-solving ones with clear teacher expectations of outcomes. We believed that an effective collaboration mandates that the students in the group must together contribute to the process of knowledge co-creation (Dillenbourg, 1999; Roschelle & Teasley, 1995) and that the outcome of the task could be something not visualised at all by us. When I initially gave the students the freedom to either work in groups or pairs or alone, it was a purely pragmatic decision, stemming from our awareness that with the whole course being online, I did not know my students enough to decide who should work with whom. Later, when I spoke to the students about this freedom to work in groups, Student E confessed that some of them had formed an "affinity" towards some of their "classmates", while some had "gelled well with" a particular student as "a partner". Student

F stated very firmly that he and a few like him had never been able to work in groups because they were "introverts with ADHD". He went on to state that he always saw himself as a "loner", or as someone who "works best alone". I made accommodations based on these statements, took the preferences of these responsible adults into account and broke all the erstwhile rules about grouping that I had read or experienced. I checked with my secondary author about 'permissions' for such freedom in grouping in available research, but she too did not have a clue about such 'student comfort based' grouping. We therefore decided to explore this new kind of grouping for assignments throughout the course, where the students' social, cognitive and emotional comfort superseded and permeated group dynamics.

By the end of the course, when asked how they felt about such grouping, Student B assured us that "it was the best ma'am as you let us work with my choice and for the first time all of us felt liberated and comfortable in our own skins." Student C corroborated when she stated that it was the "best experience" as "for the first time" as all of them "were able to put in their efforts in the assignments". Both of us learnt to use this open-to-preference-and-comfort grouping strategy in all our future classrooms and workshops sessions involving adult participants and has motivated us to research into this a little further and explore more possibilities as a professional wash-forward.

Access to Real-time Technological Tools in the Anthrogogic Classroom

With the whole course being online, there was no way by which we could have asked students, even if we had wanted to, to stay away from using available technological tools and applications either during discussions, or while they were in their breakaway rooms working on assignments. This type of Panopticon type, invigilated, regimented teaching and testing (Foucault, 1978, 1991) is not realistic and any assessment done will not carry predictive validity, for in real life, technologically enabled language users will always be able to access and use a range of these tools. During my visits to the breakaway rooms (done initially to just check if work was going on or not) I found that the students were comfortably using Google Translate and online dictionaries, and along with it, an app called Grammarly to self-edit their writing. I did not know that this app called 'Grammarly' provided linguistic reasons for its suggestive alternatives; I also had no clue about the nuances of how to negotiate my way around the application itself, until it was pointed out by the students. I further learnt that it could be activated on my phone and google docs as well and that I could outsource all my proofreading issues easily to Grammarly.

Another learning point was that, in the final exam, when I cautioned that I would use a similarity index checking tool such as Turnitin on their answers, these students chose to pass my question paper through the same tool and confessed that they found that the question paper had less than 2% similarity. From this, the two of us learnt that students are great observers and expect the teacher to be a practitioner first and a preacher next and that we ought to be careful creators of question papers or assignment developers if we expect to dissuade them from the copy-paste culture. This similarity index checking did not stop with my paper but extended to many other question papers and assignments of other faculty members: I realised that the faculty was being observed and judged for their ethical values, for these were discussed with me as issues. I maintained confidentiality but could not flee from these off-record discussions. These episodes taught us to be more truthful as question paper setters: the students even showed me the sites from which some other question papers had been downloaded! We realised that all of us as teachers must be creators of question items and not plagiarise or mindlessly copy-paste items into our test/assignment instruments, as sometimes happens when we are short of time. The students, as an appreciation of my honesty, introduced me to paraphraser tools such as Quillbot and Paraphraser.io, and to various free online artificial intelligence writing tools, OpenAI, that were mind-boggling to both of us. The introduction to OpenAI, for us, felt like the first byte, bite of the forbidden 'apple' and opened a new playground of technology that we were innocently and blissfully oblivious about. This taught us to read up on the latest developments in technology and I have been using them since then in my classroom, including the latest ChatGpt versions as a wash-forward to continue my professional development.

Plurilinguality in the Anthrogogic Classroom

The anthrogogic nature of the course enabled a celebration of plurilinguality as an asset (Deepa & Durairajan, 2022) for both us and the students. In an anthrogogic 'English as a second language classroom', located in a grassroots multilingual country like India where language users seamlessly move across languages without conscious awareness (Mohanty, 2023) it would have been erroneous, exclusive and even grossly unfair on my part, as the course instructor cum evaluator, to assume that all assessment of, for and as learning (Black & William, 1998) must be carried out only through the medium of English. The presence of English, it has to be conceded, is more than just an official language of the country that is taught as a second language in most higher education contexts: its presence stretches far beyond that, particularly post the technology boom, where there are google maps, WhatsApp messages, YouTube videos or OTT, (over-the-top) content available on the smartphone/tablet or television. English subtitles are also used as a link language to negotiate/access content in other Indian languages. My visits to the breakaway rooms to check whether the students were doing the assigned work was an eye or rather ear opener: the discussions regarding the apps they could access and how these apps could be used to either enable presentations or aid the self-editing of their own or other students' essays often took place in a host of other Indian languages. This being the case, a puritan-linguistic approach or an immersion technique will not work in India as it will be like a 'concentration camp' that is far removed from realistic multilinguistic contexts is a confirmation of our earlier demystification and ensured a renewed and re-energised wash-forward learning. Although there was no formal official assessment carried out using the other languages, in the context assessment of and for learning, I heard discussions in these breakaway chat rooms in many dialects of Telugu, Marathi, Malayalam, Kannada and Hindi, all of which were comfortably used as the language of communication and discussion. Such language use was not limited only to CLP, (Cummins, 2000), where it would have been used for non-academic interpersonal communication. It was also used to discuss the use of linkers and other cohesive devices, to check grammar points while comparing what was written to the way it would be stated in their own mother tongue and to evaluate the use of a particular word or collocation. Thus, a huge learning point through this incidental assessment as a wash-forward into other courses was that regardless of the proficiency level of the student, the other languages in the students' repertoire could be used for academic language proficiency domains (Cummins, 2000) but more in context embedded rather than in context reduced situations (Cummins, 1984): the students were careful not to use their mother tongue during official presentations. It could have been very easy for us to fall into the trap of assuming that such use is only because the students did not have the necessary proficiency to carry out their discussions in English and therefore, being deficient, had code-switched (Grosjean, 1982), or that they were other social or psychological factors which made them switch languages (Myers-Scotton, 2000; Ritchie & Bhatia, 2012). This is not necessarily the case. Adults, particularly in the Indian ESL context, are users of the language, not learners. As authors who share a common language, Tamizh[3], although our preferred language of academics is English, we did a quick introspection of our own language use and realised that very unselfconsciously, the two of us use

Tamizh, along with English to discuss the coherent ordering of arguments in an article, to cross-check references or bounce arguments off each other. The carrier language of our academic discussions could be only English or a mixture of Tamizh and English. Our content words would all be in English, but a *"nii enna nenakkaree"* (what do you think of this) or a *"idhu okayaa"* (is this okay) or even a *"inge, inda 'however' sari ille"* (in this place, this 'however' does not fit) is par for our language use.

In keeping with the mandates of a course which is a part of a larger degree programme, here, a master's programme in technology, the student assignments had to be in English. However, the students quickly learnt that they would not be penalised for using their own languages: their first reaction when they realised that I had entered their breakaway room was to whisper to each other: *"Ma'am ochhindi, raa: teluguloo maatlaadodhdhu"*. (Students F and G), "Ma'am has come: we should not talk in Telugu". Students H and I, Hindi speakers, hesitantly fumbled, *"ma'am kya hum log aapas, Hindi mein baath kar sakthe hai? Aap daantenge nahi? sachhi?"* meaning, "Ma'am, you mean we can talk amongst ourselves in Hindi and you won't scold us for doing so? Honestly ?", when I affirmed to them that they are free to use Hindi, they started literally jumping with joy and Student H remarked, *"Ma'am aap tho kamaal kardiya, ye tho jadhoo phailaaya, hum vachan dethe hai ki assignments achhese kardenge, aap ko khushi hoga aur garv bhi!"* translating to, "Ma'am you have made it magical and amazing for us. We promise you that we will do our assignments really well so that you will be pleased with our work!". I reassured them and told them to continue with their 'multilinguality'. Later it came to the stage where they would even ask me some doubts: that they were not sure they could ask, in their languages once they realized, I knew that language. The wash-forward learning for me and my students was that the other dialects and languages are an asset and part of the comfort zone, part of language use reality and that they would not be asphyxiated into an immersion system of Macaulayan colonial monolingualism. Multilinguality, and not just multilingualism is the norm for all of us (Agnihotri, 2014).

Language Potentiality in a High Proficiency Anthrogogic Classroom

This course had many students with high English language proficiency, and it was meaningless to force on them the routine proficiency related materials as they would find it boring and would have also finished them in a jiffy. Moreover, since they were technologically very sound and had access to tools like Grammarly, mundane proficiency tasks did not work with them and so we decided to get students to turn around on their own languages like a philosopher or thinker (Bruner, 1996); through this we hoped that we could move from teaching and testing the language as a mere skill, as proficiency, to assessing humane, constructive language use or language potentiality. We decided to introduce the idea of verbal disposition (Deepa, 2022d), going beyond aspects of proficiency to focus on the potentiality of language to be used in a constructive, neutral, or destructive manner. In order to do this, the theoretical framework used to enable and evaluate language potentiality was a combination of modified versions of the discourse completion questionnaire (DCQ) used in cross-cultural pragmatics research (Blum-Kulka, Deepa, 2022a; House & Kasper, 1989). In this course, however, we modified the item type to convert it to a task, weaving in shades of scenario-based testing (Purpura, 2021) to enable and assess language potentiality online, but asynchronously, using writing and not speaking as a means for language production. When used in this online high proficiency course, it became a wash-forward learning point for us with reference to the task/item type itself.

A scenario based DCQ was presented to the students first with the normal 4 options and they were asked to arrive at the answer. The options were so created that there were no language related errors, only ones that dealt with potential constructive, neutral and destructive options, a take-off from the native and non-native politeness options in the original DCQ. The students, however, arrived at the answers with their own cultural background dictating the rationales and gave us interpretations for each one of the multiple-choice options: we were initially stumped, for the rationales were quite sound. We soon learnt that multiple choice questions (MCQs) when presented to students as a discussion prompt behaved very differently online, with the open-to-preference-and-comfort grouping strategy, as the students came up with all possibilities as answers with a matching rationale (Deepa, 2022a) which would have been impossible in a closed book teaching/testing scenario. The tasks which were based on 'verbal disposition' and 'language potentiality' (Deepa, 2022d) not only worked better, but were welcomed by the students. As Student A excitedly stated: it was "refreshing and exciting" to be able to work on scenarios that demanded "higher order thinking skills rather than the need for a verbal diarrhoea like 'fluency' that is demanded by the high stakes tests". He also confessed that these tasks taught not just him but many other classmates to "think 10 times before speaking unpleasant content".

Based on this experience, we realised that we could go beyond just asking students to 'solve' such items but could ask them to even create similar ones that were based on language potentiality application scenarios with a DCQ pattern with a space for rationalisation. As a wash-forward, I tried this out in English language courses that I taught later, with great success where these items created by students with verbal disposition as a base were used as peer created materials to engage with language potentiality with a cultural interface at play. This learning experience motivated us to use the same item type with the modifications rung in, in teacher education workshops as well. It further taught us that options in an MCQ or a DCQ will need space for rationalisation and there cannot be absoluteness of the 'right' answer because perspectives decide the choice of the option in an underdeveloped scenario or context that forms the stem of the item. We learnt that the construction of the scenarios in the stem of the DCQ or even MCQ must be very tightly constructed, particularly in assessment contexts, where there will be no space for rationalisation of the option chosen by the student as a wash-forward. The spinoff learning for the students was that it dawned on them that language is a very powerful tool, which carries with it cultural biases and has the capacity to heal or destroy and therefore needs to be used with caution.

CONCLUSION

As teacher-authors and researchers, instead of being preoccupied with just washback or feedback, we continue to be persons who introspect and turn back on our own work to learn and grow as part of professional wash-forward activity. We have attempted to document the various learnings through the planned, unplanned, and incidental assessments which were a part of the online proficiency course. We learnt that we could use 'scenarios' in various ways, not just to breathe life into tasks and assessments, but also to help students turn around their own academic lives and abilities, thus helping them and us reflect on learning and teaching practices. Our eyes were opened to varied uses of technology and how plurilingualism is not just an asset but must be seen as one language, for often speakers are not even aware that there is a switch from one language to another. The most important learning however, for us is that the three prepositions that are usually linked to assessment, 'of, for and as' are insufficient: teachers and students can learn and also teach through assessment. The lines blur: the two of us have always told ourselves that the day we stop learning, we will stop teaching. We now need to add a phrase to this to state that the day we stop learning, we will also stop assessing we are all teachers, learners and doers.

We did what we had to do, to teach an online course during the pandemic: by turning the eye inward, the difficult domain became a productive area of reflection and research that would wash-forward into whatever we do. The students learnt through these assignments how to take charge of their learning, manage their time, and vocalise their preferences/comfort in group dynamics and made us aware of our own use of other languages in academic spaces, the way group dynamics works and the use of technological tools, particularly Grammarly. They also learnt that as anthrogogic students, they must bring in their strengths and add to the teaching-learning experiences to enrich, embellish, and enable one another as equal adults while maintaining mutual respect.

REFERENCES

Agnihotri, R. K. (2014). Multilinguality, Education and Harmony. *International Journal of Multilingualism*, *11*(3), 364–379. doi:10.1080/14790718.2014.921181

Alderson, J. C., & Wall, D. (1993). Does washback exist? *Applied Linguistics*, *14*(2), 115–129. doi:10.1093/applin/14.2.115

Assessment Reform Group. (2002). *Assessment for learning: 10 principles: Research-based principles to guide classroom practice*. Assessment Reform Group.

Banerjee, H. L. (2019). Investigating the construct of topical knowledge in Second language assessment: A scenario-based assessment approach. *Language Assessment Quarterly*, *16*(2), 133–160. doi:10.1080/15434303.2019.1628237

Biggs, J. (1999). *Teaching for quality learning at university*. SRHE and Open University Press.

Black, P., & Wiliam, D. (1998). *Inside the black box: Raising standards through classroom assessment*. School of Education King's College London.

Bruner, J. (1996). *The culture of Education*. Harvard University Press. doi:10.4159/9780674251083

Carless, D. (2006). Differing perceptions in the feedback process. *Studies in Higher Education*, *31*(2), 219–233. doi:10.1080/03075070600572132

Carless, D. (2007). Learning-oriented assessment: Conceptual Bases and practical implications. *Innovations in Education and Teaching International*, *44*(1), 57–66. doi:10.1080/14703290601081332

Cheng, L. (2005). *Changing language teaching through language testing: A Washback study*. Cambridge University Press.

Clarke, A. E. (2007). Grounded theory: Critiques, debates, and situational analysis. The SAGE Handbook of social science methodology, 423–442. doi:10.4135/9781848607958.n23

Cooperrider, D., Stavros, J. M., & Whitney, D. (2008). *The appreciative Inquiry handbook: For leaders of change*. Berrett-Koehler Publishers.

Creswell, J. W., & Guetterman, T. C. (2021). *Educational research: Planning, conducting and evaluating quantitative and qualitative research*. Pearson.

Cummins, J. (1984). Wanted: A theoretical framework for relating language proficiency to academic achievement among bilingual students. In: Rivera, C. (ed.). pp. 2-19. Language proficiency and academic achievement. Multilingual Matters.

Cummins, J. (2000). Academic language learning, transformative pedagogy, and information technology: Towards a critical balance. *TESOL Quarterly*, *34*(3), 537–548. doi:10.2307/3587742

Deane, P., Song, Y., van Rijn, P., O'Reilly, T., Fowles, M., Bennett, R., Sabatini, J., & Zhang, M. (2019). The case for scenario-based assessment of written argumentation. *Reading and Writing*, *32*(6), 1575–1606. doi:10.100711145-018-9852-7

Deepa, S. (2022a). Options in multiple-choice questions: Oh, Really! Yours sincerely, Adult learners! *Language and Language Teaching: A Peer-reviewed Journal*, 81-86.

Deepa, S. (2022b). Pedagogic scaffolding and anthrogogic learning contexts: Issues in metaphor mismatch. *Journal of English Language Teachers'. Interaction Forum.*, *13*(2), 3–7.

Deepa, S. (2022c). Pedagogic practices in higher education and Peter Pan syndrome: An appraisal. *Fortell*, *45*, 164–173.

Deepa, S. (2022d). Verbal disposition: The need for language potentiality in anthrogogic spaces. *Journal of English Language Teaching*, *64*(6), 17–24.

Deepa, S., & Durairajan, G. (2022). 'Warm welcome or cold shoulder': Demystifying ('positively noxious') English in the multilingual classroom. R. Kaushik & A L Khanna (eds). Critical Issues in ELT, pp. 30-51. Aakar Books.

Dillenbourg, P. (1999). What do you mean by collaborative learning? In P. Dillenbourg (Ed.), *Collaborative-learning: Cognitive and Computational Approaches* (pp. 1–19). Elsevier.

Driscoll, M., Bryant, D., & National Research Council. (1998). *Learning about assessment, learning through assessment*. National Academies Press. doi:10.17226/6217

Durairajan, G. (2015). *Assessing Learners: A Pedagogic Resource*. Cambridge University Press.

Errington, E. P. (2003). *Developing Scenario-based Learning: practical insights for tertiary educators*. Dunmore Press.

Errington, E. P. (2005). *Creating Learning Scenarios: A planning guide for adult educators*. CoolBooks.

Errington, E. P. (2011). Mission possible: Using near-world scenarios to prepare graduates for the professions. *International Journal on Teaching and Learning in Higher Education*, *23*, 84–91.

Foucault, M. (1978/1991). *Discipline and Punish: The Birth of the Prison*. Vintage Books.

Francis, D., & Hester, S. (2012). *An invitation to ethnomethodology: Language, society and social interaction*. Sage Publications. doi:10.4135/9781849208567

Freire, P. (1970/2005). *Pedagogy of the oppressed*. Penguin.

Gibbs, G. (1995). *Improving student learning through assessment and evaluation*. Oxford Centre for Staff Development, Oxford Brookes University.

Glaser, B.G. & Strauss, A.L. (1967) *The discovery of grounded theory: Strategies for qualitative research.* Aldine, Weidenfeld and Nicolson. doi:10.1093/sf/46.4.555

Gordon, A. (2020). Tests as Drivers of Change in Education: Contextualising Washback, and the possibility of Wash-forward. *VNU Journal of Foreign Studies, 36*(4). doi:10.25073/2525-2445/vnufs.4573

Grosjean, F. (1982). *Life with two languages. An introduction to bilingualism.* Harvard University Press., doi:10.2307/414002

Gutierrez, G. J., & Kouvelis, P. (1991). Parkinson's law and its Implications for Project Management. *Management Science, 37*(8), 990–1001. doi:10.1287/mnsc.37.8.990

House, J., Kasper, G., & Blum-Kulka, S. (1989). *Cross-cultural pragmatics: Requests and apologies.* Ablex Pub. Corp.

Jackson, J. (2003). Case-based Learning and Reticence in a Bilingual Context: Perceptions of Business Students in Hong Kong. *System, 31*(4), 457–469. doi:10.1016/j.system.2003.03.001

Kiley, D. (1983). *The Peter Pan syndrome: Men who have never grown up.* Dodd, Mead.

Knowles, M. S. (1968). Andragogy, not Pedagogy. *Adult Leadership, 16*(10), 350–352.

Lantolf, J. P., & Thorne, S. L. (2006). *Sociocultural theory and genesis of second language development.* Oxford University Press. doi:10.1017/S0272263108080546

Lubbe, A., Mentz, E., Olivier, J., Jacobson, T. E., Mackey, T. P., Chahine, I. C., & de Beer, J. (2021). *Learning through assessment: An approach towards self-directed learning.* AOSIS., doi:10.46925//rdluz.38.49

Mohanty, A. K. (2023). Multilingualism, mother tongue and MLE. *Language and Language Teaching, 12*(23), 155-167.

Myers-Scotton, C. (2000). Explaining the Role of Norms and Rationality in Code Switching. *Journal of Pragmatics, 32*(9), 1259–1271. doi:10.1016/S0378-2166(99)00099-5

Olleras, J. L., Dagwayan, M., Dejacto, A. M., Mangay, J. R., Ebarsabal, M., Diaz, D. J., Putian, R., Lendio, A. M., Nadera, J. C., Taneo, J. D., Cabello, C. A., & Minyamin, A. V. (2022). The Life of the Laters: Students Procrastination in Accomplishing Academic Deadlines in Online Learning. *Psychology and Education: A Multidisciplinary Journal, 2*(5), 444-454. , ISSN 2822-4353 doi:10.5281/zenodo.6791776

Parkinson, C. N. (1958). *Parkinson's Law or The Pursuit of Progress.* John Murray.

Paulus, T. M. (2005). Collaborative and Cooperative Approaches to Online Group Work: The Impact of Task Type. *Distance Education, 26*(1), 111–125. doi:10.1080/01587910500081343

Prabhu, N. S. (2021). Second thoughts about second-language teaching. In: Sudharshana, N.P., Mukhopadhyay, L. (eds). (pp. 13-16). Task-based language teaching and assessment. Springer. doi:10.1007/978-981-16-4226-5_2

Purpura, J. E. (2021). A Rationale for Using a Scenario-Based Assessment to Measure Competency-Based, Situated Second and Foreign Language Proficiency. In M. Masperi, C. Cervini, Y. Bardière (eds.) *Évaluation des acquisitions langagières: du formatif au certificatif, mediAzioni, 32*, A54-A96. http://www.mediazioni.sitlec.unibo.it.

Ritchie, W. C., & Bhatia, T. K. (2012). Social and psychological factors in language mixing. The handbook of bilingualism and multilingualism, In W. C. Ritchie, & T. K. Bhatia (Eds). (2013). Handbook of bilingualism and multilingualism. (pp. 375-390). Wiley-Blackwell. doi:10.1002/9781118332382.ch15

Roberts-Gray, C., & Gray, T. (1983). Implementing innovations: A model to bridge the gap between diffusion and utilization. *Knowledge (Beverly Hills, Calif.)*, 5(2), 213–232. doi:10.1177/107554708300500204

Roschelle, J., & Teasley, S. D. (1995). The construction of shared knowledge in collaborative problem solving. In C. O'Malley (Ed.), *Computer supported collaborative learning* (pp. 69–97). Springer., doi:10.1007/978-3-642-85098-1_5

Rothman, B. K. (2007). Writing Ourselves in Sociology. *Methodological Innovations Online*, 2(1), 11–16. doi:10.4256/mio.2007.0003

Roy, R., & Uekusa, S. (2020). Collaborative Autoethnography: "Self-Reflection" as a Timely Alternative Research Approach During the Global Pandemic. *Qualitative Research Journal*, 20(4), 383–392. doi:10.1108/QRJ-06-2020-0054

Smith, M. S., Warnes, S., & Vanhoestenberghe, A. (2018). Scenario-based learning. In J. P. Davies & N. Pachler (Eds.), *Teaching and learning in higher education: Perspectives from UCL* (pp. 144–156)., http://www.ucl-ioe-press.com/

Spencer, J. A., & Jordan, R. K. (1999). Learner centred approaches in medical education. *BMJ (Clinical Research Ed.)*, 318(7193), 1280–1283. doi:10.1136/bmj.318.7193.1280 PMID:10231266

Swain, M. (1985). Large scale communicative testing: A case study. In Y. P. Lee, A. C. Y. Y Fok, R. Lord, & G. Low (Eds.), *New Directions in Language Testing: Papers Presented at the International Symposium on Language Testing,* (pp. 35-46). Pergamon Press.

Trott, D. C. (1991, October). *Anthrogogy.* Paper presented at the meeting of the American Association for Adult and Continuing Education, Montreal, Quebec.

Turner, C. E., & Purpura, J. E. (2016). Learning-oriented assessment in second and foreign language classrooms. In D. Tsagari & J. Banerjee (Eds.), Handbook of second language assessment (pp. 255–272). De Gruyter. (pp. 255–272). De Gruyter. doi:10.1515/9781614513827-018

van Lier, L. (1989, September). Reeling, Writhing, Drawling, Stretching, and Fainting in Coils: Oral Proficiency Interviews as Conversation. *TESOL Quarterly*, 23(3), 489–508. doi:10.2307/3586922

Willatt, C., & Flores, L. M. (2022). The Presence of the Body in Digital Education: A Phenomenological Approach to Embodied Experience. *Studies in Philosophy and Education*, 41(1), 21–37. doi:10.100711217-021-09813-5

Woodward, H. (1998). Reflective Journals and Portfolios: Learning Through Assessment. *Assessment & Evaluation in Higher Education*, 23(4), 415–423. doi:10.1080/0260293980230408

ENDNOTES

[1] We would like to state here that all uses of the first person pronoun 'I' or 'me' refers only to reflections by SD the course instructor: wherever there was any consultation or discussion with GD, the pronouns 'we' and 'us' have been used.

[2] The identity of the students has been kept confidential, for ethical reasons. We have used italics and double quotation marks to indicate genuine student responses, all of which are part of informal classroom discussions. Some of these were posted in the chat box during online classes, or oral statements made either when the class met as a whole or during group discussions in the break away rooms.

[3] The 'given' spelling for this language in English 'Tamil', but that is an anglicised one. We have therefore chosen to use 'zh' rather than 'l' which is the closest approximation to the way the name is pronounced in that language.

Chapter 7
Providing Alternative Assessments Through Experiential Learning in an Online Language Teacher Training Course

Amy S. Burden
Center for Applied Linguistics, USA

ABSTRACT

In the form of a case study, the chapter focuses on the value of experiential learning and how it was adapted for the online learning environment during the pandemic. Employing Kolb's Experiential Learning Cycle, the project served as an alternative assessment that engaged in more democratic grading practices. The designed learning outcomes were for students to grow in their autonomous metacognitive reflections of their own grading and assessment practices through alternative assessments such as self and dynamic assessments. Additionally, they would employ multiple identities in the online classroom: teacher, student, and peer. Finally, through participation in the experiential learning project, they would demonstrate explicit knowledge of a variety of alternative assessments for language learning through co-constructed assessments, rubrics, and presentations. Data were collected through observation and document analysis and analyzed qualitatively. Results show growth in explicit knowledge of alternative assessments and confidence with alternative assessment design and grading.

INTRODUCTION

Experiential learning is considered to be a loaded term, as it goes by many definitions in different contexts and by different stakeholders in education and research around the world. A common complaint about adapting experiential learning for any classroom is the lack of unified theories or frameworks that confuse or misrepresent experiential learning in practice (Chan, 2022). Experiential learning is commonly

DOI: 10.4018/978-1-6684-6227-0.ch007

referred to as learning through experience. Ideally, this is a cyclical process of planning, experimentation, reflection, redesign, and further experimentation (Helate, Metaferia, & Gezahegn, 2022). Kolb, whose work this chapter relies upon, explains his framework as putting learning in the center of the learning process for the benefit of the learner. Knowledge is created through transformation, which comes from experience. His framework uses a cyclical paradigm and can begin at any point. These phases of Kolb's model include concrete experience, reflective observation, abstract conceptualization, and active experimentation (Kolb, 2012). The cyclical nature of this framework responds to common criticisms of experiential learning such as an overt focus on reflection without lens to discuss the "here and now" (Vince, 1998). Through both active experimentation and reflective observation in Kolb's model, students maintain a balanced focus. More in-depth explanations of this framework and how it was adapted in this case study will be shared in the methods section (Kolb, 2012).

The benefits of experiential learning are what make it attractive for the teacher training classroom. Residential colleges and universities across the world have embraced experiential learning for teacher training, including South Africa (Bender & Jordaan, 2007), Hong Kong (The University of Hong Kong, 2021), The United States (Furco & Ammon, 2000; Burden, 2018b) and many others, which will be further detailed later in the chapter for their merits in the current learning context. In teacher training, international studies demonstrate immense benefits, including fostering engagement with the teaching profession, growth in self-esteem and leadership abilities, and an increase in respect and understanding for diverse communities (Henderson & Brookhart, 1997). The benefits do not start and end with students. Even teachers of experiential learning courses reflect on the benefits to their professional growth, including the opportunity to learn new approaches through the experiences of their students, apply new approaches with students of diverse learning needs, and the freedom to delve deeper into course concepts that are immediately relevant to their students (Fenton & Gallant, 2016). It is in fact relevancy that is a primary purpose for incorporating or redesigning courses for experiential learning. Experiential learning directly addresses pre-service teacher complaints that the curricula are too theoretical without enough real-world training to pair alongside it. Experiential learning gives opportunities to directly connect theory to practice (Burden, 2018a; Chan, 2022).

It is often considered a core component in EFL teacher training curricula (Helate et al., 2022). For example, Primary school English language teachers in Ethiopia must take coursework in experiential learning and professional development programs through Continuous Professional Development (CPD) programs (Merriam & Bierema, 2014). In a recent study of Hong Kong pre-service EFL teachers' experiential learning projects on teaching grammar, teachers created grammar teaching materials for local in-service schoolteachers using the best practices these pre-service teachers were studying in college. The researcher-educators used Kolb's model, focusing on first observing the local teaching context, then developing grammar teaching materials from theory with the context in mind before being allowed to try those activities within the local classrooms they had observed in Kolb's first stage. They evaluated their effectiveness before revising and delivering them to local in-service educators. Results of the study demonstrated gains in multiple facets, including textbook evaluation, growth of practical skills, including teachers' core competencies, and understanding of the trends and challenges of English language teaching in mainland China (Lee, 2019).

There have always been challenges to experiential learning, despite its immense benefits to learners, teachers, and universities globally. It can be labor intensive, from training educators in the techniques of successful project design and implementation, to developing partnerships with the community of practice, the work to create and run an experiential learning course can be overwhelming to some educators (Fenton & Gallant, 2016).

EXPERIENTIAL LEARNING IN ONLINE ENVIRONMENTS

With the global pandemic in 2020, many found experiential learning, despite its benefits, to be nearly impossible. The pandemic pushed most educators online, and with it came the creative uses of experiential learning in the online course (Bayir, 2022; Bursuc & Wilsker, 2020; Satyam & Aithal, 2022; Alatni, Abubakar, & Iqbal, 2021; Blair, Gala, Tariq, Harrison & Ajjan, 2020; Inchaouh & Tchaicha, 2020). However, these examples rarely include low-resourced online classrooms or attempts to integrate anti-racist or alternative assessment forms into the experiential learning process. Most of the literature focuses on classrooms outside language learning or teacher training.

However, with the growth of telecommunication in the early 2000s came application to teacher education. Virtual exchange has been a type of experiential learning for language teachers, primarily pre-service, that engages in online environments, even if the students are not online learners(Cappellini & Hsu, 2020). In virtual exchange programs, pre-service language teacher education programs connect students across the globe to collaborate on learning projects virtually. In virtual exchange, however, there is not a heavy emphasis on experimentation but on the collaborative process, such as in the EVALUATE project in use across multiple European countries. Teachers focused on idea sharing, materials development, and problem-solving in a virtual environment (Baroni et al., 2019).

Not all virtual exchanges focus solely on theoretical problems in the online environment. Several studies in the Hong Kong context connected virtual exchange more concretely to experiential learning. One such study connected Chinese as a second/foreign language education students in their second year of their bachelor's study with French students learning Chinese with the goals of helping Chinese pre-service teachers gain pedagogical experience and for French learners of Chinese to gain communicative competence in a foreign language through virtual exchange. A similar study was conducted between pre-service French teachers from Francophone countries and French learners at Berkley in California, USA. In both studies, pre-service teachers engaged in virtual exchange to gain pedagogical experience in language teaching and refine their understanding of theoretical concepts through experience (Cappellini & Hsu, 2020).

A different manner for engaging in experiential learning through online environments for language teachers comes from a study of social media for connecting theory and practice. In this study, pre-service ESL teachers in the USA planned for experiential learning in person before experimenting with local multilingual learners at an area primary school. The third stage, reflection, happened online via the social media site Pinterest on a classroom board where students shared their lessons from the week, evidence of student learning, and obstacles they encountered during the experimentation phase. Students then engaged in an online discussion on the board and revised their lessons for the next week accordingly. Results indicated that Pinterest was a helpful resource in assisting students in metacognitive and collaborative reflection and comprehending theoretical knowledge with applications to the experiential learning environment (Burden, 2018a). The current project is novel in its use of self-contained virtual exchange in a fully online course for pre-service language teachers engaged in all four stages of Kolb's Experiential Learning Cycle.

ALTERNATIVE ASSESSMENT IN THE ONLINE ESOL AND ESL CLASSROOM

In this case study, the instructor engaged in a variety of alternative assessments both as content for pre-service teacher training, but also in practice of assessing pre-service teachers. The rationale for including alternative assessments comes from research into multimodality and equity in the content classroom for language learners. The more modes that a language learner is allowed to engage in while demonstrating understanding of content, the richer the information provided to the instructor about what that student knows and can do in the content area. This is especially helpful for students who are attending a course that is taught in a second or other language when they are not fully proficient in that language (Grapin & Llosa, 2022; Grapin, Llosa, & Haas, 2022). Within the case study framework, collecting qualitative data through alternative assessments such as dynamic assessments (explained below) allowed for interpretation of the effectiveness of the experiential learning project on research goals.

The 1990s saw the emergence of the term alternative assessment as a push back to the notion that all people and all skills could be measured through more traditional assessments such as standardized exams, multiple choice forms, and product-oriented assessments. These alternatives were designed to triangulate with one another to provide a more holistic picture of acquisition through additional measurements from journals, portfolios, observations, and peer and self-assessment (Brown & Abeywickrama, 2019). For students in the language classroom, one significant benefit of alternative assessment forms is the elicitation of meaningful communication (Lynch & Shaw, 2005). Some of the characteristics of alternative assessment are the continuous nature, more freedom in response format, context-informed tasks, far more individualized feedback, and a focus on the process and interactive performance (Bailey & Curtis, 2015). Despite the knowledge of alternative assessments being beneficial for learners and tools available that can be harnessed to bring them online, teachers and teacher-trainers are still somewhat hesitant due to curricula limitations and concerns about student buy-in (Chugai, Yamshinska, Svyrydova & Kutsenok, 2021; Chugai & Pawar, 2022).

Research on alternative assessments in online learning environments is still emerging. As this chapter focuses on online language learning and teaching, studies of interest here will reference those factors alone. For a more exhaustive look at alternative assessments in other online learning environments, see Arifuddin, Turmudi, and Rokhmah (2021). A recent study on online group dynamic language assessment in Iran focused on using the social media platform Telegram to conduct GDA with a focus on writing accuracy in English as a foreign language. By comparing GDA via Telegram with Non-GDA writing classes, the researchers found statistically significant improvements in the grammatical accuracy of student writing samples correlating positively to online GDA (Alemi, M., Miri, M., & Mozafarnezhad, A., 2019).

Peer assessment is another alternative assessment that has had emerging success in the online language learning classroom. Burden (2018b) shared the advantages of using online peer assessment via Facebook with appropriate scaffolding and preparation beforehand. Students who were reticent to share or critique another student's work felt more confident in articulating themselves via the familiar platform. Students were also more likely to complete the assessments because of the frequency with which they used the platform and the accessibility of it via student smartphones. Ariani and Febrianti also used a popular and easily accessible platform for peer assessment in an online EFL writing course in Indonesia during the pandemic. With Google Forms, students already had a familiarity that reduced the barriers to online peer assessment. The results showed that even with the distance of online learning, students could use alternative online assessments to communicate with one another and the instructor about their level of comprehension of the elements of writing being tested (2022).

Alternative Assessments With Experiential Learning in Teacher Training

Dynamic Assessment

Dynamic assessment (DA) is a practice within both formative and alternative assessments that emphasizes the learning process and student-student collaboration on learning tasks as part of the assessment. The goal is long-term learner development. Dynamic assessment (DA) is one theoretically grounded approach to interpreting and promoting learners' emergent abilities. The central rationale for DA is that traditional summative assessments focus exclusively on what learners can do on their own and miss the emerging abilities still in process for the learner (Poehner, 2009; Poehner & Infante, 2016). Dynamic Assessment studies have been primarily carried out in the language learning classroom, with only more recent studies offering glimpses into how DA can be used in content classrooms. For example, in science content classrooms delivered in students' second language, dynamic assessments involving mediation questioning techniques called *probes* allowed students to clarify their reasoning in ways that more traditional summative assessments did not. Researchers also found that during a summative activity, these probes revealed opportunities to discuss how scientific practices underpinned accurate responses(Grapin & Llosa, 2022).

Another area where dynamic assessment has seen growth is in language testing, where mediation questioning techniques were used to evaluate high-stakes exam questions in a pilot stage before administering them to the language-learning public (Choi, Wolf, Pooler, & Faulkner-Bond, 2019). Mediating probes are divided into three categories: Targeted, open-ended, and explicit. Targeted probes ask *how, what,* and *why* questions about what the student is doing now with content. Open-ended probes ask learners to elaborate on their thought processes, and explicitness probes invite them to clarify their thoughts (Gibbons, 2003).

Democratic Assessment Practices

As this course took place online in 2020 in partnership with English Language Programs of The US Department of State and a university in the Philippines, the instructor felt compelled to consider how race impacted language learning and how racial tensions could be mitigated through democratic assessment practices. The instructor decided to integrate democratic assessment practices as a lens for creating alternative assessments within the experiential learning project.

Anti-racism is defined as any proactive approach to combatting racism that empowers marginalized groups. A secondary focus is on creating equality of opportunity for more equitable outcomes (Berman and Paradies, 2010). Anti-racist assessments are typically most concerned with disconnecting feedback from grades so that students are free to focus on self-improvement and skills acquisition without an inherent focus on a grade point. Dr. Asaoe Inoue goes further to encourage practitioners of anti-racist assessment approaches to focus on student labor instead of standards, which are quite often formulated by upper class majority culture males and heavily benefit members of these intersectional groupings while simultaneously penalizing non-group students who may not adhere to these same values and ideologies within their homes and communities (Santos, 2022). Just as dynamic forms of alternative assessment value the process, so too do anti-racist assessments, which consider the labor or what students do in and around the classroom as part of the assessment for a more equitable grading system than end-products only. Labor, be its duration, quantity, or intensity, is valued more highly than quality, which is subjective. Stommel posits that grades undermine the desire to learn, replacing it with a desire to score. They discourage students from taking risks and penalize productive failures (experimenting, failing, and trying again) (2018).

One goal for this course was to create a democratic grading environment. A particular approach to anti-racist assessment attempted in this course is grading as a classroom activity. Santos, in his first- and second-year English writing classrooms allowed students to design their own grading schemes that they held themselves to. These grading schemes include quantity of labor – be it writing, reading, or time on task – and awarded extra credit for extra-labor. Additional above-and-beyond work students completed for the purpose of acquiring new skills, experimenting with writing styles, or completing additional readings to augment their understanding of a concept were all considered for extra points towards letter grades on report cards. These student-designed grading schemes constituted an anti-racist assessment because it valued student labor, student inquiry, and progress over products (Santos, 2022). When the work products are also assessed through an anti-racist lens, peer assessment and teacher assessment include linguistic, cultural, and political diversity as valuable aspects of the work product (Inoue, 2022). In this course, students engaged with grading as a classroom activity a bit closer to Inoue's approach, which included metacognitive reflection in the labor. This will be described in more detail in the next section.

Identification of Anti-Racist Practice for Current Study

Inoue published a book in 2005 explaining practical ways to implement antiracist assessments into the classroom. The strategy described here is emulated in this study - a student-created rubric for writing or speaking assessments. The rubric creation process becomes more democratic when students are involved in the creation, and results of previous research demonstrate an increase in skill acquisition when students were allowed to write proficiency goals for their writing (Fluckiger, 2010). Asoe Inoue advocated for students to create their rubrics and then use those to think reflexively about their writing. He found that the greater the students' investment in every part of the writing process, including designing the assignment and the assessment and engaging in self and peer assessment, produced more confident, more fluent writers (2005). For a language-based assessment - or one that evaluates students on their ability to demonstrate the four modalities of a second or other language - TESOL Organization contributor Larry Davis suggests dividing students into groups of 3-4 and asking them to think-pair-share what features of the upcoming assignment they would like to work on or improve on or which features would best represent high performance in the writing or speaking task. These are one-word responses like "task completion." Students then vote on each group's features until the top four features are chosen democratically (Davis, 2013). What this looks like in an intermediate classroom according to Davis is that over the course of 1–2-hour class periods, students receive their assignment and discuss what they would like to learn from completing the assignment – typically a productive task like collaborative writing or presentations. They make a list of those things they would like to learn or feel confident they should be able to demonstrate through performance on the task. The teacher then writes down each element students conceived and reduces them to short phrases on the board. Students might suggest on a writing task that they compose a central claim using terms from the academic word list for the unit. The teacher could reduce this to "Academic Claim" on the board. The teacher then requests that students do rank choice voting for their top 4-5 elements they'd like to see evaluated or worked on for the task. The top elements are placed on the rubric in place of teacher-made categories.

Students can then consider the questions they have about each category that they'd like their teacher or peer to help them answer about their own work. For example, "What words are clues to my central claim?" These questions go beneath these categories in a central column. To either side of the central columns are blank spaces where peers or teachers can respond to the questions posed with examples from student writing that demonstrate central claims, or places where they think those context clues should have been placed – giving students a chance to reflect on their writing and implement new learning in the next draft, with no regard for a grade or standard of achievement (Davis, 2013).

Application of Anti-Racist Practice in Current Study

Inoue and Poe published a short guide to integrating antiracist assessments into the English classroom in September of 2020, the month before this course began. The course integration of anti-racist grading practices relied on this guide. The guide contained seven categories of consideration. These categories and course consideration can be observed in Table 1.

Table 1. Application of Inoue and Poe's ecological guide to antiracist assessment

Category	Application to this project
Purpose: What are my goals and why are they antiracist?	create a more equitable grading environment. This is an antiracist goal because it is built on the premise of creating equitable opportunity (Berman and Paradies,2010).
Process: How is my process of assessment antiracist?	Allow students to create their own grading rubrics (2013). Encourage grading as a classroom activity by Inoue by asking students to design the assignment they would use to assess their own performance and the performances of their peers without placing grades on the work (Inoue, 2005).
Power: How do students participate and change the classroom assessment environment?	Give power to students through dynamic assessment practices through questions, not commands, and student reflection. Student labor controlled how they were assessed.
Parts: How are the mechanisms for assessment antiracist and how do I circulate them?	Students created their own assignment sheets and their own rubrics. They had full authority to make changes to these throughout the course.
People: How do people involved in the assessment understand themselves and their roles? How does the teacher reflect on their impact?	Incorporate reflective activities into student assessment. Instructor self-reflects on teaching to determine the extent to which the grading environment is equitable.
Places: Where does assessment take place in less authoritarian manner?	Create as many spaces as possible and allow students to create their own spaces through Facebook and texting so that communication could happen in areas where they felt greater control.
Products: What are the outcomes of antiracist assessment? How do you use your power to create opportunity? Are the consequences antiracist?	Focus on giving students the opportunities to create and test assignments and rubrics through experiential learning and to reflect on learning frequently through dynamic assessments. Students should leave the class with the confidence to create alternative assessments and grading schemes for their own contexts autonomously (Inoue & Poe, 2020).

Rationale and Overview for the Assessment Project

The instructor developed an online experiential learning project on assessment, focusing on rubric design for grading speaking. Because Covid would not allow students into classrooms to *experience* the impact or effects of the rubrics they designed on those studying English at lower levels, learners were provided with the opportunity to view themselves as both learners and practitioners of language and language teaching through group presentations on alternative forms of assessment given weekly during zoom meetings in which their newly designed rubric would be tested on their peers. Between these presentations, students completed self-assessment questionnaires and provided feedback using their rubric. During both the creation and subsequent revisions of their rubric, the instructor employed dynamic assessment strategies to formatively assess their growth in rubric design and alternative assessment using rubrics and modelled this type of dynamic assessment practice for them.

The designed learning outcomes in this project could be listed as follows:

1. Pre-service teachers will autonomously and metacognitively reflect on their own grading and assessment practices - consider what was working and what was not and why; what about their thinking was propelling their decisions.
2. Pre-service teachers will use critical thinking and communication skills in multiple roles – teacher to student, and student to student communication.
3. Pre-service teachers will demonstrate explicit knowledge of a variety of alternative assessments through designing alternative assessments and the rubrics for grading them and preparing an alternative assessment for a class assignment.

Instructor LO: explore forms of anti-racist assessment in practice to create a more equitable and democratic learning environment in the online classroom.

METHODS

This section walks the reader through each step of the experiential learning project. This experiential learning project stemmed from interviews with in-service teachers in the Philippines who demonstrated a desire to learn alternative assessment types. First, the instructor introduced the assignment to team-teach alternative assessments for each modality as they move through the semester. The purposes were to break up the typical class structure in the teacher-centric Zoom classroom, and for students to conduct their research based on their interests and learning goals. Students chose small groups via text and Facebook Messenger and signed up for a presentation modality topic/date in Google Docs.

Data Collection and Analysis

The analysis and results of this project constitute a case study. Yin (1994) defines "a case study [as] an empirical inquiry that investigates a contemporary phenomenon within its real-life context, especially when the boundaries between phenomenon and context are not clearly evident" (p. 13). A case study approach that is three pronged was employed: particularistic, descriptive, and heuristic (Merriam, 1998). The particularity here is the online environment in a specific developing nation with one classroom of pupils in the same degree program from the same region and of similar socioeconomic statuses. The instructor observed a particular aspect of this group; that is, she observed how they created, implemented, revised, and reflected on an experiential learning project that she attempted to instruct through an anti-racist assessment lens. The descriptive prong refers to the products of the study – the rubrics, reflections, presentations, assignment sheets, comments on the sheets as they revised, self and peer assessments they turned in, and unstructured conversations held with students before, during, and after the course completed. The heuristic prong is employed through the sections of this chapter on discussion, evidence of student learning, and teacher learning. The goals of these sections are to illuminate for the reader the meanings of findings that the reader may agree or disagree from their own experience (Merriam, 1998).

Thus, to ascertain whether the goals for this project were achieved, qualitative strategies were used to gather data from all the products of the study listed in this paragraph and to examine this documentation, observe student behaviors, speech, and collaborative writings in class to gather rich descriptive data, which was analyzed using inductive reasoning processes (Burns, 2000). Furthermore, assessment of experiential learning relies on evidence of student learning. The following sections will describe how evidence of student learning was collected from experiential learning experiences, documented, and analyzed (Qualters, 2010).

Observations

Observations in this case study included monitoring Google Chat and Facebook Messenger Chats during class time, listening to verbal communication between students and with the instructor in Google Meet, and monitoring comments and changes being made in real time to Google Documents. These included observing as students creating the assignment sheets for their group presentations, observing them as they created the rubrics for assessing these presentations, and observing them as they presented their group presentations to the class. This also included observing as they reflected verbally and in writing on the process of using their rubrics to assess the presentations as well as monitoring the changes and comments, they made in real time to the assignment sheets and the rubrics in class. This type of online observation practice has been used with success to evaluate program effectiveness and to evaluate student learning (Hu, 2015; Le, Pedro, & Park, 2015; Mundkur & Ellickson, 2012).

The instructor functioned as a participant observer and did not make changes to the document but did engage in dynamic assessment practices which involved active questioning during these reflective opportunities in class. This active involvement in the processes under observation made the instructor part of the group study (Mutch, 2005). The instructor took notes and screenshots of student writing in class (permission was obtained before the start of the course for taking photos in the online environment).

Document Analysis

A review of all assessment approaches for this project can be seen in Table 2. The assignment sheets and rubrics students co-created were analyzed weekly to follow dynamic assessment principles. So, six times during the project the instructor looked for evidence of critical thinking, metacognitive reflection, (or thinking about what worked and what didn't and why), decision-making and collaboration through communication in the online environment through turn-taking, comments back and forth between students, and requests for review from peers. She also examined their slides from their presentations to determine if explicit knowledge of a variety of alternative assessments was demonstrated. This follows from previous experiential learning case studies which engaged in online document analysis techniques such as Burden (2018a) who analyzed Pinterest posts, and Alemi et.al, (2019) who examined Telegram posts.

Table 2. Assessment approaches

Name	Learning Activity	Aligned LO	Type
Co-constructed Assignment sheet	All students work on one shared Google Doc to create a presentation group assignment	2	Formative/Dynamic
Co-constructed Grading Rubric	All students create and repeatedly adapt one shared Google Doc to create a grading rubric for the group presentations	1, 2	Formative/Dynamic
Self-assessment	Each student completes a self-assessment questionnaire on their performance in the group presentation	1	Summative
Group Presentation	In small groups, students present a 20-minute lecture on a chosen alternative assessment	3	Summative
Handout	Each small group prepares a sample alternative assessment activity to share with the class	3	Summative
Final Assessment Portfolio	Each student creates one End of Unit Traditional Assessment with specifications and rubrics. They design an alternative assessment to accompany it.	3	Summative

Participants

Students were between the ages of 20-30years old, in their 3rd year of ESL or English bachelor's programs at a mid-size private college in Central Luzon Philippines. There were 24 students in the class, and there were 14 female students and 10 male students. All students attended university full time, and several students worked part-time in addition to their education. This class was offered for the first time in a fully online format, and as campus was closed, this meant students were all designated as 'remote' learners, despite all living within commuting distance of campus.

This teaching environment is considered "low-resourced" because it was common for students to have only one electronic or "smart" device per family unit, for families to have only intermittent internet access in the home, or to have no internet within the home. This meant that students might travel to sit outside a coffee shop to use Wi-Fi, or they would use their data plans on their cell phones. Most students did not own a laptop but relied on cell phones to attend class and submit assignments. These phones might also be shared by the family unit. Students did not own books for these classes, and all materials were hand-written by professors and placed in the online learning platform for them to read.

Stage One: Concrete Experience

The following sections will follow Kolb's experiential learning cycle. This is the organizational style for this project. Beginning with Kolb's concrete experience stage, which is where the learner engages in the activity or task (Kurt, 2020). students were asked to design the presentation assignment sheets based on what they wanted to learn about different types of alternative assessments. They should consider ground rules for time, slide count, and allocation of roles within the group. Students then worked in small groups within the Zoom class to design the assignment sheet in Google Docs, with each group taking a different aspect of the assignment. They chose how they wanted to team teach (or work together to speak during the presentation), what elements of designing and grading alternative assessments they would like to learn, how long the presentations should be, and how they would like to share their presentations (Slides,

Prezi, or other presentation software/style). In this way, they acted as educators, designing an alternative assessment. This model for co-construction of assessments follows from the work of Hughes and Braun who asked pre-service special education teachers to co-construct assessments in addition to lesson plans as part of their experiential learning project. They found that these pre-service teachers increased their instructional knowledge through co-creation of content (2019).

Students also co-created grading rubrics for the assessment with an integration of anti-racist ecologies into this part of the assessment project to consider a more equitable grading system (Inoue and Poe's "Purpose", 2020), that gave students the opportunity to create and modify their own assignments and rubrics as educators (Parts and People from Inoue and Poe, 2020). To prepare students for the activity, they read Brown's chapter on grading and student evaluation (Brown & Abeywickrama, 2019). They examined the website *Cult of Pedagogy,* which featured several articles on rubric design (Gonzalez, 2020). They compared different kinds of rubrics in small groups. They then opened a shared Google Doc. Just as in Davis' lesson plan, students worked in groups of 3-4 to create dimensions for assessing the team-teaching project. These would be categories that represented elements of performance. They were asked to consider what categories would represent high-quality teaching or what they would like to learn from their classmates about alternative assessment. They wrote down 3-4 ideas and then voted on the 4 ideas that every student preferred the most, and those became categories for which they would receive feedback on the rubric.

Traditional rubrics contain performance indicators, which could be numbers from 1-4, words like "needs improvement", "okay", and "excellent" or other indicators of success (Chan, 2022). However, students should consider an alternative to the traditional rubric that is more democratic. So, students were asked to, instead of crafting performance indicators *yet*, write questions they would like answered about their team-teaching presentation for each category. They should consider what they would like the teacher and their classmates to watch for in their presentation and where they would like feedback, advice, or input on their teaching or speaking performance. This engaged anti-racist assessment using Inoue and Poe's category of "Process" by asking students to consider what they would like feedback on and what they would like their peers to pay attention to about their presentations. Students had far greater autonomy in deciding what aspects of their teaching they would like their peers to review. They took these questions and turned them into indicators within the categories. This reflexive thinking also allowed students to better prepare for their team-teaching presentation as described by Flukinger (2010). Their focus on developing the rubric and assignment sheets helped them understand how to prepare their presentations to benefit their peers' pedagogical understanding.

Integration of Dynamic Assessment Strategies

Before the first presentation, the instructor posed various probative questions on Google Docs as a comment. This was done during the Zoom class and directly after the class ended. They were asked targeted questions, such as "How will this question (highlighted in the rubric) attend to the category it is placed beneath?" This targeted question asked students to reflect on the thinking that assisted them in developing the feedback questions for the selected category and either defend their choice or suggest edits. They were also asked for elaborative probes such as: "Tell me more about this question," which engaged students in clarifying their intentions in creating a question beneath the single-trait category. Also, students engaged with explicitness probes, asking students to define pronouns without clear antecedents. This follows from the work of Grapin and Llosa in dynamic assessment in the content area classroom with English learners (2022). This allowed a very short Reflective Observation Phase to occur in Kolb's Cycle. Students took time to reflect on their products before the first presentation occurred. Through dynamic assessment practices, they were guided in their metacognitive reflections on their processes for developing the rubrics and assignments.

Second Concrete Experience

To test their products and have a concrete experience of using them, students needed to apply them to the first set of student-led presentations. Each week, before beginning assessment content review for a particular modality or skill, one team of students would present an alternative assessment they had chosen and researched. The presentations lasted between 15 and 20 minutes. During the presentations, the rest of the class held a Google Doc version of the rubric developed as a class. They were instructed to provide feedback to the presentation team using the class made rubric. After the presentation, the presenters dropped off Zoom Call to complete a self-assessment form. Then, the rest of the class discussed how they used the rubric to assess their peers. Students could not go into classrooms, and in the Philippines, low resources and sporadic access to the internet made it impossible to "enter" classrooms virtually. Thus, by creating a concrete experience of assessing one another through the lens of teacher–student, a re-envisioned experience during Kolb's first stage online was created for the students.

Stage Two: Reflective Observation

The instructor combined dynamic assessment strategies with Kolb's Reflective Observation stage at this point. Especially within the first two presentation periods, students expressed confusion over how to match the rubric to the student's performance. This think-aloud process allowed the instructor to make some corrections to future lessons to engage in a more detailed discussion of rubric use, especially anti-racist and student-centered, which adhered to Inoue and Poe's People category. Student-teachers (those who watched the presentation) completed their assessment and placed their feedback into a shared Google Doc to send to the presentation team. The presentation team uploaded their self-assessments to a discussion board within the Canvas e-learning platform for all students to review. This allowed for asynchronous review from a peer, a teacher, and a student's perspective. This method for generating reflection on student work products and the experience at the learning site has been done with success in online experiential learning and technology enhanced experiential learning. Mattera, Baena and Urena (2014) call this method rework reflection. They focused on the use of digital tools such as video, learning management systems, and virtual classroom software to help students focus on key elements of their learning experience.

Stage Three: Abstract Conceptualization

To continue with Kolb's cycle, students engaged in abstract conceptualization in class right after the presenters dropped off the call. Abstract Conceptualization asks learners to make sense of the concrete events. Learners should combine prior knowledge, course content, and peer to peer discussion to form conclusions. Students were given time in class to rewrite or revise the rubric based on how they experienced attempting to assess the team presentation. First, they held an informal conversation on what it was like giving the presentation. Then they asked the rest of the class what they thought about using the rubric. Did it "work"? Were you able to use the categories and indicators to accurately represent the performance? If not, why not? What needs to be rewritten to make the grading process clearer next time? After discussion, students were given about 10 minutes in class to get out the shared Google Doc and Messenger Chats to discuss possible changes to the rubric. A focus on revision values the labor and the learning process in this assessment of pre-service teachers. Merging Inoue's anti-racist assessment ecologies that engage the student in all stages of the learning process with Kolb's experiential learning model allowed students to have experiences in the online environment through assessing their peers and providing feedback on the student-made rubric in the team-teaching presentations. By observing their peer's assessment and use of the collaborative rubric, they could use their classmates' takes on the assessment activity and reconsider the rubric.

Stage Four: Active Experimentation

This stage encapsulates the work learners did to revise the rubrics based on their experiences using them with their peers in the online classroom and the conceptualizing discussions in class. All stages of Kolb's cycle involved ALL learners. The only time students were clearly divided into presenters and graders was *during* the presentation and immediately afterwards when the presentation team dropped off the call to complete a self-assessment and the rest of the class talked candidly about the performance.

Students were also questioned about the assignment sheet. Does it still meet your expectations for what you wanted to learn about the alternative assessment? What about what you wanted to share? How might it change to be clearer and more focused on your goals? Students realized that some of the content they had thought necessary initially was not, such as the history of the alternative assessment. They found that practical application ideas *were* needed, so they dropped the history content requirement and gave greater weight to practical application ideas.

Active experimentation is the rewriting, revising, and revisioning of the assignment and the grading rubric. Active experimentation can be considered "tinkering" with the original design of the products produced for the concrete learning experience. It is based on conceptualizing the experience through discussion and reflecting on the experience as a learner (self-assessment) and reflecting on the experience as a grader (discussions post grading and throughout the development of the rubric/assignment sheets). Through this *abstract conceptualization* of the previous week's presentation and subsequent grading, students then applied new knowledge – co-constructed knowledge – to their revisions to actively experiment with the rubric and the assignment sheets before another round of student presentations began (another concrete experience) and putting their revised rubrics to the test once again.

DISCUSSION

This section will outline evidence of students and teachers learning from this project, the obstacles encountered, and how students and teachers overcame them. A review of the project's goals and analysis of the data will determine whether these goals were met.

Designed Learning Outcomes

Promoting Enhanced Reflection on Assessment Practices

The first designed learning outcome was that students would autonomously and metacognitively reflect on their own grading and assessment practices - consider what was working and what was not and why; what about their thinking was propelling their decisions. To assess whether students metacognitively reflected on their own grading and assessment practices, their revising practices each week were observed. Students were asked to consider what was working and what was not and why. The instructor recorded the changes they made to the rubric each week based on metacognitive reflection in a private notebook. One major issue is that after the first two sessions, the revisions tapered off and students used the same rubric for the 3rd and 4th presentations. Each week from week 3 and 4, students were asked what worked and what didn't and why, but starting in week 3, they expressed that "it works," that it was clear to them, and they were happy with the rubric and the assignment sheet. This exemplifies one of the difficulties Chan described in assessing experiential learning – assessing the process. According to Chan, assessment tasks in experiential learning serve as both a marking instrument and a way to enhance and shape learning experiences, which is beneficial to the students, but increases the difficulty in assessing them (Chan, 2022).

This is also an example of some of the issues brought up by Inoue in many of his works in addition to Santos (2022) where students are so socialized to the traditional forms of assessment, that they do not shift away from it without further prompting. To mitigate this, the instructor can provide students with examples of student-created rubrics that are truly student centered as opposed to the more traditional grade centric and teacher centric models. The use of student writing samples may assist in designing these probative questions to tailor them to the unique learning experiences of the students. Healy, Flint, and Harrington described their work in student-centered experiential learning and found that student partnerships which include co-creation and viewing one another's work contributed to confidence and learning (2014). The instructor can also ask more varied probative questions when the initial questioning patterns no longer spark reflection, as Money, Dinning, Nixon, Walsh, and Magill found that when student partners feel listened to and that their thoughts and contributions are valued for their honesty, they are more likely to contribute productively to co-creation of curricular content (2016).

Facilitating Teachers' Multi-Directional Thinking and Communication Skills

The second outcome was about pre-service teachers' use of critical thinking and communication skills in multiple directions, namely teacher to student and student to student communication. Throughout this course, students were asked to communicate in a variety of ways – verbally in class after presentations and via Google Docs on rubrics and assignment sheets. These are examples of student-to-student communication that teachers initiated. Following Inoue and Poe's Guide to antiracist assessment practices, students had the autonomy to choose other modes of communication or "Places". They used Facebook Messenger, text messaging through their data plans, and Google Chat for student-to-student communication. The modes which were observed to spur the most critical thinking and communication were on Google Docs where students could comment directly on the page and make changes right away from comments. This is in line with the findings of Ariani and Febrianti who found increased engagement in online assessments when they employed Google Forms. Their belief was that it lowered the barrier to access as it was a tool which students were comfortable using outside the classroom (2022).

This experiential learning project was designed to allow students to engage in a concrete assessment experience. Through the assessment experience, they communicated via feedback on the rubrics to those student presentation groups weekly. One weakness of the experiential learning project is lack of preparation before, and time spent during the project on working with students to give effective feedback. Had the students been in actual classrooms instead of their own, they might have felt the weight of their feedback to the presenters mattered more than it did. Feedback weekly consisted of 1-2 sentences that were mostly encouraging. Chan describes some of the logistical challenges in giving effective feedback on experiential learning projects, such as how to provide constructive feedback that is not discouraging, but at the same time, balancing positive feedback so that it is still viewed by the student as constructive and has greater uptake (2022). Nicol and Macfarlane-Dick have found that effective feedback in experiential learning clarifies what good performance is, facilitates reflection, delivers high quality information, encourages dialogue, encourages self-esteem, and provides opportunities to close the gap between current and desired performances, as well as provide information that shapes instruction (2006). While student feedback on the rubrics encouraged self-esteem, it did not meet Nicol and Macfarlane's other criteria, most likely through failure to be explicitly taught feedback techniques.

Enriching Teachers' Awareness of Alternative Assessment

Finally, pre-service teachers have been expected to demonstrate increased awareness of a variety of alternative assessments through designing alternative assessments and the rubrics for grading them and preparing an alternative assessment for a class assignment.

The weekly presentations proved highly valuable in gauging this goal. All groups demonstrated a high knowledge of their chosen alternative assessment and met all criteria set by the assignment sheets they crafted. The presentation itself functioned as what Carless calls a Learning-oriented Assessment (LOA) that pulls "double-duty" in providing evidence of student learning for documentation purposes as well as being the vehicle to promote student learning. In Carless' work on LOA, he designed assessments that placed learning first by designing tasks that simulate sound learning practices amongst students and that actively engage students with their own and peer performances with thoughtfully designed criteria (Carless, 2007). This presentation served as an effective LOA because it was a task that actively engaged students in the ways Carless described and simulated these learning practices. Through the content created by the student groups, the instructor could gauge the explicit knowledge of the student presenters for adherence to the third goal in this case study. The content created by those students also served to edify the rest of the class who were serving the dual role of assessor and learner. The presentations functioned as a method for disseminating learning materials to the class on forms of alternative assessment with lesson examples for their own teaching toolboxes. The placement of the presentations alongside lectures on traditional forms of assessment provided additional opportunities for students to explore assessment methods (Carless, 2007). Through these presentations, students explored and explained journals for listening comprehension, portfolios for writing proficiency, hanging book mobiles and presentations for reading comprehension, vlogs for speaking assessment, posters for grammatical accuracy, and role-play for vocabulary assessments. Students demonstrated both explicit knowledge of the traditional forms of assessing each modality as well as innovative and creative approaches to alternative assessments. They adhered to the class-created rubric and assignment sheet, providing a researched argument for the alternative measurement and a sample activity as a virtual handout for students listening to the presentation. These sample activities adhered closely to the foundational elements of each approach to alternative assessment.

An additional LOA was a requirement when students turned in their final projects for their licensure program. They should produce the assessment of the licensure required – a traditional paper/pencil test with specifications and grading form. However, they would also describe how they could assess the same skills using an alternative assessment. This final project, while summative in nature and more traditional than the democratic and alternative assessments presented in the course, did allow for student autonomy in groupings, choice of topic, and presentation style, students reported growing in their curiosity and confidence with utilizing alternative assessments in their future classrooms.

One student wrote:

This is what we need to be learning. New and creative approaches...Tests scared me as a language student. But journals as assessment seems like fun...I liked trying out different kinds of assessments this semester. It was much more fun than simply reading about them. My favorite was building a class journal.

Seeing students thinking about the most appropriate alternative assessments for the tests they developed for their licensure program was incredibly encouraging. They each wrote rationales for their assessment choices and commonly referred to the student presentations and rubrics for assessment. Despite social distancing and lockdown requirements in their area, students still shared their references and resources from their presentations with one another, and these references built up the rationales for alternative assessment students produced.

In addition to the final products, students' skills in rubric design grew in depth as they repeatedly refined and experimented with their rubrics. Each week, they reviewed what worked and what did not. Their questions moved from surface-level confusion to tweaking wording to get at the focus of their review to best attend to the learning needs of their peers. Additionally, they became far more autonomous in learning. They created their groups, assignments, assessments, and feedback to one another, engaging in student partnerships as designed by Haley et al (2014). They researched a topic of their choosing. They were unafraid to ask for teacher input and advice, and the quality of their presentations were highly professional. They shared responsibilities and resources for the class to take away for their teaching toolboxes.

A secondary goal for this case study was to investigate the role that anti-racist, or democratic assessment could play in an online experiential learning course for pre-service ESL/EFL teachers. Because of the alternative and dynamic nature of the experiential learning process, grading was not focused on the rubric as it stood at the end of the semester but instead on the processes students worked through weekly to adjust the rubric and assignment sheets based on co-constructed knowledge of assessment theory and washback. According to Chan's work in grading the group learning process in experiential learning, aspects that should be assessed include demonstrated leadership, cooperative attitudes, application of a variety of methods to deal with different tasks and difficulties, level of engagement with the task, ability to motivate others, and a willingness to listen and responsiveness to feedback and opinions (2010). Through recorded Zoom classes and timestamped Google Docs with student names associated with edits, evidence of leadership, attitude, application of methods, level of engagement, responsiveness to feedback could all be observed in both reflection and revision practices and responses to dynamic probes within the Google Docs or the Zoom class. This provided criteria for awarding grades for engagement in the experiential learning cycle. This is aligned with the work of Santos who awarded A's to students who were the most engaged in the labor of his English course (2022).

Where this case study fell short was in making the criteria exceptionally clear to learners *before* the assessments began. As the course featured democratic and dynamic assessments through an experiential learning project, the role of assessment from the teacher needed to adapt to the autonomous decisions of the students. However, that does not excuse the need for a systematic plan on the part of the instructor that would be made available to students and adapted as the course progressed, and which allows the student and the assessor to focus on what needed to be observed and recorded, as described by Chan as an essential facet of effective observation assessments in experiential learning (2022).

Anti-racist assessment practices ask students to craft the rubrics used to assess them, giving them autonomy and "Power." Since students chose their categories and questions for feedback, the instructor did engage with those rubric criteria and honored their requests by providing feedback that students asked for in their rubrics, honoring the "Parts" they created. Several students commented that it was refreshing to contribute to their learning in this way, especially during such a difficult time in their college studies. One student noted the positive feelings of being listened to and considered valid in his desire to set learning goals through the rubric. This is aligned with the findings of Money et. al who found that involving students in the design of the curriculum contributed to their level of engagement with the course content and promoted a sense that they were taken seriously by their instructors (2016). This is also aligned with anti-racist assessment ecologies that award credit not just for correct and incorrect, which is incredibly difficult in a subjective environment like assignment and assessment creation. However, awards credit is based on consistent effort. (Inoue, 2005).

In applying concepts from Anti-racist Assessment Ecologies, several issues with the curriculum and feedback were elucidated. Inoue and Gonzalez advocate for the use of a single-trait rubric. A single-trait rubric asks the learners to craft categories they would like teacher and peer feedback on, and then to ask specific questions in each category. The responses to those questions would go either to the right meaning the answer shares with the student the positive aspects of their product that pertain to the questions asked. The responses to those questions can also be listed on the left of those questions, sharing how the work sample could be improved in the areas students asked questions about. Table 3 contains a blank example:

Table 3. Single trait rubric example

Challenging Answers	Trait	Positive Answers
Answers that challenge the student to push themselves further are here, such as suggestions to include imagery as a device in the 3rd paragraph of the argument.	1 word trait + Probing question. Ex: Persuasiveness "How did I show my use of rhetorical devices in the argument?"	Answers that affirm the student is on the right track, are written here such as examples from student writing of rhetorical devices.

It works much better in the online learning environment than a blank Google Doc because it provides light scaffolding but still relies heavily on student input and design (see Inoue, 2005 for more on single-trait rubric design).

Implications

This projects' LO's were to provide students with an experiential learning project in the online environment that exposed them to a variety of alternative assessments through multiple concrete experiences, reflection, abstract conceptualizations, and active experimentation using Kolb's Experiential Learning Cycle. This cycle can be used by practitioners to design assessment experiences for pre-service teachers in the online environment by first designing learning outcomes, or LO's. For this course, students were to be exposed to a variety of alternative assessments experientially. A second aim was to build their critical thinking and reflective skills about their own assessment practices, and finally to engage in a variety of communication practices surrounding alternative assessment practices.

From the LO's, practitioners can consider what online avenues there are for gaining experience. This could be through online tutoring programs, providing feedback to oral assessment submitted by students in an Intensive English Program or community ESL/EFL program, or assisting in-service teachers in assignment and rubric design and observing the learning environment via Zoom. Once an experience has been designed that could assist students with the LO's, teachers should design discussion questions that ask students to reflect on the concrete experience. Journalling after each learning experience is one way to engage students in reflection. Placing students into groups to discuss their thoughts about the assessment experience is another. Then, ask students to experiment with the products and processes they are exploring in the concrete experience. Provide multiple opportunities for students to engage in the assessment experience.

For those that would like to incorporate anti-racist assessment practices into their online courses, Dr. Asoe Inoue's blog posts on the topic, in addition to Davis's lesson plan on the TESOL International website are both informative and easily accessible readings on the topic. Focus on giving students power to describe how they would like to be assessed, and through dynamic assessment, probe students every week or two to reconsider how the assessment practices are influencing their work. For teachers, it is important to reflect regularly on how to communicate with students about assessments to consider how well the instructor adapts to the needs of learners and whether there are shifts from traditional forms of assessment that would benefit them.

CONCLUSION

The Global Pandemic threw all educators and students worldwide into online learning. Thankfully, educational companies and schools did not stop thinking about how to meet the needs of their learners. By getting to know students, the university, and the teaching and learning contexts, instructors can engage educational technology that gives greater access to one another. Students, with the help of their families, educators at the local university, and their communities, overcame many obstacles to their growth as language practitioners. By leaning into the resources of the local university community, educators can harness educational advancements to create an experiential learning project that promotes growth in experience and depth of knowledge about alternative assessments within an anti-racist assessment ecology, which meets the stated needs of local educators for innovative assessment practices aligned with the national curriculum. As stated in the literature review, while online teaching has promoted experiential learning online in many fields, access to experiential pre-service language teaching projects online is still a small research field.

More work must be done to develop innovative online experiential learning assessments to give language teachers worldwide access to experiences in assessing language proficiency, no matter their access to a local college or technological resources. Far more work is still to be done in anti-racist assessment design. As language educators, instruction and assessment are often given to vulnerable populations, but much of the literature around these two comes from high income academic communities that routinely cater to the needs of upper-class students. It is imperative to learn, make mistakes, and grow better to meet the needs of marginalized populations of language learners.

REFERENCES

Alatni, B. S., Abubakar, I. R., & Iqbal, S. A. (2021). Covid-19 and rapid course adaptations in Saudi Arabia: An experiential learning and recommendations for online education. *Frontiers in Psychology*, *12*, 643203. doi:10.3389/fpsyg.2021.643203 PMID:35002820

Alemi, M., Miri, M., & Mozafarnezhad, A. (2019). Investigating the Effects of Online Concurrent Group Dynamic Assessment on Enhancing Grammatical Accuracy of EFL Learners. *Tabaran Institute of Higher Education: International Journal of Language Testing*, *9*(2), 29–43.

Ariani, N., & Febrianti, Y. (2022). Compromising peer assessment using Google Forms in an online essay-writing course. In Habiddin, Karmina, & Wonorahardjo, (Eds.), Improving Assessment and Evaluation Strategies on Online Learning (1st ed., pp. 56–62). essay, Routledge. doi:10.1201/9781003261346-9

Arifuddin, A., Turmudi, T., & Rokhmah, U. N. (2021). Alternative assessments in online learning during covid-19 pandemic: The strengths and weaknesses. *International Journal of Elementary Education*, *5*(2), 240. doi:10.23887/ijee.v5i2.33532

Bailey, K. M., & Curtis, A. (2015). *Learning about language assessment: Dilemmas, decisions, and directions* (2nd ed.). National Geographic Learning/Heinle, Cengage, Learning.

Baroni, A., Dooly, M., Garcés García, P., Guth, S., Hauck, M., Helm, F., Lewis, T., Mueller-Hartmann, A., O'Dowd, R., Rienties, B., & Rogaten, J. (2019). *Evaluating the impact of virtual exchange on initial teacher education: A European policy experiment*. Research Publishing.net. doi:10.14705/rpnet.2019.29.9782490057337

Bayır, D. (2022). Impacts of the covid-19 pandemic on Experiential Learning: Development of a community-grounded online internship program. *Journal of Education for Library and Information Science*, *63*(4), 372–388. doi:10.3138/jelis.2020-0108

Bender, G., & Jordaan, R. (2007). Student Perceptions and Attitudes about Community Service-Learning in the Teacher Training Curriculum. *South African Journal of Education*, *27*(4), 631–654.

Berman, G., & Paradies, Y. (2010). Racism, disadvantage and multiculturalism: Towards effective anti-racist praxis. *Ethnic and Racial Studies*, *33*(2), 214–232. doi:10.1080/01419870802302272

Blair, J., Gala, P., Tariq, A., Harrison, D., & Ajjan, H. (2020). Online Experiential Learning: Methods, Advantages, and Challenges. Society for Marketing Advances Proceedings, 111–113.

Brown, H. D., & Abeywickrama, P. (2019). *Language assessment: Principles and classroom practices*. Pearson.

Burden, A. (2018). a. Pinterest: Pinning the gap between SoTL and SLCE in higher education. *The International Journal of Research on Service-Learning and Community Engagement*, 6(1). Advance online publication. doi:10.37333/001c.6816

Burden, A. (2018) b. Three Methods to Enhance Peer Review in Your Classroom. In M. Weimer (Ed.), The College Teacher's Handbook: A Resource Collection for New Faculty (pp. 73- 76). Madison, WI: Magna Publications.

Bursac, V., & Wilsker, A. (2020). Thriving During a Crisis: Transferring Experiential Learning Online. *Business Education Innovation Journal*, 12(2), 30–39.

Cappellini, M., & Hsu, Y.-Y. (2020). When future teachers meet real learners through telecollaboration: An experiential approach to learn how to teach languages online. *Journal of Virtual Exchange*, 3, 1–11. doi:10.21827/jve.3.35751

Carless, D. (2007). Learning-Oriented assessment: Conceptual bases and practical implications. *Innovations in Education and Teaching International*, 44(1), 57–66. Advance online publication. doi:10.1080/14703290601081332

Chan, C. K. Y. (2010). Group assessment. CETL. https://ar.cetl.hku.hk/group.htm#6

Chan, C. K. Y. (2022). *Assessment for Experiential Learning*. Routledge. doi:10.4324/9781003018391

Chappuis, J., & Stiggins, R. J. (2020). *Classroom assessment for student learning: Doing it right — using it well* (2nd ed.). Pearson.

Choi, I., Wolf, M. K., Pooler, E., Sova, L., & Faulkner-Bond, M. (2019). Investigating the benefits of scaffolding in assessments of young English learners: A case for scaffolded retell tasks. *Language Assessment Quarterly*, 16(2), 161–179. doi:10.1080/15434303.2019.1619180

Chugai, O., & Pawar, A. (2022). Using alternative assessment during the pandemic by Indian and Ukrainian teachers of English. *Facta Universitatis*, 6(1), 001–009.

Chugai, O. Y., Yamshinska, N. V., Svyrydova, L. H., & Kutsenok, N. M. (2018). Alternative assessment during the pandemic: teachers of English perspective. *SWorldJournal*, (09-02), 90–99. doi:10.30888/2663-5712.2021-09-02-039

Davis, L. (2013). *Building rubrics democratically - TESOL international association*. tesol.org. https://www.tesol.org/docs/default-source/books/6P/building-rubrics-democratically_full.pdf?status=Temp&sfvrsn=0.9838654 007180547

Fenton, L., & Gallant, K. (2016). Integrated experiential education: Definitions and a conceptual model. *The Canadian Journal for the Scholarship of Teaching and Learning*, 7(2), 7. doi:10.5206/cjsotl-rcacea.2016.2.7

Fluckiger, J. (2010). Single Point Rubric: A Tool for Responsible Student Self-Assessment. *The Delta Kappa Gamma Bulletin: International Journal of Professional Educators*, 76(4), 18–25.

Furco, A., & Ammon, M. S. (2000). Highlights from service-learning in California's teacher education programs: A White Paper. *Service Learning, General*, 155. https://digitalcommons.unomaha.edu/slceslgen/155

Gibbons, P. (2003). Mediating language learning: Teacher interactions with ESL students in a content-based classroom. *TESOL Quarterly*, *37*(2), 247. doi:10.2307/3588504

GonzalezJ. (2020, April 13). *Cult of Pedagogy*. Cult of Pedagogy. https://www.cultofpedagogy.com/

Grapin, S., Llosa, L., & Haas, A. (2022, January 1). An illustration of four types of formative assessment in a fifth-grade physical science unit. *Science and Children*, (January/February), 58–63.

Grapin, S. E., & Llosa, L. (2022). Dynamic assessment of English learners in the content areas: An exploratory study in fifth-grade science. *TESOL Quarterly*, *56*(1), 201–229. doi:10.1002/tesq.3059

Healey, M., Flint, A., & Harrington, K. (2014). *Engagement through Partnership: Students as Partners in Learning and Teaching in Higher Education.* York: HEA. https://www.heacademy.ac.uk/engagement-through-partnership-s tudents-partners -learning-and-teaching-higher-education

Helate, T. H., Metaferia, T. F., & Gezahegn, T. H. (2022). English language teachers' engagement in and preference for experiential learning for professional development. *Heliyon*, *8*(10), e10900. doi:10.1016/j.heliyon.2022.e10900 PMID:36237971

Henderson, J., & Brookhart, S. (1997, March 24). *Service Learning for Aspiring School Leaders: An Exploratory Study* [Paper presented at the Annual Meeting of Educational Research Association]. US Department of Education.

Herrera, L., Cuesta Melo, C. H., & Lucero Zambrano, M. A. (2022). Influence of self-assessment on the English Language Learning process. *Colombian Applied Linguistics Journal*, *24*(1), 89–104. doi:10.14483/22487085.17673

Hu, H. (2015). Building virtual teams: Experiential learning using emerging technologies. *E-Learning and Digital Media*, *12*(1), 17–33. doi:10.1177/2042753014558373

Hughes, M. T., & Braun, G. (2019). Experiential Learning Experiences to Enhance Preservice Special Educators' Literacy Instruction. *International Electronic Journal of Elementary Education*, *12*(1), 93–101. doi:10.26822/iejee.2019155341

Inchaouh, G., & Tchaïcha, J. D. (2020). Online collaboration and Experiential Learning in higher education: Designing an online cross-border collaborative project for Business Students. *International Journal of Technology, Knowledge and Society*, *16*(4), 37–56. doi:10.18848/1832-3669/CGP/v16i04/37-56

Inoue, A. B. (2020, April 6). *Thinking about one-point rubrics, standards, and dimensions*. Thinking about One Point Rubrics, Standards, and Dimensions. http://asaobinoue.blogspot.com/2015/07/thinking-about-one-po int-rubrics.html

Inoue, A. B., & Poe, M. (2020). How to stop harming your students: An ecological guide to Antiracist writing assessment. *Composition Studies*, *48*(3), 14–15.

Kolb, A. (2012). *What is Experiential Learning?* [Video]. Youtube. https://www.youtube.com/watch?v=1ZeAdN4FB5A

Kolb, A., & Kolb, D. A. (2017). *The experiential educator: Principles and practices of experiential learning*. Experience Based Learning Systems Inc.

Kurt, S. (2020, December 28). *Kolb's Experiential Learning Theory & Learning Styles*. Educational Technology. https://educationaltechnology.net/kolbs-experiential-learnin g-theory-learning-styles/

Le, Q. T., Pedro, A., & Park, C. S. (2015). A social virtual reality based construction safety education system for experiential learning. *Journal of Intelligent & Robotic Systems*, *79*(3-4), 487–506. doi:10.100710846-014-0112-z

Lee, J. (2019). Experiential teacher education – preparing preservice teachers to teach English grammar through an experiential learning project. *The Australian Journal of Teacher Education*, 1–20. doi:10.14221/ajte.2018v44n1.1

Lynch, B., & Shaw, P. (2005). Portfolios, power, and Ethics. *TESOL Quarterly*, *39*(2), 263. doi:10.2307/3588311

Mattera, M., Baena, V., Ureña, R., & Moreno, M. D. F. (2014). Creativity in technology-enhanced experiential learning: Videocast implementation in higher education. *International Journal of Technology Enhanced Learning*, *6*(1), 46–64. doi:10.1504/IJTEL.2014.060026

Merriam, S. B. (1998). *Qualitative research and case study applications in education*. Jossy-Bass.

Merriam, S. B., & Bierema, L. L. (2014). *Adult learning: Bridging theory and practice*. Jossey Bass.

Money, J., Dinning, T., Nixon, S., Walsh, B., & Magill, C. (2016). Co-Creating a Blended Learning Curriculum in Transition to Higher Education: A Student Viewpoint. *Creative Education*, *7*(9), 1205–1213. doi:10.4236/ce.2016.79126

Mundkur, A., & Ellickson, C. (2012). Bringing the real world in: Reflection on building a virtual learning environment. *Journal of Geography in Higher Education*, *36*(3), 369–384. doi:10.1080/03098265.2012.692073

Mutch, C. (2005). *Doing educational research: A practitioner's guide to getting started*. NZCER.

Nicol, D. J., & Macfarlane-Dick, D. (2006). Formative assessment and self-regulated learning: A model and seven principles of good feedback practice. *Studies in Higher Education*, *31*(2), 199–218. doi:10.1080/03075070600572090

Poehner, E. M., & Infante, P. (2016). Dynamic Assessment in the Language Classroom. In D. Tsagari & J. Banerjee (Eds.), Handbook of Second Language Assessment (pp. 275–290). DeGruyter Mouton. doi:10.1515/9781614513827-019

Poehner, M. (2009). Group dynamic assessment: Mediation for the L2 classroom. *TESOL Quarterly*, *43*(3), 471–491. doi:10.1002/j.1545-7249.2009.tb00245.x

Qualters, D. M. (2010). Bringing the outside in: Assessing experiential education. *New Directions for Teaching and Learning*, *2010*(124), 55–62. doi:10.1002/tl.421

Santos, M. C. (2022). How I Implemented Asao B. Inoue's Labor-Based Grading and Other Antiracist Assessment Strategies. *CEA Critic, 84*(2), 160–179. doi:10.1353/cea.2022.0019

Satyam, & Aithal, R. K. (2022). Reimagining an experiential learning exercise in times of crisis: Lessons learned and a proposed framework. *Journal of Marketing Education, 44*(2), 191–202. doi:10.1177/02734753221084128

Stommel, J. (2018). *How to Ungrade.* Jesse Stommel. www.jessestommel.com/how-to-ungrade/

University of Hong Kong. (2021). *Theory and practice as one: Experiential learning @ HKU.* HKU. https://tl.hku.hk/reform/experiential-learning/4/

Vince, R. (1998). Behind and beyond Kolb's learning cycle. *Journal of Management Education, 22*(3), 304–319. doi:10.1177/105256299802200304

Yin, R. K. (1994). *Case study research design and methods* (2nd ed.). Sage.

Chapter 8
Participant Evaluation of an Online Course on Language Assessment Literacy

Asli Lidice Gokturk Saglam
University of South Eastern Norway, Norway

Ece Sevgi-Sole
University of Milan, Italy

ABSTRACT

This chapter reports on participant evaluations of an online professional development course on language assessment literacy (LAL) for practitioners interested in the field. With the introduction and widespread of online courses following the Covid era, the need to evaluate the effectiveness of the new modalities and platforms to deliver these courses as well as the online course content has become inevitable. To serve for this purpose, this chapter presents the analysis of data collected from a multinational online community of language teachers through the end-of-course questionnaire (n=13) and focused interviews (n=6). The results of the analysis suggested three main issues indicated by the course participants: learning in an online community, course design, and course content. The chapter which discusses the emerging sub-themes has implications for teacher educators, researchers, and course designers interested in learning about the participant perspective towards an online course in a multicultural LAL context.

INTRODUCTION

Distance education, which dates back to the 1920s, gained a sharp impetus, and spread much more widely during the Covid pandemic, which broke out towards the end of 2019. Soon after, a variety of online learning platforms and tools were available to educators, and in a very short time, the vast majority of the educational institutions all around the world turned into virtual classrooms. In a similar way, teacher education was also carried onto online platforms. A number of these courses made use of educational technologies to promote collaborative and dialogic interaction and co-construction of knowledge within

DOI: 10.4018/978-1-6684-6227-0.ch008

online professional learning and sharing communities. In Lave and Wenger's (1991) terms, these online courses create Communities of Practice (CoP), in which groups come together to share their experience and discover possibilities development through social, collaborative, and regular interaction.

One such community was the online teacher training program called Language Assessment Literacy for Practitioners (LAL4P), the focus of this current chapter. The course was designed to promote teachers' LAL literacy, identified as a key area in teacher education (Chow & Leung, 2011; Coombe et al., 2012; Fulcher, 2012; Vogt & Tsagari, 2014). LAL4P aimed at improving the assessment literacy of the language teachers through exposure to, and discussion of, key concepts in language assessment, as well as supporting the production of assessment tasks. Within a collaborative network of online communities of practice, language assessment literacy was explored and discussed among a group of international practitioners from diverse educational contexts.

The inclusion of online modality into the practices of information exchange and developing expertise in specific fields of inquiry have however, also raised concerns regarding the effectiveness of the emerging methods and platforms. These concerns over effectiveness have added another dimension to the already existing issues in educational evaluation, such as seeking institutional accreditation, improving the curriculum design, monitoring student performance, and governing instructional activities (Haberstroh et al., 2014; Hegji, 2017; Steyn et al., 2019). Following the Covid era, lines of research have been developed and conducted to investigate the impact of the virtual classrooms on participants, educators, and educational policies (Aristovnik et al., 2020; Marinoni, 2020; Schleicher, 2020). However, little attention has been given to the systematic and valid investigation of participants' evaluation of these online courses, even though this area can shed important light on participant perceptions and expectations of these courses (Hew et al., 2020). To address this gap, this chapter reports on participant evaluations of LAL4P aimed at increasing our understanding participants' perspectives of the elements of an online course design and bring further insight to the practices of online course developers, and improve the quality of online courses, potentially leading to participant benefit. Thus, the research question is How do multinational participants of a CoP evaluate an online course on language assessment literacy?

The chapter will explain the background in further detail by presenting a brief overview of literature review, outlining research settings including the program, participants, data collection/analysis tools, and discussing findings and implications.

BACKGROUND

The incorporation of participant viewpoints in the evaluation of instructional courses has become an increasingly common practice. A review of course evaluation studies suggest that the three main motivations behind eliciting learner perceptions are providing the students with their learning needs, acknowledging the positive correlation between learner satisfaction and learning, and identifying any barriers to the intended course goals (Tsimaras et al., 2022). To elaborate, the first reason for such a step is the idea that educators constantly seek to find innovative methods to cater for the needs of the 21st century learners, and transform traditional classrooms into interactive, student-centered environments in which there is active engagement learning journeys (Oflaz et al., 2022; Tsimaras et al., 2022).

Another line of research investigating the reasons for including participant voices in course evaluations points to the significantly positive relationship between online learning and student satisfaction, engagement, and interaction (e.g., Yousaf et al., 2022). Mixed opinions and attitudes have emerged in the literature regarding the studies on participant satisfaction in online courses in diverse disciplines. In addition to the participant satisfaction level, these studies can reveal the participant's perspective on several key features of online courses. The results of this line of research reveal that a common issue in this area appears to be course design and quality of content. It has been reported that participants expressed higher satisfaction when they found the online course goals meaningful, the course content comprehensible, and the course platform navigation intuitive (Conache et al., 2016; Mehall, 2020; Sun et al., 2008; Xi et al., 2018). Unclear course expectations and task instructions, on the other hand, lead to dissatisfaction (Kucuk & Richardson, 2019; Young, 2013). Online interaction with the other participants also appears to be a facilitating element, playing a key role in participant satisfaction (Banerjee & Duflo, 2014; Dinh & Ngyuen, 2020; Shea et al., 2001). Several studies report that course participants who engage in online dialogic interaction through discussion boards or chat rooms develop overall higher opinions. Regarding social interaction, constructive feedback from course tutors has emerged as a factor positively affecting attitudes (Shea et al., 2001). Similarly, Aloni and Harrington (2018) assert that asynchronous discussion boards are valuable in promoting content knowledge and critical thinking skills.

Additionally, several studies discuss the importance of listening to students' voices to identity barriers to online learning, and, to gain insights that could improve implementation of instructional activities (e.g. Ali, Uppal & Gulliver, 2017). Participant characteristics, which might include (lack of) tech familiarity, tendency to aggression, and even factors related to emotional intelligence, have been identified as potential factors in decreasing level of online course satisfaction (Berenson et al., 2008; Halimi et al., 2020; Kauffman, 2015). Finally, the inclusion of peer assessment tasks in some courses emerged as a point of complaint, hence participant dissatisfaction. Some participants found their peer feedback "fierce" (Kirschner, 2012), while others claimed that it was poorly executed and insufficiently thoughtful (Krause, 2013). In the current chapter, there is a discussion of the aforementioned features of online courses, which reportedly affect participant evaluations, with an emphasis on an online, multicultural Community of Practice (CoP) which is specialized in language assessment literacy.

Systematic Analysis of Participant Evaluations

At this point, methodological concerns might arise regarding the appropriate validation of methods regarding the collection and interpretation of participant perceptions. In their review of the advantages and disadvantages of e-learning, Choudhury & Pattnaik (2020) focus on inadequacies found in the practices regarding collecting perceptions of the stakeholders, including learners, designers, implementers, and designers, and they identified the challenges in acquiring accurate learner feedback and ways to include their voice in the evaluation of the educational potential of e-learning programs. The shortcomings of participation perception studies, due to their lack of systematicity is a serious problem but has been responded to by adopting validated course evaluation models into study design (Gokmenoglu et al., 2021; Oflaz et al., 2022; Shih & Yuan, 2019; Tsimaras et al., 2022). For example, Tsimaras et al. (2022) gathered and classified online learners' feedback on multiple courses given at Patras University, Greece within the framework of Stufflebeam's Content, Input, Process, Product (CIPP) Model (2003), involving the analysis of learners' feedback on open-ended questionnaire items to evaluate 27 online courses. The wide-ranging evaluation focused on three areas: (a) the supportive framework of these courses (infrastructure, content, support, organization, and coordination), (b) the teachers themselves, and (c) the course implementation, focusing on learning approaches and outcomes. Digital formative and summative questionnaires implied that the introduced programmes met learner expectations, both in terms of scientific knowledge advancement, and the practical application to their work. However, areas for further improvement were identified like the course duration as well as the availability of the instructional activities on a weekly basis.

The current study also adapts the CIPP Model (Stufflebeam, 2003), aiming to contribute to the systematic analysis of participant perceptions about an online Language Assessment Literacy course. The CIPP Model (2003) defines *'context evaluation'* as the identification of a program's strengths and weaknesses and establishing plans for improvement; and *'input'* as the initial implementation strategy for the program. In their definition, the term *'process'* refers to the monitoring, evaluating, and reviewing the program's progress towards its objectives. The goal of this phase is to provide the stakeholders with feedback regarding the achievement of the objectives established in the previous phase, and ways to improve the efficiency of the utilization of available resources. Finally, Stufflebeam (2003) defines the *'product'* as assessment and interpretation of the program outcomes via documenting and examining the observed implications. In the current study, the term 'context evaluation' corresponds to the program goals and objectives and participants' needs in enhancing their language assessment literacy, and 'input', to instructional design, and accordingly, the selected materials. 'Process' can be defined as the implementation of the web course in an online community of practice, while 'course satisfaction' and participants' 'perceived learning', refers to the notion of product.

The Online Course Language Assessment for Practitioners (LAL4P)

The course under evaluation, Language Assessment Literacy for Practitioners (LAL4P), was a component of TESOL's Electronic Village Online (EVO) program. The online training was designed to improve teachers' language assessment literacy (LAL), and the rationale behind its design and implementation was rather complex. First, the premise of the study presented in this chapter is language assessment literacy, which some consider to be a rather neglected area in teacher education. Vogt and Tsagari (2014) report that LAL in in-service training is insufficient to cope with assessment challenges, which means that this area should be prioritized. It is also argued that educational technology (Malone, 2008) and online communities of practice (Hargreaves, 2013) both have a role in promoting teacher professional development. Finally, more prominently during the last decade, an online course has been considered to be advantageous over a traditional face-to-face course in that: a) it leads to democratization of education, because all that is needed is a computer and internet connection; b) it demolishes classroom walls and reaches larger populations; and c) its flexible, self-directed nature alleviates the "working hours" barrier and is accessible to professionals at their convenience.

LAL4P was conducted over five weeks, mainly on the free online platform Canvas. Each week was presented in the form of a separate module, with each consisting of embedded input in the form of videos, visuals, or articles on the weekly topic, followed by online discussions facilitated through the involvement of guest experts, tasks for the participants, and an online meeting with a well-known scholar in the field. The only synchronous component of the course was the online meetings, and the course's generally asynchronous nature enabled the participants to follow the training at their own pace and availability. The online meetings recordings were freely available on the Canvas platform. This blended course design was intended to provide flexibility to the participants and experts alike, both in developing their own reflections, and providing feedback for course improvement (Garrison, 2016; Hew & Cheung, 2014; Vaughan et al., 2013).

The choice of the online course platform appears to be another point of consideration in the course evaluation process. The educational evaluation literature highlights the differences between face-to-face and Web-based or e-learning courses, indicating that traditional course evaluation standards and criteria may be in adequate and misleading for an online course evaluation (Breslow et al., 2013; Literat, 2015). This clearly indicates a need for the creation of reliable criteria in the evaluation of courses designed on various online platforms. The current chapter intends to address this research area by investigating the operation of an online course on language assessment literacy,, by outlining the prominent issues as indicated by the course participants, potentially contributing to the formulation of criteria for the design and systematic evaluation of online LAL courses.

Participant Evaluations on an Online LAL Training

LAL4P participants consisted of English teachers from geographically diverse educational settings who shared an interest in language assessment. 13 teachers completed the course evaluation questionnaire and 6 took part in in-depth one-to-one interviews. Due to guarantees of anonymity, the participant profile will be presented here collectively rather than detailed individually. The vast majority of the participants obtained their post-graduate degrees in Language Education (43% PhD.; 25% Masters), and the lowest teaching qualification was reported to be a teaching certificate that was internationally recognized (7.5%). Field experience in teaching and assessment practices reportedly ranged between 0-2 years (9.6%) and 15+ years (42%). Some worked in managerial positions and as teacher trainers, but most were tertiary level English language teachers (87.8%). The remaining participants were secondary school, high school, or primary school teachers in a descending order of population size, with the smallest group being the preschool teachers (4.9%).

The study presented in this chapter collected data with the participants permission, from LAL4P using two main sources: an end-of-course questionnaire (n=13), and one-on-one interviews (n=6). The online questionnaire consisted of 10 items, and delivered via Google forms (see App. A). Items 1, 2 and 9 required long-text answers for qualitative analysis. Item 1 was designed to investigate the perceived benefits of the LAL4P course, while item 2 focused on the participants' main difficulties. Item 9 was designed to elicit further information about the online course components. The remaining items were quantitatively analyzed and formulated as a Likert scale; items 3-8 investigated the participants' level of (dis)agreement on course-related statements, and item 10, the perceived confidence level in assessment activities.

Online interviews were held with six participants after giving their written consent. The purpose was to triangulate the questionnaire data and obtain more in-depth information from the participant perspective. Each one-on-one interview lasted around 40 minutes and were recorded, transcribed, and analyzed through thematic coding through NVivo software. The quantitative data were analyzed through descriptive statistics using Statistical Package for the Social Sciences (SPSS). The data were analyzed iteratively in three stages: individual coding by the two researchers, meetings for calibration purposes, and finally, coding-agreement meetings.

EMERGING ISSUES IN AN ONLINE LAL COURSE EVALUATION AND THEIR IMPLICATIONS

The discussion in this section will involve a thorough examination of the interview and questionnaire data, with due consideration to the CIPP Model of evaluation. This analysis will allow an in-depth evaluation of the program through the participants' eyes. Table 1 exhibits how Stufflebeam's CIPP Model corresponds to the online course evaluation in the context of Language Assessment Literacy of Practitioners enumerating the questions and focal points guiding the evaluation for each component (see Table 1). The adaptation of the model was achieved through rounds of researcher discussions, supported by opinions from other experts in the field.

Table 1. Adaptation of the CIPP model to an online language assessment literacy course evaluation (LAL4P)

CIPP Model Component	Correspondence to the LAL Context
Context evaluation	Do the goals of the program reflect the needs of the participants of the program? Needs analysis; What are the perceived needs in LAL training? Setting the course objectives
Input evaluation	What is required to achieve course goals? Analysis of target groups characteristics Adaptation of the course to the specific needs of the target group Development of instructional materials Development of course Canvas
Process evaluation	How is course content disseminated? Implementation of the course in an online community of practice Use of resources Dissemination of information
Product evaluation	What is the evidential outcome? Participation of the learners Knowledge and observable skills of participants Participant satisfaction Achievement of initial objectives

The interviews (n=6) enabled a deeper analysis of the participant course evaluations and resonated with the questionnaire outcomes. In addition, qualitative data analysis of the factors affecting participant views on course evaluation revealed four emerging themes, namely (1) course design based on participant needs, (2) course content, (3) delivery of course content, and (4) learning in an online community. The emerging themes and their corresponding sub themes are summarized below and then explained further in detail in the relevant sections (see Table 2).

Course Design: Creating the Context

The first item elaborated on in the course evaluation concerns the course design. Teachers pointed out several aspects of merit in the course design. Responses indicated that such well-structured, self-paced, and multimodal online courses were perceived as very effective, in line with other studies providing evidence that structured content contributes to participant satisfaction (Sun et al., 2008; Conache et al.,

2016; Xi et al., 2018). The most appreciated aspect was the blended course design presenting theory, and then asking for suggestions as to its practical application. Two other elements which the participants found relevant were multimodality and self-paced learning.

Table 2. Issues mentioned by Online LAL course participants in their course evaluations

CIPP Framework	Themes	Sub-themes	Example Statements
Context	Course design based on participant needs	A blend of theory and practice	The course content was very structured.
		Multimodality	The videos shared by you, each week, they are very up to the point, and they give us ideas about that task and how to assess them
		Self-paced learning	There were wide range of sources that I can download and use later
Input	Course Content	Course input	Course covered assessment of skills, theoretical assessment on test, creating assessment, and all these principles of assessment. These were helpful.
		Hands on practice	I guess, the part where we were supposed to design the tests and receive feedback from our peers, and moderators was the best.
		Live sessions	The weekly live sessions with eminent guests, who gave the attendees ample time for questions, were extremely satisfying.
		ICT Tools	It was great that I was introduced to digital tools which can be used for formative assessment.
Process	Delivery of Course Content	Interaction	I also love the communication on the platform. So, they do have discussions where people have... where people share the ideas and ask for some ideas. It was really helpful.
		Peer Feedback	Having my work peer reviewed and reviewed by competent scholars specializing in language assessment was the best.
		Moderators	The moderators were always there to help us out, I liked it the most.
Product	Learning in an online community	Enhancement of LAL Course Satisfaction	I have learned a lot about key concepts of assessments and assessment tools. (in percentages)

A Blend of Theory and Practice

T1 believed that the course was well structured, stating that:

The work was really harmonious. I mean, being online with discussion, suggesting offering work, theoretical work and loads of practice. So, all skills were balanced overall? as a course. I love that all the skills and theoretical ideas, which are essential in our professional world, were also given just as a background for development.

Multimodality

The inclusion of both visual and written sources of information seems to have been appreciated. T1 focused on how the use of multimodality in the course design facilitated the learning process, as shown in the following:

The videos shared by you each week were to the point and they give us great ideas about that task and how to assess them. I like videos, because they are very easy to understand, in my context. I think we generally don't want to read a lot. But the videos give us very valuable information in a short time.

Similarly, T3 confirmed that the use of images and other visual representations complemented the oral and written input, saying:

The symbols you used in reliability and validity, the dart figures were really good, because some people have some problems understanding these concepts. Making it a little bit easier was good. It's a little bit of an abstract thing for them, maybe. But you put it on the ground for us.

Self-Paced Learning

Another important aspect of course design remarked on was the opportunity of working with the course content in a self-paced approach. The interview analysis provided evidence for earlier studies' claims that self-paced course work is a great advantage in online course design (Garrison, 2016; Hew & Cheung, 2014; Vaughan et al., 2013). "Unfortunately, I was not able to join the webinars, but we shared the recordings of the webinars, ppt slides among us after the webinar had ended. Therefore, I had a chance to catch up. Thank you" stated T2.

Both in questionnaires and interviews, teachers indicated that they were challenged by time constraints in their interaction with the course content and community members for a variety of reasons (e.g., workload). As an example, T3 elaborated on such challenges, as demonstrated below.

The pacing can be a little bit difficult for me because I have lots of things to do. So, it was a self-paced course. So, trying to catch up with everything was kind of difficult for me. But I created time ... I was careful with my time, and I caught up with you. But I couldn't respond to questions that other participants or mentors asked me because I was trying to catch up with the topic. That's why I couldn't respond to some of the questions. (T3)

Findings from the questionnaire confirmed this. One of the participants remarked: "Making time despite my busy work schedule to do justice to this session and read the suggested resources has meant sacrificing rest, sleep and some personal commitment in the last five weeks". Despite time restriction, however, the encouragement of participants to work at their own pace, sharing notes and recordings of meetings, a view recording and/or revisit resources all seemed to have a positive impact on the perception of the course. "Unfortunately, I was not able to join the webinars, but we shared the recordings of the webinars, and PowerPoint slides among ourselves after the webinar had ended. Therefore, I had a chance to catch up. I thank you" (T2). This sharing and accumulation of the online content also leaves a sustainable digital trail for participants to pursue. T4 called this feature "foreverness", commenting:

You need to touch people, and all the knowledge shared makes that. How can I say this, I don't know. But foreverness... even though you are not in this world, it ends...you give a kind of..., as a flower that goes everywhere. So, this is something that I want to comment on this course. (T4)

This comment implies that life of an online professional community may extend beyond the lifespan of the course (5 weeks in this case) if it is designed to leave a digital and 'everlasting' trail for members to sustain their interaction with the course content and shared materials .

Course Content: Deciding on the Input

Another factor which teachers considered to be one of the main benefits was the course content. According to the responses, several features of the online course were considered invaluable, including hands-on practice, the wide ranging input, live sessions with language assessment experts to wrap up the weekly content, as well as focus and guidance on Information and Communication Technologies (ICT) tools for use in classroom-based assessment.

Scope of the Input

Some stated that scope of the course input, i.e., classroom-based assessment, closely matched the teachers' assessment needs.

I haven't ever participated in a course which is covered all areas in assessment. So, if I managed to attend some courses, or webinars, it was specifically related to one skill, for example, speaking, or writing or just formative or summative assessment, but this course helped me to brush up all my knowledge together, just to get all the ideas and it was kind of intensive, concentrated source of skills on assessments, it was really valuable. (T5)

Many other participants similarly deemed the course input beneficial for their professional development and classroom practice. T2, for example, suggested: "The resources you have provided are also very important and useful for us". In addition, T1 affirmed that these input materials would guide their future practice as well, saying: "I keep them, and I will use them and out whenever I need them".

Hands-On Practice

Course participants expressed positive perceptions regarding the follow-up tasks, which required teachers to put into practice the theoretical knowledge conveyed in the course input. To illustrate, T5 asserted that "weekly tasks were really essential in enhancing my knowledge". Hands-on tasks also seemed to improve teachers' attitudes to designing their own assessment tools. T4, for example, noted that although for some participants, a task involving designing an assessment task elicited negative attitudes such as reluctance and even withdrawal from the course, personally, T4 regained her/his confidence, as demonstrated in the following comment.

You know, when you asked us to design our own tasks, I would say 'I would never do that', and I wanted to, you know, delete my old messages, email, and account, and just leave the course. But the discussion boards were really helpful, because I could see that others are working on it, and they have delivered the tasks, and I just had a look at what they did. And, you know, it increased my level of confidence. And I started to think about my own assessment tasks, and I designed one, and right now, I can talk about assessment criteria, I can talk about the, you know, maybe technology in assessment, how important is peer feedback, how important is in alternative assessment. So, it really helped. (T4)

Consequently, T4 reported being able to complete the required task, and came to consider this hand-on experience as 'the best part' of the assessment course: "I guess, the part that we were supposed to design the tests and receive feedback from our peers, and, you know, the course, developers Yeah, that was the best part of it".

Live Sessions

Weekly synchronous sessions with educators and researchers in the domain were scheduled to conclude each week's work, and these were deemed 'helpful', as indicated in the following comment: "Each module we had webinars, and they were really helpful" (T1). In addition, the opportunity to interact with assessment experts was seen as the 'strength', which increased overall interest in the course, as pointed out by T1: "I was so interested. I was so excited because I always read their work. And I had a chance to listen to them in a live webinar. And they were the strength of our course". It is also noteworthy that the words "our course" T1 tended to highlight a sense of belonging, an ownership of the course and the community. Synchronous meetings allowing communication between teachers from diverse educational backgrounds seemed to contribute to this social bonding and professional sharing.

T4 also suggested that these meetings brought encouragement to gain a wider perspective into the work already done in the field, and the work that remains to be done: "The lecturers talked about their own research and the work that they have done in the area, I could see, you know, maybe some gaps that can be better identified". It can be inferred that these meetings may have encouraged teachers to identify their own assessment needs and inspired them to adopt an inquiry-based approach into their assessment practices.

Interview findings are in line with questionnaires, particularly, on the benefits of guest speakers with relevant expertise. One of the comments indicated that "the most enlightening part was the live meetings with experts and researchers in language assessment". Another participant concurs that these meetings were enlightening because they provided the opportunity to interact with the speakers: "The weekly live sessions with eminent guests, who gave the attendees ample time for questions, were extremely satisfying". The synchronous live sessions were generally perceived to support teacher learning in assessment: "Weekly webinars were really supportive for me. Thanks to these webinars, I took some important notes".

Information Communication Technologies (ICT) Tools

Teachers reported being satisfied with their learning about online tools for integration into their assessment and teaching practices.

I really like that we learned about the digital tools that we can use while we are assessing our students formatively. For example, I have newly learned Flipgrid. These digital tools are really important, and I believe that they will be very helpful for my assessment and teaching practices. As you know, we sometimes have online learning. I am lucky to have known about these tools. (T1)

Another teacher stated that participants had become 'deeply engaged' in the use of ICT in the course. This deep engagement into online tools was made possible through the follow up tasks, "projects", which required sharing of response to these tasks via the suggested web tools listed on the course website.

Online tools are a really popular topic these days and after? I gained some background on online tools, we were engaged deeply in a lot of projects related to that. And it was interesting for me to see what other people could share with that, and I was happy to share my ideas...the online tools I used in my practice. (T5)

In addition, according to T5, sharing and interaction within the community through engagement with tasks and activities guided her, allowing her to better contextualize the use of ICT in assessment. Similarly, T4 concurred that resources shared in the course guided her learning about educational technology in assessment, and enabled her to operationalize ideas and theory in daily practice:

I'm interested in the role of technology in assessment. And some of these sources were introduced. You introduced one book that I found in the resource materials. And yeah, I guess it can help me much better to get to know how we can use technology in our system". (T4)

Consequently, teachers tended to appreciate the course content because it integrated and showcased a wide range of information about educational technology in assessment, bringing more positive attitudes, and this, in turn, impacted their course evaluation.

Delivery of the Course Content: The Process

According to the participants, the success of the process was attributable to three key factors: facilitative interaction, constructive peer-feedback, and the existence of supportive moderators.

Facilitative Interaction

The course design allowed asynchronous and synchronous participant interaction, which was appreciated, as indicated in the following: "Interaction happened in our discussion boards, and in our online meetings, also weekly meetings" (T1). Clearly, interaction was deemed among the most beneficial aspects of the course since it facilitated critical reflection. This interaction was reported as existing within the whole community and influenced the development of positive perceptions towards the course, in line with other studies (Shea et al., 2001; Banerjee & Duflo, 2014). In addition, one participant indicated:

Reflection from the peers on the platforms from other participants, really enriched my professional growth in assessment because you see that these people are engaged in assessment. It was very interesting to learn from other people and learn more. Seeing what they think was really helpful. (T5)

The same participant also explained that the community interaction helped her to develop a better understanding of her own existing assessment knowledge and ideas, and she reports that this interaction helped her redesign her schemata of the key concepts regarding language assessment.

I'm really grateful to be here on this course, because exactly this course helped me to brush up all my knowledge and revealed a lot of ideas that, probably, I had heard before, but now, it was more clearly out in the light for me, probably because of the communication because of discussion. (T5)

T5 concluded that she was better able to construct meaning thanks to dialogic interaction in the community, and T2 concurred, saying: "Thanks to these interactions, I had the chance to remember my previous practices, and I had a chance to reinforce to validate my knowledge, for example, assessing young learners". Another participant suggested that interaction acted as a mechanism for benchmarking one's assessment ideas and beliefs: "You write your comments in the discussion and when people give you comments, maybe you understand that some of your ideas can be wrong" (T4). It is important to note here that many participants pointed out that efficient communication requires a context that is 'stress free' and socially amicable, as demonstrated in the following: "Actually, the atmosphere was totally stress free. We shared our feelings, our opinions" (T2).

It was also suggested that interaction within the community contributed to the positive perception of the course since participants had an opportunity to hear about practices in diverse educational contexts. "It was always interesting to see how other people, how other professionals, colleagues from other countries think about classroom assessment". This interaction appeared to raise teachers' awareness towards assessment practices in different contexts, exemplified by the following comment: "When I read their comments, I understand that! Wow…They have a different way of assessing than my country. I mean, in some cases, so I get this benefit" (T4).

Constructive Peer-Feedback

Another dimension that contributes to learning in this online community was perceived as peer feedback. To illustrate, T4 explained how the process contributed to her professional learning within the course: "There was a teacher, she sent us feedback after we sent our documents assessment document. I got a better concept about, you know, the rating scales, and the related topic about rating scales". T5, had a slightly different experience, and reported that although initially skeptical towards peer feedback practices, they experienced a change in attitude after observing how freely accessible peer feedback was in the online community through open-access written dialogue.

I always consider peer feedback a bit of a dull and boring topic. And I must admit that when my colleagues and I attend each other's classes at my school, I hate giving feedback. So that's all very formal. In my case, feedback, that was really a thing I hated. But here I see that people will deal with that calmly and professionally. This course helped me to accept it and convinced me to look at it again and use it in my teaching because I saw it in practice. I mean, I saw it in real life that people do use feedback in their practice. It convinced me that it's not such a dreary thing. (T5)

Consequently, participants came to consider peer feedback as a valuable course component which provides counterevidence to Kirschner (2012) and Krause (2013), two prominent studies claiming that peer feedback tasks are a source of dissatisfaction. One participant even stated: "Giving feedback was the most beautiful thing about the course" (T6).

Supportive Moderators

Participants tended to emphasize the contribution of moderators in their positive evaluation of the course and seemed to equate working with the mentors as valuable experience in 'training'. T2 indicated: "Without hesitation, our moderators also supported us. Actually. It was training for me. When I had a problem, and I wrote one of the mentors an email, you immediately answered my email, and you facilitated me throughout the process, then I was able to finish this course. I learned many things from mentors". Mentors' timely response and moderation were seen as fundamental to learning and these helpful attitudes contributed to community members' course satisfaction.

Perceived Learning and Course Satisfaction: The Product

A clear, but rather intangible end-product was the participants' reference to their perceived learning about LAL in the interviews, while the percentages obtained through the end-of-course questionnaire provided a more tangible statistical basis for their course satisfaction.

Learning in an Online Community and Improvement of LAL Knowledge

In their course evaluation, participants referred to the affordances of learning professionally in an online community, which they reported was enabled by a perceived improvement in their LAL knowledge. One expressed her appreciation of the course, stressing that it covered a deficiency in LAL that was left by her formal teacher education:

I must mention that I've never studied assessment at our university. We didn't have any subject related to assessment. Assessment was covered really very generally. For example, if it's good, that is the high grade, and if it's poor, that is the low grade. So, we never studied formative assessment or validity, reliability. These ideas were really difficult for me and another reason why this course was really unique and invaluable for me that it had a lot of suggested literature on these topics, and I had to go through validity and reliability again and again, because these terms are quite confusing. (T5)

In contrast, another participant highlighted that despite receiving training in assessment in formal teacher education, nevertheless, the course made an important further contribution to professional development in LAL: "I have known some of these issues, these topics, but I believe that I have learned new things. For example, for assessing the speaking for assessing the productive skills such as speaking and writing (T2)".

In a similar vein, T1 outlined the benefits of the course, stating:

This course benefited me in learning more about the basic assessment skills. How to assess them, and also for the validity and reliability of the assessment. So, for assessing listening and speaking skill, I learned that we need to fix the criteria or rubrics first, then we have to move forward. (T1)

Consequently, gains in experience and information were cited by those participating in the course, and these gains were facilitated by teachers' reflection, and better-informed assessment practices. To illustrate these benefits, the quotation below shows how T3 was able to influence her/his own institution's assessment practices.

So, after taking this course, I started to evaluate my assessment activities in the class, especially the formative ones. I try to evaluate myself and my assessment task more. And I even contribute to the testing office about their formative assessment when I evaluate the task they created. And I told them maybe we can make it more reliable by adding another rater in the class. And they find it really useful. And maybe next year, not this semester, but next year, we'll be using that too. (T3)

Interviews findings resonate with the questionnaire outcomes, as responses also indicate perceived improvement of LAL through "better understanding and reliability and validity of an assessment". Another anonymous comment indicated: "I have learned a lot about key concepts of assessments and assessment tools" (T5). Others noted the expansion of knowledge in different domains of LAL:

While taking the LAL EVO22 course I learned a lot about the language assessment principles as a whole and its peculiarities for each of four skills (reading, listening, speaking, and writing). I have become more aware of the authenticity and validity of the tests I use in my classroom. I am sure it will help me select more appropriate ones (T4).

The course was seen by one as "a useful refresher on the basic notions of assessment", i.e., it helped participants gain insights into LAL. Furthermore, the course was considered to have raised awareness about assessment literacy needs, and encouraged teachers to set themselves further goals for improvement of LAL, as reflected in the following comment:

Before this course, I had thought that my knowledge about testing and assessment in language teaching was good enough, but I realized that I learnt many things, especially teaching and assessment of reading and speaking. I was introduced to digital tools which can be used for formative assessment. Also, I was provided with extra information about washback. I really like assessment. I want to learn a lot of information about preparing tests, writing test items and item analysis (T6).

In sum, the above-mentioned aspects of learning in an online community seemed to reinforce participants' generally positive views of the course.

Course Satisfaction

The results of the questionnaire indicated positive perceptions of the course. A majority of the participants (77%) expressed positive opinions in terms of their satisfaction, and considerable number (69%) also conceived that they were able to improve their LAL. The interaction within the online community was perceived as 'good' by most (69%). Course content (77%), weekly tasks (77%), and synchronous meetings (6%2) were also deemed highly positive, due to their contribution to contributed to the participants' perceived LAL development (see Table 3).

Table 3. Participants' overall course satisfaction

	SD	D	PA	TA	Mean	Mode	Std
I am satisfied with the course	23	0	0	77	3.3	4	1.31
My knowledge in LAL expanded	23	0	8	69	3.2	4	1.30
Interaction within the online community was good	15	8	8	69	3.3	4	1.18
Weekly synchronous meetings were beneficial for my professional development.	23	15	0	62	3.1	4	1.28
Weekly tasks helped me improve my LAL knowledge	23	0	0	77	3.3	4	1.32
I liked and learnt from the course content presented on Canvas platform.	23	0	0	77	3.3	4	1.32

CONCLUSION

This chapter has outlined the components for the evaluation of an online training (LAL4P) specifically designed to improve language teachers' assessment literacy, and how these components are seen in the eyes of the participants. Following the premises of Stufflebeam's (2003) CIPP model of course evaluation, the findings indicated four main focal areas in the evaluation of an online course on Language Assessment Literacy for Practitioners: a course design based on learners' needs, course content, delivery of the content, and the product.

The results support findings of the earlier studies, which emphasize the importance of putting learner needs and needs analysis at the heart of course design. First, the participants described an effective online LAL course design, citing the factors of blending theory and practice, involving multimodality using visual and textual sources, and enabling self-paced learning. Secondly, the results offer a sub-categorization of the elements involved in a favorable course content. The participants considered that course content was meaningful due to its clarity in goals and instructions, which were clearly outlined to them, in line with the views of Young (2013), and Kucuk & Richardson (2019). Other reported elements of meaningful content included purposeful selection of the weekly tasks, supporting Sun et al. (2008), Conache et al. (2016), Xi et al. (2018), and Mehall (2020), as well as live sessions on Zoom in providing consolidation, and use of ICT tools appropriate for the purpose of the tasks. Third, the facilitative interaction among participants through online discussion boards, (c.f. Aloni and Harrington, 2018), peer feedback tasks, and moderator support were identified as favorable methods for delivering online course content in a LAL setting, supporting others' similar findings on interaction (Banerjee & Duflo, Dinh & Ngyuen, 2020; 2014; Shea et al., 2001). Finally, the LAL course participants cited benefits of a successful course outcome regarding their perceived LAL improvement, and their overall course satisfaction included elements from all three other components of course evaluation. The reported positive associations between perceived learning and course satisfaction further confirms Yousaf et al.'s (2022) conclusions.

As a final remark, it is possible to conclude that delving into the participants' world eventually leads not only to an understanding of benefits, but also, towards the identification of challenges; their perceptions can reveal challenges faced in the online course, such as technical difficulties, course navigation issues, or unclear instructions. As stated by Huang & Liaw (2018), identifying and addressing these challenges can improve the overall user experience and reduce barriers to successful course completion. In addition, eliciting students' perceptions can serve as an authentic form of assessment, allowing instructors to measure the course's impact on knowledge, skills, and attitudes. This approach can provide evidence of the course's effectiveness in meeting its learning objectives and identifying areas for further improvement. Finally, participant perceptions are vital for continuous improvement; online courses are dynamic, and subject to constant updates and revisions, and eliciting students' perceptions can serve as a feedback loop for continuous improvement. Regularly analyzing students' perceptions can help instructors and course designers make informed decisions about updates and modifications to maintain the relevance and effectiveness of courses. These findings naturally have implications for online course designers and teacher educators in the field of Language Assessment Literacy, but the nature of this research, i.e., the investigation of online courses features with the aim of increasing quality standards, has a wider application to online courses in general, regardless of disciplines.

ACKNOWLEDGMENT

This research received no specific grant from any funding agency in the public, commercial, or not-for-profit sectors.

REFERENCES

Ali, S., Uppal, M. A., & Gulliver, S. R. (2018). A conceptual framework highlighting e-learning implementation barriers. *Information Technology & People*, *31*(1), 156–180. doi:10.1108/ITP-10-2016-0246

Aloni, M., & Harrington, C. (2018). Research based practices for improving the effectiveness of asynchronous online discussion boards. *Scholarship of Teaching and Learning in Psychology*, *4*(4), 271–289. doi:10.1037tl0000121

Aristovnik, A., Keržič, D., Ravšelj, D., Tomaževič, N., & Umek, L. (2020). Impacts of the COVID-19 pandemic on life of higher education students: A global perspective. *Sustainability (Basel)*, *12*(20), 8438. doi:10.3390u12208438

Banerjee, A. V., & Duflo, E. (2014). (Dis) organization and success in an economics MOOC. *The American Economic Review*, *104*(5), 514–518. doi:10.1257/aer.104.5.514 PMID:25214652

Berenson, R., Boyles, G., & Weaver, A. (2008). Emotional intelligence as a predictor of success in online learning. *International Review of Research in Open and Distance Learning*, *9*(2), 1–17. doi:10.19173/irrodl.v9i2.385

Breslow, L., Pritchard, D. E., DeBoer, J., Stump, G. S., Ho, A. D., & Seaton, D. T. (2013). Studying learning in the worldwide classroom research into edX's first MOOC. *Research & Practice in Assessment*, *8*, 13–25.

Choudhury, S., & Pattnaik, S. (2020). Emerging themes in e-learning: A review from the stakeholders' perspective. *Computers & Education*, *144*, 103657. doi:10.1016/j.compedu.2019.103657

Chow, A., & Leung, P. (2011). Assessment for learning in language classrooms. In *R*. Berry and B.

Conache, M., Dima, R., & Mutu, A. (2016). A comparative analysis of MOOC (Massive Open Online Course) platforms. *Informatica Economica*, *20*(2).

Coombe, C., Troudi, S., & Al-Hamly, M. (2012). Foreign and second language teacher assessment literacy: Issues, challenges and recommendations. In C. Coombe, P. Davidson, B. O'Sullivan, & S. Stoynoff (Eds.), *The Cambridge Guide to Second Language Assessment* (pp. 20–29). Cambridge University Press.

Dinh, L. P., & Nguyen, T. T. (2020). Pandemic, social distancing, and social work education: Students' satisfaction with online education in Vietnam. *Social Work Education*, *39*(8), 1074–1083. doi:10.1080/02615479.2020.1823365

Fulcher, G. (2012). Assessment literacy for the language classroom. *Language Assessment Quarterly*, *9*(2), 113–132. doi:10.1080/15434303.2011.642041

Garrison, D. R. (2016). *E-learning in the 21st century: A community of inquiry framework for research and practice*. Routledge.

Gokmenoglu, T., Dasci Sonmez, E., Yavuz, I., & Gok, I. (2021). Turkish Ministry of National Education school-based disaster education program: A preliminary results of the program evaluation. *International Journal of Disaster Risk Reduction*, *52*, 101943. doi:10.1016/j.ijdrr.2020.101943

Haberstroh, S., Duffey, T., Marble, E., & Ivers, N. N. (2014). Assessing student-learning outcomes within a counselor education program. *Counseling Outcome Research and Evaluation*, *5*(1), 28–38. doi:10.1177/2150137814527756

Halimi, F., AlShammari, I., & Navarro, C. (2020). Emotional intelligence and academic achievement in higher education. *Journal of Applied Research in Higher Education*.

Hargreaves, E. (2013). Assessment for learning and teacher learning communities: UK teachers' experiences. *Teaching Education*, *24*(3), 327–344. doi:10.1080/10476210.2012.713931

Hegji, A. (2017). An overview of accreditation of higher education in the United States. *CRS Report No. R43826*. CRS. https://fas.org/sgp/crs/misc/R43826.pdf

Hew, K. F., & Cheung, W. S. (2014). Students' and instructors' use of massive open online courses (MOOCs): Motivations and challenges. *Educational Research Review*, *12*, 45–58. doi:10.1016/j.edurev.2014.05.001

Hew, K. F., Jia, C., Gonda, D. E., & Bai, S. (2020). Transitioning to the "new normal" of learning in unpredictable times: Pedagogical practices and learning performance in fully online flipped classrooms. *International Journal of Educational Technology in Higher Education*, *17*(1), 1–22. doi:10.118641239-020-00234-x PMID:34778516

Kauffman, H. (2015). A review of predictive factors of student success in and satisfaction with online learning. *Research in Learning Technology*, *23*. doi:10.3402/rlt.v23.26507

Kirschner, A. (2012). A pioneer in online education tries a MOOC. *The Chronicle of Higher Education*.

Krause, S. D. (2013). MOOC Response about "Listening to World Music.". *College Composition and Communication*, *64*(4), 689–695. https://www.jstor.org/stable/43490786

Kucuk, S., & Richardson, J. C. (2019). A Structural Equation Model of Predictors of Online Learners' Engagement and Satisfaction. *Online Learning : the Official Journal of the Online Learning Consortium*, *23*(2), 196–216. doi:10.24059/olj.v23i2.1455

Lave, J., & Wenger, E. (1991). *Situated learning: Legitimate peripheral participation*. Cambridge University Press. doi:10.1017/CBO9780511815355

Literat, I. (2015). Implications of massive open online courses for higher education: Mitigating or reifying educational inequities? *Higher Education Research & Development*, *34*(6), 1164–1177. doi:10.1080/07294360.2015.1024624

Malone, M. (2008). Training in language assessment. In E. Shoha-my & N. Hornberger (Eds.), Encyclopedia of language and education. Language Testing and Assessment (2nd ed., pp. 225-239). New York: Springer Science+Business Media. doi:10.1007/978-0-387-30424-3_178

Marinoni, G., Van't Land, H., & Jensen, T. (2020). The impact of Covid-19 on higher education around the world. *IAU global survey report, 23*.

Mehall, S. (2020). Purposeful Interpersonal Interaction in Online Learning: What Is It and How Is It Measured? *Online Learning : the Official Journal of the Online Learning Consortium*, *24*(1), 182–204. doi:10.24059/olj.v24i1.2002

Oflaz, M., Diker Coskun, Y., & Bolat, O. (2022). The Effects of the Technology-Integrated Writing Lessons: CIPP Model of Evaluation. *The Turkish Online Journal of Educational Technology*, *21*(1), 157–179.

Schleicher, A. (2020). *The impact of COVID-19 on education: Insights from education at a glance 2020*. OECD. https://www. oecd. org/education/the-impact-of-covid-19-on-e ducation-insights-education-at-a-glance-2020. pdf

Shea, P., Swan, K., Fredericksen, E., & Pickett, A. (2001). Student Satisfaction and Reported Learning in the SUNY Learning Network: Interaction and Beyond-Social Presence in Asynchronous Learning Networks. SUNY.

Shih, Y. C., & Yuan, Y. P. (2019). Evaluating an English Elite Program in Taiwan using the CIPP Model. *Journal of Asia TEFL*, *16*(1), 200–219. doi:10.18823/asiatefl.2019.16.1.13.200

Steyn, C., Davies, C., & Sambo, A. (2019). Eliciting student feedback for course development: The application of a qualitative course evaluation tool among business research students. *Assessment & Evaluation in Higher Education*, *44*(1), 11–24. doi:10.1080/02602938.2018.1466266

Stufflebeam, D. L. (2003). The CIPP Model for evaluation. In T. Kellaghan & D. L. Stufflebeam (Eds.), *International Handbook of Educational Evaluation* (pp. 31–62). Springer. doi:10.1007/978-94-010-0309-4_4

Sun, P. C., Tsai, R. J., Finger, G., Chen, Y. Y., & Yeh, D. (2008). What drives successful e-Learning? An empirical investigation of the critical factors influencing learner satisfaction. *Computers & Education*, *50*(4), 1183–1202. doi:10.1016/j.compedu.2006.11.007

Tsimaras, D. O., Mystakidis, S., Christopoulos, A., Zoulias, E., & Hatzilygeroudis, I. (2022). E-Learning Courses Evaluation on the Basis of Trainees' Feedback on Open Questions Text Analysis. *Education Sciences*, *12*(9), 633. doi:10.3390/educsci12090633

Vaughan, N. D., Cleveland-Innes, M., & Garrison, D. R. (2013). *Teaching in blended learning environments: Creating and sustaining communities of inquiry*. Athabasca University Press. doi:10.15215/aupress/9781927356470.01

Vogt, K., & Tsagari, D. (2014). Assessment literacy of foreign language teachers: Findings of a European study. *Language Assessment Quarterly*, *11*(4), 374–402. doi:10.1080/15434303.2014.960046

Xi, J., Chen, Y., & Wang, G. (2018). Design of a Personalized Massive Open Online Course Platform. *International Journal of Emerging Technologies in Learning*, *13*(4), 58–70. doi:10.3991/ijet.v13i04.8470

Young, J. R. (2013). What professors can learn from 'hard core' MOOC students. *The Chronicle of Higher Education*, *59*(37), 58–70. doi:10.3991/ijet.v13i04.8470

Yousaf, H. Q., Rehman, S., Ahmed, M., & Munawar, S. (2022). Investigating students' satisfaction in online learning: The role of students' interaction and engagement in universities. *Interactive Learning Environments*, 1–18. doi:10.1080/10494820.2022.2061009

KEY TERMS AND DEFINITIONS

Collaborative Learning: Collaborative learning is an educational approach in which learners work in groups and/or pairs to process and synthesize information and concepts through working together.

Community of Practice: A community of practice (CoP) refers to a group of people who come together, face to face or online, to share a common concern, a set of problems, and best practices to construct knowledge to improve a field of professional practice.

Continuous Professional Development: Continuous professional development (CPD) refers to the life-long learning and the learning activities professionals engage in to develop, maintain and improve their knowledge, skills, experience, and understanding.

Course Evaluation: The process of surveying learner ideas at the end of a class or course to elicit general information on what learners liked and disliked about the course with the goal of improving the instructional design and educational experience.

Language Assessment Literacy: Language Assessment Literacy (LAL) refers to the knowledge and skills that stakeholders involved in assessment practices are required to have to conduct and use assessment tasks.

Online Learning: Learning in a virtual environment on the internet.

Online Learning Platforms: An online learning platform is a webspace which is used to host educational content and provide learners with resources (i.e. videos, oral and written materials) and means (i.e. Discussion boards) for learning.

APPENDIX

End-of-Course Questionnaire

Purpose of the Survey

Please complete this questionnaire (based on Vogt, Tsagari & Spanoudis 2014) in order to help us to adapt future LAL EVOs to your needs, and evaluate the success of LAL EVO22 at the end. We would also like to report about the impact of EVO 2022 to a wider audience and in various academic work. Your responses to the survey will help us to do this.

Data Protection

Data collected in this survey will be treated confidentially and will not be used except for the purposes mentioned above. When we report on responses your responses will remain anonymous.

Informed Consent

By filling out and submitting this survey you indicate your acceptance of the uses of your data explained under 'Purpose of the survey' above. If you have any questions and/or concerns, please email researchers.

Survey

There are 10 questions, and it will probably take around 10 minutes. Please read each statement carefully and respond to the questions in each item.

1. What have been the main benefits of LAL EVO22 for you? (Please write as much as you like)
2. What have been the main difficulties related to this EVO for you, and what (if anything) have you done to overcome them? (Please write as much as you like)
   (Items 3-8) To what extent do you agree or disagree with the following statements.
   I totally agree / I partially agree. / I disagree. / I totally disagree.
3. I am satisfied with the course.
4. LAL EVO22 helped me to expand my knowledge in LAL.
5. I liked interacting with colleagues and reading their comments on the Discussion boards.
6. Weekly online (and recorded) meetings were beneficial for my professional development.
7. Weekly tasks helped me improve my LAL knowledge.
8. I liked and learnt from the content presented on Canvas platform.
9. Are there any features of LAL EVO23 about which you'd like to tell us more?
10. How confident do you feel to engage in assessment activities?

Chapter 9
Digital Assessment Literacy:
English Assessment Practice in Vietnam

Thuy Thai
University of Huddersfield, UK

Susan Sheehan
https://orcid.org/0000-0003-4471-3929
University of Huddersfield, UK

Quynh Thi Ngoc Nguyen
https://orcid.org/0000-0001-6286-5139
University of Languages and International Studies, Vietnam National University, Hanoi, Vietnam

Thao Thi Phuong Nguyen
University of Languages and International Studies, Vietnam National University, Hanoi, Vietnam

Yen Thi Quynh Nguyen
https://orcid.org/0009-0004-2378-7472
University of Languages and International Studies, Vietnam National University, Hanoi, Vietnam

Hien Thi Thu Tran
University of Languages and International Studies, Vietnam National University, Hanoi, Vietnam

Chi Thi Nguyen
University of Languages and International Studies, Vietnam National University, Hanoi, Vietnam

Hoa Quynh Nguyen
University of Languages and International Studies, Vietnam National University, Hanoi, Vietnam

Sao Bui
University of Languages and International Studies, Vietnam National University, Hanoi, Vietnam

ABSTRACT

This chapter reports on a project explored which classroom-based English language assessment practices, with a particular emphasis on digital assessments, in Vietnam. A mixed-method approach to data collection was adopted to understand the current assessment landscape. The methods include questionnaire (N = 2569) and teaching observations with follow-up interviews (N =7). The results of the project revealed what were behind teachers' choices of assessment tasks in their classroom, the use of assess-

DOI: 10.4018/978-1-6684-6227-0.ch009

Digital Assessment Literacy

ment feedback and the challenges faced by the teachers in their practices in online environment. The project has extended an understanding of the current assessment landscape in Vietnam. Discussions on how the data has informed an online toolkit which will provide assessment and testing resources and recommendation for best practices will be presented as effective assessment can support and promote learning, and as Crusan et al. point out it is the students who lose out if assessment practices are poor.

INTRODUCTION

This chapter reports on a project which explored classroom-based English language assessment practices, with a particular emphasis on digital assessments, in Vietnam. The project used a mixed-method approach to data collection to understand the current assessment landscape. The methods include questionnaire and teaching observations with follow-up interviews. The participants came from all stages of education and from both state and private provision. This chapter, thus, examines literature around digital assessment, focusing on three core themes: teachers' choices of online assessments, the challenges of conducting online assessments in general and the use of feedback in online classes in particular. These themes are explored through the prism of Language Assessment Literacy (LAL). A discussion of our project's findings in relation to the literature will be presented, followed by a conclusion and recommendations.

Assessment refers to the activities of measuring learners' achievement and progress in a learning process. Assessment plays a crucial role in all kinds of teaching and learning systems in formal education (Wiliam, 2011) as it can provide useful information to determine if the goals of education are being met. Effective assessment can support and promote learning (Berry et. al., 2019); thus, it is important that teachers are able to conduct assessment activities effectively and efficiently. It is argued that for the success of assessment activities to be guaranteed, teachers may need to acquire certain "knowledge, skills and abilities [...] to design, develop, maintain, or evaluate, large-scale standardized and/or classroom-based tests, familiarity with test processes, and awareness of principles and concepts that guide and underpin practice, including ethics and codes of practice" (Fulcher, 2012, p. 125). The term language assessment literacy is used to encapsulate this body of knowledge, skills and abilities.

Numerous studies have explored teachers' assessment knowledge and practice, for example teachers' knowledge and practice in assessment task design in Asia (Koh et al., 2018), teachers' beliefs regarding assessment literacy materials in North America (Malone, 2013), assessment training needs in Europe (Fulcher, 2012; Vogt & Tsagari, 2014), writing assessment from a worldwide perspective (Crusan et al., 2016). These studies seem to suggest that teachers have inadequate levels of assessment knowledge, and that teaching context may have an impact on assessment literacy and teachers' assessment philosophy. However, while research exists on how teachers engage in assessment in traditional classroom settings, little work has examined the nature of assessment in online classrooms (Krishnan et al., 2021). The key features of online learning and assessment are considered below.

Online learning refers to a form of education whereby instructions and interactions between teachers and learners are conducted in a fully virtual environment with the support of the internet and/or web-based technologies (Gikandi et al., 2011). This new method of instruction has received increased attention from different stakeholders, including teachers, researchers, parents and students (Pu & Xu, 2021); one of the main concerns is the quality of assessment (Alavi et al., 2021). There has been a call for online assessment to be redesigned so that it can meet the primary purpose of assisting learners to achieve their learning goals in an online learning environment (Akimov et al., 2018). This is because teachers found it challenging to monitor their students' learning progress effectively without seeing their students in the same physical place (Cheng et al., 2013). Pu and Xu's (2021) study further supported this finding as they provided evidence that teachers were found to face difficulties in implementing assessments in the online environment. Pu and Xu suggested that the difficulties can be explained by the fact that teachers may not have a thorough understanding of the connection between learning and assessment in an online curriculum. In addition, Waycott et al. (2010; 2013) argue that similar to traditional learning settings, differences in learners' ability and backgrounds (nations and/or socio-economic groups) may contribute to variations in the effectiveness levels of online learning.

For these reasons, in this study we explored what assessment practices were conducted in remote teaching in Vietnam, including teachers' attitudes towards online assessment, teachers' choices of assessment instruments, the challenges teachers have experienced in this new teaching environment and teachers' feedback delivery. This study is part of a bigger project which investigated the current practice of English language assessment in Vietnam with an aim to develop an understanding of teachers' experience with assessment in online classes. The following research questions (RQ) have been explored.

RQ1: What were teachers' attitude towards online assessments?
RQ2: What were the reasons for their choices of assessment in their online classes?
RQ3: How was feedback implemented by teachers?
RQ4: What challenges were experienced by teacher when conducting online assessments?

LITERATURE REVIEW

As this study examined teachers' online assessment practice by exploring their choices of assessment activities, and the challenges they face while implementing the activities, this section reviews relevant literature related to these issues. Additionally, as feedback plays an important role in transforming learning, the study also aimed to unpack how feedback was delivered in online classes. Thus, a third sub-theme of this section reviews previous studies which investigated how teachers delivered their feedback in online learning environment.

Teachers' Choices of Online Assessments

There are a multitude of assessment instruments which can be employed in classrooms for teachers to collect observable evidence to make inferences about students' learning. These include both conventional ones such as tests or written assignments and unconventional examples such as one-sentence summaries, student-generated test questions or minute papers (Brookhart, 2013). Regarding the online learning environment, the majority of online assessments rely on written outputs from students as evidence of their performance, manifest in online exams, in virtual discussion boards, in portfolios, and by written essays (Cheng et al., 2013; Gikandi et al., 2011). In order to evaluate learners' spoken outputs, oral examinations and video presentations are also conducted (Fluck, 2019). A range of tools are available for collecting and displaying evidence for online assessment, including web-based testing software, internet-based audio and video platforms, electronic portfolio software, and other digital tools like Google docs and other word-processing software (Moffitt et al., 2020). However, the effectiveness of using these tools is still in question.

Recent research, which investigated how teachers used online assessment activities during the pandemic, seem to indicate that teachers had an inconsistent approach to adapting their assessment activities to an online learning environment. For example, Almossa and Alzaharani (2022) revealed that during the pandemic, formative assessments were rarely used in Saudi universities. The results of their investigation also indicated that the least frequently employed assessment practices involved incorporating curriculum expectations into summative assessments, addressing the cultural and linguistic diversity of students, and providing accommodations for students with special needs or exceptionalities. In Spain, group assignments became less frequent, while exams contained more multiple-choice questions and fewer essay questions (Panadero et al., 2022). These findings align with other recent studies (Bartolic et al., 2021; Senel & Senel, 2021), which all seem to indicate that selecting and adapting assessment activities to an online learning environment may not be a simple process to teachers. Thus, more research into this area would be able to reveal if the inconsistent approach to assessments may lie in teachers' digital competence and/or they may be a result of inadequate assessment literacy.

Challenges of Implementing Online Assessments

Online learning has become increasingly popular, thanks to the development of modern technologies and learning tools and systems. Language teachers are not only learning to navigate online education but also how to assess language in an online environment, especially in the pandemic when teaching was all conducted online. The design and implementation of assessment in online learning environments has long been a challenge for teachers (Akimov et al., 2018; Benson, 2003). Among different aspects involved in online assessment, understanding the way teachers implemented online assessment, and the challenges they faced is important. The following are some of the studies conducted to understand teachers' assessment practices in online learning environment in different contexts.

Pu and Xu (2021) studied the challenges faced by English as a foreign language (EFL) teachers during the pandemic in China and found that their assessment literacy was a major challenge, particularly in regards to integrating assessment into the online curriculum. The study revealed that the participating teachers were aware of the importance of online assessment but struggled to incorporate it systematically into their online teaching and learning processes. As a result, online assessment was disconnected from the overall online curriculum (Pu & Xu, 2021). In similar vein, Forrester (2020) studied the challenges and the possible solutions associated with moving a group speaking assessment task from face-to-face to online mode upon the outbreak of the pandemic at a university in Hong Kong. The results showed that while teachers had a positive view on the new one-to-one discussion assessment, the students were ambivalent with some preferring the original group discussion mode. The study recommends that a body of administrative, pedagogical, and integrity concerns should be considered along with the teachers and the students' feedback on the new assessment task. Abduh (2021) also investigated teachers' perceptions of the assessment methods used in full-time online learning during a COVID-19 lockdown in a Saudi EFL context. The results showed that the teachers were ambivalent toward online assessment. In addition, it was found that the teachers faced serious challenges in assessing students online.

Furthermore, studies have shown teachers encountered challenges in using self- and peer assessment in online teaching despite a positive face-to-face experience in a fully remote teaching environment (Panadero et al., 2022; Senel & Senel, 2021). This has posed a detrimental effect on student engagement.

For example, over half of the participants in Panadero et al.'s (2022) study reported no benefits from online self-assessment, with an even higher percentage for peer assessment, which saw a sharp decrease in use during remote teaching and learning. The problems encountered by the teachers were primarily related to the online environment, rather than face-to-face teaching. The finding seems to suggest that even though teachers were generally positive about the value of online assessment, students' involvement had diminished. Thus, it is important to understand the reasons behind this phenomenon. Studies which involve observing teachers' implementation of assessment activities in their online classes could enhance the understanding of the extent to which these activities are effective.

The Use of Feedback in Online Classes

Feedback has been widely acknowledged as a vital yet challenging aspect of teaching across a range of global contexts and disciplines, including but not limited to second language education (Evans, 2013; Lee, 2017). The COVID-19 pandemic has exacerbated this challenge, as school closures and the shift to online education have created a novel feedback environment for many teachers. Jiang and Yu's (2021) research revealed that the shift to online teaching heightened teachers' recognition of the importance of feedback and their willingness to provide it, along with the necessity to learn how to use new technologies for feedback. According to Gamage et al. (2020), secondary education showed an increase in feedback delivery, while primary and early childhood education experienced a decrease. This could be due to students in these latter stages relying heavily on teachers for feedback and needing direct observation, which was challenging to achieve in a remote learning setting.

Prior studies on teacher feedback have primarily focused on evaluating its impact on student learning outcomes (Guo & Wei, 2019; Lee, 2017), exploring its relationship with teacher identity (Donaghue, 2020), examining teacher beliefs and practices surrounding feedback (Haniff Mohd Tahir, 2022; Ninković et al., 2021; Thi et al., 2022), or contrasting it with other forms of feedback, such as automated feedback (Link et al., 2020). However, research on teachers' feedback practices in an online learning remains limited. Wilson and Czik (2016) provided insight into the ways in which teachers provided feedback in online learning environments. They proposed that the amount, type, and level of feedback may be altered when incorporating technology-generated feedback into teaching practice. Feedback amount refers to the workload involved in providing feedback whereas feedback type reflects different forms of feedback such as directive, query, informative, and praise (Link et al., 2020). Hattie and Timperly (2007) suggested that the type of feedback and the way it is delivered could vary its effectiveness. Moreover, among different forms of feedback, praise seems to be the least ineffective due to the amount of learning-related information it can provide (Hattie & Timperly, 2007). Feedback level refers to the level of language skills which can be classified as lower-level and higher-level subskills (surface-level and content-level skills) (Link et al., 2020). These studies seem to indicate that teachers' feedback practice could have an impact on students' learning outcomes.

However, enhanced student learning outcomes may not necessarily result from changes in feedback amount, type, and level (Lee, 2021). Jiang et al. (2020) conducted a sociocultural examination and found that for feedback to positively impact student learning, there must also be considerations in four dimensions of feedback: intentionality (being intentional and focused), reciprocity (teacher-student interaction), transcendence (transfer of learning to new situations), and meaning (providing a meaningful learning experience). Technology and feedback tools can aid these practices. However, the extent and longevity of these adaptions and implementations are contingent on individual teacher beliefs, their willingness to offer guidance, and contextual elements such as class size (Jiang et al., 2020).

In terms of teacher beliefs about feedback, previous studies show that teachers have traditionally viewed feedback as a mere transfer of information, resulting in limited student use of the feedback received (Jiang et al., 2019; Lee, 2017). In recent years, there is a growing scholarly call to view feedback as dialogic communication between teachers and students (Carless & Winstone, 2020; Winstone & Carless, 2019). Yet it remains unclear whether such calls have been taken up by teachers and to what extent teachers may adapt their feedback practice accordingly (Jiang & Yu, 2021). Additionally, in light of the pandemic, insights into teachers' online feedback practices, the factors that may shape their practices, and the impact on learning are important (Jiang & Yu, 2021). As teachers' feedback plays a central role in helping students understand their performance, the method or quality of feedback delivery may have a significant impact on students' learning outcomes. Thus, it is necessary to analyse the effects of the emergency remote teaching context on feedback practices.

Regarding Vietnam's context, before the Covid-19 pandemic, online assessment was not popular; thus, research into teachers' online assessment practices is limited. Several attempts have been made to understand teachers' use of online platform such as Kahoot (Nguyen & Yukawa, 2019) and teachers' intentions to use technology in assessments (Tang & Tran, 2022). Tang and Tran's (2022) study seem to indicate that technical support and training may enhance teachers' willingness to use online assessment tools and technology in their classrooms. This finding is consistent with Nguyen and Yukawa's (2019) study which provides more specific evidence that teachers' technology usage may vary depending on different levels of ages. However, the studies have not dealt with what assessment activities were conducted in teachers' online classes and what difficulties, apart from technological skills, they faced in their online assessment practices.

Reviewing the literature reveals several issues about digital assessment practice. The new learning environment, enforced by the Covid-19 pandemic, has witnessed changes in teachers' choices of assessment instruments and in teachers' delivery and use of feedback. Although there are a few studies which tried to unpack the reasons behind these changes, more studies are needed to add further insights into these issues. In addition, it is evident in the literature that teachers seem to be struggling with conducting assessments in their online classrooms and that the quality of their assessments is in question from the researchers' perspective. However, the questions of how teachers view their experiences of online assessments in online classrooms, what they do and why they do what they are doing need more attention in future studies. Answers to these questions are significant as they can provide relevant recommendations to theories and practice, including informing content of training in teacher training programmes, and support in-service teachers, etc.

THEORETICAL FRAMEWORK

Research which explores assessment practices in language classrooms is often considered as being within the field of Language Assessment Literacy (LAL). LAL has been defined by Fulcher (2012) as:

The knowledge, skills and abilities required to design, develop, maintain or evaluate, large scale standardized and/or classroom-based tests, familiarity with test processes, and awareness of principles and concepts that guide and underpin practice, including ethics and codes of practice. The ability to place knowledge, skills, processes, principles and concepts within wider historical, social, political and philosophical frameworks in order [sic] understand why practices have arisen as they have, and to evaluate the role and impact of testing on society, institutions, and individuals. (Fulcher, 2012, p. 125)

As the project sought to determine the rationale for the assessment activities deployed by the teachers who participated in the project, it adopted the Language Assessment Literacy Model for the Teaching Profession (LAL-TEP) model (Villa Larenas, 2021). This model informed both data collection and data analysis. The model (see Figure 1 below) identifies the following as key components of LAL: context, language assessment learning, language assessment knowledge, conceptions of language assessment and language assessment practices.

Figure 1. The LAL-TEP Model
Source: Larenas (2021)

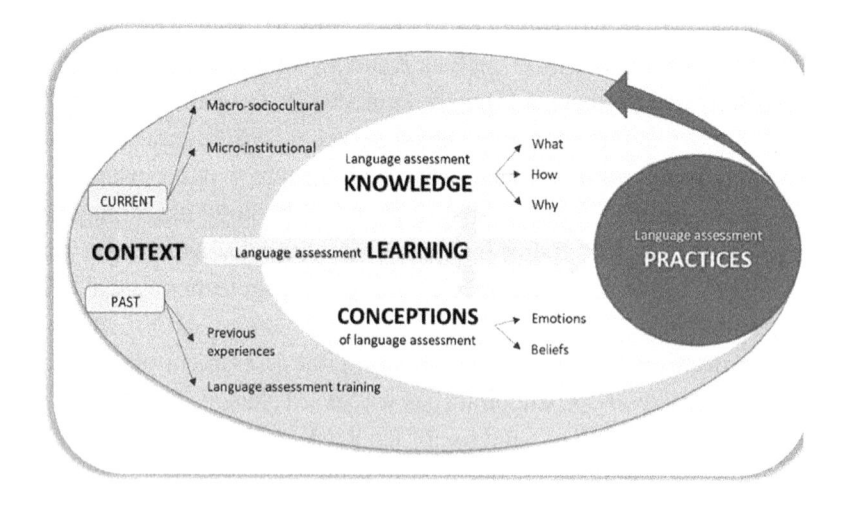

The model is multi-directional, so the context influences language assessment practices and these practices also influence the context. For example, the use of multiple-choice items focussing on knowledge of grammar influences the stakeholders' understanding of the ways in which language should be assessed. In the LAL-TEP model, the importance of context is emphasised. LAL is "… socially constructed (and re-constructed) from and for the specific context in which stakeholders' practices are immersed." (Villa Larenas and Brunfaut, 2022, p. 27)

METHODOLOGY

Design

Following Berry, Sheehan and Munro (2017, p. 203) the study adopted:

Digital Assessment Literacy

"... a social constructivist model of learning and meaning-making, with the language classroom representing the community of practice. It focuses on the sociocultural context in relation to actual assessment literacy practices in the language classroom, since an investigation into what is happening in classes may be of little value without exploring why it is happening."

Context and Participants

Data were collected in Vietnam where education is divided into four stages: primary, secondary, high school and tertiary. English is taught at all four levels of education and is a compulsory subject for students at all levels. The state sector is significantly larger than the private one. Private schools often focus on the quality of English language provision when marketing themselves. A total of 2569 Vietnamese teachers participated in this study, 524 responses of which were incomplete. The participants came from 59 out of 64 provinces in Vietnam; the majority of whom were from the north of the country. A total of 1820 participant teachers worked in public institutions and 181 in private institutions. In terms of qualifications, 65.8% of them (n=1690) had a university degree; 177 (6.9%) had a master's degree and 20 (0.8%) had a PhD. Figure 2 illustrates the participants in terms of education levels they were teaching. Table 1 shows their English teaching experience.

Figure 2. Types of institutions

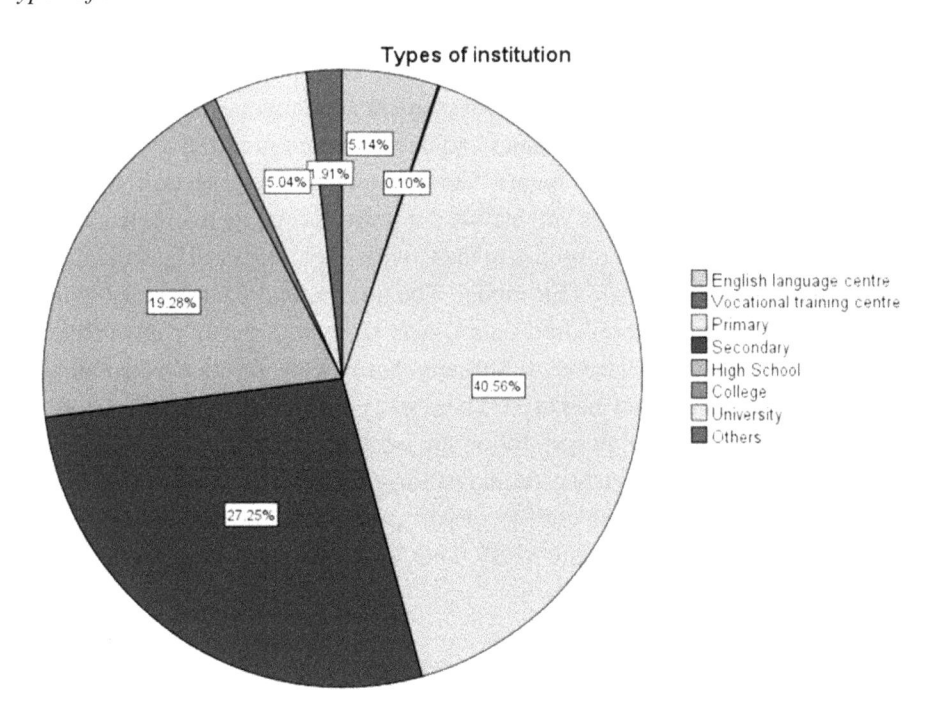

Table 1. Years of teaching experience

	Years	Percent	Count
1	0 - 4	16.43%	336
2	5 - 9	17.80%	364
3	10 - 14	20.44%	418
4	15 - 19	19.27%	394
5	20 - 24	22.20%	454
6	25+	3.86%	79
Missing			524

Research Instruments and Data Collection

A mixed-method approach to data collection was adopted to understand the current assessment landscape. The methods include questionnaire and teaching observations with follow-up interviews. The overall methodology and the data collection instruments were reviewed and approved by Ethics Committees from a British higher education institution and the project sponsor.

Questionnaire

The online questionnaire was distributed through Qualtrics. The questionnaire was divided into three sections. The first section explored experiences of assessment as a language learner. The second section explored training and how the topic of assessment had been covered in initial teacher education and in subsequent training undertaken by the participants. The final questionnaire section, which is the focus of this study, considered assessment practices and included questions relating to online assessment and the pivot to online teaching and assessing in response to the Covid-19 pandemic. This matches the Language Assessment Practices section of the LAL-TEP model. The questionnaire was available in both English and Vietnamese. The survey items were based on a Likert scale with participants selecting from five options which ranged from Strongly Disagree to Strongly Agree. One question asked the participants to state which digital assessment tools they had used. There were no open-response questions in the survey as the project used classroom observation with follow-up interviews to collect qualitative data. Many of the questionnaire items had been previously used and validated in a previous study (Sheehan and Munro, 2019). Probability sampling strategy was used to recruit participants to respond to the questionnaire. Data from questionnaire was analysed, using SPSS. Due to the scope of this chapter, only data in the final questionnaire section is presented.

Classroom Observations and Follow-Up Interviews

Observations were conducted to obtain insights into teachers' practice in their classrooms and follow-up interviews were to understand teachers' thoughts on their practice. Non-probability sampling strategy was employed to recruit the participants for observations and follow-up interviews. Seven teachers were invited at this stage. This number reflects the four stages of education in Vietnam and includes institutions from both the state and private sectors. The teachers were all experienced educators with at least 10 years of experience and one teacher had 20 years. The observations related to the Language Assessment Practices aspect of the LAL-TEP model. The structured observations used an observation schedule which included 15 assessment activities. The schedule was based on one used in two previous projects (Sheehan and Munro, 2017, 2019) which was adapted for the Vietnamese context. The observers recorded each time an assessment activity occurred. The schedule included space for notes in which the observers could record the student reactions to the assessment activities or the comments used by the teachers when assessing the students. As soon as schedules allowed, the observer and the teacher met for the follow-up interview. The semi-structured interview included questions which related to the observed assessment activities and other broader questions about the language assessment practices and training.

The interviews provided the teachers an opportunity to talk about the thinking behind the assessment activities used and how the observed activities related to their overall assessment practices. This broader discussion covered many aspects of the LAL-TEP model such as institutional context and language assessment training. Table 2 summarises our data collection methods. Data from observations and interviews were thematically analysed. The themes were taken from the LAL-TEP model, including language assessment knowledge, language assessment learning, conceptions of language assessment, language assessment practices and context. The additional themes considered in the literature review, which were choices of assessments, challenges of implementing assessments and feedback, were also used. Coding was undertaken by one member of the research team. Other team members reviewed the codes and coding and were satisfied with coding process.

Table 2. Summary of data collection methods

Questionnaire	2569 responses
Observation	7, including 1 lesson in a public primary school 1 lesson in a private primary school 1 lesson in a public secondary school 1 lesson in a private secondary school 1 lesson in a public high school 1 lesson in a private high school 1 lesson in a public university
Follow-up interview	7

Credibility in qualitative research deals with the question "How congruent are the findings with reality?" (Merriam, 2009). Different techniques can be used to establish the credibility and trustworthiness of research, namely prolonged engagement, persistent observation, triangulation, referential adequacy, peer debriefing and member checking (Lincoln & Guba, 1985). This study used several techniques that are relevant such as triangulation and thick description. Regarding triangulation, the study combined three different data collection instruments, namely questionnaire, observation and interview. This helps achieve the validity of data as the researchers search for convergence among multiple and different sources of information to form themes or categories in a study (Creswell & Miller, 2000). It is argued by Geertz (1973) that any single behaviour or interaction, when extracted from its context, could mean a number of things. Thus, thick description requires that researchers account for the complex specificity and circumstantiality of their data. In this study, we provided details about the context of the study, the participants, and a detailed description of each step which helps in transporting the readers into the setting and/or the situation. In this sense, it promotes credibility as it assists the researcher in interpretation and makes the phenomenon clear to readers (Shenton, 2004).

FINDINGS

Teachers' Attitude Towards Online Assessment

The participant teachers seemed to have positive experiences with online assessments as 47.4% of the participants reported to prefer digital assessments to paper-based assessments and 62% felt comfortable when using digital platforms (tools, techniques, softwares, apps, etc.) to create assessments (Table 3). 65.6% agreed that digital platforms were helpful and 41.4% frequently used digital platforms to assess their students. This seems to be concurrent with previous findings in Jiang and Yu's (2021) study. Although the majority of the participants had an idea about their experience of assessing students online, around one third of the participants were unsure if they liked or disliked the experience. In addition, 40.1% of the participants stated that they had difficulty in assessing students online. This is an interesting finding as it seems to suggest that there might be a difference between the comfort of using digital platforms and the quality of using them. Being comfortable with digital platforms may not necessarily mean knowing how to use them to assess students' learning effectively. 41.4% of the participants also stated that there were differences in the assessments they used when teaching online and when in offline classes.

Table 3. Teachers' experience of assessing students online

	Strongly disagree	Disagree	Neutral	Agree	Strongly agree
I prefer digital assessments to paper-based assessments.	3.7	10.5	38.3	36.3	11.1
I feel comfortable when using digital platforms (tools, techniques, softwares, apps, etc.) to create assessments.	2.1	5.9	30.1	47.7	14.3
I have difficulty in assessing students online.	6.3	17.9	35.7	32.3	7.8
The assessments I use when teaching online are similar to what I use in face-to-face teaching mode.	7.2	34.2	32.8	21.1	4.6
I find it helpful to use digital platforms (tools, techniques, softwares, apps, etc.) to assess students.	2.6	5.4	26.4	50.3	15.3
I use the assessment information that digital platforms (tools, techniques, softwares, apps, etc.) provide to plan my lessons.	1.9	9.1	34.8	44.3	9.8
I use digital platforms (tools, techniques, softwares, apps, etc.) to assess students frequently.	3.1	13.5	42.0	33.3	8.1

There was a statistically significant interaction between the effects of teaching experience and qualifications on teachers' difficulty in assessing students online, $F(22, 1509) = 1.622, p = 0.34$. There was also a statistically significant interaction between the effects of teaching experience and qualifications on preference towards digital assessments to paper-based assessments, $F(22, 1512) = 1.876, p = 0.008$.

The Post Hoc test analysis showed that teachers who have a doctorate and have been teaching between 20-24 years significantly find it more difficult in assessing students online (p = 0.021) and that teachers who have a master's degree or a college degree and have been teaching less than 4 years significantly have more preference towards digital assessments to paper-based assessments (p=0.40, p=0.42). The study showed that there might be groups of teachers who may find digital assessments more challenging than the other groups. However, it is worth a note here that the data set met all of the assumptions of factor analysis, except the normality test, in order to go forward with factor analysis. The decision of running ANOVA was still made due to the large data set; thus, the violation of normality test might not have created considerably negative impact on the interpretation of the results.

Teachers' Choices of Assessment

In the observed online sessions, we found that teachers used different assessment activities, including quizzes, word game, sentence correction, repeating or summarising students' responses, and peer assessment. We also observed that there was one session in which no assessment activities were conducted. The follow-up interviews contributed to unpacking what were behind teachers' choices of assessment tasks in their classroom. These will be presented in this section.

Teachers seemed to be creative and be able to make use of online environment as they found it convenient to conduct quizzes. Extracts 1 and 2 typically summarises the reason why teachers used quizzes frequently. It was the digital platform which helped teachers access and implement the activity to accommodate the goals they set for their students. In this case, as teachers were aware of the significance of vocabulary, they decided to do the activities to ensure that their students not only remembered the meaning of the words/phrases but also knew how to use them properly. The teachers seem to realise that the new learning environment can be helpful for particular purposes and types of assessment, in this case it is assessing vocabulary. This finding seems to support what Panadero et al. (2022) found in their study, which suggests that more multiple-choice questions and fewer essay questions are more favoured by teachers in their online classes.

When I teach students online, I always, in each class, I always use quizzes to help students review new words, but in real life class we need to change, we cannot always use quizzes. We cannot use quizzes with devices, students do not bring their mobile phones, just some students bring, so I cannot use this as online. (T2)

Well, I think vocabulary is foundation for students to do many kinds of activities so I really focus on this activity and I want students to use the vocabulary they learn in class, right in class. So that's why I always give them chances to make their own sentences or conversations using the new vocabulary so that they will feel the words are just, uhm, they don't learn the words in a passive way, I want they learn them in an active way and they can use them later. (T3)

Peer assessment was observed to be used in the lessons, however, for different reasons. One of the reasons reported by the teachers was convenience as she said: "when students do a test, to be honest, when I do not have time to mark students' papers, I let them peer assess." (T4). It might have been due to the large class size and the amount of work she needed to complete that she decided to conduct peer assessment activity in her class. While implementing this activity, the teacher was also aware of its effectiveness as she realised that students needed to receive adequate training so that they would know how to do the peer assessment "carefully and properly". This seems to suggest that when a challenge for teachers to balance their workload is posed, teachers may select what assessment tasks are more convenient to them. Although this did not seem to be an appropriate justification for selecting different assessment types, this finding shed light on the influence of context on a teacher's choice of assessment activity.

Other reasons for the implementation of peer assessment were to boost students' engagement with their peers and to encourage their critical thinking, as suggested by the public university teacher in extract 3.

I ask them to have peer assessment to make them more attentive to their peer's performance. Because you know, people often think that it's none of their business when their friends stood up and talk. And the second reason I think that I want to trigger the students' critical thinking, in that way er I might require them to think, to dig deeper more about the self-assessment and what should be done to improve their proficiency. (T1)

The extract suggests that the teacher was clear about the purposes of the assessment she selected. She was also aware of the benefits that the assessment could bring to her students, which is to help them to be an active learner. This finding appears to contrast with previous studies (Panadero & Brown, 2017; Panadero et al., 2014) which reveal that their participants did not identify any advantages in online peer assessment and self- assessment. Our study showed evidence that the teachers implemented peer assessment and self-assessment for their own benefits and for their students' benefits although at some points the assessments were not organised systematically.

In one session there were no observed assessment activities. In the follow-up interview the teacher made the following comments about the choice not to include opportunities for assessment in the lesson.

I think the purpose of the lesson in the video is to inform students how an essay should be structured and what criteria should be considered when rating or writing the essay, so I think the purpose was purely informational, so just give students some ideas so I think that nature determines my decision was very how to say easy-going and the students didn't take it seriously and I myself didn't take it seriously either, and no score-related matter was discussed. So I think it made the lesson less stressful for them. (T1)

The teacher seems to consider assessment as a stressful process for both teachers and students. It may be the case that the teacher has conflated assessment and testing, and this has led her to the association of assessment with stress. This type of conflation has been noted in other LAL studies, (Sheehan and Munro, 2017, Berry et al., 2017). In this observed session, the teacher made the choice to avoid assessments as she wanted to reduce the stress levels of students and allow herself the opportunity to teach without a focus on the aspects of assessment which relate to grading or scoring. This separation of teaching and assessment has been reported in other studies (Berry et al., 2019; Pu & Xu, 2021), which could be problematic as the teacher might not have been able to understand the extent of students' learning. The interviewed teacher's comments about the stressful nature of assessment may reflect the teaching and learning context in which students have to take high-stakes tests. These tests are used as gate-keepers throughout the education system in Vietnam. The use of high-stakes tests has, in some ways, distorted attitudes to assessment as a whole and seems to have obscured the differences between testing and assessment.

Digital Assessment Literacy

Another important finding of our study is that the national assessment policy and the associated national examinations influenced digital assessment practices. A good knowledge of vocabulary is needed to do well in these examinations. The interviewed teachers were conscious of the examinations when they prepared assessment activities. The teachers reported to frequently use online quizzes via Microsoft forms or Quizzizz, Quizlet, Liveworksheet.com, etc to assess their students' knowledge of vocabulary. As can be seen in the extract below teachers in rural locations were especially anxious to ensure their students did well in these examinations. Students from rural schools tend to be in a less favourable position than their counterparts from city schools.

You know, in the countryside, in my setting here, apart from the purpose of learning a foreign language. I want my student to use the foreign language to communicate, alright? But they also have to learn English as a core subject. They have to follow some route to have a good place in the university, so I just want them to do the question on pronunciation well enough, to get enough mark for pronunciation. Beside that, I always believe my students can do it. So I repeat the rules. I repeat the rules because I know one day they can do it for sure. (T5)

The context in which teachers and learners are in tend to influence their choices of assessments. This finding is of importance since it reveals another factor for consideration – the context of assessments. What we mean by context is not only the online context that teachers and learners were forced to be in during the pandemic but also the policy and the associated national exams teachers and learners were required to adhere to and to perform well. This has further supported the importance of understanding the context suggested by Villa Larenas and Brunfaut (2022).

The Use of Assessment Feedback

In the observed sessions there were many examples of teachers praising the students. This seems to support Jiang and Yu's (2021) study which reported that praise appears to be one of the most commonly used forms of feedback. Below is one example of the reasons given for using praise in the digital classroom.

I think the comments and gestures to respond to the students are beneficial. They motivate students to learn. When students write new words on the board and get many scores for their team, they are motivated, and they are encouraged to join meaningful competitions with others. (T4)

The teacher considers praise to be source of motivation for her students. She also notes that teamwork can motivate students. The use of praise and teamwork can reduce the sense of isolation which may occur when students are working in a digital classroom. A strong sense of community can be cultivated through positive classroom relationships. This finding has added to the literature which witnesses the increase in feedback delivery (Gamage et al., 2020; Jiang & Yu, 2021) by providing an explanation to teachers' use of feedback.

Teamwork was considered to be beneficial to motivation by the teachers. It might be due to wider pressure from tests that the students responded to all assessment activities as though they were taking a test, irrespective of the nature of task and assessment focus. Competition or being overly competitive could have negative consequences on the classroom. Students, in an effort to gain the best marks, may deploy strategies associated with test wiseness to get the right answer and not use their language knowledge. To avoid students relying on test wiseness to answer quiz questions, one teacher incorporated a review of quiz answers into her lesson as can be observed below.

Uhm, well, as I said, there are two kinds of students, they want to get to the top or they want to get all the correct answers. That may lead to some negative aspects that students do not really understand why they choose that answer. They just remember all, this one is wrong, so next time I will choose another one. So I review it, so students can have the chance to explain why they chose that answer, why they chose the wrong one, what signal they didn't pay attention to and lead them to choose the wrong answer. So I review it, and it's also another way for me to summarize the theory. (T6)

The teacher promotes higher order thinking skills by encouraging the students to consider more than just the correctness or incorrectness of the answer. This was done as a follow-up activity when the students completed the quiz. She wants the learners to think about the language patters being assessed and to develop their understanding of them through consideration of the quiz answers. This indicates the observed teacher used quizzes as dialogic communication between teachers and students. However, this type of engagement was not frequently found in the data. In other words, more evidence would be needed to demonstrate if teachers in Vietnam have taken up the new approach of feedback suggested by recent studies (Carless, 2020; Carless & Boud, 2018; Winstone & Carless, 2019).

The Challenges Faced by the Teachers in Their Practices in Online Environment

There was acceptance amongst the participants that digital assessment was part of the assessment landscape. As one teacher noted, hybrid learning is now an accepted teaching mode so digital assessments will continue to be used. Digital assessment brings with it an associated need for digital feedback. One of the participants stressed the need to incorporate digital feedback into her assessment practices when she said: *"Because you know hybrid learning is very important, it's the current trend of education right now. So I think giving online feedback is also very important."* (T1). Whilst accepting that digital assessment was now part of daily life the teachers were aware of the limitations of digital assessment with particular concern about the issue of technological distraction. Some of the participants speculated that the students find less novelty in digital assessments than the teachers do.

Maybe because we do not tackle the real part of learning when we use [technology] because we just use that to get more interactive, use tool like maybe to mix or match. Maybe it sounds more fun to us. We think we assume that the students will find it fun and less tired when they do the task but sometimes it's a source of distraction. (T2)

A decrease in students' involvement was found in emergency remote teaching (Panadero et al., 2022; Senel & Senel, 2021) while a range of digital tools was available. The teachers in our study appeared to be comfortable with using digital platforms and tools but their concern was about how to use them effectively in their classrooms.

DISCUSSION

We aimed to explore teachers' assessment practices in an online learning environment by looking at their experience with digital tools, their selection of online assessment activities and the challenges they had to cope with. The first finding of our study reveals that the participant teachers were generally comfortable with conducting and implementing assessment activities in digital platforms (softwares, online tools, techniques, apps, etc). There follows a list of the most used digital platforms: Class Dojo, Classkick, Quizzizz, quizlet, Kahoot, Richmonddlp, Nearpod, Liveworksheet.com and Google/Microsoft form. However, there were groups of teachers who find it more difficult to assess their students online than the other groups. In particular, newly trained teachers reported to be more comfortable of using digital platforms than those with 20-24 years of teaching. A possible explanation for this is that younger teachers may have more familiarity and experience with modern technologies than mature teachers. This finding seems to support Nguyen and Yukawa's (2019) study which suggests that different levels of ages may need additional support in terms of technical skills. In addition, it is interesting to observe that most participants reported they had difficulty in assessing students online. There is an apparent inconsistency in the data as the participants find online assessments difficult but using the platforms is not difficult. This inconsistency could be explained by the fact that the teachers find the interpretation of the results and how these results can be used to inform future teaching to be difficult. Thus, the assessment activities are quick and easy for the teachers to create using relevant tools, but the overall assessment process is more complicated, and the challenges presented to teachers of online assessment should not be underestimated.

The second finding of our study is that the teachers seemed to be creative and be able to make use of the online environment. There were reasons behind their selection of assessment activities. However, it was evident that tests had an immense impact on the content and methods of the assessments in their classrooms in both public and private schools. This can also explain why teachers may consider tests and assessment more broadly as a source of stress for their students. As a result, they may avoid assessment in their classrooms to avoid inducing feelings of stress in their students. This finding confirms the impact of social contexts on teachers' assessment practice, as suggested by previous studies (Sheehan & Munro, 2017).

The third finding was about the way teacher delivered feedback to their students. The teachers seemed to overuse praise to motivate and perhaps to reduce the feeling of stress in their students; however, the use of praise was not always effective. This seems to echo what is suggested by Hatti and Timperly (2007) that praise is the least effective form of feedback. Although there was insufficient evidence that the teachers tried to engage the students in understanding why they selected the wrong answer in the quizzes completed. However, in the observed lessons, most of the time the teachers did not point out what the students did well and what they can do to improve. In other words, the feedback delivered did not seem to reflect the four dimensions suggested in the literature: intentionality, reciprocity, transcendence and meaning (Jiang et al., 2020). The element of using feedback as dialogic communication between teachers and students (Carless & Winstone, 2020; Winstone & Carless, 2019) was not clear in our study. This may indicate that the delivery of feedback could have been improved and that digital competence may not play a role in determining the effectiveness of feedback from teachers to their students.

Our fourth finding is about the challenges faced by the teachers. It reveals that the teachers were concerned about the effectiveness of their online assessment activities to assess their students. This finding is consistent with the findings of previous studies (Pu & Xu, 2021; Panadero et al., 2022) which stated that teachers were aware of the importance of online assessment but struggled to incorporate it systematically and effectively into their online teaching and learning processes.

Viewing online assessment through the prism of LAL and using the LAL-TEP model generated important insights into assessment processes in Vietnam. In terms of the LAL-TEP model, the teachers were able to provide a clear rationale for their assessment activities. They demonstrated some levels of knowledge relating to the how, what, and why of assessment. The macro-sociocultural context impacted on assessment practices in ways which can be categorised as immediate and ongoing. The immediate impact was the pivot to online teaching and assessment. The ongoing one was the impact of national policy and examinations on how the teachers assessed their students. The findings support the contention of the authors of the LAL-TEP model that LAL is constructed "from and for" a particular teaching context. The LAL-TEP model highlights the role of emotion in LAL. The findings relating to emotion in this study are concentrated on negative emotions as assessment can be a source of stress for both teachers and students, which seems to support the results reported by Berry, Sheehan and Munro (2017, 2019).

CONCLUSION AND RECOMMENDATION

The project has extended an understanding of the current assessment landscape in Vietnam, with the focus on digital assessment practices. The survey data seemed to reveal that teachers are comfortable with online platforms and digital tools. However, there seems to be a difference in the self-report data and the observation and interview data. The qualitative data showed they seem to be struggling with using them to assess their students in their online classes. The teachers also seem to worry about quality of assessments they selected to conduct, and the quality of feedback based on the assessments. More importantly, there are particular groups of teachers who find it more difficult in assessing students, which may mean there might be groups of learners who lose out if assessment practices are poor, as suggested by Crusan et al. (2016). Therefore, the main conclusion of the study is that the issue for teachers is not the digital part but the assessment part. Better digital assessment needs teachers who have a good grounding in assessment. Assessment knowledge is the foundation which the teachers need to have before they embark on any type of assessment, including digital assessment. The pandemic has highlighted gaps in assessment knowledge which existed before the shift to digital assessment.

The study can offer several important implications regarding teacher training and institutional practices. First, it is crucial to improve teachers' assessment literacy as the emergency remote teaching has confirmed this. Considerable attention to assessments in teacher training programmes can help teachers better resolve assessment related issues in different learning environments. Assessments, teaching and learning should be integrated and not separated. It is also important to consider the impact of the macro-sociocultural context on assessment practices and address the related issues in teacher training programmes. Second, the professional development of teachers is as important as what teachers learn during their initial training programmes. Thus, institutions should provide support and resources to offer greater opportunities for change in teachers' assessment practices. Teachers' efforts of applying innovative practices should be recognised by their institutions. A community of practice can be created so that teachers can share their practices and can receive constructive feedback on how they are conducting their assessments. Timely support regarding this can help reduce teachers' stress and enhance students' learning experience. Moreover, accessible resources can be created so teachers can learn at their own pace to update with current knowledge of assessments.

REFERENCES

Akimov, A., Kobinger, S., & Malin, M. (2018). Determinants of student success in finance courses. *Journal of Financial Education*, *44*(2), 223–245. https://www.jstor.org/stable/10.2307/26775505

Alavi, S. M., Dashtestani, R., & Mellati, M. (2021). Crisis and Changes in Learning Behaviours: Technology-Enhanced Assessment in Language Learning Contexts. *Journal of Further and Higher Education*, *46*(4), 461–474. doi:10.1080/0309877X.2021.1985977

Almossa, S. Y., & Alzahrani, S. M. (2022). Assessment practices in Saudi higher education during the COVID-19 pandemic. *Humanities & Social Sciences Communications*, *9*(1), 5. doi:10.105741599-021-01025-z

Balloo, K., Evans, C., Hughes, A., Zhu, X., & Winstone, N. (2018). Transparency Isn't Spoon-Feeding: How a Transformative Approach to the Use of Explicit Assessment Criteria Can Support Student Self-Regulation. *Frontiers in Education*, *3*, 69. doi:10.3389/feduc.2018.00069

Bartolic, S. K., Boud, D., Agapito, J., Verpoorten, D., Williams, S., Lutze-Mann, L., Matzat, U., Moreno, M. M., Polly, P., Tai, J., Marsh, H. L., Lin, L., Burgess, J.-L., Habtu, S., Rodrigo, M. M. M., Roth, M., Heap, T., & Guppy, N. (2021). A multi-institutional assessment of changes in higher education teaching and learning in the face of COVID-19. *Educational Review*, *74*(3), 517–533. doi:10.1080/00131911.2021.1955830

Benson, A. D. (2003). Assessing participant learning in online environments. *New Directions for Adult and Continuing Education*, *2003*(100), 69–78. doi:10.1002/ace.120

Berry, V., Sheehan, S., & Munro, S. (2017). Exploring teachers' language assessment literacy: A social constructivist approach to understanding effective practices. In *ALTE (2017). Learning and Assessment: Making the Connections–Proceedings of the ALTE 6th International Conference*, (pp. 201-207). ALTE.

Berry, V., Sheehan, S., & Munro, S. (2019). What does language assessment literacy mean to teachers? *ELT Journal*, *73*(2), 113–123. doi:10.1093/elt/ccy055

Bozkurt, A., Jung, I., Xiao, J., Vladimirschi, V., Schuwer, R., Egorov, G., & Olcott, D. Jr. (2020). A global outlook to the interruption of education due to COVID-19 pandemic: Navigating in a time of uncertainty and crisis. *Asian Journal of Distance Education*, *15*(1), 1–126. https://eric.ed.gov/?id=EJ1290039

Brookhart, S. M. (2013). *How to create and use rubrics for formative assessment and grading*. Ascd.

Carless, D., & Winstone, N. (2020). Teacher feedback literacy and its interplay with student feedback literacy. *Teaching in Higher Education*, *28*(1), 150–163. doi:10.1080/13562517.2020.1782372

Cheng, A.-C., Jordan, M. E., & Schallert, D. L. (2013). Reconsidering assessment in online/hybrid courses: Knowing versus learning. *Computers & Education*, *68*, 51–59. doi:10.1016/j.compedu.2013.04.022

Creswell, J. W., & Miller, D. L. (2000). Determining Validity in Qualitative Inquiry. *Theory into Practice*, *39*(3), 124–130. doi:10.120715430421tip3903_2

Crusan, D., Plakans, L., & Gebril, A. (2016). Writing assessment literacy: Surveying second language teachers' knowledge, beliefs, and practices. *Assessing Writing, 28*, 43–56. doi:10.1016/j.asw.2016.03.001

Dawson, P., Henderson, M., Ryan, T., Mahoney, P., Boud, D., Phillips, M., & Molloy, E. (2018). Technology and Feedback Design. In *Learning* (pp. 1–45). Design, and Technology. doi:10.1007/978-3-319-17727-4_124-1

Donaghue, H. (2020). Feedback Talk as a Means of Creating, Ratifying and Normalising an Institutionally Valued Teacher Identity. *Journal of Language, Identity, and Education, 19*(6), 395–411. doi:10.1080/15348458.2019.1696683

Evans, C. (2013). Making Sense of Assessment Feedback in Higher Education. *Review of Educational Research, 83*(1), 70–120. doi:10.3102/0034654312474350

Fluck, A. E. (2019). An international review of eExam technologies and impact. *Computers & Education, 132*, 1–15. doi:10.1016/j.compedu.2018.12.008

Fulcher, G. (2012). Assessment literacy for the language classroom. *Language Assessment Quarterly, 9*(2), 113–132. doi:10.1080/15434303.2011.642041

Gamage, K. A. A., Silva, E. K., & Gunawardhana, N. (2020). Online Delivery and Assessment during COVID-19: Safeguarding Academic Integrity. *Education Sciences, 10*(11), 301. doi:10.3390/educsci10110301

Geertz, C. (1993). *The interpretation of cultures : selected essays*.

Gikandi, J. W., Morrow, D., & Davis, N. E. (2011). Online formative assessment in higher education: A review of the literature. *Computers & Education, 57*(4), 2333–2351. doi:10.1016/j.compedu.2011.06.004

Guo, W., & Wei, J. (2019). Teacher Feedback and Students' Self-regulated Learning in Mathematics: A Study of Chinese Secondary Students. *The Asia-Pacific Education Researcher, 28*(3), 265–275. doi:10.100740299-019-00434-8

Haniff Mohd Tahir, M. (2022). Factors Influencing Secondary English as a Second Language Teachers' Intentions to Utilize Google Classroom for Instructions during the Covid-19 Pandemic. *Arab World English Journal, 13*(2), 17–36. doi:10.24093/awej/vol13no2.2

Hattie, J., & Timperley, H. (2007). The Power of Feedback. *Review of Educational Research, 77*(1), 81–112. doi:10.3102/003465430298487

Hodges, C. B., Moore, S., Lockee, B. B., Trust, T., & Bond, M. A. (2020). *The difference between emergency remote teaching and online learning*.

Jiang, L., & Yu, S. (2021). Understanding Changes in EFL Teachers' Feedback Practice During COVID-19: Implications for Teacher Feedback Literacy at a Time of Crisis. *The Asia-Pacific Education Researcher, 30*(6), 509–518. doi:10.100740299-021-00583-9

Jiang, L., Yu, S., & Wang, C. (2020). Second language writing instructors' feedback practice in response to automated writing evaluation: A sociocultural perspective. *System*, *93*, 102302. doi:10.1016/j.system.2020.102302

Jiang, L., Yu, S., & Zhao, Y. (2019). Teacher engagement with digital multimodal composing in a Chinese tertiary EFL curriculum. *Language Teaching Research*, *25*(4), 613–632. doi:10.1177/1362168819864975

Koenka, A. C., Linnenbrink-Garcia, L., Moshontz, H., Atkinson, K. M., Sanchez, C. E., & Cooper, H. (2019). A meta-analysis on the impact of grades and comments on academic motivation and achievement: A case for written feedback. *Educational Psychology*, *41*(7), 922–947. doi:10.1080/01443410.2019.1659939

Koh, K., Burke, L. E. C.-A., Luke, A., Gong, W., & Tan, C. (2018). Developing the assessment literacy of teachers in Chinese language classrooms: A focus on assessment task design. *Language Teaching Research*, *22*(3), 264–288. doi:10.1177/1362168816684366

Krishnan, J., Black, R. W., & Olson, C. B. (2021). The power of context: Exploring teachers' formative assessment for online collaborative writing. *Reading & Writing Quarterly*, *37*(3), 201–220. doi:10.1080/10573569.2020.1764888

Lee, I. (2017). *Classroom writing assessment and feedback in L2 school contexts*. Springer. doi:10.1007/978-981-10-3924-9

Lee, I. (2021). The Development of Feedback Literacy for Writing Teachers. *TESOL Quarterly*, *55*(3), 1048–1059. doi:10.1002/tesq.3012

Lincoln, Y. S., & Guba, E. G. (1985). *Naturalistic inquiry*. Sage. doi:10.1016/0147-1767(85)90062-8

Link, S., Mehrzad, M., & Rahimi, M. (2020). Impact of automated writing evaluation on teacher feedback, student revision, and writing improvement. *Computer Assisted Language Learning*, *35*(4), 605–634. doi:10.1080/09588221.2020.1743323

Malone, M. E. (2013). The essentials of assessment literacy: Contrasts between testers and users. *Language Testing*, *30*(3), 329–344. doi:10.1177/0265532213480129

Merriam, S. B. (2009). Qualitative research: a guide to design and implementation. San Francisco, California: Jossey-Bass.

Moffitt, R. L., Padgett, C., & Grieve, R. (2020). Accessibility and emotionality of online assessment feedback: Using emoticons to enhance student perceptions of marker competence and warmth. *Computers & Education*, *143*, 103654. doi:10.1016/j.compedu.2019.103654

Nguyen, T. T. T., & Yukawa, T. (2019). Kahoot with smartphones in testing and assessment of language teaching and learning, the need of training on mobile devices for Vietnamese teachers and students. *International Journal of Information and Education Technology (IJIET)*, *9*(4), 286–296. http://www.ijiet.org/vol9/1214-JR328.pdf. doi:10.18178/ijiet.2019.9.4.1214

Ninković, S., Olić Ninković, S., Lazarević, T., & Adamov, J. (2021). Serbian teachers' perceptions of online assessment during COVID-19 school closure: The role of teachers' self-efficacy. *Educational Studies*, 1–13. doi:10.1080/03055698.2021.1960151

Panadero, E., Fraile, J., Pinedo, L., Rodríguez-Hernández, C., & Díez, F. (2022). Changes in classroom assessment practices during emergency remote teaching due to COVID-19. *Assessment in Education: Principles, Policy & Practice*, *29*(3), 361–382. doi:10.1080/0969594X.2022.2067123

Pu, S., & Xu, H. (2021). Examining Changing Assessment Practices in Online Teaching: A Multiple-Case Study of EFL School Teachers in China. *The Asia-Pacific Education Researcher*, *30*(6), 553–561. doi:10.100740299-021-00605-6

Rapanta, C., Botturi, L., Goodyear, P., Guàrdia, L., & Koole, M. (2020). Online University Teaching During and After the Covid-19 Crisis: Refocusing Teacher Presence and Learning Activity. *Postdigital Science and Education*, *2*(3), 923–945. doi:10.100742438-020-00155-y

Senel, S., & Senel, H. C. (2021). Remote Assessment in Higher Education during COVID-19 Pandemic. *International Journal of Assessment Tools in Education*, 181-199. doi:10.21449/ijate.820140

Sheehan, S., & Munro, S. (2017). *Assessment: attitudes, practices and needs*. ELT research paper.

Shenton, A. K. (2004). Strategies for ensuring trustworthiness in qualitative research projects. *Education for Information*, *22*(2), 63–75. doi:10.3233/EFI-2004-22201

Tang, T. T., Nguyen, T. N., & Tran, H. T. T. (2022). Vietnamese Teachers' Acceptance to Use E-Assessment Tools in Teaching: An Empirical Study Using PLS-SEM. *Contemporary Educational Technology*, *14*(3), ep375. doi:10.30935/cedtech/12106

Thi, N. K., Nikolov, M., & Simon, K. (2022). Higher-proficiency students' engagement with and uptake of teacher and Grammarly feedback in an EFL writing course. *Innovation in Language Learning and Teaching*, 1–16. doi:10.1080/17501229.2022.2122476

Villa Larenas, S. (2021, June 14-17). *A revised multidimensional model for LAL: relationships between beliefs, knowledge, practices, learning, and context* [Paper presentation]. Language Testing Research Colloquium (LTRC).

Villa Larenas, S., & Brunfaut, T. (2022). But who trains the language teacher educator who trains the language teacher? An empirical investigation of Chilean EFL teacher educators' language assessment literacy. *Language Testing*, *02655322221134218*. doi:10.1177/02655322221134218

Vogt, K., & Tsagari, D. (2014). Assessment literacy of foreign language teachers: Findings of a European study. *Language Assessment Quarterly*, *11*(4), 374–402. doi:10.1080/15434303.2014.960046

Waycott, J., Bennett, S., Kennedy, G., Dalgarno, B., & Gray, K. (2010). Digital divides? Student and staff perceptions of information and communication technologies. *Computers & Education*, *54*(4), 1202–1211. doi:10.1016/j.compedu.2009.11.006

Waycott, J., Sheard, J., Thompson, C., & Clerehan, R. (2013). Making students' work visible on the social web: A blessing or a curse? *Computers & Education*, *68*, 86–95. doi:10.1016/j.compedu.2013.04.026

Wiliam, D. (2011). What is assessment for learning? *Studies in Educational Evaluation*, *37*(1), 3–14. doi:10.1016/j.stueduc.2011.03.001 PMID:22114905

Wilson, J., & Czik, A. (2016). Automated essay evaluation software in English Language Arts classrooms: Effects on teacher feedback, student motivation, and writing quality. *Computers & Education*, *100*, 94–109. doi:10.1016/j.compedu.2016.05.004

Winstone, N., & Carless, D. (2019). *Designing effective feedback processes in higher education: A learning-focused approach*. Routledge. doi:10.4324/9781351115940

Chapter 10
"We Don't Know What We Don't Know":
Classroom Assessment Literacy for Remote and Online Contexts – Insights From an Inter-Country Comparative Study

Toni Mäkipää
https://orcid.org/Orcid
University of Helsinki, Finland

Anna Soltyska
https://orcid.org/0000-0003-4587-6113
Ruhr-Universität Bochum, Germany

ABSTRACT

This chapter studies post-pandemic assessment literacy and professional development related to assessment literacy for English teachers in Finland and Germany. The aim of the research is to determine the extent to which language instructors in both countries have been prepared for designing, performing, and evaluating assessment activities, particularly in remote teaching contexts. The study also explores available training options to enhance teachers' assessment literacy. The current study addresses teachers at all levels of education, including primary, secondary, tertiary, and vocational. Qualitative and quantitative data were collected through an online survey (N = 124) and structured video conference interviews (N = 27). The results indicate a significant gap in assessment literacy regarding online assessment (irrespective of the country of the participants, their age, or teaching experience). Furthermore, the results corroborate that there is ample demand for training in online assessment design and administration, suggesting the preferred modes and topics of such training.

DOI: 10.4018/978-1-6684-6227-0.ch010

INTRODUCTION

This chapter aims to compare English teachers' perceived capabilities for (online) assessment in Finland and Germany. The study follows the principle of constructive alignment (Biggs & Tang, 2011), whereby learning objectives, teaching methods, and assessment procedures should be interconnected and influence one another. Thus, the study examines if and how teachers adjusted their classroom assessment practices reflecting changes to teaching and learning methodologies enforced during the COVID-19 pandemic. The role of the teacher is fundamental in both effective classroom instruction (Berry et al., 2019; Mellati & Khademi, 2018) and the selection and implementation of appropriate assessment practices (Mellati & Khademi, 2018; Popham, 2018). Therefore, understanding teachers' experiences in evaluating learners' progress under remote conditions could shed light on future teacher training in pre-service and in-service settings.

Research suggests that the efficient use of multifaceted and germane assessment practices has been marginalised or overlooked in teacher education (e.g., Berry et al., 2019; Green, 2018; Mellati & Khademi, 2018; Vogt & Tsagari, 2014). The literature has also raised questions about teachers' perceived inability to master assessment-related tasks and decisions within their courses (e.g., Green, 2018; Tsagari & Vogt, 2017; Vogt & Tsagari, 2014). In turn, these results accentuate the need for greater attention in assessment activities.

Many studies have not considered the interplay of emergency remote teaching (ERT), online assessment, and assessment literacy. Put differently, the constraints caused by the pandemic have not been explored in conjunction with assessment literacy. The unprecedented and rapid change to remote teaching has, therefore, heightened the need to explore the relationship between ERT and assessment literacy. Further, comparative studies regarding assessment literacy across Europe have been conducted (e.g., Tsagari & Vogt, 2017; Vogt & Tsagari, 2014; Vogt et al., 2020), but the authors have not found research that compares Finland and Germany.

The aspect of users' potential familiarity with and access to digital tools for teaching, learning, and assessment has not been studied in connection with assessment literacy. There were substantial differences in levels of digitalisation in Finland and Germany, which according to European Commission's Digital Economy and Society Index for 2020 ranked 1 and 11, respectively. Thus, it is worthwhile to analyse teachers' preparedness for online assessment overall and assessing students under the circumstances of ERT and testing, particularly in these two countries.

This chapter aims to contribute to current research in assessment literacy by describing language teachers' perceived assessment literacy in ERT and comparing English teachers of Finland and Germany. Based primarily on practitioners' self-reported gaps in the field of assessment, the results can inform future pedagogy of language teaching. It can also propose that both student teachers and in-service teachers be equipped with research-based knowledge of diverse and efficacious assessment practices through suitable training measures. Ideally, such professional development is tailor-made and implemented considering local preferences for delivery mode and content.

The following research questions are presented:

1. To what extent have English teachers in Finland and Germany been prepared for designing, performing, and evaluating assessment activities, particularly in remote teaching contexts?
2. What training can be used to enhance teachers' assessment literacy, particularly related to the focus, scope, and delivery of training?

ASSESSMENT LITERACY

Assessment literacy is an increasingly important focus area in the field of education (DeLuca et al., 2016; Lam, 2019; Popham, 2018). However, assessment literacy is still a novel concept because it was only first defined in the early 1990s (Fulcher, 2012). The American Federation of Teachers (AFT, 1990) asserted that there were seven standards of assessment. These standards require teachers to be skilled in choosing appropriate assessment methods, interpreting assessment methods, making decisions about students with assessment results, and recognising unethical assessment methods (AFT, 1990). These standards do not, however, include the words "assessment literacy."

Currently, these standards are regarded as being outdated as they do not consider standard-based assessment or formative assessment (Brookhart, 2011). Since the publication of the seven standards, more comprehensive definitions have been proposed. These now focus on a range of skills that teachers should obtain. For example, Brookhart (2011) asserted that 11 standards of knowledge and skills are pertinent for every teacher. These include understanding the content area of teaching, articulating clear learning intentions, displaying a range of communication strategies, and administering external assessments (Brookhart, 2011). Xu and Brown (2016) underscored that assessment literacy is a dynamic and evolving system, contingent on the context and changes in the environment. To rephrase, assessment literacy refers to levels of mastery rather than a dichotomy of being assessment-literate or assessment-illiterate (Xu & Brown, 2016).

In the field of language teaching, language assessment literacy (LAL) is viewed as a focal concept to assess students' language skills. This, in turn, requires additional competence (Inbar-Lourie, 2008). However, no consensus exists regarding what LAL refers to (Bøhn & Tsagari, 2022; Harding & Kremmel, 2016; Vogt et al., 2020). For example, LAL has been defined as:

the ability to design, develop, and critically evaluate tests and other assessment procedures, as well as the ability to monitor, evaluate, grade, and score assessments on the basis of theoretical knowledge. (Vogt & Tsagari, 2014, p. 377)

In contrast, Butler and Peng (2021, p. 430) conceptualised LAL as "stakeholders' knowledge of language assessment and the skills they use to design assessments and use their results." A widely cited definition by Fulcher (2012) conceptualised LAL as:

The knowledge, skills and abilities required to design, develop, maintain or evaluate, large-scale standardized and/or classroom based tests, familiarity with test processes, and awareness of principles and concepts that guide and underpin practice, including ethics and codes of practice. The ability to place knowledge, skills, processes, principles and concepts within wider historical, social, political and philosophical frameworks in order to understand why practices have arisen as they have, and to evaluate the role and impact of testing on society, institutions, and individuals. (p. 125)

As the definitions imply, LAL fundamentally necessitates the acquisition of several skills, such as producing tests, interpreting scores, or understanding the functions of assessment (O'Loughlin, 2013). Basically, LAL involves knowledge, skills, and principles (Butler & Peng, 2021).

The use of assessment practices to foster learning requires more than simply mastering the theoretical knowledge of assessment. Teachers must put their knowledge into practice (Xu & Brown, 2016; Yan &

Fan, 2021). Essentially, LAL development is apprenticeship-based. In other words, teachers must substantiate their skills and theoretical knowledge in assessment-related activities (Yan & Fan, 2021). Put differently, supporting the enhancement of LAL is a fundamental aspect of every teacher's professional development (Harding & Kremmel, 2016; Xu & Brown, 2016). Essentially, LAL is a co-constructed, social construct (Yan & Fan, 2021). Taylor (2013) delineated four profiles of LAL, focusing on the following stakeholders: (1) test writers; (2) classroom teachers; (3) university administrators; and (4) professional language testers. According to Taylor (2013), the profile for classroom teachers encapsulates the knowledge of theory, technical skills, principles and concepts, language pedagogy, sociocultural values, local practices, personal beliefs or attitudes, scores, and decision making. Taylor (2013) argued that out of these components, language pedagogy is the most important for language teachers. In other words, the need of LAL varies across stakeholder groups (Kremmel & Harding, 2020; O'Loughlin, 2013; Taylor, 2013; Yan & Fan, 2021).

The profiles described by Taylor (2013) were validated by Kremmel and Harding (2020); however, they added a few expansions and distinctions. The pitfall of the model is that the components and the dimensions are not specified (Bøhn & Tsagari, 2021). Bøhn and Tsagari (2021) also argued that more components need to be included in Taylor's (2013) model, namely disciplinary competence and collaboration competence. Moreover, more research is required to investigate how the components of Taylor's (2013) model should be operationalised (Bøhn & Tsagari, 2022).

Research on LAL has focused on language teachers, who are important stakeholders in assessment-related research (Lam, 2019; O'Loughlin, 2013; Vogt et al., 2020). Several studies conducted on LAL in Europe and Iran indicate cause for concern. For example, some institutions decide what assessment practices their teachers should use. Teachers cannot affect the decisions (Mansouri et al., 2021). Thus, teachers use assessment practices that they might consider to be ineffective (Mansouri et al., 2021). Moreover, several studies indicate that language teachers are dissatisfied with the assessment practices they use. They are not prepared to meet the requirements of classroom assessment due to poor training (e.g., Mansouri et al., 2021; Tsagari & Vogt, 2014; Vogt & Tsagari, 2017). These results, however, contrast with Lam's (2019) study of Chinese teachers, in which most teachers displayed pertinent assessment knowledge. Yet, some of the teachers employed teacher-centred assessment practices in writing and were unable to choose alternative assessment practices (Lam, 2019). Teachers also need more training in curriculum knowledge, ethics, test fairness, and communication skills (Bøhn & Tsagari, 2021).

These studies suggest that more training is required to enhance LAL. However, teachers require targeted and differentiated training as they have individual needs and preferences for development (DeLuca et al., 2016; Drackert et al., 2020). In addition to increasing language teachers' knowledge of assessment, training is beneficial because it reshapes their teaching practices (Delgado & Rodriguez, 2022).

WIDER CONTEXT

Emergency Remote Teaching

Remote teaching increased around the world due to the COVID-19 pandemic. Scholars differentiate this type of remote teaching from regular online learning. The sudden shift to remote teaching due to the pandemic is referred to as ERT (Milman, 2020). The term "pandemic pedagogy" has also been employed (Milman, 2020). Planning and timing factors distinguish ERT from online learning. Online learning is meticulously planned before the start of the teaching unit. ERT is used out of necessity. In addition, remote teaching is temporary as compared to the permanence of online learning (Hodges et al., 2020).

Due to the unprecedented shift to ERT and online platforms, several language teachers perceived remote teaching and its advantages more positively than prior to the COVID-19 pandemic (Jin et al., 2021). In other words, the ERT experience could normalise remote teaching in post-pandemic education (Can & Silman-Karanfil, 2022; Jin et al., 2021). Therefore, it is important to investigate ERT from multifaceted perspectives to ascertain how instructive remote teaching can be organised in the "new pedagogy" (Can & Silman-Karanfil, 2022).

A proliferation of studies has investigated language learning in ERT; however, few studies have examined online assessment practices. Mäkipää et al. (2021) explored foreign language teachers' assessment and feedback practices in ERT in Finland. According to the teachers, assessment was more problematic in ERT than in contact teaching. Still, the teahceres were able to assess students equally. The teachers also considered their assessment to be fair (Mäkipää et al., 2021). Vurdien and Puranen (2022) noted advantages and disadvantages of online assessment in "challenging times," as reported by English teachers from various levels of schooling in Finland and Spain. The researchers concluded that overall flexibility (seen as a positive feature) and questionable authorship of test-takers' responses (seen as a major drawback) are the aspects of online assessment that need to be addressed.

Reports from American higher education institutions were collected in a special edition of *Language Assessment Quarterly* (Ockley, 2021). The reports demonstrate how assessment procedures for placement purposes were adapted to overcome challenges in the initial stage of the pandemic. Moreover, a study by Al Shlowiy et al. (2021) explored education-related problems in ERT in Saudi Arabia. They found that language teachers expressed concerns about cheating in an online context, a view also shared by Soltyska (2022) regarding German higher education. Al Shlowiy et al. (2021) pointed out that not all students possess the skills required for using online platforms. However, students disagreed with these perceptions. Bruce and Stakounis (2021) focused on the early response of the British university sector to the pandemic, studying changes in English for academic purposes (EAP) assessment procedures in the United Kingdom during the pandemic. Their work emphasised the contribution of emergency remote assessment (ERA) to ongoing discussions on the validity of assessment practices.

As reflected in recent studies, ERA concentrates on formative assessment and displaces large-scale assessments (Cooper et al., 2022). This new focus could reprioritise students' progression and authentic problem-based activities vs. make comparisons across students (Cooper et al., 2022).

Teacher Education

Finland

Teacher education in Finland is university-based. To become a qualified language teacher, one needs a master's degree (300 credits), which includes teachers' pedagogical studies (60 credits). Students usually have one language as their major and another as a minor. Most language teachers in Finland teach several languages (but it is not a requirement). The pedagogical studies focus on various aspects of teaching, such as social and philosophical foundations of education, pedagogy of teaching, and assessment. Out of the 60 credits in teacher education, one-third (20) are devoted to practicums. Contrary to the practice in many countries, students are not graded in their teaching practicums. They either pass or fail. Moreover, differences exist regarding the implementation of teacher education at Finnish universities. At most universities, the 60 credits are completed within one academic year. At others, the courses are divided over several years.

Finnish teacher education is described as research based, in which theory and practice converge (Säntti et al., 2018). In essence, pre-service teachers should immerse themselves in current research on pedagogy. They should be able to transform the theories and research findings for use in their classrooms. Language assessment has been subject to a myriad of studies over the last few decades. The latest trends are considered in the preparation of new curricula. Although the requirement of diverse assessment is prevalent in Finnish core curricula, questions have been raised about the teaching of assessment in Finnish teacher education.

According to Atjonen (2017), assessment is marginally considered in teacher education and the number of courses that focus on assessment is scarce. Nevertheless, the data in Atjonen's (2017) study were collected in 2015 (seven years before this publication). According to the latest research, English teachers in Finland need more training in creating multifaceted teaching and assessment practices, as well as rendering assessment more transparent (Härmälä & Marjanen, 2022). Therefore, one can argue that greater attention to assessment is required in Finnish teacher education.

Germany

In accordance with the federal structure of Germany, education at all levels of schooling (including teacher education) falls within the remit of 16 regional governments. Federal states aimed to guarantee the comparable quality of university training and enable pre-service teachers' mobility across the federal states. Thus, common content requirements for teacher education in 19 major general and vocational schooling subjects were agreed upon as they worked to form the basis for teacher education (KMK, 2008). Irrespective of the subject, teacher education comprises four key areas: (1) subject knowledge (*Fachwissenschaften*); (2) subject didactics (*Fachdidaktik*); (3) pedagogy (*Bildungswissenschaften*); and (4) and practical training (*Praxisphasen*).

Within their master of education degree programmes, prospective teachers must select two subjects to study. These subjects much align with the level and type of schooling they want to work in:

- **Primary School:** *Grundschule*, in most federal states years 1-4
- **Either Level of Secondary School:** *Sekundarstufe I*, in most federal states years 5-10 or *Sekundarstufe II*, years 11-13
- **Vocational School:** *Berufsschule*, for graduates of *Sekundarstufe I* who do not pursue academic education)

Teachers in the secondary setting are qualified to teach in their specific fields (*Fachlehrer:innen*). Educators in the primary area usually obtain qualifications in several subjects (*Klassenlehrer:innen*).

The subject-specific and pedagogical competencies to be achieved by a prospective teacher in any degree programme (regardless of specialisation) only briefly mentions assessment. One of the five key competencies that graduates must obtain is "basic knowledge of subject-specific assessment" (KMK, 2008, p. 4). This knowledge is expanded during the mandatory period of practical training, *Vorbereitungsdienst (Referendariat)*, that teachers-to-be must attend post-graduation and prior to official deployment in a school. However, the durations and core curricula of this practical phase vary across federal states.

Teachers of modern foreign languages should have, among other competencies:

Initial reflective experience in the competence-oriented planning and implementation of foreign language teaching in heterogeneous learning groups, e.g., with regard to target-differentiated and target-equal teaching and know the basics of performance diagnosis and assessment in the subject. (KMK, 2008, p. 44, author's translation)

Again, only rudimentary knowledge of assessment is expected of pre-service teachers of foreign languages.

Regarding educating for teaching and assessment in remote conditions or, more broadly, the role of digitalisation in teacher education, the minimum uniform requirements are even more vague. Admittedly, prospective teachers should:

Be able to assess and take on board developments in the field of digitalisation considering their subject-specific field and its pedagogical requirements, and to critically reflect on the possibilities and limits of digitalisation ... and contribute to further development of curricula and teaching methodologies" based on their experience with and reflection of digitalisation. (KMK, 2008, p. 44, author's translation)

Finally, they should "be aware of the opportunities that digital learning media may provide with regard to accessibility and use them for differentiation and individual support in their classes" (KMK, 2008, p. 44, author's translation). During their practical training, teachers should gain hands-on experience in using digital technologies to support teaching and learning processes, as well as organise their daily routines at school.

The "education in the digital world" strategy (author's own translation) was adopted in 2016 (KMK, 2016) to bridge digitalisation gaps in schooling at all levels. Yet, the goals were not achieved across all areas in the following five years. For instance, educating teachers in using digital media remains a major challenge as was shown with the data collected at the height of the pandemic and remote teaching in 2020 (Monitor Lehrerbildung, 2021). The results of previous studies with students, pre-service teachers, and teacher educators confirm that all stakeholder groups lacked routine with and confidence in using digital solutions in their professional activities (Schiefner-Rohs, 2021).

These facts conclude that current teacher education in Germany does not sufficiently address any of the key areas found in the present study. These include assessment literacy and preparedness for acting in remote online conditions.

DIGITAL ECONOMY AND SOCIETY INDEX (DESI)

The DESI is a body of data used to analyse Europe's overall digital performance and track the progress of countries within the European Union (EU) in terms of digital competitiveness. DESI is based on five key indicators, the first three of which are relevant in teacher education and autonomous professional development:

1. **Connectivity:** Accessibility of fixed and mobile broadband internet access and related costs
2. **Human Capital:** Aspects of internet use or basic and advanced digital skills
3. **Use of Internet Services:** Related to citizens' use of digital content, the use of the internet for communication, and diverse online transactions)

4. **Integration of Digital Technology:** Business digitalisation and the popularity of e-commerce
5. **Digital Public Services:** Online government and health services

Teachers' views on assessment in ERT and training needs can be better understood by knowing the extent to which participants in a particular country can rely on stable and financially accessible internet access in their work (educators who teach and assess learners) and professional development (organised training sessions or self-study). It is also beneficial to identify the level of teachers' overall digital skills (for example, familiarity and confidence when using the internet or how they plan to use it in their daily life).

DESI 2020 (European Commission, 2020), which retrospectively provided information about the months in which the COVID-19 pandemic commenced in Europe, showed Finland leading the ranking of 29 countries. Germany ranked 11th. According to the data for the subsequent year, which was published in November 2021 (European Commission, 2021a) when the present study was underway, Finland ranked 2nd and Germany 10th. One year later, based on DESI 2022 (European Commission, 2022), Finland regained the top position and Germany moved down to the 13th ranking. This trend and considerable discrepancy between Finnish and German societies and economies justifies the purposefulness of analysing English teachers' assessment skills for digital contexts and comparing them against the country indicators of overall digitalisation trends.

Several individual indicators can be identified that might explain the reasons for teachers' attitudes about and preparedness for engaging in any professional activity in online contexts. These indicators, as well as data for Finland and Germany based on the information provided by the European Commission (2021a, 2021b, 2021c), are presented in Table 1.

Table 1. Selected DESI indicators for Finland and Germany (2021)

	Finland	**Germany**	**EU Average**
Human Capital	Rank: 1	Rank: 7	-
o Basic skills*	76%	70%	56%
o Above-basic skills*	50%	39%	31%
Connectivity	Rank: 13	Rank: 6	-
Integration of digital technology	Rank: 1	Rank: 19	-
Digital public services	Rank: 3	Rank: 17	-

* Percentage of citizens in a given country who possess basic or above-basic digital skills

In 2021, Finland led the ranking for human capital and the level of digital skills among its citizens was well above the EU average. Finland was also the leading country in terms of the integration of digital technology by businesses and the third most advanced regarding the digitalisation of public services. German citizens had a generally high level of basic digital skills; however, the country ranked considerably lower than Finland regarding the implementation of digital solutions in entrepreneurial and public sectors.

These results, likely to reflect the actual extent of citizens' contact with and exposure to digitalisation in everyday contexts, might indicate different levels of familiarity with online solutions among Finnish and German teachers. However, other assumptions can be made based on the indicators for connectivity and access to broadband internet connection across the country, which show Germany (rank 6) ranked higher than Finland (rank 13).

Worth noting are the similarities related to technical accessibility. For instance, both countries had significant urban-rural digital divides in internet access. This is due to a large number of citizens who rely on mobile broadband and the comparable price of internet connections.

The 2021 DESI reports mention several measures that were introduced in Finland and Germany to increase the overall level of digitalisation and address the contemporary COVID-19 challenges for educators and pupils. It is likely that these projects and additional sources of funding and support, which came into force in 2020, influenced teachers' views on assessment literacy in ERT. Before the pandemic, Finnish schools had successfully implemented platforms and applications that went on to be used throughout the lockdowns. The measures in 2020 focused on equipping pupils with laptops for home use as part of the *Kaikille Kone – Device for All* campaign (https://www.oph.fi/fi/hankkeet/kaikille-kone-kampanja) and providing adequate learning materials for distance learning at no charge (European Commission, 2021b, p. 5). Germany's *DigitalPact School* funding programme (https://www.bundesregierung.de/breg-de/service/archiv/initiative-digitale-bildung-1860856), which was aimed at improving the digital infrastructure in schools, became operative in 2019. In 2020, its initial budget and scope was increased in view of the dramatic infrastructural and training shortages unveiled by the pandemic. The funds were used to employ additional staff to support technical services in schools, providing teachers and pupils with equipment for remote learning and teaching (European Commission, 2021c).

Both Finland and Germany implemented several measures to boost the general level of digitalisation within their societies. However, the data derived from the relevant DESI indicators show noteworthy differences between the two countries in this regard.

METHODOLOGY

Two instruments were designed and applied to collect data for this study. First, an online questionnaire was created in line with Dörnyei and Taguchi (2010). Its 25 open and closed items were grouped into six thematic sections. See Table 2 for details on sections, number, and types of items and sources of inspiration.

Table 2. Details of online questionnaire

Section	No. of Items (Total/Closed/Open)	Source of Inspiration
1. General information	8/8/-	-
2. Assessment-related teacher education	2/1*/1	Vogt and Tsagari (2014)
3. Assessment-related knowledge, abilities, and confidence	3/3*/-	Kremmel and Harding (2020)
4. Experience with emergency online teaching and assessment	2/1*/1	Zhang et al. (2021)
5. Professional development in language assessment	6/4*+1/1	Vogt and Tsagari (2014)
6. Concluding questions	4/-/4	-

* Matrix items with several statements and responses based on the Likert scale

Most of the closed items were on a three- or four-point Likert scale, whereby the respondents were asked to specify their level of disagreement or agreement with a given statement so trends in feelings and attitudes toward aspects of assessment and training can be inferred. Nine experts in assessment literacy from Finland, Germany, and the UK provided feedback on the draft questionnaire, which was subsequently improved and digitalised. Responses were collected by Qualtrics, a survey tool, between October 2021 and January 2022. The online survey link was shared via regional teachers' organisations and social media; therefore, a non-representative snowball sample was obtained.

Structured interviews constituted the other research instrument (Dörnyei, 2007). Each interview followed a set pattern, with 22 questions or prompts divided into four thematic blocks: (1) online assessment and assessment in ERT; (2) providing feedback with others in ERT; (3) self- and peer-assessment with others in ERT; and (4) culture-related aspects of assessment. The respondents to the online questionnaire who volunteered to serve as interviewees were contacted by both researchers involved in the project. Twenty-seven online interviews were conducted via Zoom between January and March 2022. All interviews were recorded with participants' permission; the responses were transcribed. Following the perspectivist approach (the analysis conducted by the practitioners from two countries with different professional experience in pre-service and in-service teacher training), the responses were thematically coded by both researchers independently of each other. The codes were compared and streamlined to an agreed interpretation (Cornish et al., 2014).

Regarding the quantitative data, descriptive statistics were computed because they summarise the general tendencies of the dataset (Dörnyei, 2007). ANOVA was not deemed suitable due to the uneven distribution of participants across countries. With its scope clearly focused on teachers' preparedness for assessment in online settings, including in the context of ERT, this chapter is based on a selection of data originating from both sources. Quantitative data was derived from questionnaire sections four and five, as well as selected sub-items from sections two and three pertinent to assessment in ERT and online settings. The qualitative data originates mainly from the first section of the interview.

Participants

Participants included 91 English teachers from Germany and 33 English teachers from Finland. The latter parts of the questionnaire were answered by 80 teachers from Germany and 26 from Finland. This may be because not all questions were mandatory. See Table 3 for detailed information on participants' backgrounds.

As described in Table 3, most participants were female, middle-aged, relatively experienced in teaching, and worked in higher education. The data from Germany reflects attitudes and views of English language instructors active in higher education. Moreover, the number of educational levels exceeds the number of participants because some teachers work at several levels.

Additional trends related to survey participation can be noticed (the reasons for which may be speculated). First, a comparatively low number of respondents from Finland (one-third of the figure for Germany) can be explained by the excessive number of educational surveys conducted in Finland. This resulted in teachers' reluctance to participate in another study (as anecdotal evidence and informal conversations with Finnish teachers confirmed). Second, contemporary needs for professional development in the field of assessment literacy in Finland might have been satisfied through the ARVO project (*Kieltenopettajien arviointiosaamisen päivittäminen* – Updating the assessment skills of language teachers), funded by the Finnish National Board of Education and conducted in 2021. The project, which focused on three assessment topics (formative, summative, and oral language assessment) included extensive teacher training offered by the University of Jyväskylä's Language Campus in spring 2021 and autumn 2021. It was attended by 400 teachers from the primary and upper secondary schools (Jyväskylän yliopisto, 2022). Third, with regard to homogenous teaching contexts of German teachers (only 14 out of 91 acting beyond the field of higher education), it can be assumed that the unequal support provided by teachers' organisations in disseminating the information about the survey (extensive support from the AKS, *Arbeitskreis der Sprachenzentren* – Association of Language Centres in Higher Education and limited support of regional associations of language teachers in primary and secondary education, *Philologenverbände*) might have led to this striking imbalance of teaching backgrounds.

Table 3. Participants of the study

		Germany	Finland
Gender	Male	28	25
	Female	61	7
	Other	1	-
	Prefer not to say	1	1
Age (Years)	20–29	3	3
	30–39	21	8
	40–49	26	12
	50–59	21	9
	60+	20	1
Teaching Experience (Years)	1–5	10	5
	6–10	16	7
	11–20	31	10
	20+	34	11
Institution	Primary school	2	8
	Secondary school	13	22
	Vocational education	2	2
	Higher education	77	8

Regarding the geographical background of the respondents, there was a significantly higher number of participants from Germany. Thus, the results of the study might not adequately reflect the attitudes and needs of the practitioners from both countries. However, considering the difference in population sizes (Germany's 84.3 million in January 2023 per the Federal Statical Office1 and Finland's 5.6 million in September 2022 per Statistics Finland2), the overall proportion of respondents seems justifiable.

Participation in this study was voluntary. All direct quotes from the open-ended questions and interviews are anonymous. Further, all participants consented to the use of their responses for research purposes.

RESULTS

Teacher Preparedness

The survey results provide evidence that a substantial percentage of teachers in both countries received no training in online assessment during their formal education, irrespective of age and level of teaching experience. These figures (82% Finnish and 74% German respondents) are indicative of a gap in teachers' assessment literacy regarding online evaluation (see Table 4).

As shown in Table 4, designing online assessment and creating rating scales were the two fields in which the teachers in both countries had not received training during their formal education. Similarly, training in using rating scales, interpreting test results, and forms of alternative assessment were scarce. These data also reveal that the teachers had received training in purposes of language assessment, principles of good assessment, and providing meaningful feedback.

Table 4. Assessment-related fields that participants received training in during formal education

	Germany (N = 91)				Finland (N = 33)			
	No Training	Some Training	Extensive Training	Do Not Remember	No Training	Some Training	Extensive Training	Do Not Remember
Purposes of language assessment	14%	53%	27%	6%	3%	55%	21%	21%
Principles of good assessment	18%	47%	31%	4%	12%	43%	33%	12%
Formative assessment	22%	40%	19%	19%	12%	61%	18%	9%
Summative assessment	23%	37%	18%	22%	-	67%	24%	9%
Forms of alternative assessments	28%	46%	17%	9%	27%	37%	15%	21%
Assessment-related terminology	22%	51%	25%	2%	15%	52%	18%	15%
Providing meaningful feedback	20%	31%	44%	5%	15%	49%	30%	6%
Creating rating scales	39%	41%	14%	6%	58%	18%	6%	18%
Using rating scales	28%	44%	22%	6%	33%	43%	15%	9%
Interpreting test results	31%	45%	18%	6%	40%	30%	18%	12%
Designing online assessment	74%	18%	6%	2%	82%	9%	6%	3%

Regarding information about their general perceptions of online assessment practices in ERT, the respondents were asked to use a four-point Likert scale to indicate the extent to which they agreed with the statements in Table 5 (1 is "I don't agree at all" and 4 is "I fully agree").

Interestingly, in both countries, few respondents were confident that the changes they introduced in their online assessment practices during ERT were based on theory and research. However, the level of support the teachers received from their institutions and regional or national organisations differed, with German teachers acknowledging more organised support than their Finnish counterparts. Overall, the means of the German teachers were slightly higher in several items, but no statistically significant differences were detected.

Table 5. Participants' views on assessment practices during ERT

	Germany		Finland	
	M	S.D.	M	S.D.
The changes in my assessment practices have been initiated by the institution/school (e.g., not to lower students' grades).	2.89	1.52	2.30	1.53
I have made substantial changes to my assessment practices during remote teaching.	3.33	1.48	3.21	1.47
The changes that I have introduced to my assessment practices are based on theory and research rather than impromptu decisions.	2.97	1.35	3.00	1.44
I have received some external support (training and/or resources) from my institution/school or from a regional/national organisation when reshaping assessment for remote teaching.	2.67	1.50	2.24	1.44
Overall, I am open-minded to developing new assessment methods.	3.41	1.19	3.12	1.39

Note: M = mean, SD = standard deviation
(Germany N = 91, Finland N = 33)

The qualitative data on online assessment-related challenges that practitioners faced in emergency remote conditions originates from open items in the survey and structured interviews. Common challenges were associated with lack of time (for designing, administering, and evaluating assessment tasks) and pressures related to time and workload under which the respondents and their colleagues had to work. These barriers were followed by having to overcome technical difficulties and addressing concerns related to cheating, test malpractice, academic integrity, and ensuring fairness of assessment overall. Considerable modifications to classroom assessment practices have been implemented in both countries. Yet, more often in Germany than Finland, the driving force behind such revisions and the key decision maker was often each respondent's institution rather than the teachers themselves.

As reported, the newly employed assessment methods comprised offline (non-digital) and online (digital) procedures. The former included portfolio assessment based on written or paper-based work, written assignments, and take-home exams. All were submitted on paper or photographed/scanned and sent as an e-mail attachment. Traditional in-person interviews took place under restricted pandemic conditions. The latter ranged from automatically assessed online tests in various virtual learning environments (the most common being Moodle), synchronous (sometimes invigilated in real time) and asynchronous online written exams or assignments, recorded oral responses submitted via cloud sharing or virtual learning environments, live oral presentations delivered via video conferencing systems like Zoom or MS Teams, and individual or group oral exams via video calls.

Perceived Training Needs and Assessment Literacy Gaps

The second research question focused on teachers' training needs in assessment. The results of the study corroborate ample demand for training in online assessment design and other areas.

Based on the qualitative data, most respondents, during their formal education, had been instructed on how to create (online) assessment tools and how to apply the tools in their education contexts. Teachers regretted not being taught about test validity, reliability, and fairness. They would welcome training in data (statistical) analysis for assessment purposes. Several interviewees admitted that "they wished they had been taught anything about that topic" or described their experience of shifting to remote teaching and testing as "it was like we were in a darkened room looking for a switch on the wall." The expressed mindsets share many parallels irrespective of interviewees' backgrounds and length of professional experience.

Surprisingly, voices for more training in online assessment appeared as frequently as for training in the use of Common European Framework of Reference (CEFR) for assessment purposes (among Finnish teachers) and in choosing suitable assessment methods for their learners (among German teachers). When asked to name specific areas of online assessment in which training is required, some interviewees confirmed their fragmentary knowledge of online assessment. They confessed that "they don't know (what they would like to learn about online assessment), because they don't know what they don't know." Other interviewees suggested familiarising themselves with tools for online assessment, receiving guidelines on designing cheat-proof or assessment tasks that could not be plagiarised, managing legal issues, and handling technical setbacks. Table 6 shows the domains in which teachers felt they needed more opportunities for professional development and an indication of the amount of training requested (ranging from no training to extensive training).

As Table 6 illustrates, the teachers highlighted a need for training in choosing assessment procedures for their learners, designing and implementing rating scales, and integrating peer-assessment in their class or course. Compared with Finnish teachers, German teachers need more training in designing online tests or assessments, preparing classroom tests or assessments, integrating self-assessments in their class or course, and using portfolio assessment. In contrast, Finnish teachers needed more training than German teachers in using CEFR for assessment purposes.

Another question targeted individual sub-skills that are commonly assessed in isolation or integrated tasks. Table 7 summarises respondents' views on their training needs in these five domains.

Table 6. Domains participants need additional training

	No Training		Some Training		Extensive Training	
	Germany	Finland	Germany	Finland	Germany	Finland
Choosing assessment procedures for learners	38%	50%	62%	46%	-	4%
Designing online tests/assessment	24%	42%	60%	58%	16%	-
Preparing classroom tests/assessment	68%	92%	31%	8%	1%	-
Designing and implementing rating scales	48%	42%	46%	54%	6%	4%
Giving feedback to students based on information from various forms of assessment	59%	65%	41%	31%	-	4%
using informal, continuous, non-test type of assessment	53%	62%	41%	34%	6%	4%
Integrating self-assessment in a class/course	35%	73%	59%	19%	6%	8%
Integrating peer-assessment in a class/course	46%	54%	48%	42%	6%	4%
Using portfolio assessment	45%	58%	44%	38%	11%	4%
Using CEFR for assessment	62%	38%	31%	58%	6%	4%

(Germany N = 80, Finland N = 26)

Table 7. Domains participants need additional training

	No Training		Some Training		Extensive Training	
	Germany	Finland	Germany	Finland	Germany	Finland
Assessing receptive skills (reading/listening)	60%	65%	40%	35%	-	-
Assessing productive skills (speaking/writing)	65%	46%	35%	50%	-	4%
Assessing micro-linguistic aspects (e.g., grammar/vocabulary)	64%	69%	35%	31%	1%	-
Assessing integrated language skills like language mediation	40%	27%	53%	69%	7%	4%
Assessing aspects of the target-language cultures	40%	34%	48%	58%	12%	8%

(Germany N = 80, Finland N = 26)

Teachers in both countries felt they need more training, particularly in assessing aspects of the target-language cultures (intercultural competence) and assessing integrated language skills like language mediation (reading-into-writing). However, Finnish teachers need more training in assessing productive skills (speaking/ writing) as compared to German teachers.

As can be seen in Figure 1, more than half of the German teachers expressed the need for additional training in all the items. They would appreciate training in using statistics to analyse assessment quality and designing assessment for multicultural groups. These two areas were also chosen by most Finnish respondents, although slightly less often. In contrast, further training in the remaining fields of assessment literacy (establishing fairness, reliability, and validity) would not be necessary according to the Finnish teachers. It can be concluded that German teachers indicated significantly more assessment areas that they would like to learn about than their Finnish counterparts.

Figure 1. Participants' training needs according to topic
(Germany N = 80, lefthand bars; Finland N = 26, righthand bars)

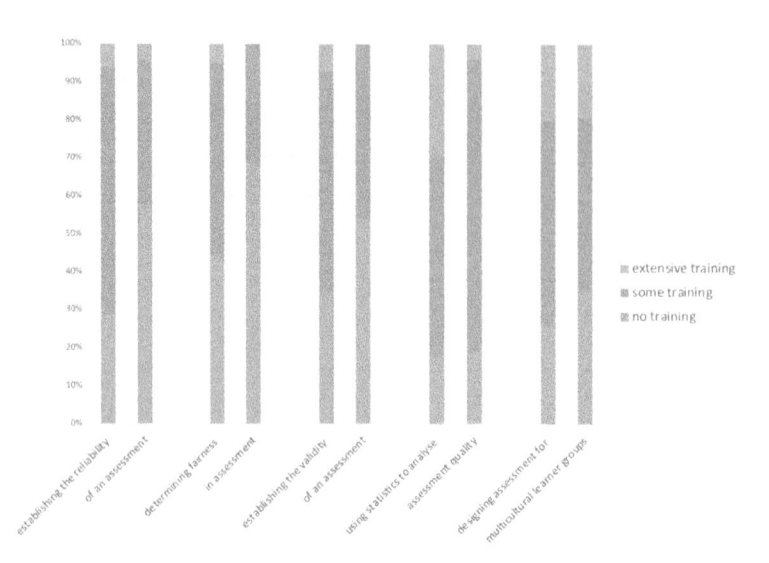

Possible Training Formats

In addition to potential content areas of future training, the quantitative data offer practical suggestions for preferred formats and delivery modes. It also includes temporal and financial aspects of training that need to be considered when planning professional development measures for these target groups.

As can be seen in Figure 2, according to the respondents from both countries, two teaching units or one full day were the most appropriate lengths of time for assessment training. The appropriate format would be online if the training were to take two teaching units. By contrast, if the training were to last one full day, the appropriate format would be face-to-face (German teachers) or blended (Finnish teachers). Remarkably, a significant percentage of respondents irrespective of the country was uninterested in any training provided face-to-face or in a blended format. Only minor fractions were not interested in online training.

Figure 2. Overview of the type and intensity of requested training
(Germany N = 80, lefthand bars; Finland N = 26, righthand bars); *2TU equals 90 minutes.

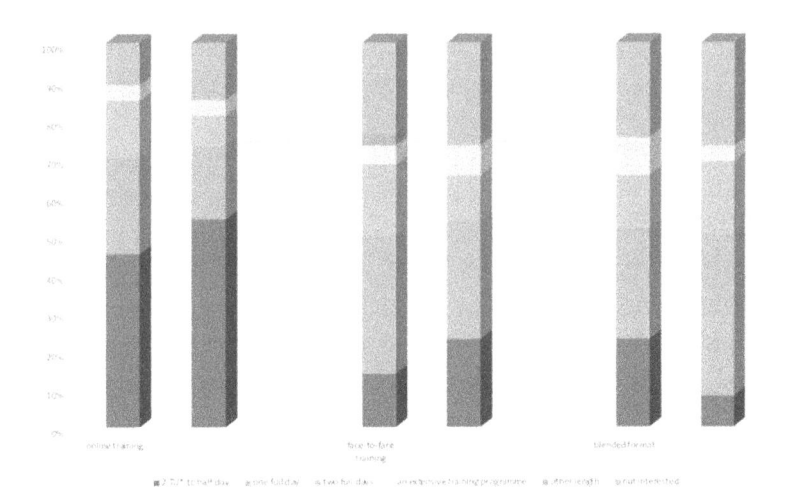

In addition to commenting on the format of training, the teachers shed light on the temporal and financial aspects of training. The results are shown in Table 8. A large majority of respondents would attend training if it were provided within their regular working hours. About half of the respondents from each country would attend training beyond regular working hours if they were remunerated for their participation. Overall, charging no fees for the training seemed far more significant for German teachers than their Finnish counterparts.

Table 8. Participants' opinions on scheduling and sources of financing the training

	Germany	Finland
Only provided within regular working hours	64%	77%
Offered after hours (beyond regular working hours)	49%	38%
Offered after hours (beyond regular working hours) and receive remuneration for training duration	53%	46%
Free of charge	63%	31%

(Germany N = 80; Finland N = 26)

DISCUSSION

This study compared the perceived preparedness of English teachers in Finland and Germany for designing, performing, and evaluating assessment activities, particularly in remote teaching contexts. It also explored potential areas for additional training. It is important to study the effects of the pandemic on education and assessment to enhance future practices for ERT and pandemic pedagogy (Milman, 2020). Based on the experience, it seems justified to claim that remote teaching may become more prominent in education (Can & Silman-Karanfil, 2022; Jin et al., 2021). Therefore, more research is required to elucidate how teaching, learning, and assessment in remote contexts can be reshaped to provide an effective instructive learning environment for every student.

Assessment literacy in English courses in Finland and Germany has not been compared previously. This, the contribution of this study is twofold. First, it provides an account of English teachers' assessment-related practices and decisions. Second, it offers insights into future training in assessment in the context of both countries.

Concerning the first research question, according to the participants, training for online assessment was non-existent (with few exceptions). On the one hand, this result was expected as most teachers had completed their education before the expansion of digital materials and communication modes in education. On the other hand, based on DESI indicators collated and published annually by the European Commission, the overall level of digitalisation in Finland is higher than in Germany. Therefore, it was surprising to learn that this difference did not affect the training on online assessment.

Further, the respondents noted that topics like interpreting test results and creating rating scales were overlooked in teacher education in both countries. These results suggest that training in many focal aspects of assessment literacy had been marginalised in Finland and Germany, which corroborates the findings of previous research (Berry et al., 2019; Green, 2018; Mellati & Khademi, 2018; Vogt & Tsagari, 2014). The teacher plays a key role in selecting appropriate assessment practices for instruction (Mellati & Khademi, 2018; Popham, 2018). Thus, one wonders how instructors could be expected to succeed in the implementation of assessment with limited training in the subject.

In addition, differences in assessment literacy across countries were detected as summative and formative assessment are more prevalent in Finnish teacher education. This highlights the country-specific feature of teacher education and the aspects of assessment, which are valued more in some countries than in others. In recent years, the art of formative assessment has been emphasised in Finnish education. This might explain the prevalence of formative assessment in Finnish teacher education and teachers' confidence in designing and applying this form of evaluation.

The second research question focused on teachers' training needs in assessment. The results show that the respondents perceived their knowledge of assessing integrated language skills and aspects of target-language cultures to be insufficient. Thus, they opted for more training. Furthermore, teachers in Finland and Germany require additional training in using statistics and assessing multicultural learner groups.

Differences between the countries were also detected. For example, teachers in Finland did not indicate a strong need for training on choosing assessment procedures for learners or creating classroom tests (as opposed to their colleagues in Germany). However, Finnish teachers expressed the need for additional training on the use of CEFR.

Given that assessment literacy training should be individualised and context-specific (DeLuca et al., 2016; Drackert et al., 2020), the results of this study contribute to the literature by outlining the perceived need for English teachers' training in Finland and Germany. In other words, assessment literacy training in both countries should focus on online assessment, integrated language skills, and multicultural learner groups. However, in Germany, greater attention is required in summative and formative assessment. Finnish teachers need training in the use of CEFR. In terms of the mode of training, to match the preferences of most of the respondents, it could be delivered in a blended format (i.e., partially online and partially in-person for teachers in Finland or face-to-face for teachers in Germany.

Fundamentally, LAL is conceptualised as an apprenticeship-based initiative (Yan & Fan, 2021). This alludes to the interplay of both theory and practice. However, the decisions the teachers made regarding online assessment in ERT were not primarily based on theories or research. This is alarming because language teachers need a solid theoretical ground for assessment-related decisions (Fulcher, 2012; Xu & Brown, 2016). This visibly attests to the fact that teachers need more support in combining theories and research findings with decisions made in the classroom and remote teaching.

Assessment is an inherent part of learning (DeLuca et al., 2016; Lam, 2019; Popham, 2018), which is why assessment decisions cannot be made haphazardly. Therefore, assessment literacy training should focus on addressing the relationship between theory and practice. It should explore how a solid knowledge of theory can contribute to effectively using assessment practices in both contact teaching and online classrooms. Moreover, teachers' decisions did not originate from their institutions/schools. From the point view of enhancing LAL, these results are promising. If institutions initiated the decisions and guidelines for all assessment-related decisions, this would hinder teachers' development of LAL (Mansouri et al., 2021).

The contributions of this study provide multifaceted theoretical and practical suggestions to augment the literature. First, teacher education should incorporate more comprehensive training in assessment. Although several topics have been addressed in sufficient depth, a range of topics has been overlooked or considered only marginally. Similar results have been emphasised in previous studies. Therefore, one wonders how the teaching of assessment should be enhanced to educate teachers who are mindful of the opportunities that could arise from the better use of diverse assessment practices. One solution for this conundrum could be to increase credits for assessment courses, which would naturally allow for a more in-depth consideration of assessment. Furthermore, future teachers would be more familiar with current research and better equipped with knowledge and practical tools for assessing students' proficiency.

Second, online assessment and remote teaching should be placed among the primary concerns in contemporary teacher education. After the lessons learned from ERT during the pandemic, research has elucidated diverse ways for organising high-quality instruction in online contexts. Incorporating these results into current practices will allow for various types of teaching in the future (i.e., blended courses, online courses, or distance learning). Instead of the conventional way of arranging education as a face-to-face instruction, remote teaching would diversify the implementation of teaching.

As the results of this study indicate, neither online assessment nor online pedagogy have been sufficiently considered in teacher education. In addition, unprepared teachers faced numerous challenges with online assessment, such as technical problems and issues related to the fairness of assessment and academic integrity. To meet the requirements of future education, it is of the utmost importance to revisit course programmes and include the notions of online assessment, ERA, and online pedagogy.

The main limitation of this study is the unbalanced number of participants from Finland and Germany. Furthermore, the levels of education of the respondents from both countries were unevenly represented. For example, the German data centres on higher education teachers, in which the pedagogy differs substantially from those in primary schools. Therefore, the results concerning the differences are tentative.

Despite the uneven number of participants across countries and levels of education, the results enlighten researchers about English teachers' perceptions of assessment practices in ERT. The results provide insights for further inquiry with larger datasets and a different sampling strategy. Moreover, the questionnaire was distributed through e-mail lists and groups on social media. Interviews were conducted via videoconferencing. Thus, teachers were unreachable if they are not active users of social media, do not regularly read their e-mail, or are not at ease with communicating via Zoom. These limitations must be considered when reviewing the implications of the results.

Remote teaching might become more prominent in future education. Therefore, additional research is required to form a more comprehensive understanding of assessment and ERT. More specifically, research targeting a range of stakeholders (like language learners at various levels of schooling, foreign language instructors, and decision makers at all levels of education) is important. Furthermore, future studies should address the lessons learnt from ERT: instructive assessment practices created by teachers; novel practices used by teachers; and ways to apply these practices in future instruction (contact teaching and remote contexts). From the point of view of assessment literacy, it is vital to explore teachers' knowledge of the pedagogy of ERT, particularly focusing on digital assessment practices to unravel deficiencies and provide training.

CONCLUSION

The data obtained through this study provide a valuable source of recommendations for designing and conducting teacher professional development. To meet the perceived training and upskilling the needs of in-service teachers, opportunities for professional development should address both contemporary (originating from the experience of teaching remotely in recent years) and long-term (teachers' education curricula overall) assessment literacy deficits. The training should be tailor-made, considering country-specific preferences related to delivery mode, length, timing, and cost of training. Divergent thematic areas of assessment expertise and reported knowledge gaps among practitioners from both countries should be considered.

The results of the study must be treated with caution. In addition, the results may not apply to all other contexts as they are based on a relatively small, non-representative sample. However, they may be relevant to teachers' educators and practitioners' experiences of ERT and assessing around the world. The results bore similar characteristics, such as insufficient theoretical preparation, lack of familiarity with digital technologies used for teaching and assessment purposes, time pressure, and growing concerns about the fairness of applied assessment tools and methods.

The overall level of digitalisation in teachers' countries of employment did not seem to affect their perceived preparedness for remote or online assessment. Thus, there is hope that LAL training, if designed and administered in line with local requirements, may be successful, irrespective of a given country's progress in digitalisation as measured by the Digital Economy and Society Index. In the contemporary world, educators can rarely opt out of applying digital and online solutions in their teaching and assessment practices. Understanding what teachers need to know and how they prefer to close the gaps in their assessment literacy should guide professional development and contribute to optimising assessment practices.

DISCLOSURE STATEMENT

The authors declare no conflict of interest.

FUNDING

This research received no particular funding.

REFERENCES

Al Shlowiy, A., Al-Hoorie, A. H., & Alharbi, M. (2021). Discrepancy between language learners and teachers concerns about emergency remote teaching. *Journal of Computer Assisted Learning*, *37*(6), 1528–1538. doi:10.1111/jcal.12543

American Federation of Teachers (AFT). (1990). *Standards for teacher competence in educational assessment of students.* https://buros.org/standards-teacher-competence-educational-a ssessment-students

Atjonen, P. (2017). Arviointiosaamisen kehittäminen yleissivistävän koulun opettajien koulutuksessa – opetussuunnitelmatarkastelun virittämiä näkemyksiä [Development of assessment literacy in the training of teachers in general education – views generated by reviewing the national core curriculum]. In V. Britschgi, & J. Rautopuro (Eds.), Kriteerit puntarissa (pp. 131–169). Suomen kasvatustieteellinen seura.

Berry, V., Sheehan, S., & Munro, S. (2019). What does language assessment literacy mean to teachers? *ELT Journal*, *73*(2), 113–123. doi:10.1093/elt/ccy055

Biggs, J., & Tang, C. (2011). *Teaching for quality learning at university* (4th ed.). Open University Press.

Bøhn, H., & Tsagari, D. (2021). Teacher educators' conceptions of language assessment literacy in Norway. *Journal of Language Teaching and Research*, *12*(2), 222–233. doi:10.17507/jltr.1202.02

Bøhn, H., & Tsagari, D. (2022). Language assessment literacy: Understanding the construct from Norwegian EFL teachers' perspective. *Studies in Language Assessment*, *11*(1), 119–148. doi:10.58379/UNUD5510

Brookhart, S. (2011). Educational assessment knowledge and skills for teachers. *Educational Measurement: Issues and Practice, 30*(1), 3–12. doi:10.1111/j.1745-3992.2010.00195.x

Bruce, E., & Stakounis, H. (2021). *The impact of Covid-19 on the UK EAP sector during the initial six months of the pandemic. BALEAP-funded report.* https://www.baleap.org/wp-content/uploads/2021/06/BALEAP-Rep ort-Covid-and-EAP-May-2021.pdf

Bruce, E., & Stakounis, H. (2022). Emergency remote assessment (ERA) narratives from the UK English for academic purposes (EAP) sector. In K. Sadeghi (Ed.), *Technology-assisted language assessment in diverse contexts. Lessons from the transition to online testing during COVID-19* (pp. 34–53). Routledge. doi:10.4324/9781003221463-4

Butler, Y. G., Peng, X., & Lee, J. (2021). Young learners' voices: Towards a learner-centered approach to understanding language assessment literacy. *Language Testing, 38*(3), 429–455. doi:10.1177/0265532221992274

Can, I., & Silman-Karanfil, L. (2022). Insights into emergency remote teaching in EFL. *ELT Journal, 76*(1), 34–43. doi:10.1093/elt/ccab073

Cooper, A., DeLuca, C., Holden, M., & MacGregor, S. (2022). Emergency assessment: Rethinking classroom practices and priorities amid remote teaching. *Assessment in Education: Principles, Policy & Practice, 29*(5), 534–554. doi:10.1080/0969594X.2022.2069084

Cornish, F., Gillespie, A., & Zittoun, T. (2014). Collaborative analysis of qualitative data. In U. Flick (Ed.), *The SAGE handbook of qualitative data analysis* (pp. 79–93). SAGE Publications Ltd. doi:10.4135/9781446282243.n6

Delgado, J. Z., & Rodriguez, C. (2022). Language assessment literacy of language teachers in the context of adult education in Spain. *Studies in Language Assessment, 11*(1), 64–91. doi:10.58379/RRDV2344

DeLuca, C., LaPointe-McEwan, D., & Luhanga, U. (2016). Approaches to classroom assessment inventory: A new instrument to support teacher assessment literacy. *Educational Assessment, 21*(4), 248–266. doi:10.1080/10627197.2016.1236677

Dörney, Z., & Taguchi, N. (2010). *Questionnaires in second language research: Construction, administration, and processing* (2nd ed.). Routledge.

Dörnyei, Z. (2007). *Research methods in applied linguistics.* Oxford University Press.

Drackert, A., Konzett-Firth, C., Stadler, W., & Visser, J. (2020). An empirical study on Romance language teachers' subjective theories regarding assessment purposes and good tests. In D. Tsagari (Ed.), *Language assessment literacy: From theory to practice* (pp. 50–70). Cambridge Scholars Publishing.

European Commission. (2020). *Digital economy and society index (DESI) 2021. Thematic chapters.* https://digital-strategy.ec.europa.eu/en/library/digital-eco nomy-and-society-index-desi-2020

European Commission. (2021a). *Digital economy and society index (DESI) 2021. Thematic chapters.* https://digital-strategy.ec.europa.eu/en/library/digital-eco nomy-and-society-index-desi-2021

European Commission. (2021b). *Digital economy and society index (DESI) 2021. Finland.* https://digital-strategy.ec.europa.eu/en/library/digital-eco nomy-and-society-index-desi-2021

European Commission. (2021c). *Digital economy and society index (DESI) 2021. Germany.* https://digital-strategy.ec.europa.eu/en/library/digital-eco nomy-and-society-index-desi-2021

European Commission. (2022). *Digital economy and society index (DESI) 2021. Thematic chapters.* https://digital-strategy.ec.europa.eu/en/library/digital-eco nomy-and-society-index-desi-2022

Fulcher, G. (2012). Assessment literacy for the language classroom. *Language Assessment Quarterly*, *9*(2), 113–132. doi:10.1080/15434303.2011.642041

Green, A. (2018). Teacher assessment literacy for the classroom. In T. Aksit, H. I. Mengu, & R. Turner (Eds.), *Bridging Teaching, Learning and Assessment in the English Language Classroom* (pp. 2–7). Cambridge Scholars Publishing.

Harding, L., & Kremmel, B. (2016). Teacher assessment literacy and professional development. In D. Tsagari & J. Banerjee (Eds.), *Handbook of Second Language Assessment* (pp. 413–427). De Gruyter. doi:10.1515/9781614513827-027

Härmälä, M., & Marjanen, J. (2022). *Englantia koronapandemian aikaan. A-englannin osaaminen 9. luokan lopussa keväällä 2021* [English during the corona pandemic. Learning outcomes of A level English at the end of the 9th grade in spring 2021]. Kansallinen koulutuksen arviointikeskus.

Hodges, C., Moore, S., Lockee, B., Trust, T., & Bond, A. (2020). *The difference between emergency remote teaching and online learning.* https://er.educause. edu/articles/2020/3/the-difference-betw een-emergency-remote-teaching-and-online-learning

Inbar-Lourie, O. (2008). Constructing a language assessment knowledge base: A focus on language assessment courses. *Language Testing*, *25*(3), 385–402. doi:10.1177/0265532208090158

Jin, L., Xu, Y., Deifell, E., & Angus, K. (2021). Emergency remote language teaching and U.S.-based college-level world language educators' intention to adopt online teaching in postpandemic times. *Modern Language Journal*, *105*(2), 412–434. doi:10.1111/modl.12712

Jyväskylän yliopisto. (2022). *ARVO – Kieltenopettajien arviointiosaamisen päivittäminen* [Updating language teachers' assessment literacy]. https://www.jyu.fi/hytk/fi/laitokset/solki/arvo-2013-kielten opettajien-arviointiosaamisenpaivittaminen

Kremmel, B., & Harding, L. (2020). Towards a comprehensive, empirical model of language assessment literacy across stakeholder groups: Developing the language assessment literacy survey. *Language Assessment Quarterly*, *17*(1), 100–120. doi:10.1080/15434303.2019.1674855

Kultusministerkonferenz (2008). *Ländergemeinsame inhaltliche Anforderungen für die Fachwissenschaften und Fachdidaktiken in der Lehrerbildung. KMK Beschluss vom 16.10.2008 i.d.F. vom 16.05.2019* [Resolution of the Standing Conference of the Ministers of Education and Cultural Affairs dated 16.10.2008 as amended on 16.05.2019]. https://www.kmk.org/fileadmin/veroeffentlichungen_be-schluess e/2008/2008_10_16-Fachprofile-Lehrerbildung.pdf

Kultusministerkonferenz (2016). *Bildung in der digitalen Welt. Strategie der Kultusministerkonferenz* [Education in the Digital World. Strategy of the Standing Conference of the Ministers of Education and Cultural Affairs]. https://www.kmk.org/fileadmin/Dateien/veroeffentlichungen_be schluesse/2018/Strategie_Bildung_in_der_digitalen_Welt_idF._ vom_07.12.2017.pdf

Lam, R. (2019). Teacher assessment literacy: Surveying knowledge, conceptions and practices of classroom-based writing assessment in Hong Kong. *System, 81*, 78–89. doi:10.1016/j.system.2019.01.006

Mäkipää, T., Hahl, K., Luodonpää-Manni, M. (2021). Teachers' perceptions of assessment and feedback practices in Finland's foreign language classes during the COVID-19 pandemic. *CEPS Journal, 11*, 219–240. .1108 doi:10.26529/cepsj

Mansouri, B., Molana, K., & Nazari, M. (2021). The interconnection between second language teachers' language assessment literacy and professional agency: The mediating role of institutional policies. *System, 103*, 102674. doi:10.1016/j.system.2021.102674

Mellati, M., & Khademi, M. (2018). Exploring teachers' assessment literacy: Impact on learners' writing achievements and implications for teacher development. *The Australian Journal of Teacher Education, 43*(6), 1–19. doi:10.14221/ajte.2018v43n6.1

Milman, N. B. (2020). *This is emergency remote teaching, not just online teaching.* https://www.edweek.org/leadership/opinion-this-is-emergency- remote-teaching-not-just-online-teaching/2020/03

Monitor Lehrerbildung. (2021). *Lehrkräfte vom ersten Semester an für die digitale Welt qualifizieren* [Qualifying teachers for the digital world from the very first semester of their studies]. https://2020.monitor-lehrerbildung.de/export/sites/default/. content/Downloads/Monitor-Lehrerbildung_Digitale-Welt_Policy -Brief-2021.pdf

O'Loughlin, K. (2013). Developing the assessment literacy of university proficiency test users. *Language Testing, 30*(3), 363–380. doi:10.1177/0265532213480336

Ockey, G. J. (2021). An overview of COVID-19's impact on English language university admissions and placement tests. *Language Assessment Quarterly, 18*(1), 1–5. doi:10.1080/15434303.2020.1866576

Popham, W. J. (2018). *Assessment literacy for educators in a hurry.* ACSD.

Säntti, J., Puustinen, M., & Salminen, J. (2018). Theory and practice in Finnish teacher education: A rhetorical analysis of changing values from the 1960s to the present day. *Teachers and Teaching, 24*(1), 5–21. doi:10.1080/13540602.2017.1379387

Schiefner-Rohs, M. (2021). Lehrer*innenbildung (in) der Post-Digitalität: erste Impulse zur Diskussion [Teacher education (in) the post-digital age: initial impulses for discussion]. In R. Arnold, C. Gómez Tutor, & R. Ulber (Eds.), *Professionalisierungsprozesse in der Lehrkräftebildung. Rückblicke – Einblicke – Ausblicke.* Schneider Verlag Hohengehren.

Soltyska, A. (2022). Von cheating zu e-cheating: Gefahren und Chancen aktueller Entwicklungen im Bereich des Prüfungsbetrugs beim Fremdsprachentesten [From cheating to e-cheating: risks and opportunities of current developments in the field of academic misconduct in foreign language assessment]. In A. Brandt (Ed.), *Quo vadis Sprachenlehre? Neue Unterrichtsformen vor der Tür. Dokumentation der 1. AKS-Online-Konferenz. Fremdsprachen in Lehre und Forschung* (pp. 19–35). AKS Verlag.

Taylor, L. (2013). Communicating the theory, practice and principles of language testing to test stakeholders: Some reflections. *Language Testing*, *30*(3), 403–412. doi:10.1177/0265532213480338

Tsagari, D., & Vogt, K. (2017). Assessment literacy of foreign language teachers around Europe: Research, challenges, and future prospects. *Papers in Language Testing and Assessment*, *6*(1), 41–63. doi:10.58379/UHIX9883

Vogt, K., & Tsagari, D. (2014). Assessment literacy of foreign language teachers: Findings of a European study. *Language Assessment Quarterly*, *11*(4), 374–402. doi:10.1080/15434303.2014.960046

Vogt, K., Tsagari, D., Csépes, I., Green, A., & Sifakis, N. (2020). Linking learners' perspectives on language assessment practices to teachers' assessment literacy enhancement (TALE): Insights from four European countries. *Language Assessment Quarterly*, *17*(4), 410–433. doi:10.1080/15434303.2020.1776714

Vurdien, R., & Puranen, P. (2022). Teacher attitudes toward online assessment in challenging times. In B. Arnbjörnsdóttir, B. Bédi, L. Bradley, K. Friðriksdóttir, H. Garðarsdóttir, S. Thouësny, & M. J. Whelpton (Eds.), Intelligent CALL, granular systems, and learner data: short papers from EUROCALL 2022 (pp. 370–374). Research-publishing.net. doi:10.14705/rpnet.2022.61.1486

Xu, Y., & Brown, G. T. L. (2016). Teacher assessment literacy in practice: A reconceptualization. *Teaching and Teacher Education*, *58*, 149–162. doi:10.1016/j.tate.2016.05.010

Yan, X., & Fan, J. (2021). "Am I qualified to be a language tester?": Understanding the development of language assessment literacy across three stakeholder groups. *Language Testing*, *38*(2), 219–246. doi:10.1177/0265532220929924

Zhang, C., Yan, X., & Wang, J. (2021). EFL teachers' online assessment practices during the COVID-19 pandemic: Changes and mediating factors. *The Asia-Pacific Education Researcher*, *30*(6), 499–507. doi:10.100740299-021-00589-3

ADDITIONAL READING

Mäkipää, T. (2023). Students' perceptions of teacher assessment practices in foreign language emergency remote teaching during Covid-19 in Finland. *Studies in Language Assessment*. Advance online publication.

Sadeghi, K. (Ed.). (2022). *Technology-assisted language assessment in diverse contexts. Lessons from the transition to online testing during COVID-19*. Routledge. doi:10.4324/9781003221463

Sadeghi, K., & Douglas, D. (Eds.). (2023). *Fundamental considerations in technology mediated language assessment*. Routledge. doi:10.4324/9781003292395

Tsagari, D., & Vogt, K. (Eds.). (2022). Special issue: Contextualising language assessment literacy. Studies in Language Assessment, 11(1), 1–153.

KEY TERMS AND DEFINITIONS

Assessment Literacy: The knowledge and skills needed to create and evaluate examinations and tests, as well as the ability to make research-based decisions when creating and scoring tests. The ability to use various types of assessment to enhance students' learning in contact teaching, hybrid teaching, and remote teaching environments. An understanding of wider assessment-related theoretical and ethical frameworks is an integral aspect of assessment literacy.

Assessment of Integrated Language Skills: This combines the assessment of two or more language skills using the same assessment task to simulate an authentic target language use situation. Typically, integrated assessment tasks are based on performance, leading to speaking or writing based on the input obtained through reading or listening.

Digitalisation: The incorporation of digital technologies in social or business activities and processes, typically aimed to make improvements and provide value-producing outcomes. In education, the use of digital technologies includes desktop computers, portable devices, the internet, and software applications to teach, enhance learning, and assess learners' progress.

Emergency Remote Assessment (ERA): The employment of teacher-, student-, and learning-centred assessment practices in emergency remote teaching to assess students' skills and knowledge and enhance students' learning and well-being. This method does not necessarily adhere to the demands of high-quality assessment.

Emergency Remote Teaching (ERT): Teaching that was originally planned to occur in a classroom but, due to unforeseen circumstances, had to be implemented in a remote format. This teaching method is created of out necessity. Thus, it may not meet the requirements of high-quality instruction.

Formative Assessment: The term used to denote planned and ongoing assessment activities and tasks aimed at monitoring student learning. These observations are used to inform teachers' practices and assist students to improve their learning.

Online Assessment: The evaluation of a test-taker's abilities and/or knowledge. This assessment is conducted online, either remotely or in a test venue.

Summative Assessment: This assessment occurs at the end of the learning cycle. It aims to measure whether and to what extent students have achieved the learning goals of a teaching/learning unit.

ENDNOTES

[1] https://www.destatis.de/EN/Themes/Society-Environment/Population/Current-Population/_node.html

[2] https://www.stat.fi/en/publication/cl7rl42jefkdd0cw3zww9grdg

Compilation of References

Abbasian, M. (2016). Dynamic Assessment: Review of Literature. *International Journal of Modern Language Teaching and Learning*, *1*(3), 116–120.

Abduh, M. (2021). Full-time online assessment during COVID-19 lockdown: EFL teachers' perceptions. *Asian EFL Journal Research Articles*, *28*(01), 26–46.

Aghazadeh, Z., & Soleimani, M. (2020). The effect of e-portfolio on EFL learners' writing accuracy, fluency and complexity. *The Reading Matrix: An International Online Journal*, *20*(2), 182–199.

Agnihotri, R. K. (2014). Multilinguality, Education and Harmony. *International Journal of Multilingualism*, *11*(3), 364–379. doi:10.1080/14790718.2014.921181

Akimov, A., Kobinger, S., & Malin, M. (2018). Determinants of student success in finance courses. *Journal of Financial Education*, *44*(2), 223–245. https://www.jstor.org/stable/10.2307/26775505

Al Shlowiy, A., Al-Hoorie, A. H., & Alharbi, M. (2021). Discrepancy between language learners and teachers concerns about emergency remote teaching. *Journal of Computer Assisted Learning*, *37*(6), 1528–1538. doi:10.1111/jcal.12543

Alatni, B. S., Abubakar, I. R., & Iqbal, S. A. (2021). Covid-19 and rapid course adaptations in Saudi Arabia: An experiential learning and recommendations for online education. *Frontiers in Psychology*, *12*, 643203. doi:10.3389/fpsyg.2021.643203 PMID:35002820

Alavi, S. M., Dashtestani, R., & Mellati, M. (2021). Crisis and Changes in Learning Behaviours: Technology-Enhanced Assessment in Language Learning Contexts. *Journal of Further and Higher Education*, *46*(4), 461–474. doi:10.1080/0309877X.2021.1985977

Alderson, J. C., & Wall, D. (1993). Does washback exist? *Applied Linguistics*, *14*(2), 115–129. doi:10.1093/applin/14.2.115

Alemi, M., Miri, M., & Mozafarnezhad, A. (2019). Investigating the Effects of Online Concurrent Group Dynamic Assessment on Enhancing Grammatical Accuracy of EFL Learners. *Tabaran Institute of Higher Education: International Journal of Language Testing*, *9*(2), 29–43.

Alexiou, A., & Paraskeva, F. (2010). Enhancing self-regulated learning skills through the implementation of an e-portfolio tool. *Procedia: Social and Behavioral Sciences*, *2*(2), 3048–3054. doi:10.1016/j.sbspro.2010.03.463

Ali, S., Uppal, M. A., & Gulliver, S. R. (2018). A conceptual framework highlighting e-learning implementation barriers. *Information Technology & People*, *31*(1), 156–180. doi:10.1108/ITP-10-2016-0246

Aljaafreh, A., & Lantolf, J. P. (1994). Negative feedback as regulation and second language learning in the zone of proximal development. *Modern Language Journal*, *78*(4), 465–483. doi:10.1111/j.1540-4781.1994.tb02064.x

Allaei, S. K., & Connor, U. (1990). Using performative assessment instruments with ESL student writers. In L. Hamp-Lyons (Ed.), *Assessing second language writing in academic contexts* (pp. 227–240). Ablex.

Allehaiby, W. H., & Al-Bahlani, S. (2021). Applying Assessment Principles during Emergency Remote Teaching: Challenges and Considerations. *Arab World English Journal*, *12*(4), 3–18. doi:10.24093/awej/vol12no4.1

Almossa, S. Y., & Alzahrani, S. M. (2022). Assessment practices in Saudi higher education during the COVID-19 pandemic. *Humanities & Social Sciences Communications*, *9*(1), 5. doi:10.105741599-021-01025-z

Aloni, M., & Harrington, C. (2018). Research based practices for improving the effectiveness of asynchronous online discussion boards. *Scholarship of Teaching and Learning in Psychology*, *4*(4), 271–289. doi:10.1037tl0000121

American Federation of Teachers (AFT). (1990). *Standards for teacher competence in educational assessment of students*. https://buros.org/standards-teacher-competence-educational-a ssessment-students

Amir, Z., Ismail, K., & Hussin, S. (2011). Blogs in language learning: Maximizing students' collaborative writing. *Procedia: Social and Behavioral Sciences*, *18*, 537–543. doi:10.1016/j.sbspro.2011.05.079

Anam, S., Akhiriyah, S., & Iswati, H. D. (2023). Advances in Social Science, Education and Humanity Research: Looking into the Role of Dynamic Assessment in English Grammar Mastery of Indonesian EFL Learners. *Paper presented at the Unima International Conference on Social Sciences and Humanity 2022*. Atlantic Press. https://www.atlantis-press.com/proceedings/unicssh-22/125984 028

Anastasiadou, A. (2015). EFL Curriculum Design: The Case of the Greek State School Reality in the Last Two Decades (1997-2014). *International Journal of Applied Linguistics and English Literature*, *4*(2), 112–119.

Angouri, J., Mattheoudakis, M., & Zigrika, M. (2010). Then how will they get 'the much-wanted paper'? A multifaceted study of English as a foreign language in. Greece. In A. Psaltou-Joycey & M. Mattheoudakis (Eds.), *Advances in Research on Language Acquisition and Teaching: Selected Papers* (pp. 179–194). Greek Applied Linguistics Association.

Ariani, N., & Febrianti, Y. (2022). Compromising peer assessment using Google Forms in an online essay-writing course. In Habiddin, Karmina, & Wonorahardjo, (Eds.), Improving Assessment and Evaluation Strategies on Online Learning (1st ed., pp. 56–62). essay, Routledge. doi:10.1201/9781003261346-9

Arifuddin, A., Turmudi, T., & Rokhmah, U. N. (2021). Alternative assessments in online learning during covid-19 pandemic: The strengths and weaknesses. *International Journal of Elementary Education*, *5*(2), 240. doi:10.23887/ijee.v5i2.33532

Aristovnik, A., Keržič, D., Ravšelj, D., Tomaževič, N., & Umek, L. (2020). Impacts of the COVID-19 pandemic on life of higher education students: A global perspective. *Sustainability (Basel)*, *12*(20), 8438. doi:10.3390u12208438

Assessment Reform Group. (2002). *Assessment for learning: 10 principles: Research-based principles to guide classroom practice*. Assessment Reform Group.

Atjonen, P. (2017). Arviointiosaamisen kehittäminen yleissivistävän koulun opettajien koulutuksessa – opetussuunnitelmatarkastelun virittämiä näkemyksiä [Development of assessment literacy in the training of teachers in general education – views generated by reviewing the national core curriculum]. In V. Britschgi, & J. Rautopuro (Eds.), Kriteerit puntarissa (pp. 131–169). Suomen kasvatustieteellinen seura.

Babaee, M., & Tikoduadua, M. (2013). E-portfolios: A New Trend in Formative Writing Assessment [IJMEF]. *International Journal of Modern Education Forum*, *2*(2), 49–56.

Babamoradi, P., Nasiri, M., & Mohammadi, E. (2018). Learners' attitudes toward using dynamic assessment in teaching and assessing IELTS writing task one. *International Journal of Language Testing*, *8*(1), 1–11.

Compilation of References

Bailey, K. M., & Curtis, A. (2015). *Learning about language assessment: Dilemmas, decisions, and directions* (2nd ed.). National Geographic Learning/Heinle, Cengage, Learning.

Baleni, Z. G. (2015). Online formative assessment in higher education: Its pros and cons. *Electronic Journal of e-Learning*, *13*, 228–236.

Ball, H. L. (2019). Conducting Online Surveys. *Journal of Human Lactation*, *35*(3), 413–417. doi:10.1177/0890334419848734 PMID:31084575

Balloo, K., Evans, C., Hughes, A., Zhu, X., & Winstone, N. (2018). Transparency Isn't Spoon-Feeding: How a Transformative Approach to the Use of Explicit Assessment Criteria Can Support Student Self-Regulation. *Frontiers in Education*, *3*, 69. doi:10.3389/feduc.2018.00069

Banerjee, A. V., & Duflo, E. (2014). (Dis) organization and success in an economics MOOC. *The American Economic Review*, *104*(5), 514–518. doi:10.1257/aer.104.5.514 PMID:25214652

Banerjee, H. L. (2019). Investigating the construct of topical knowledge in Second language assessment: A scenario-based assessment approach. *Language Assessment Quarterly*, *16*(2), 133–160. doi:10.1080/15434303.2019.1628237

Bangun, I., Li, Z., & Mannion, P. (2019). Future teacher educators in critical evaluation of educational technology through collaborative digital storytelling projects. In K. Graziano (Ed.), Proceedings of Society for Information Technology & Teacher Education International Conference (pp. 595-600). Las Vegas, NV, United States: Association for the Advancement of Computing in Education (AACE). Retrieved from https://www.learntechlib.org/primary/p/207702/

Bangun, I., Mannion, P., & Li, Z. (2023). EAP writing with peer and instructor e-feedback: A qualitative study. Manuscript submitted for publication.

Baroni, A., Dooly, M., Garcés García, P., Guth, S., Hauck, M., Helm, F., Lewis, T., Mueller-Hartmann, A., O'Dowd, R., Rienties, B., & Rogaten, J. (2019). *Evaluating the impact of virtual exchange on initial teacher education: A European policy experiment*. Research Publishing.net. doi:10.14705/rpnet.2019.29.9782490057337

Barram, K. (2017). *How to Use Formative Feedback to Help Students Achieve Better Marks in Summative Assesment*. The University of Manchester. https://www.elearning.fse.manchester.ac.uk

Barrett, H., & Carney, J. (2005). Conflicting paradigms and competing purposes in electronic portfolio development. *Educational Assessment*. https://electronicportfolios.org/portfolios/LEAJournal-Barre ttCarney.pdf

Bartolic, S. K., Boud, D., Agapito, J., Verpoorten, D., Williams, S., Lutze-Mann, L., Matzat, U., Moreno, M. M., Polly, P., Tai, J., Marsh, H. L., Lin, L., Burgess, J.-L., Habtu, S., Rodrigo, M. M. M., Roth, M., Heap, T., & Guppy, N. (2021). A multi-institutional assessment of changes in higher education teaching and learning in the face of COVID-19. *Educational Review*, *74*(3), 517–533. doi:10.1080/00131911.2021.1955830

Baturay, M. H., & Daloğlu, A. (2010). E-portfolio assessment in an online English language course. *Computer Assisted Language Learning*, *23*(5), 413–128. doi:10.1080/09588221.2010.520671

Bayır, D. (2022). Impacts of the covid-19 pandemic on Experiential Learning: Development of a community-grounded online internship program. *Journal of Education for Library and Information Science*, *63*(4), 372–388. doi:10.3138/jelis.2020-0108

Beach, R., & Friedrich, T. (2006). Response to writing. In C. A. MacArthur, S. Graham, & J. Fitzgerald (Eds.), *Handbook of writing research* (pp. 222–234).

Bender, G., & Jordaan, R. (2007). Student Perceptions and Attitudes about Community Service-Learning in the Teacher Training Curriculum. *South African Journal of Education*, *27*(4), 631–654.

Benson, A. D. (2003). Assessing participant learning in online environments. *New Directions for Adult and Continuing Education*, *2003*(100), 69–78. doi:10.1002/ace.120

Berenson, R., Boyles, G., & Weaver, A. (2008). Emotional intelligence as a predictor of success in online learning. *International Review of Research in Open and Distance Learning*, *9*(2), 1–17. doi:10.19173/irrodl.v9i2.385

Berman, G., & Paradies, Y. (2010). Racism, disadvantage and multiculturalism: Towards effective anti-racist praxis. *Ethnic and Racial Studies*, *33*(2), 214–232. doi:10.1080/01419870802302272

Berry, V., Sheehan, S., & Munro, S. (2017). Exploring teachers' language assessment literacy: A social constructivist approach to understanding effective practices. In *ALTE (2017). Learning and Assessment: Making the Connections–Proceedings of the ALTE 6th International Conference*, (pp. 201-207). ALTE.

Berry, V., Sheehan, S., & Munro, S. (2019). What does language assessment literacy mean to teachers? *ELT Journal*, *73*(2), 113–123. doi:10.1093/elt/ccy055

Biggs, J. (1999). *Teaching for quality learning at university*. SRHE and Open University Press.

Bin Mubayrik, H. F. (2020). New Trends in Formative-Summative Evaluations for Adult Education. *SAGE Open*, *10*(3). doi:10.1177/2158244020941006

Bitchener, J., & Storch, N. (2016). Written Corrective [*Development*. Multilingual Matters.]. *Feedback*, L2.

Black, P., & Wiliam, D. (1998). *Inside the black box: Raising standards through classroom assessment*. School of Education King's College London.

Blair, J., Gala, P., Tariq, A., Harrison, D., & Ajjan, H. (2020). Online Experiential Learning: Methods, Advantages, and Challenges. Society for Marketing Advances Proceedings, 111–113.

Bøhn, H., & Tsagari, D. (2021). Teacher educators' conceptions of language assessment literacy in Norway. *Journal of Language Teaching and Research*, *12*(2), 222–233. doi:10.17507/jltr.1202.02

Bøhn, H., & Tsagari, D. (2022). Language assessment literacy: Understanding the construct from Norwegian EFL teachers' perspective. *Studies in Language Assessment*, *11*(1), 119–148. doi:10.58379/UNUD5510

Bolliger, D. U., & Shepherd, C. E. (2010). Student perceptions of ePortfolio integration in online courses. *Distance Education*, *31*(3), 295–314. doi:10.1080/01587919.2010.513955

Bolotov, V., Kovaleva, G., Pinskaya, M., & Valdman, I. (2013). *Developing the Enabling Context for Student Assessment in Russia*. The International Bank for Reconstruction and Development. https://documents1.worldbank.org/curated/en/6733714683365358 23/pdf/Developing-the-enabling-context-for-student-assessmen t-in-Russia.pdf

Boulaid, F., & Moubtassime, M. (2019). Investigating the role of Kahoot in the enhancement of English vocabulary among Moroccan university students : English department as a case study. *International Journal of Innovation and Applied Studies*, *27*(3), 797–808.

Bozkurt, A., Jung, I., Xiao, J., Vladimirschi, V., Schuwer, R., Egorov, G., & Olcott, D. Jr. (2020). A global outlook to the interruption of education due to COVID-19 pandemic: Navigating in a time of uncertainty and crisis. *Asian Journal of Distance Education*, *15*(1), 1–126. https://eric.ed.gov/?id=EJ1290039

Braun, V., & Clarke, V. (2006). Using thematic analysis in psychology. *Qualitative Research in Psychology*, *3*(2), 77–101. doi:10.1191/1478088706qp063oa

Breslow, L., Pritchard, D. E., DeBoer, J., Stump, G. S., Ho, A. D., & Seaton, D. T. (2013). Studying learning in the worldwide classroom research into edX's first MOOC. *Research & Practice in Assessment*, *8*, 13–25.

Compilation of References

Brookhart, S. (2011). Educational assessment knowledge and skills for teachers. *Educational Measurement: Issues and Practice*, *30*(1), 3–12. doi:10.1111/j.1745-3992.2010.00195.x

Brookhart, S. (2013). *How to create and use rubrics for formative assessment and grading*. Association for Supervision and Curriculum Development.

Brown, D. H. (1990). *Language assessment: Principles and classroom practices*. Longman.

Brown, J. D. (2005). *Testing in language programs: A comprehensive guide to English language assessment*. Prentice Hall Regents.

Bruce, E., & Stakounis, H. (2021). *The impact of Covid-19 on the UK EAP sector during the initial six months of the pandemic. BALEAP-funded report*. https://www.baleap.org/wp-content/uploads/2021/06/BALEAP-Rep ort-Covid-and-EAP-May-2021.pdf

Bruce, E., & Stakounis, H. (2022). Emergency remote assessment (ERA) narratives from the UK English for academic purposes (EAP) sector. In K. Sadeghi (Ed.), *Technology-assisted language assessment in diverse contexts. Lessons from the transition to online testing during COVID-19* (pp. 34–53). Routledge. doi:10.4324/9781003221463-4

Bruner, J. (1996). *The culture of Education*. Harvard University Press. doi:10.4159/9780674251083

Burden, A. (2018) b. Three Methods to Enhance Peer Review in Your Classroom. In M. Weimer (Ed.), The College Teacher's Handbook: A Resource Collection for New Faculty (pp. 73- 76). Madison, WI: Magna Publications.

Burden, A. (2018). a. Pinterest: Pinning the gap between SoTL and SLCE in higher education. *The International Journal of Research on Service-Learning and Community Engagement*, *6*(1). Advance online publication. doi:10.37333/001c.6816

Bursac, V., & Wilsker, A. (2020). Thriving During a Crisis: Transferring Experiential Learning Online. *Business Education Innovation Journal*, *12*(2), 30–39.

Burzynski Bullard, S. B., & Anderson, N. (2014). "I'll take commas for $200": An instructional intervention using games to help students master grammar skills. *Journalism & Mass Communication Educator*, *69*(1), 5–16. doi:10.1177/1077695813518778

Butler, Y. G., Peng, X., & Lee, J. (2021). Young learners' voices: Towards a learner-centered approach to understanding language assessment literacy. *Language Testing*, *38*(3), 429–455. doi:10.1177/0265532221992274

Canals, L., Granena, G., Yilmaz, Y., & Malkicka, A. (2020). Second language learners' and teachers' perceptions of delayed immediate corrective feedback in an asynchronous online setting: An exploratory study. *TESL Canada Journal*, *37*(2), 181–209. doi:10.18806/tesl.v37i2.1336

Can, I., & Silman-Karanfil, L. (2022). Insights into emergency remote teaching in EFL. *ELT Journal*, *76*(1), 34–43. doi:10.1093/elt/ccab073

Cappellini, M., & Hsu, Y.-Y. (2020). When future teachers meet real learners through telecollaboration: An experiential approach to learn how to teach languages online. *Journal of Virtual Exchange*, *3*, 1–11. doi:10.21827/jve.3.35751

Cardoso, A. C. S. (2011). Feedback em contextos de ensino-aprendizagem on-line. *Linguagens e Diálogos*, *2*(2), 17–34.

Carifio, J., Jackson, I., & Dagostino, L.James Carifio, Ina Jackson, Lorrain. (2001). Effects of diagnostic and prescriptive comments on the revising behaviors of community college students. *Community College Journal of Research and Practice*, *25*(2), 109–122. doi:10.1080/10668920150218498

Carless, D. (2006). Differing perceptions in the feedback process. *Studies in Higher Education*, *31*(2), 219–233. doi:10.1080/03075070600572132

Carless, D. (2007). Learning-oriented assessment: Conceptual Bases and practical implications. *Innovations in Education and Teaching International*, *44*(1), 57–66. doi:10.1080/14703290601081332

Carless, D., & Winstone, N. (2020). Teacher feedback literacy and its interplay with student feedback literacy. *Teaching in Higher Education*, *28*(1), 150–163. doi:10.1080/13562517.2020.1782372

Carstairs, J., & Myors, B. (2009). Internet testing: A natural experiment reveals test score inflation on a high-stakes, unsupervised cognitive test. *Computers in Human Behavior*, *25*(3), 738–742. https://www.sciencedirect.com/science/article/pii/S074756320 9000260. doi:10.1016/j.chb.2009.01.011

Center for the Greek Language. (2013). *Common European Framework of Reference for Languages: Learning, Teaching, Assessment. Assessment criteria*. Greek trans. Centre for the Greek Language. https://www.greeklanguage.gr/certification/node/112.html

Challis, D. (2005). Towards the mature ePortfolio: Some implications for higher education. *Canadian Journal of Learning and Technology*, *31*(3). https://www.learntechlib.org/p/43166/. doi:10.21432/T2MS41

Chamot, A. U. (2005). Language learning strategy instruction: Current issues and research. [Cambridge University Press.]. *Annual Review of Applied Linguistics*, *25*, 112–130. doi:10.1017/S0267190505000061

Chan, C. K. Y. (2010). Group assessment. CETL. https://ar.cetl.hku.hk/group.htm#6

Chan, C. K. Y. (2022). *Assessment for Experiential Learning*. Routledge. doi:10.4324/9781003018391

Chapelle, C. A., Cotos, E., & Lee, J. (2015). Validity arguments for diagnostic assessment using automated writing evaluation. *Language Testing*, *32*(3), 385–405. doi:10.1177/0265532214565386

Chappuis, J., & Stiggins, R. J. (2020). *Classroom assessment for student learning: Doing it right — using it well* (2nd ed.). Pearson.

Chen, C.-M., Wang, J.-Y., Chen, Y.-T., & Wu, J.-H. (2016). Forecasting reading anxiety for promoting English-language reading performance based on reading annotation behavior. *Interactive Learning Environments*, *24*(4), 681–705. doi:10.1080/10494820.2014.917107

Cheng, A.-C., Jordan, M. E., & Schallert, D. L. (2013). Reconsidering assessment in online/hybrid courses: Knowing versus learning. *Computers & Education*, *68*, 51–59. doi:10.1016/j.compedu.2013.04.022

Cheng, L. (2005). *Changing language teaching through language testing: A Washback study*. Cambridge University Press.

Choi, I., Wolf, M. K., Pooler, E., Sova, L., & Faulkner-Bond, M. (2019). Investigating the benefits of scaffolding in assessments of young English learners: A case for scaffolded retell tasks. *Language Assessment Quarterly*, *16*(2), 161–179. doi:10.1080/15434303.2019.1619180

Choudhury, S., & Pattnaik, S. (2020). Emerging themes in e-learning: A review from the stakeholders' perspective. *Computers & Education*, *144*, 103657. doi:10.1016/j.compedu.2019.103657

Chow, A., & Leung, P. (2011). Assessment for learning in language classrooms. In *R*. Berry and B.

Chugai, O. Y., Yamshinska, N. V., Svyrydova, L. H., & Kutsenok, N. M. (2018). Alternative assessment during the pandemic: teachers of English perspective. *SWorldJournal*, (09-02), 90–99. doi:10.30888/2663-5712.2021-09-02-039

Chugai, O., & Pawar, A. (2022). Using alternative assessment during the pandemic by Indian and Ukrainian teachers of English. *Facta Universitatis*, *6*(1), 001–009.

Ciesielkiewicz, M. (2019). The use of e-portfolio in higher education: From the students' perspective. *Issues in Educational Research, 29*(3), 649–667.

Clarke, A. E. (2007). Grounded theory: Critiques, debates, and situational analysis. The SAGE Handbook of social science methodology, 423–442. doi:10.4135/9781848607958.n23

Conache, M., Dima, R., & Mutu, A. (2016). A comparative analysis of MOOC (Massive Open Online Course) platforms. *Informatica Economica, 20*(2).

Coombe, C., Troudi, S., & Al-Hamly, M. (2012). Foreign and second language teacher assessment literacy: Issues, challenges and recommendations. In C. Coombe, P. Davidson, B. O'Sullivan, & S. Stoynoff (Eds.), *The Cambridge Guide to Second Language Assessment* (pp. 20–29). Cambridge University Press.

Cooper, A., DeLuca, C., Holden, M., & MacGregor, S. (2022). Emergency assessment: Rethinking classroom practices and priorities amid remote teaching. *Assessment in Education: Principles, Policy & Practice, 29*(5), 534–554. doi:10.1080/0969594X.2022.2069084

Cooperrider, D., Stavros, J. M., & Whitney, D. (2008). *The appreciative Inquiry handbook: For leaders of change*. Berrett-Koehler Publishers.

Cornish, F., Gillespie, A., & Zittoun, T. (2014). Collaborative analysis of qualitative data. In U. Flick (Ed.), *The SAGE handbook of qualitative data analysis* (pp. 79–93). SAGE Publications Ltd. doi:10.4135/9781446282243.n6

Council of Europe. (2001). *Common European Framework of Reference for Languages: Learning, teaching, assessment*. Cambridge University Press.

Council of Europe. (2010). *Common European Framework of Reference for Languages: learning, teaching, assessment*. Council of Europe Publishing. www.coe.int/lang-CEFR

Creswell, J. W. (2014). *Research design: Qualitative, quantitative, and mixed methods approaches* (4th ed.). Sage.

Creswell, J. W., & Guetterman, T. C. (2021). *Educational research: Planning, conducting and evaluating quantitative and qualitative research*. Pearson.

Creswell, J. W., & Miller, D. L. (2000). Determining Validity in Qualitative Inquiry. *Theory into Practice, 39*(3), 124–130. doi:10.120715430421tip3903_2

Crusan, D., Plakans, L., & Gebril, A. (2016). Writing assessment literacy: Surveying second language teachers' knowledge, beliefs, and practices. *Assessing Writing, 28*, 43–56. doi:10.1016/j.asw.2016.03.001

Cummins, J. (1984). Wanted: A theoretical framework for relating language proficiency to academic achievement among bilingual students. In: Rivera, C. (ed.). pp. 2-19. Language proficiency and academic achievement. Multilingual Matters.

Cummins, J. (2000). Academic language learning, transformative pedagogy, and information technology: Towards a critical balance. *TESOL Quarterly, 34*(3), 537–548. doi:10.2307/3587742

Cummins, P. W., & Davesne, C. (2009). Using electronic portfolios for second language assessment. *Modern Language Journal, 93*, 848–867. doi:10.1111/j.1540-4781.2009.00977.x

Darren, G., & Mallery, P. (2020). *IBM SPSS Statistics 26 Step by Step. A Simple Guide and Reference* (7th ed.). Routledge.

Davis, L. (2013). *Building rubrics democratically - TESOL international association*. tesol.org. https://www.tesol.org/docs/default-source/books/6P/building- rubrics-democratically_full.pdf?status=Temp&sfvrsn=0.9838654 007180547

Dawson, P., Henderson, M., Ryan, T., Mahoney, P., Boud, D., Phillips, M., & Molloy, E. (2018). Technology and Feedback Design. In *Learning* (pp. 1–45). Design, and Technology. doi:10.1007/978-3-319-17727-4_124-1

Deane, P., Song, Y., van Rijn, P., O'Reilly, T., Fowles, M., Bennett, R., Sabatini, J., & Zhang, M. (2019). The case for scenario-based assessment of written argumentation. *Reading and Writing*, *32*(6), 1575–1606. doi:10.100711145-018-9852-7

Deepa, S. (2022a). Options in multiple-choice questions: Oh, Really! Yours sincerely, Adult learners! *Language and Language Teaching: A Peer-reviewed Journal*, 81-86.

Deepa, S., & Durairajan, G. (2022). 'Warm welcome or cold shoulder': Demystifying ('positively noxious') English in the multilingual classroom. R. Kaushik & A L Khanna (eds). Critical Issues in ELT, pp. 30-51. Aakar Books.

Deepa, S. (2022b). Pedagogic scaffolding and anthrogogic learning contexts: Issues in metaphor mismatch. *Journal of English Language Teachers'. Interaction Forum.*, *13*(2), 3–7.

Deepa, S. (2022c). Pedagogic practices in higher education and Peter Pan syndrome: An appraisal. *Fortell*, *45*, 164–173.

Deepa, S. (2022d). Verbal disposition: The need for language potentiality in anthrogogic spaces. *Journal of English Language Teaching*, *64*(6), 17–24.

Delgado, J. Z., & Rodriguez, C. (2022). Language assessment literacy of language teachers in the context of adult education in Spain. *Studies in Language Assessment*, *11*(1), 64–91. doi:10.58379/RRDV2344

DeLuca, C., LaPointe-McEwan, D., & Luhanga, U. (2016). Approaches to classroom assessment inventory: A new instrument to support teacher assessment literacy. *Educational Assessment*, *21*(4), 248–266. doi:10.1080/10627197.2016.1236677

Demirel, M., & Duman, H. (2015). The use of portfolio in English Language Teaching and its effects on achievement and attitude. *Procedia: Social and Behavioral Sciences*, *191*, 2634–2640. doi:10.1016/j.sbspro.2015.04.598

Dillenbourg, P. (1999). What do you mean by collaborative learning? In P. Dillenbourg (Ed.), *Collaborative-learning: Cognitive and Computational Approaches* (pp. 1–19). Elsevier.

Dinh, L. P., & Nguyen, T. T. (2020). Pandemic, social distancing, and social work education: Students' satisfaction with online education in Vietnam. *Social Work Education*, *39*(8), 1074–1083. doi:10.1080/02615479.2020.1823365

Donaghue, H. (2020). Feedback Talk as a Means of Creating, Ratifying and Normalising an Institutionally Valued Teacher Identity. *Journal of Language, Identity, and Education*, *19*(6), 395–411. doi:10.1080/15348458.2019.1696683

Dörney, Z., & Taguchi, N. (2010). *Questionnaires in second language research: Construction, administration, and processing* (2nd ed.). Routledge.

Dörnyei, Z. (2007). *Research methods in applied linguistics*. Oxford University Press.

Dörnyei, Z. (2007). *Research Methods in Applied Linguistics: Quantitative, Qualitative and Mixed Methodologies*. Oxford University Press.

Dörnyei, Z. (2007). *Research methods in applied linguistics: Quantitative, qualitative, and mixed methodologies*. Oxford University Press.

Dörnyei, Z., & Taguchi, T. (2010). *Questionnaires in Second Language Acquisition: Construction, Administration and Processing* (2nd ed.). Routledge.

Compilation of References

Drackert, A., Konzett-Firth, C., Stadler, W., & Visser, J. (2020). An empirical study on Romance language teachers' subjective theories regarding assessment purposes and good tests. In D. Tsagari (Ed.), *Language assessment literacy: From theory to practice* (pp. 50–70). Cambridge Scholars Publishing.

Driscoll, M., Bryant, D., & National Research Council. (1998). *Learning about assessment, learning through assessment*. National Academies Press. doi:10.17226/6217

Durairajan, G. (2015). *Assessing Learners: A Pedagogic Resource*. Cambridge University Press.

Du, W. Y., & Zhou, C. Y. (2019). Web-based scaffolding teaching of EAP reading and writing. *Creative Education*, *10*(8), 1863–1872. doi:10.4236/ce.2019.108134

Ekahitanond, V. (2014). Promoting university students' critical thinking skills through peer feedback activity in an online discussion forum. *The Alberta Journal of Educational Research*, *59*(2), 247–265. doi:10.11575/ajer.v59i2.55617

Elboshi, A. (2021). Web-enhanced peer feedback in ESL writing classrooms: A literature review. *English Language Teaching*, *14*(4), 66–76. doi:10.5539/elt.v14n4p66

Ellis, R. (2009). Corrective Feedback and Teacher Development. *Journal of Linguistics and Language Teaching*, *1*(1), 3–18.

ElSaheli-Elhage, R. (2021). Access to students and parents and levels of preparedness of educators during the COVID-19 emergency transition to e-learning. *International Journal on Studies in Education*, *3*(2), 61–69. doi:10.46328/ijonse.35

Elsalem, L., Al-Azzam, N., Jum'ah, A. A., & Obeidat, N. (2021). Remote E-exams during Covid-19 pandemic: A cross-sectional study of students' preferences and academic dishonesty in faculties of medical sciences. *Annals of Medicine and Surgery (London)*, *62*, 326–333. doi:10.1016/j.amsu.2021.01.054 PMID:33520225

Errington, E. P. (2003). *Developing Scenario-based Learning: practical insights for tertiary educators*. Dunmore Press.

Errington, E. P. (2005). *Creating Learning Scenarios: A planning guide for adult educators*. CoolBooks.

Errington, E. P. (2011). Mission possible: Using near-world scenarios to prepare graduates for the professions. *International Journal on Teaching and Learning in Higher Education*, *23*, 84–91.

Etemadi, S. H., & Abbasian, G.-R. (2023). Dynamic assessment and EFL learners' writing journey: Focus on DA modalities and writing revision types. *Teaching English Language*, *17*(1), 53-79. https://www.teljournal.org/article_162923.html

European Commission (2020). *Digital Education Action Plan 2021-2027. Resetting education and training for the digital age*. COM (2020) 624.

European Commission. (2020). *Digital economy and society index (DESI) 2021. Thematic chapters*. https://digital-strategy.ec.europa.eu/en/library/digital-eco nomy-and-society-index-desi-2020

European Commission. (2021a). *Digital economy and society index (DESI) 2021. Thematic chapters*. https://digital-strategy.ec.europa.eu/en/library/digital-eco nomy-and-society-index-desi-2021

European Commission. (2021b). *Digital economy and society index (DESI) 2021. Finland*. https://digital-strategy.ec.europa.eu/en/library/digital-eco nomy-and-society-index-desi-2021

European Commission. (2021c). *Digital economy and society index (DESI) 2021. Germany*. https://digital-strategy.ec.europa.eu/en/library/digital-eco nomy-and-society-index-desi-2021

European Commission. (2022). *Digital economy and society index (DESI) 2021. Thematic chapters*. https://digital-strategy.ec.europa.eu/en/library/digital-eco nomy-and-society-index-desi-2022

Evans, C. (2013). Making Sense of Assessment Feedback in Higher Education. *Review of Educational Research*, *83*(1), 70–120. doi:10.3102/0034654312474350

Farahian, M., & Avarzamani, F. (2018). The impact of portfolio on EFL learners' metacognition and writing performance. *Cogent Education*, *5*(1), 1–21. doi:10.1080/2331186X.2018.1450918

Farhady, H. (1982). Measures of language proficiency from the learner's perspective. *TESOL Quarterly*, *16*(1), 43. doi:10.2307/3586562

Farrokh, P., & Rahmani, A. (2017). Dynamic assessment of writing ability in transcendence tasks based on Vygotskian perspective. *Asian-Pacific Journal of Second and Foreign Language Education*, *2*(10), 1–23. doi:10.118640862-017-0033-z

Fask, A., Englander, F., & Wang, Z. (2014). Do Online Exams Facilitate Cheating? An Experiment Designed to Separate Possible Cheating from the Effect of the Online Test Taking Environment. *Journal of Academic Ethics*, *12*(2), 101–112. https://www.researchgate.net/publication/272018789. doi:10.100710805-014-9207-1

Fenton, L., & Gallant, K. (2016). Integrated experiential education: Definitions and a conceptual model. *The Canadian Journal for the Scholarship of Teaching and Learning*, *7*(2), 7. doi:10.5206/cjsotl-rcacea.2016.2.7

Fernandes, S., Flores, M. A., & Lima, R. M. (2010). Students' views of assessment in project-led engineering education: Findings from a case study in Portugal. *Assessment & Evaluation in Higher Education*, *37*(2), 163–178. htps:// doi:10.1080/02602938.2010.515015

Ferracane, M. F., & Lee-Makiyama, H. (2017). *China's technology protectionism and its non-negotiable rationales*. European Centre for International Political Economy. https://euagenda.eu/upload/publications/untitled-96376-ea.pd f

Feuerstein, R., Rand, Y., & Rynders, J. E. (1988). *Don't Accept Me as I Am. Helping Retarded Performers Excel*. Plenum. doi:10.1007/978-1-4899-6128-0

Finstad, K. (2010). Response interpolation and scale sensitivity: Evidence against 5-point scales. *Journal of Usability Studies*, *5*(3), 104–110.

Fluck, A. E. (2019). An international review of eExam technologies and impact. *Computers & Education*, *132*, 1–15. doi:10.1016/j.compedu.2018.12.008

Fluckiger, J. (2010). Single Point Rubric: A Tool for Responsible Student Self-Assessment. *The Delta Kappa Gamma Bulletin: International Journal of Professional Educators*, *76*(4), 18–25.

Fluminhan, C. S. L., Arana, A. S. A., & Fluminhan, A. (2013). A importância do feedback como ferramenta pedagógica na educação a distância. *Colloquium Humanarum, 10*(Especial), 721-728.

Foucault, M. (1978/1991). *Discipline and Punish: The Birth of the Prison*. Vintage Books.

Francis, D., & Hester, S. (2012). *An invitation to ethnomethodology: Language, society and social interaction*. Sage Publications. doi:10.4135/9781849208567

Freire, P. (1970/2005). *Pedagogy of the oppressed*. Penguin.

Fulcher, G. (2012). Assessment literacy for the language classroom. *Language Assessment Quarterly*, *9*(2), 113–132. doi:10.1080/15434303.2011.642041

Fulcher, G. (2013). *Practical Language Testing*. Routledge. doi:10.4324/980203767399

Furco, A., & Ammon, M. S. (2000). Highlights from service-learning in California's teacher education programs: A White Paper. *Service Learning, General*, 155. https://digitalcommons.unomaha.edu/slceslgen/155

Galetić, F., & Herceg, T. (2022). Student Preferences for Online and Onsite Learning and Exams - How Credible at the Grades Obtained in Online Exams? *FEB Zagreb International Odyssey Conference on Economics, 4*(1), 198-211. https://www.researchgate.net/publication/366067341

Gamage, K. A. A., Silva, E. K., & Gunawardhana, N. (2020). Online Delivery and Assessment during COVID-19: Safeguarding Academic Integrity. *Education Sciences, 10*(11), 301. doi:10.3390/educsci10110301

Garrison, D. R. (2016). *E-learning in the 21st century: A community of inquiry framework for research and practice.* Routledge.

Geertz, C. (1993). *The interpretation of cultures : selected essays.*

Ghahremani, D., & Azarizad, R. (2013). The Effect of Dynamic Assessment on EFL Process Writing: Content and Organization. *International Research Journal of Applied and Basic Sciences, 4*, 874–878.

Giannikas, C. (2020). Facebook in tertiary education: The impact of social media in e-learning. *Journal of University Teaching & Learning Practice, 17*(1), 3. https://eric.ed.gov/?id=EJ1247596. doi:10.53761/1.17.1.3

Gibbons, P. (2003). Mediating language learning: Teacher interactions with ESL students in a content-based classroom. *TESOL Quarterly, 37*(2), 247. doi:10.2307/3588504

Gibbs, G. (1995). *Improving student learning through assessment and evaluation.* Oxford Centre for Staff Development, Oxford Brookes University.

Giessen, H. W. (2015). Serious games effects: An overview. *Procedia: Social and Behavioral Sciences, 174*, 2240–2244. doi:10.1016/j.sbspro.2015.01.881

Gikandi, J. W., Morrow, D., & Davis, N. E. (2011). Online formative assessment in higher education: A review of the literature. *Computers & Education, 57*(4), 2333–2351. doi:10.1016/j.compedu.2011.06.004

Gil, A. C. (2021). *Métodos e técnicas de pesquisa social* (7th ed.). Atlas.

Glaser, B.G. & Strauss, A.L. (1967) *The discovery of grounded theory: Strategies for qualitative research.* Aldine, Weidenfeld and Nicolson. doi:10.1093/sf/46.4.555

Göb, R., Mccollin, C., & Ramalhoto, M. F. (2007). Ordinal methodology in the analysis of Likert scales. *Quality & Quantity, 41*(5), 601–626. doi:10.100711135-007-9089-z

Gokmenoglu, T., Dasci Sonmez, E., Yavuz, I., & Gok, I. (2021). Turkish Ministry of National Education school-based disaster education program: A preliminary results of the program evaluation. *International Journal of Disaster Risk Reduction, 52*, 101943. doi:10.1016/j.ijdrr.2020.101943

Göksün, D. O., & Gürsoy, G. (2019). Comparing success and engagement in gamified learning experiences via Kahoot and Quizizz. *Computers & Education, 135*, 15–29. doi:10.1016/j.compedu.2019.02.015

GonzalezJ. (2020, April 13). *Cult of Pedagogy.* Cult of Pedagogy. https://www.cultofpedagogy.com/

Gordon, A. (2020). Tests as Drivers of Change in Education: Contextualising Washback, and the possibility of Washforward. *VNU Journal of Foreign Studies, 36*(4). doi:10.25073/2525-2445/vnufs.4573

Graf, S. T., Rasmussen, F., & Ruge, D. (2021). *Online oral examinations during Covid-19. A survey study at University College level.* Tidsskriftet Læring og Medier (LOM), Nr. 24 2021ISSN: 1903-248X. https://tidsskrift.dk/lom/article/view/125805/174782

Graham, S., Hebert, M., & Harris, K. R. (2015). Formative assessment and writing: A meta-analysis. *The Elementary School Journal*, *115*(4), 523–547. doi:10.1086/681947

Grapin, S. E., & Llosa, L. (2022). Dynamic assessment of English learners in the content areas: An exploratory study in fifth-grade science. *TESOL Quarterly*, *56*(1), 201–229. doi:10.1002/tesq.3059

Grapin, S., Llosa, L., & Haas, A. (2022, January 1). An illustration of four types of formative assessment in a fifth-grade physical science unit. *Science and Children*, (January/February), 58–63.

Gratz, E., & Looney, L. (2020). Faculty resistance to change: An examination of motivators and barriers to teaching online in higher education. *International Journal of Online Pedagogy and Course Design*, *10*(1), 1–14. doi:10.4018/IJOPCD.2020010101

Gray, L. (2008). Effective practice with e-portfolios. *JISC*, 5-40.

Greek Ministry of Education and Religious Affairs. (2016). *Teaching of English in the first grade of elementary school.* https://www.aftodioikisi.gr/mediafiles/2016/05/%CE%91%CE%93% CE%93%CE%9B%CE%99%CE%9A%CE%91-%CE%99%CE%9D%CE%A3%CE%A4%CE%99 %CE%A4%CE%9F%CE%A5%CE%A4%CE%9F.pdf

Greek Ministry of Education and Religious Affairs. (2021). *Circular: English in Kindergarten*. Ministry of Education. https://www.minedu.gov.gr/ypapegan/ypour-apof/50174-23-09-21 -egkyklios-agglika-sta-nipiagogeia-2

Green, A. (2018). Teacher assessment literacy for the classroom. In T. Aksit, H. I. Mengu, & R. Turner (Eds.), *Bridging Teaching, Learning and Assessment in the English Language Classroom* (pp. 2–7). Cambridge Scholars Publishing.

Grigorenko, E., & Sternberg, J. R. (1998). Dynamic Testing. *Psychological Bulletin*, *124*(1), 75–111. doi:10.1037/0033-2909.124.1.75

Grijalva, T., Nowell, C., & Kerkvliet, J. (2006). Academic Honesty and Online Courses. Coll. *Student J.*, *40*(1), 180–185.

Griva, E., & Kofou, I. (2017). *Alternative assessment in Language learning: challenges and practices*. Kyriakidis Editions.

Grosjean, F. (1982). *Life with two languages. An introduction to bilingualism.* Harvard University Press., doi:10.2307/414002

Guo, W., & Wei, J. (2019). Teacher Feedback and Students' Self-regulated Learning in Mathematics: A Study of Chinese Secondary Students. *The Asia-Pacific Education Researcher*, *28*(3), 265–275. doi:10.100740299-019-00434-8

Gutierrez, G. J., & Kouvelis, P. (1991). Parkinson's law and its Implications for Project Management. *Management Science*, *37*(8), 990–1001. doi:10.1287/mnsc.37.8.990

Haberstroh, S., Duffey, T., Marble, E., & Ivers, N. N. (2014). Assessing student-learning outcomes within a counselor education program. *Counseling Outcome Research and Evaluation*, *5*(1), 28–38. doi:10.1177/2150137814527756

Halimi, F., AlShammari, I., & Navarro, C. (2020). Emotional intelligence and academic achievement in higher education. *Journal of Applied Research in Higher Education*.

Haniff Mohd Tahir, M. (2022). Factors Influencing Secondary English as a Second Language Teachers' Intentions to Utilize Google Classroom for Instructions during the Covid-19 Pandemic. *Arab World English Journal*, *13*(2), 17–36. doi:10.24093/awej/vol13no2.2

Hanrahan, S., & Isaacs, G. (2001). Assessing self-and peer-assessment: The students' view. *Higher Education Research & Development*, *20*(1), 53–66. doi:10.1080/07294360123776

Harding, L., & Kremmel, B. (2016). Teacher assessment literacy and professional development. In D. Tsagari & J. Banerjee (Eds.), *Handbook of Second Language Assessment* (pp. 413–427). De Gruyter. doi:10.1515/9781614513827-027

Compilation of References

Hargreaves, E. (2013). Assessment for learning and teacher learning communities: UK teachers' experiences. *Teaching Education*, *24*(3), 327–344. doi:10.1080/10476210.2012.713931

Härmälä, M., & Marjanen, J. (2022). *Englantia koronapandemian aikaan. A-englannin osaaminen 9. luokan lopussa keväällä 2021* [English during the corona pandemic. Learning outcomes of A level English at the end of the 9th grade in spring 2021]. Kansallinen koulutuksen arviointikeskus.

Hartle, S. (2022). University student perceptions of English language study changes: Reactions to remote emergency teaching during the COVID-19 emergency. *Language Learning in Higher Education*, *12*(2), 429–451. doi:10.1515/cercles-2022-2056

Hattie, J., & Timperley, H. (2007). The Power of Feedback. *Review of Educational Research*, *77*(1), 81–112. doi:10.3102/003465430298487

Healey, M., Flint, A., & Harrington, K. (2014). *Engagement through Partnership: Students as Partners in Learning and Teaching in Higher Education.* York: HEA. https://www.heacademy.ac.uk/engagement-through-partnership-s tudents-partners -learning-and-teaching-higher-education

Hegji, A. (2017). An overview of accreditation of higher education in the United States. *CRS Report No. R43826*. CRS. https://fas.org/sgp/crs/misc/R43826.pdf

Heidari, K. (2020). Critical thinking and EFL learners' performance on textually-explicit, textually-implicit, and script-based reading items. *Thinking Skills and Creativity*, *37*, 100703. doi:10.1016/j.tsc.2020.100703

Helate, T. H., Metaferia, T. F., & Gezahegn, T. H. (2022). English language teachers' engagement in and preference for experiential learning for professional development. *Heliyon*, *8*(10), e10900. doi:10.1016/j.heliyon.2022.e10900 PMID:36237971

Henderson, J., & Brookhart, S. (1997, March 24). *Service Learning for Aspiring School Leaders: An Exploratory Study* [Paper presented at the Annual Meeting of Educational Research Association]. US Department of Education.

Hendrickson, M. J. (1978). Error Correction in Foreign Language Teaching: Recent Theory, Research, and Practice. *Modern Language Journal*, *62*(8), 387–398.

Herrera, L., Cuesta Melo, C. H., & Lucero Zambrano, M. A. (2022). Influence of self-assessment on the English Language Learning process. *Colombian Applied Linguistics Journal*, *24*(1), 89–104. doi:10.14483/22487085.17673

Hew, K. F., & Cheung, W. S. (2014). Students' and instructors' use of massive open online courses (MOOCs): Motivations and challenges. *Educational Research Review*, *12*, 45–58. doi:10.1016/j.edurev.2014.05.001

Hew, K. F., Jia, C., Gonda, D. E., & Bai, S. (2020). Transitioning to the "new normal" of learning in unpredictable times: Pedagogical practices and learning performance in fully online flipped classrooms. *International Journal of Educational Technology in Higher Education*, *17*(1), 1–22. doi:10.118641239-020-00234-x PMID:34778516

Hodges, C. B., Moore, S., Lockee, B. B., Trust, T., & Bond, M. A. (2020). *The difference between emergency remote teaching and online learning.*

Hodges, C., Moore, S., Lockee, B., Trust, T., & Bond, A. (2020). *The difference between emergency remote teaching and online learning.* https://er.educause. edu/articles/2020/3/the-difference-betw een-emergency-remote-teaching-and-online-learning

Hodges, Ch., Moore, S., Lockee, B., Trust, T., & Bond, A. (2020). The Difference Between Emergency Remote Teaching and Online Learning. *EDUCAUSE Review,* https://er.educause.edu/articles/2020/3/the-difference-betwe en-emergency-remote-teaching-and-online-learning

Holden, O. L., Norris, M. E., & Kuhlmeier, V. A. (2021). Academic Integrity in Online Assessment: A Research Review. *Frontiers in Education, 6 - 2021*, NA. https://doi.org/https://doi.org/10.3389/feduc.2021.639814

Holden, O. L., Norris, M. E., & Kuhlmeier, V. A. (2021). Academic Integrity in Online Assessment: A Research Review. *Front. Educ., 14 July 2021 Sec. Frontiers in Education*, *6*, 639814. Advance online publication. doi:10.3389/feduc.2021.639814

Hollister, K. K., & Berenson, M. L. (2009). Proctored versus Unsupervised Online Exams: Studying the Impact of Exam Environment on Student Performance. *Decision Sciences Journal of Innovative Education*, *7*(1). https://www.learntechlib.org/p/157703

House, J., Kasper, G., & Blum-Kulka, S. (1989). *Cross-cultural pragmatics: Requests and apologies*. Ablex Pub. Corp.

Hsieh, P.-H., Lee, C.-I., & Chen, W.-F. (2015). Students' perspectives on e-portfolio development and implementation: A case study in Taiwanese higher education. *Australasian Journal of Educational Technology*, *31*(5), 641–656. doi:10.14742/ajet.1605

Hughes, A. (2003). Testing for Language Teachers. (2nd or 3rd edition). Cambridge: CUP.

Hughes, M. T., & Braun, G. (2019). Experiential Learning Experiences to Enhance Preservice Special Educators' Literacy Instruction. *International Electronic Journal of Elementary Education*, *12*(1), 93–101. doi:10.26822/iejee.2019155341

Hu, H. (2015). Building virtual teams: Experiential learning using emerging technologies. *E-Learning and Digital Media*, *12*(1), 17–33. doi:10.1177/2042753014558373

Hung, S. T. (2011). Pedagogical applications of vlogs: An investigation into ESP learners' perceptions. *British Journal of Educational Technology*, *42*(5), 736–746. doi:10.1111/j.1467-8535.2010.01086.x

Hung, S. T. A. (2012). A washback study on e-portfolio in an English as a Foreign Language teacher preparation program. *Computer Assisted Language Learning*, *25*(1), 21–36. doi:10.1080/09588221.2010.551756

Hyland, F., & Hyland, K. (2006). *Feedback in second language writing: Contexts and issues*. Cambridge University Press. doi:10.1017/CBO9781139524742

Hyland, K. (2019). *Second language writing* (2nd ed.). Cambridge University Press.

Ikeda, M. (2020). *Were schools equipped to teach – and were students ready to learn – remotely? PISA in Focus, No. 108*. OECD Publishing., doi:10.1787/4bcd7938-

Inbar-Lourie, O. (2008). Constructing a language assessment knowledge base: A focus on language assessment courses. *Language Testing*, *25*(3), 385–402. doi:10.1177/0265532208090158

Inchaouh, G., & Tchaïcha, J. D. (2020). Online collaboration and Experiential Learning in higher education: Designing an online cross-border collaborative project for Business Students. *International Journal of Technology, Knowledge and Society*, *16*(4), 37–56. doi:10.18848/1832-3669/CGP/v16i04/37-56

Inoue, A. B. (2020, April 6). *Thinking about one-point rubrics, standards, and dimensions*. Thinking about One Point Rubrics, Standards, and Dimensions. http://asaobinoue.blogspot.com/2015/07/thinking-about-one-po int-rubrics.html

Inoue, A. B., & Poe, M. (2020). How to stop harming your students: An ecological guide to Antiracist writing assessment. *Composition Studies*, *48*(3), 14–15.

Ioannou, S., & Tsagari, D. (2022). Effects of Recasts, Metalinguistic Feedback, and Students' Proficiency on the Acquisition of Greek Perfective Past Tense. *Languages (Basel, Switzerland)*, *7*(1), 40. doi:10.3390/languages7010040

Compilation of References

Jaap, A., Dewar, A., Duncan, C., Fairhurst, K., Hope, D., & Kluth, D. (2021). Effect of remote online exam delivery on student experience and performance in applied knowledge tests. *BMC Medical Education*, *21*(1), 86. doi:10.118612909-021-02521-1 PMID:33530962

Jabeen, S. S., & Thomas, A. J. (2015). *Effectiveness of Online Language Learning*. Proceedings of the World Congress on Engineering and Computer Science (WCECS 2015), San Francisco, USA.

Jackson, J. (2003). Case-based Learning and Reticence in a Bilingual Context: Perceptions of Business Students in Hong Kong. *System*, *31*(4), 457–469. doi:10.1016/j.system.2003.03.001

Jansem, A. (2021). The Feasibility of Foreign Language Online Instruction During the Covid-19 Pandemic: A Qualitative Case Study of Instructors' and Students' Reflections. *International Education Studies*, *14*(4), 93–101. https://doi.org/doi. doi:10.5539/ies.v14n4p93

Jeffs, C., Nelson, N., Grant, K. A., Nowell, L., Paris, B., & Viceer, N. (2021). Feedback for teaching development: Moving from a fixed to growth mindset. *Professional Development in Education*, *47*, 1–14. doi:10.1080/19415257.2021.1876149

Jiang, L., & Yu, S. (2021). Understanding Changes in EFL Teachers' Feedback Practice During COVID-19: Implications for Teacher Feedback Literacy at a Time of Crisis. *The Asia-Pacific Education Researcher*, *30*(6), 509–518. doi:10.100740299-021-00583-9

Jiang, L., Yu, S., & Wang, C. (2020). Second language writing instructors' feedback practice in response to automated writing evaluation: A sociocultural perspective. *System*, *93*, 102302. doi:10.1016/j.system.2020.102302

Jiang, L., Yu, S., & Zhao, Y. (2019). Teacher engagement with digital multimodal composing in a Chinese tertiary EFL curriculum. *Language Teaching Research*, *25*(4), 613–632. doi:10.1177/1362168819864975

Jin, L., Xu, Y., Deifell, E., & Angus, K. (2021). Emergency remote language teaching and U.S.-based college-level world language educators' intention to adopt online teaching in postpandemic times. *Modern Language Journal*, *105*(2), 412–434. doi:10.1111/modl.12712

Jones, B., & Gerzon, N. (2020). *The power of evidence use in formative assessment*. WestED. https://csaa.wested.org/

Jyväskylän yliopisto. (2022). *ARVO – Kieltenopettajien arviointiosaamisen päivittäminen* [Updating language teachers' assessment literacy]. https://www.jyu.fi/hytk/fi/laitokset/solki/arvo-2013-kielten opettajien-arviointiosaamisenpaivittaminen

Kauffman, H. (2015). A review of predictive factors of student success in and satisfaction with online learning. *Research in Learning Technology*, *23*. doi:10.3402/rlt.v23.26507

Khan, Z., & Balasubramanian, S. (2012). Students Go Click, Flick and Cheat… e-Cheating, Technologies, and More. *Journal of Academic and Business Ethics*, *6*, 1–26.

Kiley, D. (1983). *The Peter Pan syndrome: Men who have never grown up*. Dodd, Mead.

King, D. L., & Case, C. J. (2014). E-cheating: Incidence and Trends Among College Students. *Issues in Information Systems*, *15*(I), 20–27.

Kirschner, A. (2012). A pioneer in online education tries a MOOC. *The Chronicle of Higher Education*.

Knezek, G., Christensen, R., & Rice, D. (1997). Changes in Teacher Attitudes During Information Technology Training. In J. Willis, J. Price, S. McNeil, B. Robin & D. Willis (Eds.), *Proceedings of SITE 1997--Society for Information Technology & Teacher Education International Conference* (pp. 763-766). Waynesville, NC USA: Association for the Advancement of Computing in Education (AACE). https://www.learntechlib.org/primary/p/47182

Knowles, M. S. (1968). Andragogy, not Pedagogy. *Adult Leadership*, *16*(10), 350–352.

Koenka, A. C., Linnenbrink-Garcia, L., Moshontz, H., Atkinson, K. M., Sanchez, C. E., & Cooper, H. (2019). A meta-analysis on the impact of grades and comments on academic motivation and achievement: A case for written feedback. *Educational Psychology*, *41*(7), 922–947. doi:10.1080/01443410.2019.1659939

Koh, K., Burke, L. E. C.-A., Luke, A., Gong, W., & Tan, C. (2018). Developing the assessment literacy of teachers in Chinese language classrooms: A focus on assessment task design. *Language Teaching Research*, *22*(3), 264–288. doi:10.1177/1362168816684366

Kolb, A. (2012). *What is Experiential Learning?* [Video]. Youtube. https://www.youtube.com/watch?v=1ZeAdN4FB5A

Kolb, A., & Kolb, D. A. (2017). *The experiential educator: Principles and practices of experiential learning*. Experience Based Learning Systems Inc.

Koşar, G. (2021). The progress a pre-service English language teacher made in her feedback giving practices in distance teaching practicum. *Journal of English Teaching*, *7*(3), 366–381.

Kozulin, A., & Garb, E. (2002). Dynamic assessment of EFL text comprehension of at-risk students. *School Psychology International*, *23*(1), 112–127. doi:10.1177/0143034302023001733

Krabbe, H. (2014). Digital concept mapping for formative assessment. In: D. Ifenthaler, R. & Hanewald. (Eds) Digital knowledge maps in education (pp. 275–297). Springer. doi:10.1007/978-1-4614-3178-7_15

Krause, S. D. (2013). MOOC Response about "Listening to World Music.". *College Composition and Communication*, *64*(4), 689–695. https://www.jstor.org/stable/43490786

Kremmel, B., & Harding, L. (2020). Towards a comprehensive, empirical model of language assessment literacy across stakeholder groups: Developing the language assessment literacy survey. *Language Assessment Quarterly*, *17*(1), 100–120. doi:10.1080/15434303.2019.1674855

Krishnan, J., Black, R. W., & Olson, C. B. (2021). The power of context: Exploring teachers' formative assessment for online collaborative writing. *Reading & Writing Quarterly*, *37*(3), 201–220. doi:10.1080/10573569.2020.1764888

Kucuk, S., & Richardson, J. C. (2019). A Structural Equation Model of Predictors of Online Learners' Engagement and Satisfaction. *Online Learning : the Official Journal of the Online Learning Consortium*, *23*(2), 196–216. doi:10.24059/olj.v23i2.1455

Kultusministerkonferenz (2008). *Ländergemeinsame inhaltliche Anforderungen für die Fachwissenschaften und Fachdidaktiken in der Lehrerbildung. KMK Beschluss vom 16.10.2008 i.d.F. vom 16.05.2019* [Resolution of the Standing Conference of the Ministers of Education and Cultural Affairs dated 16.10.2008 as amended on 16.05.2019]. https://www.kmk.org/fileadmin/veroeffentlichungen_beschluess e/2008/2008_10_16-Fachprofile-Lehrerbildung.pdf

Kultusministerkonferenz (2016). *Bildung in der digitalen Welt. Strategie der Kultusministerkonferenz* [Education in the Digital World. Strategy of the Standing Conference of the Ministers of Education and Cultural Affairs]. https://www.kmk.org/fileadmin/Dateien/veroeffentlichungen_be schluesse/2018/Strategie_Bildung_in_der_digitalen_Welt_idF._vom_07.12.2017.pdf

Kurt, S. (2020, December 28). *Kolb's Experiential Learning Theory & Learning Styles*. Educational Technology. https://educationaltechnology.net/kolbs-experiential-learnin g-theory-learning-styles/

Ladyshewsky, R. K. (2015). Post-graduate student performance in 'supervised in-class' vs. 'unsupervised online' multiple choice tests: Implications for cheating and test security. *Assessment & Evaluation in Higher Education*, *40*(7), 883–897. doi:10.1080/02602938.2014.956683

Compilation of References

Lam, R. (2019). Teacher assessment literacy: Surveying knowledge, conceptions and practices of classroom-based writing assessment in Hong Kong. *System*, *81*, 78–89. doi:10.1016/j.system.2019.01.006

Lanier, M. M. (2006). Academic Integrity and Distance Learning. *Journal of Criminal Justice Education*, *17*(2), 244–261. doi:10.1080/10511250600866166

Lantolf, J. P., Kurtz, L., & Kisselev, O. (2017). Understanding the revolutionary character of L2 development in the ZPD: Why levels of mediation matter. *Journal of Applied Linguistics*, *3*(2), 153–171. https://journal.equinoxpub.com/LST/article/view/608

Lantolf, J. P., & Poehner, M. E. (2004). Dynamic assessment of L2 development: Bringing the past into the future. *Journal of Applied Linguistics*, *1*(2), 49–72. doi:10.1558/japl.1.1.49.55872

Lantolf, J. P., & Thorne, S. (2006). *Sociocultural Theory and the Genesis of Second Language Development*. Oxford University Press.

Lantolf, J. P., & Thorne, S. L. (2006). *Sociocultural theory and genesis of second language development*. Oxford University Press. doi:10.1017/S0272263108080546

Latimer, N., & Chan, S. (2022). Eye-tracking L2 students taking online multiple-choice reading tests: Benefits and challenges. *International Journal of TESOL Studies*, *4*(1), 83–104. doi:10.46451/ijts.2022.01.07

Lave, J., & Wenger, E. (1991). *Situated learning: Legitimate peripheral participation*. Cambridge University Press. doi:10.1017/CBO9780511815355

Lee, I. (2017). *Classroom writing assessment and feedback in L2 school contexts*. Springer. doi:10.1007/978-981-10-3924-9

Lee, I. (2021). The Development of Feedback Literacy for Writing Teachers. *TESOL Quarterly*, *55*(3), 1048–1059. doi:10.1002/tesq.3012

Lee, J. (2019). Experiential teacher education – preparing preservice teachers to teach English grammar through an experiential learning project. *The Australian Journal of Teacher Education*, 1–20. doi:10.14221/ajte.2018v44n1.1

Lee, L. (2010). Exploring wiki-mediated collaborative writing: A case study in an elementary Spanish course. *CALICO Journal*, *27*(2), 260–276. doi:10.11139/cj.27.2.260-276

Lefever, S., Dal, M., & Matthíasdóttir, A. (2007). Online data collection in academic research: Advantages and limitations. *British Journal of Educational Technology*, *38*(4), 574–582. doi:10.1111/j.1467-8535.2006.00638.x

Leontjev, D. (2016). Dynamic assessment of word derivational knowledge: Tracing the development of a learner. *Eesti Rakenduslingvistika Ühingu aastaraamat Estonian Papers in Applied Linguistics, 12,* 141-160. https://www.researchgate.net/publication/303320043_Dynamic_assessment_of_word_derivational_knowledge_Tracing_the_development_of_a_learner

Le, Q. T., Pedro, A., & Park, C. S. (2015). A social virtual reality based construction safety education system for experiential learning. *Journal of Intelligent & Robotic Systems*, *79*(3-4), 487–506. doi:10.100710846-014-0112-z

Lidz, S. C. (1997). Dynamic Assessment Approaches. In D. P. Flanagan, J. L. Genshaft, & P. L. Harrison (Eds.), *Contemporary Approaches to Assessment of Intelligence* (pp. 285–293). The Guilford Press.

Li, L., Liu, X., & Zhou, Y. (2012). Give and take: A re-analysis of assessor and assessee's roles in technology-facilitated peer assessment. *British Journal of Educational Technology*, *43*(3), 376–384. doi:10.1111/j.1467-8535.2011.01180.x

Li, M. (2021). Computer-mediated teacher feedback. In *Researching and Teaching Second Language Writing in the Digital Age*. Palgrave Macmillan. doi:10.1007/978-3-030-87710-1_3

Lincoln, Y. S., & Guba, E. G. (1985). *Naturalistic inquiry*. Sage. doi:10.1016/0147-1767(85)90062-8

Link, S., Dursun, A., Karakaya, K., & Hegelheimer, V. (2014). Towards Better ESL Practices for Implementing Automated Writing Evaluation. *CALICO Journal, 31*(3), 323–344. doi:10.11139/cj.31.3.323-344

Link, S., Mehrzad, M., & Rahimi, M. (2020). Impact of automated writing evaluation on teacher feedback, student revision, and writing improvement. *Computer Assisted Language Learning, 35*(4), 605–634. doi:10.1080/09588221.2020.1743323

Lin, W.-C., & Yang, S.-C. (2011). Exploring students' perceptions of integrating Wiki technology and peer feedback into English writing courses. *English Teaching, 10*(2), 88–103.

Literat, I. (2015). Implications of massive open online courses for higher education: Mitigating or reifying educational inequities? *Higher Education Research & Development, 34*(6), 1164–1177. doi:10.1080/07294360.2015.1024624

Liu, S. H.-J., & Lan, Y.-J. (2016). Social constructivist approach to web-based EFL learning: Collaboration, motivation, and perception on the use of Google Docs. *Journal of Educational Technology & Society, 19*(1), 171–186.

Lo, J.-J., Yeh, S.-W., & Sung, C.-S. (2013). Learning paragraph structure with online annotations: An interactive approach to enhancing EFL reading comprehension. *System, 41*(2), 413–427. doi:10.1016/j.system.2013.03.003

Lorenzo, G. & Ittelson, J. (2005). An overview of e-portfolios. *Educause Learning Initiative*, 1-27.

Lubbe, A., Mentz, E., Olivier, J., Jacobson, T. E., Mackey, T. P., Chahine, I. C., & de Beer, J. (2021). *Learning through assessment: An approach towards self-directed learning*. AOSIS., doi:10.46925//rdluz.38.49

Lynch, B., & Shaw, P. (2005). Portfolios, power, and Ethics. *TESOL Quarterly, 39*(2), 263. doi:10.2307/3588311

Lyu, B., & Lai, C. (2022). Learners' engagement on a social networking platform: An ecological analysis. *Language Learning & Technology, 26*(1), 1–22.

Mahapatra, S. K. (2021). Online formative assessment and feedback practices of ESL teachers in India, Bangladesh and Nepal: A Multiple Case Study. *The Asia-Pacific Education Researcher, 30*(6), 519–530. doi:10.100740299-021-00603-8

Mak, B., & Coniam, D. (2008). Using wikis to enhance and develop writing skills among secondary school students in Hong Kong. *System, 36*(3), 437–455. doi:10.1016/j.system.2008.02.004

Mäkipää, T., Hahl, K., Luodonpää-Manni, M. (2021). Teachers' perceptions of assessment and feedback practices in Finland's foreign language classes during the COVID-19 pandemic. *CEPS Journal, 11*, 219–240. .1108 doi:10.26529/cepsj

Malone, M. (2008). Training in language assessment. In E. Shoha-my & N. Hornberger (Eds.), Encyclopedia of language and education. Language Testing and Assessment (2nd ed., pp. 225-239). New York: Springer Science+Business Media. doi:10.1007/978-0-387-30424-3_178

Malone, M. E. (2013). The essentials of assessment literacy: Contrasts between testers and users. *Language Testing, 30*(3), 329–344. doi:10.1177/0265532213480129

Mansouri, B., Molana, K., & Nazari, M. (2021). The interconnection between second language teachers' language assessment literacy and professional agency: The mediating role of institutional policies. *System, 103*, 102674. doi:10.1016/j.system.2021.102674

Ma, Q. (2020). Examining the role of inter-group peer online feedback on wiki writing in an EAP context. *Computer Assisted Language Learning, 33*(3), 197–216. doi:10.1080/09588221.2018.1556703

Marinoni, G., Van't Land, H., & Jensen, T. (2020). The impact of Covid-19 on higher education around the world. *IAU global survey report, 23*.

Compilation of References

Markova, Y. S. (2020). About the consequences and problems in the higher education system during the pandemic. *Scientific interdisciplinary research, 5*, 226-229. https://cyberleninka.ru/article/n/o-posledstviyah-i-problema h-v-sisteme-vysshego-obrazovaniya-vo-vremya-pandemii

Marks, A. M., & Cronjé, J. C. (2008). Randomised Items in computer-based tests: Russian roulette in assessment? *International Forum of Educational Technology and Society. 11*(4), 41–50. https://digitalknowledge.cput.ac.za/handle/11189/3519

Martin, J., & Collins, R. (2011). Formative and summative evaluation in the assessment of adult learning. In V. C. X. Wang (Ed.), *Assessing and evaluating adult learning in career and technical education* (pp. 127–142). IGI Global. doi:10.4018/978-1-61520-745-9.ch008

Mason, R., & Lockwood, F. (1994). *Using communications media in open and flexible learning*. Routledge.

Mattera, M., Baena, V., Ureña, R., & Moreno, M. D. F. (2014). Creativity in technology-enhanced experiential learning: Videocast implementation in higher education. *International Journal of Technology Enhanced Learning, 6*(1), 46–64. doi:10.1504/IJTEL.2014.060026

Mattheoudakis, M., & Alexiou, T. (2009). Early Foreign Language Instruction in Greece: Socioeconomic Factors and Their Effect on Young Learners' Language Development. In M. Nikolov (Ed.), *The Age Factor and Early Language Learning* (pp. 227–252). http://rcel.enl.uoa.gr/docsforpeap/Mattheoudakis%20and%20Alexiou.pdf doi:10.1515/9783110218282.227

Mauludin, L. A., & Ardianti, T. M. (2017). The Role of Dynamic Assessment in EFL Writing Class. *METATHESIS: Journal of English Language, Literature, and Teaching, 1*(2), 82–93.

Mehall, S. (2020). Purposeful Interpersonal Interaction in Online Learning: What Is It and How Is It Measured? *Online Learning : the Official Journal of the Online Learning Consortium, 24*(1), 182–204. doi:10.24059/olj.v24i1.2002

Mehrabany, Z., & Bagheri, M. (2017). Which one is superior; The cake approach or the sandwich approach? The effect of dynamic assessment on EFL undergraduates' vocabulary knowledge. [IJLLALW]. *International Journal of Language Learning and Applied Linguistics World, 15*(2), 1–13.

Mellati, M., & Khademi, M. (2018). Exploring teachers' assessment literacy: Impact on learners' writing achievements and implications for teacher development. *The Australian Journal of Teacher Education, 43*(6), 1–19. doi:10.14221/ajte.2018v43n6.1

Merriam, S. B. (2009). Qualitative research: a guide to design and implementation. San Francisco, California: Jossey-Bass.

Merriam, S. B. (1998). *Qualitative research and case study applications in education*. Jossy-Bass.

Merriam, S. B., & Bierema, L. L. (2014). *Adult learning: Bridging theory and practice*. Jossey Bass.

Miao, T., & Mian, L. (2013). Dynamic Assessment in ESL Writing Classroom. *International Conference on Education Technology and Management Science*, (Icetms), 676–679. https://download.atlantis-press.com/proceedings/icetms-13/6996

Milman, N. B. (2020). *This is emergency remote teaching, not just online teaching*. https://www.edweek.org/leadership/opinion-this-is-emergency- remote-teaching-not-just-online-teaching/2020/03

Moffitt, R. L., Padgett, C., & Grieve, R. (2020). Accessibility and emotionality of online assessment feedback: Using emoticons to enhance student perceptions of marker competence and warmth. *Computers & Education, 143*, 103654. doi:10.1016/j.compedu.2019.103654

Mohamadi Zenouzagh, Z. (2019). The effect of online summative and formative teacher assessment on teacher competences. *Asia Pacific Education Review, 20*(3), 343–359. doi:10.100712564-018-9566-1

Mohamadi, Z. (2018). Comparative effect of online summative and formative assessment on EFL student writing ability. *Studies in Educational Evaluation*, *59*, 29–40. https://doi-org.sdl.idm. oclc.org/10.1016/j.stueduc.2018.02. 003. doi:10.1016/j.stueduc.2018.02.003

Mohammadi, M., Jabbari, A., & Fazilatfar, A. (2018). The Impact of the Asynchronous Online Discussion Forum on the Iranian EFL Students' Writing Ability and Attitudes. *Applied Research on English Language*, *7*(4), 457–486. doi:10.22108/are.2018.112792.1351

Mohanty, A. K. (2023). Multilingualism, mother tongue and MLE. *Language and Language Teaching, 12*(23), 155-167.

Money, J., Dinning, T., Nixon, S., Walsh, B., & Magill, C. (2016). Co-Creating a Blended Learning Curriculum in Transition to Higher Education: A Student Viewpoint. *Creative Education*, *7*(9), 1205–1213. doi:10.4236/ce.2016.79126

Monitor Lehrerbildung. (2021). *Lehrkräfte vom ersten Semester an für die digitale Welt qualifizieren* [Qualifying teachers for the digital world from the very first semester of their studies]. https://2020.monitor-lehrerbildung.de/export/sites/default/. content/Downloads/Monitor-Lehrerbildung_Digitale-Welt_Policy -Brief-2021.pdf

Morgan, D. (2019). *Basic and Advanced Focus Groups*. SAGE Publications. doi:10.4135/9781071814307

Mu, C., & Carrington, S. (2007). An Investigation of Three Chinese Students' English Writing Strategies. *TESL-EJ: The Electronic Journal for English as a Second Language*, *11*(1), 1–23.

Muin, C. F., & Hafidah, H. (2020). Students' perceptions on the use of e-portfolio for learning assessment: A case study. *ELITE Journal*, *3*(1), 13–20.

Mundkur, A., & Ellickson, C. (2012). Bringing the real world in: Reflection on building a virtual learning environment. *Journal of Geography in Higher Education*, *36*(3), 369–384. doi:10.1080/03098265.2012.692073

Munoz, A., & Mackay, J. (2019). An online testing design choice typology towards cheating threat minimisation. *Journal of University Teaching & Learning Practice*, *16*(3), 54–70. doi:10.53761/1.16.3.5

Muravev, Y. (2022). Improving second language acquisition by extensive and analytical reading in a digital environment. *Journal of College Reading and Learning*, 1–17. doi:10.1080/10790195.2022.2084798

Mutch, C. (2005). *Doing educational research: A practitioner's guide to getting started*. NZCER.

Myers-Scotton, C. (2000). Explaining the Role of Norms and Rationality in Code Switching. *Journal of Pragmatics*, *32*(9), 1259–1271. doi:10.1016/S0378-2166(99)00099-5

Namaziandost, E., Alekasir, S., Sawalmeh, M. H. M., & Miftah, M. Z. (2020). Investigating the Iranian EFL learners' attitudes towards the implementation of e-portfolios in English learning and assessment. *Cogent Education*, *7*(1), 1–32. doi:10.1080/2331186X.2020.1856764

Naz, R., Nusrat, A., Tariq, S., Farooqi, R., & Ashraf, F. (2022). Mobile assisted vocabulary learning (M learning): A quantitative study targeting ESL Pakistani learners. *Webology*, *19*(3), 1342–1364.

Nenyuk, E. A. (2021). The first results of distance learning: the evolution of opinions. *The world of science, culture, education, 3*(88), 221-223. https://cyberleninka.ru/article/n/pervye-itogi-distantsionno go-obucheniya-evolyutsiya-mneniy

Nepivodova, L. (2007) *On Communicative Language Ability, Validity and Different Modes of Administration (The analysis of the second-year Practical English Examination)*. [Unpublished MA dissertation, Masaryk University, Brno].

Nepivodova, Linda. (2023) *Computer or Paper? Comparison of two modes of test administration*. Brno: Masarykova univerzita. Cizí jazyky a jejich didaktiky: teorie, empirie, praxe.

Compilation of References

Newman, D. R., Webb, B., & Cochrane, C. (1995). A content analysis method to measure critical thinking in face to face and computer supported group learning. *Interpersonal Computing and Technology*, *3*(2), 56–77.

Nguyen, T. T. T., & Yukawa, T. (2019). Kahoot with smartphones in testing and assessment of language teaching and learning, the need of training on mobile devices for Vietnamese teachers and students. *International Journal of Information and Education Technology (IJIET)*, *9*(4), 286–296. http://www.ijiet.org/vol9/1214-JR328.pdf. doi:10.18178/ijiet.2019.9.4.1214

Nicol, D. J., & Macfarlane-Dick, D. (2006). Formative assessment and self-regulated learning: A model and seven principles of good feedback practice. *Studies in Higher Education*, *31*(2), 199–218. doi:10.1080/03075070600572090

Nikolopoulou, K., Akriotou, D., & Gialamas, V. (2019). Early Reading Skills in English as a Foreign Language via ICT in Greece: Early Childhood Student Teachers' Perceptions. *Early Childhood Education Journal*, *47*(5), 597–606. doi:10.100710643-019-00950-8

Ninković, S., Olić Ninković, S., Lazarević, T., & Adamov, J. (2021). Serbian teachers' perceptions of online assessment during COVID-19 school closure: The role of teachers' self-efficacy. *Educational Studies*, 1–13. doi:10.1080/03055698.2021.1960151

Nor, N. F. M., Razak, N. A., & Aziz, J. (2010). E-learning: Analysis of online discussion forums in promoting knowledge construction through collaborative learning. *WSEAS Transactions on Communications*, *9*(1), 53–62.

Noyes, J. M., & Garland, K. J. (2008). Computer-vs. paper-based tasks: Are they equivalent? *Ergonomics*, *51*(9), 1352–1375. doi:10.1080/00140130802170387 PMID:18802819

O'Loughlin, K. (2013). Developing the assessment literacy of university proficiency test users. *Language Testing*, *30*(3), 363–380. doi:10.1177/0265532213480336

Ockey, G. J. (2021). An overview of COVID-19's impact on English language university admissions and placement tests. *Language Assessment Quarterly*, *18*(1), 1–5. doi:10.1080/15434303.2020.1866576

Odo, D. M. (2022). An action research investigation of the impact of using online feedback videos to promote self-reflection on the microteaching of pre-service EFL teachers. *Systemic Practice and Action Research*, *35*(3), 327–343. doi:10.100711213-021-09575-8 PMID:34248347

Oflaz, M., Diker Coskun, Y., & Bolat, O. (2022). The Effects of the Technology-Integrated Writing Lessons: CIPP Model of Evaluation. *The Turkish Online Journal of Educational Technology*, *21*(1), 157–179.

Olleras, J. L., Dagwayan, M., Dejacto, A. M., Mangay, J. R., Ebarsabal, M., Diaz, D. J., Putian, R., Lendio, A. M., Nadera, J. C., Taneo, J. D., Cabello, C. A., & Minyamin, A. V. (2022). The Life of the Laters: Students Procrastination in Accomplishing Academic Deadlines in Online Learning. *Psychology and Education: A Multidisciplinary Journal*, *2*(5), 444-454. , ISSN 2822-4353 doi:10.5281/zenodo.6791776

Omar, N. N. (2017). The Effectiveness of Kahoot Application Towards Students' Good Feedback Practice. *The International Journal of Social Sciences (Islamabad)*, *3*(2), 2551–2562.

Pachler, N., Daly, C., Mor, Y., & Mellar, H. (2010). Formative e-assessment: Practitioner cases. *Computers & Education*, *54*(3), 715–721. doi:10.1016/j.compedu.2009.09.032

Pahamzah, J., Syafrizal, S., & Nurbaeti, N. (2022). The effects of EFL course enriched with Kahoot on students' vocabulary mastery and reading comprehension skills. *The Journal of Language and Linguistic Studies*, *18*(1), 643–652. doi:10.3316/informit.400435517746294

Paiva, V. L. M. de O. (2003). Feedback em ambiente virtual. In V. Leffa (Ed.), *Interação na aprendizagem das línguas* (pp. 219–254). Educat.

Panadero, E., Fraile, J., Pinedo, L., Rodríguez-Hernández, C., & Díez, F. (2022). Changes in classroom assessment practices during emergency remote teaching due to COVID-19. *Assessment in Education: Principles, Policy & Practice*, *29*(3), 361–382. doi:10.1080/0969594X.2022.2067123

Parkinson, C. N. (1958). *Parkinson's Law or The Pursuit of Progress*. John Murray.

Paulus, T. M. (2005). Collaborative and Cooperative Approaches to Online Group Work: The Impact of Task Type. *Distance Education*, *26*(1), 111–125. doi:10.1080/01587910500081343

Perifanou, M., Economides, A. A., & Tzafilkou, K. (2022). Greek teachers' difficulties & opportunities in emergency distance teaching. *E-Learning and Digital Media*, *19*(4), 361–379. doi:10.1177/20427530221092854

Poehner, E. M., & Infante, P. (2016). Dynamic Assessment in the Language Classroom. In D. Tsagari & J. Banerjee (Eds.), Handbook of Second Language Assessment (pp. 275–290). DeGruyter Mouton. doi:10.1515/9781614513827-019

Poehner, M. E. (2008). *Dynamic Assessment: A Vygotskian Approach to Understanding and Promoting L2 Development. Educational Linguistics*. Springer. https://link.springer.com/book/10.1007/978-0-387-75775-9

Poehner, M. (2009). Group dynamic assessment: Mediation for the L2 classroom. *TESOL Quarterly*, *43*(3), 471–491. doi:10.1002/j.1545-7249.2009.tb00245.x

Poehner, M., & Wang, Z. (2021). Dynamic Assessment and second language development. *Language Teaching*, *54*(4), 472–490. doi:10.1017/S0261444820000555

Popham, W. J. (2018). *Assessment literacy for educators in a hurry*. ACSD.

Prabhu, N. S. (2021). Second thoughts about second-language teaching. In: Sudharshana, N.P., Mukhopadhyay, L. (eds). (pp. 13-16). Task-based language teaching and assessment. Springer. doi:10.1007/978-981-16-4226-5_2

Prilop, C. N., Weber, K. E., & Kleinknecht, M. (2021a). The role of expert feedback in the development of pre-service teachers' professional vision of classroom management in an online blended learning environment. *Teaching and Teacher Education*, *99*, 103276. doi:10.1016/j.tate.2020.103276

Prilop, C. N., Weber, K. E., Prins, F. J., & Kleinknecht, M. (2021). Connecting feedback to self-efficacy: Receiving and providing peer feedback in teacher education. *Studies in Educational Evaluation*, *70*, 101062. doi:10.1016/j.stueduc.2021.101062

Prince, D. J., Fulton, R. A., & Garsombke, T. W. (2009). Comparisons Of Proctored Versus Non-Proctored Testing Strategies In Graduate Distance Education Curriculum. [TLC]. *Journal of College Teaching and Learning*, *6*(7). doi:10.19030/tlc.v6i7.1125

Purpura, J. E. (2021). A Rationale for Using a Scenario-Based Assessment to Measure Competency-Based, Situated Second and Foreign Language Proficiency. In M. Masperi, C. Cervini, Y. Bardière (eds.) *Évaluation des acquisitions langagières: du formatif au certificatif, mediAzioni, 32*, A54-A96. http://www.mediazioni.sitlec.unibo.it.

Pu, S., & Xu, H. (2021). Examining Changing Assessment Practices in Online Teaching: A Multiple-Case Study of EFL School Teachers in China. *The Asia-Pacific Education Researcher*, *30*(6), 553–561. doi:10.100740299-021-00605-6

Compilation of References

Pyrtsiou, F., & Rousoulioti, T. (2022). *Perceptions and Attitudes towards Assessment: Focusing on the Use of Portfolios in Formal and Informal Secondary Education in Greece*. ResearchGate. https://www.researchgate.net/publication/362903598_Pyrtsiou_F_Rousoulioti_T_2022Perceptions_and_Attitudes_towards_Assessment_Focusing_on_the_Use_of_Portfolios_in_Formal_and_Informa l_Secondary_Education_in_Greece_In_IPapadopolous_S_Chiper_Ed s_Internati

Qualters, D. M. (2010). Bringing the outside in: Assessing experiential education. *New Directions for Teaching and Learning, 2010*(124), 55–62. doi:10.1002/tl.421

Quevedo-Camargo, G. (2021). *Avaliação online: um guia para professores*. Letraria.

Radosavlevikj, N. (2021). Students´ Attitudes and Preferences to Online Teaching During the Pandemic COVID -19 Period. *Yearbook - Faculty of Philology, 12*(17), 103-115. https://eds.s.ebscohost.com

Radu, M. C., Schnakovszky, C., Herghelegiu, E., Ciubotariu, V. A., & Cristea, I. (2020). The impact of the COVID-19 pandemic on the quality of educational process: A student survey. *International Journal of Environmental Research and Public Health, 17*(21), 1–15. doi:10.3390/ijerph17217770 PMID:33114192

Rahmani, A., Rashtchi, M., & Yazdanimoghadam, M. (2020). Interactionist and interventionist dynamic assessment approaches to teaching argumentative writing: Do complexity, accuracy, and fluency develop? *Journal of English Language Pedagogy and Practice, 13*(27), 100–128. doi:10.30495/jal.2021.680912

Raimes, A. (1983). *Techniques in Teaching Writing*. Oxford University Press.

Ranalli, J., Link, S., & Chukharev-Hudilainen, E. (2017). Automated writing evaluation for formative assessment of second language writing: Investigating the accuracy and usefulness of feedback as part of argument-based validation. *Educational Psychology, 37*(1), 8–25. doi:10.1080/01443410.2015.1136407

Rapanta, C., Botturi, L., Goodyear, P., Guàrdia, L., & Koole, M. (2020). Online University Teaching During and After the Covid-19 Crisis: Refocusing Teacher Presence and Learning Activity. *Postdigital Science and Education, 2*(3), 923–945. doi:10.100742438-020-00155-y

Ritchie, W. C., & Bhatia, T. K. (2012). Social and psychological factors in language mixing. The handbook of bilingualism and multilingualism, In W. C. Ritchie, & T. K. Bhatia (Eds.). (2013). Handbook of bilingualism and multilingualism. (pp. 375-390). Wiley-Blackwell. doi:10.1002/9781118332382.ch15

Ritonga, M., Farhangi, F., Ajanil, B., & Ayman, F. K. (2022). Interventionist vs. interactionist models of dynamic assessment (DA) in the EFL classroom: Impacts on speaking accuracy and fluency (SAF), foreign language classroom anxiety (FLCA), and foreign language learning motivation (FLLM). *Language Testing in Asia, 12*(1), 43. doi:10.118640468-022-00195-0

Roberts-Gray, C., & Gray, T. (1983). Implementing innovations: A model to bridge the gap between diffusion and utilization. *Knowledge (Beverly Hills, Calif.), 5*(2), 213–232. doi:10.1177/107554708300500204

Roschelle, J., & Teasley, S. D. (1995). The construction of shared knowledge in collaborative problem solving. In C. O'Malley (Ed.), *Computer supported collaborative learning* (pp. 69–97). Springer., doi:10.1007/978-3-642-85098-1_5

Rothman, B. K. (2007). Writing Ourselves in Sociology. *Methodological Innovations Online, 2*(1), 11–16. doi:10.4256/mio.2007.0003

Rousoulioti, T. (2015). Alternative assessment. In Th. Roussoulioti & V. Panagiotidou (Eds.), *Curricula Models for the teaching of Greek as a second/foreign language*. Zitis publication. https://www.researchgate.net/publication/340771917_Enallakti ke_axiologese

Rousoulioti, Th., & Karagkouni, I. (2019). The assessment of writing: The present and the future. Kathedra: Vol. 4. *1. Department of Byzantine and Modern Greek Literature*. Lomonosov University. http://kathedra-ens.ru/hellenika/teukhi/.

Rovai, A. P. (2003). Strategies for grading online discussions: Effects on discussions and classroom community in Internet-based university courses. *Journal of Computing in Higher Education, 15*(1), 89–107. doi:10.1007/BF02940854

Roy, R., & Uekusa, S. (2020). Collaborative Autoethnography: "Self-Reflection" as a Timely Alternative Research Approach During the Global Pandemic. *Qualitative Research Journal, 20*(4), 383–392. doi:10.1108/QRJ-06-2020-0054

Ruiz-Primo, M. (2000). On the use of concept maps as an assessment tool in science: What we have learned so far. *Revista Electrónica de Investigación Educativa, 2*(1), 29–52.

Saberi, P. (2020). Research in the time of coronavirus: Continuing ongoing studies in the midst of the COVID-19 pandemic. *AIDS and Behavior, 24*(8), 2232–2235. doi:10.100710461-020-02868-4 PMID:32303924

Sadek, N. (2015). Dynamic Assessment (DA): Promoting Writing Proficiency through Assessment. *International Journal of Bilingual & Multilingual Teachers of English, 2*(2), 59–70. doi:10.12785/ijbmte/030201

Santos, M. C. (2022). How I Implemented Asao B. Inoue's Labor-Based Grading and Other Antiracist Assessment Strategies. *CEA Critic, 84*(2), 160–179. doi:10.1353/cea.2022.0019

Säntti, J., Puustinen, M., & Salminen, J. (2018). Theory and practice in Finnish teacher education: A rhetorical analysis of changing values from the 1960s to the present day. *Teachers and Teaching, 24*(1), 5–21. doi:10.1080/13540602.2017.1379387

Sapkota, A. (2012). Developing Students' Writing Skill through Peer and Teacher Correction: An Action Research. *Journal of NELTA, 17*(1-2), 70–82. doi:10.3126/nelta.v17i1-2.8094

Satyam, & Aithal, R. K. (2022). Reimagining an experiential learning exercise in times of crisis: Lessons learned and a proposed framework. *Journal of Marketing Education, 44*(2), 191–202. doi:10.1177/02734753221084128

Schiefner-Rohs, M. (2021). Lehrer*innenbildung (in) der Post-Digitalität: erste Impulse zur Diskussion [Teacher education (in) the post-digital age: initial impulses for discussion]. In R. Arnold, C. Gómez Tutor, & R. Ulber (Eds.), *Professionalisierungsprozesse in der Lehrkräftebildung. Rückblicke – Einblicke – Ausblicke*. Schneider Verlag Hohengehren.

Schleicher, A. (2020). *The impact of COVID-19 on education: Insights from education at a glance 2020*. OECD. https://www.oecd.org/education/the-impact-of-covid-19-on-e ducation-insights-education-at-a-glance-2020.pdf

School Education Gateway. (2020) *Survey on online and distance learning – Results*. School Education Gateway. https://www.schooleducationgateway.eu/en/pub/viewpoints/surv eys/survey-on-online- teaching.htm

Schwartz, F., & White, K. (2000). Making sense of it all: giving and getting on-line course feedback. In K. W. White & B. H. Weight (Eds.), *The on-line teaching guide* (pp. 167–182). Allyn & Bacon.

Senel, S., & Senel, H. C. (2021). Remote Assessment in Higher Education during COVID-19 Pandemic. *International Journal of Assessment Tools in Education*, 181-199. doi:10.21449/ijate.820140

Serhan, D. (2020). Transitioning from face-to-face to remote learning: Students' attitudes and perceptions of using Zoom during Covid-19 pandemic. [IJTES]. *International Journal of Technology in Education and Science, 4*(4), 335–342. https://ijtes.net/index.php/ijtes/article/view/148. doi:10.46328/ijtes.v4i4.148

Shabani, K. (2018). Group dynamic assessment of L2 learners' writing abilities. *Iranian Journal of Language Teaching Research, 6*(1), 129–149. doi:10.30466/ijltr.2018.20494

Compilation of References

Shea, P., Swan, K., Fredericksen, E., & Pickett, A. (2001). Student Satisfaction and Reported Learning in the SUNY Learning Network: Interaction and Beyond-Social Presence in Asynchronous Learning Networks. SUNY.

Sheehan, S., & Munro, S. (2017). *Assessment: attitudes, practices and needs.* ELT research paper.

Shenton, A. K. (2004). Strategies for ensuring trustworthiness in qualitative research projects. *Education for Information*, *22*(2), 63–75. doi:10.3233/EFI-2004-22201

Shih, Y. C., & Yuan, Y. P. (2019). Evaluating an English Elite Program in Taiwan using the CIPP Model. *Journal of Asia TEFL*, *16*(1), 200–219. doi:10.18823/asiatefl.2019.16.1.13.200

Sifakis, N. C., & Sougari, A.-M. (2005). Pronunciation issues in EIL pedagogy in the periphery: A survey of Greek state schoolteachers' beliefs. *TESOL Quarterly*, *39*(3), 467–488. doi:10.2307/3588490

Silverman, D. (2006). *Interpreting qualitative data: Methods for analyzing talk, text and interaction.* Sage Publications.

Smith, H. (2008). Assessing student contributions to online discussion boards. *Practitioner Research in Higher Education*, *2*(1), 22–28.

Smith, M. S., Warnes, S., & Vanhoestenberghe, A. (2018). Scenario-based learning. In J. P. Davies & N. Pachler (Eds.), *Teaching and learning in higher education: Perspectives from UCL* (pp. 144–156)., http://www.ucl-ioe-press.com/

Solnyshkina, M. I., Harkova, E. V., & Kiselnikov, A. S. (2014). Unified (Russian) State Exam in English: Reading Comprehension Tasks. *English Language Teaching*, *7*(12), 1–11. doi:10.5539/elt.v7n12p1

Soltyska, A. (2022). Von cheating zu e-cheating: Gefahren und Chancen aktueller Entwicklungen im Bereich des Prüfungsbetrugs beim Fremdsprachentesten [From cheating to e-cheating: risks and opportunities of current developments in the field of academic misconduct in foreign language assessment]. In A. Brandt (Ed.), *Quo vadis Sprachenlehre? Neue Unterrichtsformen vor der Tür. Dokumentation der 1. AKS-Online-Konferenz. Fremdsprachen in Lehre und Forschung* (pp. 19–35). AKS Verlag.

Song, B. K. (2021). E-portfolio implementation: Examining learners' perception of usefulness, self-directed learning process and value of learning. *Australasian Journal of Educational Technology*, *37*(1), 68–81.

Son, J.-B. (2002). Online Discussion in a CALL Course for Distance Language Teachers. *CALICO Journal*, *20*(1), 127–144. https://www.jstor.org/stable/24149612. doi:10.1558/cj.v20i1.127-144

Spencer, J. A., & Jordan, R. K. (1999). Learner centred approaches in medical education. *BMJ (Clinical Research Ed.)*, *318*(7193), 1280–1283. doi:10.1136/bmj.318.7193.1280 PMID:10231266

Steyn, C., Davies, C., & Sambo, A. (2019). Eliciting student feedback for course development: The application of a qualitative course evaluation tool among business research students. *Assessment & Evaluation in Higher Education*, *44*(1), 11–24. doi:10.1080/02602938.2018.1466266

Stommel, J. (2018). *How to Ungrade.* Jesse Stommel. www.jessestommel.com/how-to-ungrade/

Storch, N. (2013). *Collaborative writing in L2 classrooms.* Multilingual Matters. doi:10.21832/9781847699954

Stuber-McEwen, D., Wiseley, P., & Hoggatt, S. (2009). Point, Click, and Cheat: Frequency and Type of Academic Dishonesty in the Virtual Classroom. *Online Journal of Distance Learning Administration*, *12*(3), 1.

Stufflebeam, D. L. (2003). The CIPP Model for evaluation. In T. Kellaghan & D. L. Stufflebeam (Eds.), *International Handbook of Educational Evaluation* (pp. 31–62). Springer. doi:10.1007/978-94-010-0309-4_4

Sue, V. M., & Ritter, L. A. (2012). *Conducting Online Surveys* (2nd ed.). SAGE Publications, Inc. doi:10.4135/9781506335186

Sun, P. C., Tsai, R. J., Finger, G., Chen, Y. Y., & Yeh, D. (2008). What drives successful e-Learning? An empirical investigation of the critical factors influencing learner satisfaction. *Computers & Education*, *50*(4), 1183–1202. doi:10.1016/j.compedu.2006.11.007

Sun, Y., Wang, T.-H., & Wang, L.-F. (2021). Implementation of Web-Based Dynamic Assessments as Sustainable Educational Technique for Enhancing Reading Strategies in English Class during the COVID-19 Pandemic. *Sustainability (Basel)*, *13*(11), 5842. doi:10.3390u13115842

Suvorov, R., & Hegelheimer, V. (2014). *Computer-assisted language testing. The 167 companion to language assessment*. Wiley. http://onlinelibrary.wiley.com/doi/10.1002/9781118411360.wbc la083/full

Švaříček, R., & Šeďová, K. (2007). Kvalitativní výzkum v pedagogických vědách. *Portal (Baltimore, Md.)*.

Swain, M. (1985). Large scale communicative testing: A case study. In Y. P. Lee, A. C. Y. Y Fok, R. Lord, & G. Low (Eds.), *New Directions in Language Testing: Papers Presented at the International Symposium on Language Testing*, (pp. 35-46). Pergamon Press.

Syafei, M., Mujiyanto, J., Yuliasri, I., & Pratama, H. (2021). Students' perception of the application of portfolio assessment during the COVID-19 pandemic. *Academic International Conference on Literacy and Novelty*, pp. 61–70). KnE Social Sciences. doi 10.18502/kss.v5i7.9320

Syzdykova, Z., Koblandin, K., Mikhaylova, N., & Akinina, O. (2021). Assessment of e-portfolio in higher education. *International Journal of Emerging Technologies in Learning*, *16*(2), 120–134. doi:10.3991/ijet.v16i02.18819

Tang, T. T., Nguyen, T. N., & Tran, H. T. T. (2022). Vietnamese Teachers' Acceptance to Use E-Assessment Tools in Teaching: An Empirical Study Using PLS-SEM. *Contemporary Educational Technology*, *14*(3), ep375. doi:10.30935/cedtech/12106

Tao, Y., & Zou, B. (2021). Students' perceptions of the use of Kahoot! in English as a foreign language classroom learning context. *Computer Assisted Language Learning*, *0*, 1–20. doi:10.1080/09588221.2021.2011323

Tavakoli, M., & Nezakat-Alhossaini, M. (2014). Implementation of corrective feedback in an English as a foreign language classroom through dynamic assessment. *Journal of Language and Linguistic Studies*, *10*(1), 211–232.

Taylor, L. (2013). Communicating the theory, practice and principles of language testing to test stakeholders: Some reflections. *Language Testing*, *30*(3), 403–412. doi:10.1177/0265532213480338

Ter-Misanova, S. G. (2005). Traditions and innovations: English language teaching in Russia. *World Englishes*, *24*(4), 445–454. doi:10.1111/j.0883-2919.2005.00427.x

Thi, N. K., Nikolov, M., & Simon, K. (2022). Higher-proficiency students' engagement with and uptake of teacher and Grammarly feedback in an EFL writing course. *Innovation in Language Learning and Teaching*, 1–16. doi:10.1080/17501229.2022.2122476

Thoms, J. J., & Poole, F. (2017). Investigating linguistic, literary, and social affordances of L2 collaborative reading. *Language Learning & Technology*, *21*(1), 139–156. 10125/44615

To, J., & Carless, D. (2016). Making productive use of exemplars: Peer discussion and teacher guidance for positive transfer of strategies. *Journal of Further and Higher Education*, *40*(6), 746–764. doi:10.1080/0309877X.2015.1014317

Tootkaboni, A. A., & Khatib, M. (2014). The Efficiency of Various Kinds of Error Feedback on Improving Writing Accuracy of EFL Learners. *Bellaterra Journal of Teaching & Learning Language & Literature*, *7*(3), 30–46. doi:10.5565/rev/jtl3.529

Topuz, A. C., Saka, E., & Faruk Fatsa, Ö. (2022). Emerging trends of online assessment systems in the emergency remote teaching period. *Smart Learning Environments*, *9*(17), 1–21. doi:10.118640561-022-00199-6

Tripp, D. (2005). Pesquisa-ação: Uma introdução metodológica. *Educação e Pesquisa*, *31*(3), 443–466. doi:10.1590/S1517-97022005000300009

Trott, D. C. (1991, October). *Anthrogogy*. Paper presented at the meeting of the American Association for Adult and Continuing Education, Montreal, Quebec.

Trumbull, E., & Lash, A. (2013). *Understanding Formative Assessment: Insights from Learning Theory and Measurement Theory*. Wested. https://www.wested.org/online_pubs/resource1307.pdf

Tsagari, D., & Vogt, K. (2017). Assessment literacy of foreign language teachers around Europe: Research, challenges, and future prospects. *Papers in Language Testing and Assessment*, *6*(1), 41–63. doi:10.58379/UHIX9883

Tseng, S.-S., & Yeh, H.-C. (2019). The impact of video and written feedback on student preferences of English speaking practice. *Language Learning & Technology*, *23*(2), 145–158.

Tseng, S.-S., Yeh, H.-C., & Yang, S. (2015). Promoting different reading comprehension levels through online annotations. *Computer Assisted Language Learning*, *28*(1), 41–57. doi:10.1080/09588221.2014.927366

Tsimaras, D. O., Mystakidis, S., Christopoulos, A., Zoulias, E., & Hatzilygeroudis, I. (2022). E-Learning Courses Evaluation on the Basis of Trainees' Feedback on Open Questions Text Analysis. *Education Sciences*, *12*(9), 633. doi:10.3390/educsci12090633

Tsiplakides, I. (2018). Shadow Education and Social Class Inequalities in Secondary Education in Greece: The Case of Teaching English as a Foreign Language. [online]. *The International Journal of Social Education*, *7*(1), 71–93. doi:10.17583/rise.2018.2987

Turner, C. E., & Purpura, J. E. (2016). Learning-oriented assessment in second and foreign language classrooms. In D. Tsagari & J. Banerjee (Eds.), Handbook of second language assessment (pp. 255–272). De Gruyter. (pp. 255–272). De Gruyter. doi:10.1515/9781614513827-018

Tzifopoulos, M. (2020). In the shadow of Coronavirus: Distance education and digital literacy skills in Greece. *International Journal of Social Science and Technology*, *5*(2), 1–14.

Underwood, J. (2006). Digital Technologies and Dishonesty in Examinations and Tests. *Review, Qualifications and Curriculum Authority*, *10*(5). https://www.researchgate.net/publication/253936339

University of Hong Kong. (2021). *Theory and practice as one: Experiential learning @ HKU*. HKU. https://tl.hku.hk/reform/experiential-learning/4/

Ur, P. (1996). *A Course in Language Teaching: Practice and theory*. Cambridge University Press.

van Lier, L. (1989, September). Reeling, Writhing, Drawling, Stretching, and Fainting in Coils: Oral Proficiency Interviews as Conversation. *TESOL Quarterly*, *23*(3), 489–508. doi:10.2307/3586922

Varble, D. (2014). Reducing Cheating Opportunities in Online Test. *Atlantic Marketing J.*, *3*(3), 131–149.

Vasileiou, S., Papadima-Sophocleous, S., & Giannikas, C. N. (2023). Technologies in Second Language Formative Assessment: As Systematic Review. *Research Papers in Language Teaching and Learning*, *13*(1), 50–63.

Vaughan, N. D., Cleveland-Innes, M., & Garrison, D. R. (2013). *Teaching in blended learning environments: Creating and sustaining communities of inquiry*. Athabasca University Press. doi:10.15215/aupress/9781927356470.01

Villa Larenas, S. (2021, June 14-17). *A revised multidimensional model for LAL: relationships between beliefs, knowledge, practices, learning, and context* [Paper presentation]. Language Testing Research Colloquium (LTRC).

Villa Larenas, S., & Brunfaut, T. (2022). But who trains the language teacher educator who trains the language teacher? An empirical investigation of Chilean EFL teacher educators' language assessment literacy. *Language Testing, 02655322221134218*. doi:10.1177/02655322221134218

Villas Boas, B. M. F. (2014). Avaliação para aprendizagem na formação de professores. *Cadernos de Educação, 26*, 57–77.

Vince, R. (1998). Behind and beyond Kolb's learning cycle. *Journal of Management Education, 22*(3), 304–319. doi:10.1177/105256299802200304

Vogt, K., & Tsagari, D. (2014). Assessment literacy of foreign language teachers: Findings of a European study. *Language Assessment Quarterly, 11*(4), 374–402. doi:10.1080/15434303.2014.960046

Vogt, K., Tsagari, D., Csépes, I., Green, A., & Sifakis, N. (2020). Linking learners' perspectives on language assessment practices to teachers' assessment literacy enhancement (TALE): Insights from four European countries. *Language Assessment Quarterly, 17*(4), 410–433. doi:10.1080/15434303.2020.1776714

Vogt, K., Tsagari, D., & Spanoudis, G. (2020). What Do Teachers Think They Want? A Comparative Study of In-Service Language Teachers' Beliefs on LAL Training Needs. *Language Assessment Quarterly, 17*(4), 386–409. doi:10.1080/15434303.2020.1781128

Vurdien, R., & Puranen, P. (2022). Teacher attitudes toward online assessment in challenging times. In B. Arnbjörnsdóttir, B. Bédi, L. Bradley, K. Friðriksdóttir, H. Garðarsdóttir, S. Thouësny, & M. J. Whelpton (Eds.), Intelligent CALL, granular systems, and learner data: short papers from EUROCALL 2022 (pp. 370–374). Research-publishing.net. doi:10.14705/rpnet.2022.61.1486

Vygotsky, L. S. (1987). The Collected Works of L. S. Vygotsky. Volume 1. Problems of General Psychology. Including the Volume Thinking and Speech. R. W. Rieber and A. S. Carton (Eds). Plenum.

Vygotsky, L. S. (1978). *Mind in society: The development of higher psychological processes* (M. Cole, Ed. & Trans.). Harvard University Press.

Wagener, D. (2006). Promoting independent learning skills. *Computer Assisted Language Learning, 19*(4-5), 279–286. doi:10.1080/09588220601043180

Wang, A. I., & Tahir, R. (2020). The effect of using Kahoot! for learning – A literature review. *Computers & Education, 149*, 183818. doi:10.1016/j.compedu.2020.103818

Wang, P., & Jeffrey, R. (2017). Listening to learners: An investigation into college students' attitudes towards the adoption of e-portfolios in English assessment and learning. *British Journal of Educational Technology, 48*(6), 1451–1463. doi:10.1111/bjet.12513

Wang, Y. J., Shang, H. F., & Briody, P. (2013). Exploring the impact of using automated writing evaluation in English as a foreign language university students' writing. *Computer Assisted Language Learning, 26*(3), 234–257. doi:10.1080/09588221.2012.655300

Wang, Z. (2020). Computer-assisted EFL writing and evaluations based on artificial intelligence: A case from a college reading and writing course. *Library Hi Tech, 40*(1), 80–97. doi:10.1108/LHT-05-2020-0113

Waycott, J., Bennett, S., Kennedy, G., Dalgarno, B., & Gray, K. (2010). Digital divides? Student and staff perceptions of information and communication technologies. *Computers & Education, 54*(4), 1202–1211. doi:10.1016/j.compedu.2009.11.006

Compilation of References

Waycott, J., Sheard, J., Thompson, C., & Clerehan, R. (2013). Making students' work visible on the social web: A blessing or a curse? *Computers & Education*, *68*, 86–95. doi:10.1016/j.compedu.2013.04.026

Weir, C., O'Sullivan, B., Yan, J., & Bax, S. (2007). Does the computer make a difference? Reaction of candidates to a computer-based versus a traditional handwritten form of the IELTS writing component: Effects and impact. *IELTS Research Report.*, *7*(6), 1–37.

Wiliam, D. (2011). What is assessment for learning? *Studies in Educational Evaluation*, *37*(1), 3–14. doi:10.1016/j.stueduc.2011.03.001 PMID:22114905

Willatt, C., & Flores, L. M. (2022). The Presence of the Body in Digital Education: A Phenomenological Approach to Embodied Experience. *Studies in Philosophy and Education*, *41*(1), 21–37. doi:10.100711217-021-09813-5

Wilson, J., & Czik, A. (2016). Automated essay evaluation software in English Language Arts classrooms: Effects on teacher feedback, student motivation, and writing quality. *Computers & Education*, *100*, 94–109. doi:10.1016/j.compedu.2016.05.004

Winstone, N., & Carless, D. (2020). *Designing effective feedback processes in higher education: A learning-focused approach*. Routledge.

Woodward, H. (1998). Reflective Journals and Portfolios: Learning Through Assessment. *Assessment & Evaluation in Higher Education*, *23*(4), 415–423. doi:10.1080/0260293980230408

Xiaoxiao, L., & Yan, L. (2010). A Case Study of Dynamic Assessment in EFL Process Writing. *Chinese Journal of Applied Linguistis (Bimonthly)*, *33*(1), 24–40.

Xi, J., Chen, Y., & Wang, G. (2018). Design of a Personalized Massive Open Online Course Platform. *International Journal of Emerging Technologies in Learning*, *13*(4), 58–70. doi:10.3991/ijet.v13i04.8470

Xu, Y., & Brown, G. T. L. (2016). Teacher assessment literacy in practice: A reconceptualization. *Teaching and Teacher Education*, *58*, 149–162. doi:10.1016/j.tate.2016.05.010

Yang, M., Mak, P., & Yuan, R. (2021). Feedback experience of online learning during the COVID-19 pandemic: Voices from pre-service English language teachers. *The Asia-Pacific Education Researcher*, *30*(6), 611–620. doi:10.100740299-021-00618-1

Yan, X., & Fan, J. (2021). "Am I qualified to be a language tester?": Understanding the development of language assessment literacy across three stakeholder groups. *Language Testing*, *38*(2), 219–246. doi:10.1177/0265532220929924

Yarahmadzehi, N., & Goodarzi, M. (2020). Investigating the role of formative mobile based assessment in vocabulary learning of pre-intermediate EFL learners in comparison with paper based assessment. *Turkish Online Journal of Distance Education*, *21*(1), 181–196. doi:10.17718/tojde.690390

Yastibas, A. E., & Yastibas, G. C. (2015). The use of e-portfolio-based assessment to develop students' self-regulated learning in English language teaching. *Procedia: Social and Behavioral Sciences*, *176*, 3–13. doi:10.1016/j.sbspro.2015.01.437

Yin, R. K. (1994). *Case study research design and methods* (2nd ed.). Sage.

Yousaf, H. Q., Rehman, S., Ahmed, M., & Munawar, S. (2022). Investigating students' satisfaction in online learning: The role of students' interaction and engagement in universities. *Interactive Learning Environments*, 1–18. doi:10.1080/10494820.2022.2061009

Zeng, G., & Takatsuka, S. (2009). Text-based peer-peer collaborative dialogue in a computer-mediated learning environment in the EFL context. *System*, *37*(3), 434–446. doi:10.1016/j.system.2009.01.003

Zhang, C., Yan, X., & Wang, J. (2021). EFL teachers' online assessment practices during the COVID-19 pandemic: Changes and mediating factors. *The Asia-Pacific Education Researcher*, *30*(6), 499–507. doi:10.100740299-021-00589-3

Zhang, Y. H. (2010). Constructing Dynamic Assessment Mode in College English Writing Class. *Journal of PLA University of Foreign Languages*, *1*, 46–50.

Zhang, Z. V. (2020). Engaging with automated writing evaluation (AWE) feedback on L2 writing: Student perceptions and revisions. *Assessing Writing*, *43*, 100439. doi:10.1016/j.asw.2019.100439

Zhao, R., & Hirvela, A. (2015). Undergraduate ESL students' engagement in academic reading and writing in learning to write a synthesis paper. *Reading in a Foreign Language*, *27*(2), 219–241.

Zocaratto, B. L., & Quevedo-Camargo, G. (2022). Feedback on-line na formação inicial de professores de línguas: Estado da arte. *Estudos Em Avaliação Educacional*, *33*, e09532. doi:10.18222/eae.v33.9532

Related References

To continue our tradition of advancing academic research, we have compiled a list of recommended IGI Global readings. These references will provide additional information and guidance to further enrich your knowledge and assist you with your own research and future publications.

Aburezeq, I. M., & Dweikat, F. F. (2017). Cloud Applications in Language Teaching: Examining Pre-Service Teachers' Expertise, Perceptions and Integration. *International Journal of Distance Education Technologies*, *15*(4), 39–60. doi:10.4018/IJDET.2017100103

Acharjya, B., & Das, S. (2022). Adoption of E-Learning During the COVID-19 Pandemic: The Moderating Role of Age and Gender. *International Journal of Web-Based Learning and Teaching Technologies*, *17*(2), 1–14. https://doi.org/10.4018/IJWLTT.20220301.oa4

Adams, J. L., & Thomas, S. K. (2022). Non-Linear Curriculum Experiences for Student Learning and Work Design: What Is the Maximum Potential of a Chat Bot? In S. Ramlall, T. Cross, & M. Love (Eds.), *Handbook of Research on Future of Work and Education: Implications for Curriculum Delivery and Work Design* (pp. 299–306). IGI Global. https://doi.org/10.4018/978-1-7998-8275-6.ch018

Adera, B. (2017). Supporting Language and Literacy Development for English Language Learners. In J. Keengwe (Ed.), *Handbook of Research on Promoting Cross-Cultural Competence and Social Justice in Teacher Education* (pp. 339–354). Hershey, PA: IGI Global. doi:10.4018/978-1-5225-0897-7.ch018

Ahamer, G. (2017). Quality Assurance for a Developmental "Global Studies" (GS) Curriculum. In I. Management Association (Ed.), Educational Leadership and Administration: Concepts, Methodologies, Tools, and Applications (pp. 438-477). Hershey, PA: IGI Global. https://doi.org/ doi:10.4018/978-1-5225-1624-8.ch023

Akayoğlu, S., & Seferoğlu, G. (2019). An Analysis of Negotiation of Meaning Functions of Advanced EFL Learners in Second Life: Negotiation of Meaning in Second Life. In M. Kruk (Ed.), *Assessing the Effectiveness of Virtual Technologies in Foreign and Second Language Instruction* (pp. 61–85). IGI Global. https://doi.org/10.4018/978-1-5225-7286-2.ch003

Akella, N. R. (2022). Unravelling the Web of Qualitative Dissertation Writing!: A Student Reflects. In A. Zimmerman (Ed.), *Methodological Innovations in Research and Academic Writing* (pp. 260–282). IGI Global. https://doi.org/10.4018/978-1-7998-8283-1.ch014

Alegre de la Rosa, O. M., & Angulo, L. M. (2017). Social Inclusion and Intercultural Values in a School of Education. In S. Mukerji & P. Tripathi (Eds.), *Handbook of Research on Administration, Policy, and Leadership in Higher Education* (pp. 518–531). Hershey, PA: IGI Global. doi:10.4018/978-1-5225-0672-0.ch020

Alexander, C. (2019). Using Gamification Strategies to Cultivate and Measure Professional Educator Dispositions. *International Journal of Game-Based Learning*, 9(1), 15–29. https://doi.org/10.4018/IJGBL.2019010102

Anderson, K. M. (2017). Preparing Teachers in the Age of Equity and Inclusion. In I. Management Association (Ed.), Medical Education and Ethics: Concepts, Methodologies, Tools, and Applications (pp. 1532-1554). Hershey, PA: IGI Global. doi:10.4018/978-1-5225-0978-3.ch069

Awdziej, M. (2017). Case Study as a Teaching Method in Marketing. In D. Latusek (Ed.), *Case Studies as a Teaching Tool in Management Education* (pp. 244–263). Hershey, PA: IGI Global. doi:10.4018/978-1-5225-0770-3.ch013

Bakos, J. (2019). Sociolinguistic Factors Influencing English Language Learning. In N. Erdogan & M. Wei (Eds.), *Applied Linguistics for Teachers of Culturally and Linguistically Diverse Learners* (pp. 403–424). IGI Global. https://doi.org/10.4018/978-1-5225-8467-4.ch017

Banas, J. R., & York, C. S. (2017). Pre-Service Teachers' Motivation to Use Technology and the Impact of Authentic Learning Exercises. In L. Tomei (Ed.), *Exploring the New Era of Technology-Infused Education* (pp. 121–140). Hershey, PA: IGI Global. doi:10.4018/978-1-5225-1709-2.ch008

Barton, T. P. (2021). Empowering Educator Allyship by Exploring Racial Trauma and the Disengagement of Black Students. In C. Reneau & M. Villarreal (Eds.), *Handbook of Research on Leading Higher Education Transformation With Social Justice, Equity, and Inclusion* (pp. 186–197). IGI Global. https://doi.org/10.4018/978-1-7998-7152-1.ch013

Benhima, M. (2021). Moroccan English Department Student Attitudes Towards the Use of Distance Education During COVID-19: Moulay Ismail University as a Case Study. *International Journal of Information and Communication Technology Education*, 17(3), 105–122. https://doi.org/10.4018/IJICTE.20210701.oa7

Beycioglu, K., & Wildy, H. (2017). Principal Preparation: The Case of Novice Principals in Turkey. In I. Management Association (Ed.), Educational Leadership and Administration: Concepts, Methodologies, Tools, and Applications (pp. 1152-1169). Hershey, PA: IGI Global. https://doi.org/ doi:10.4018/978-1-5225-1624-8.ch054

Bharwani, S., & Musunuri, D. (2018). Reflection as a Process From Theory to Practice. In M. Khosrow-Pour, D.B.A. (Ed.), Encyclopedia of Information Science and Technology, Fourth Edition (pp. 1529-1539). Hershey, PA: IGI Global. doi:10.4018/978-1-5225-2255-3.ch132

Related References

Bhushan, A., Garza, K. B., Perumal, O., Das, S. K., Feola, D. J., Farrell, D., & Birnbaum, A. (2022). Lessons Learned From the COVID-19 Pandemic and the Implications for Pharmaceutical Graduate Education and Research. In C. Ford & K. Garza (Eds.), *Handbook of Research on Updating and Innovating Health Professions Education: Post-Pandemic Perspectives* (pp. 324–345). IGI Global. https://doi.org/10.4018/978-1-7998-7623-6.ch014

Bintz, W., Ciecierski, L. M., & Royan, E. (2021). Using Picture Books With Instructional Strategies to Address New Challenges and Teach Literacy Skills in a Digital World. In L. Haas & J. Tussey (Eds.), *Connecting Disciplinary Literacy and Digital Storytelling in K-12 Education* (pp. 38–58). IGI Global. https://doi.org/10.4018/978-1-7998-5770-9.ch003

Bohjanen, S. L., Cameron-Standerford, A., & Meidl, T. D. (2018). Capacity Building Pedagogy for Diverse Learners. In J. Keengwe (Ed.), *Handbook of Research on Pedagogical Models for Next-Generation Teaching and Learning* (pp. 195–212). Hershey, PA: IGI Global. doi:10.4018/978-1-5225-3873-8.ch011

Brewer, J. C. (2018). Measuring Text Readability Using Reading Level. In M. Khosrow-Pour, D.B.A. (Ed.), Encyclopedia of Information Science and Technology, Fourth Edition (pp. 1499-1507). Hershey, PA: IGI Global. doi:10.4018/978-1-5225-2255-3.ch129

Brookbanks, B. C. (2022). Student Perspectives on Business Education in the USA: Current Attitudes and Necessary Changes in an Age of Disruption. In A. Zhuplev & R. Koepp (Eds.), *Global Trends, Dynamics, and Imperatives for Strategic Development in Business Education in an Age of Disruption* (pp. 214–231). IGI Global. doi:10.4018/978-1-7998-7548-2.ch011

Brown, L. V., Dari, T., & Spencer, N. (2019). Addressing the Impact of Trauma in High Poverty Elementary Schools: An Ecological Model for School Counseling. In K. Daniels & K. Billingsley (Eds.), *Creating Caring and Supportive Educational Environments for Meaningful Learning* (pp. 135–153). IGI Global. https://doi.org/10.4018/978-1-5225-5748-7.ch008

Brown, S. L. (2017). A Case Study of Strategic Leadership and Research in Practice: Principal Preparation Programs that Work – An Educational Administration Perspective of Best Practices for Master's Degree Programs for Principal Preparation. In V. Wang (Ed.), *Encyclopedia of Strategic Leadership and Management* (pp. 1226–1244). Hershey, PA: IGI Global. doi:10.4018/978-1-5225-1049-9.ch086

Brzozowski, M., & Ferster, I. (2017). Educational Management Leadership: High School Principal's Management Style and Parental Involvement in School Management in Israel. In V. Potocan, M. Üngan, & Z. Nedelko (Eds.), *Handbook of Research on Managerial Solutions in Non-Profit Organizations* (pp. 55–74). Hershey, PA: IGI Global. doi:10.4018/978-1-5225-0731-4.ch003

Cahapay, M. B. (2020). Delphi Technique in the Development of Emerging Contents in High School Science Curriculum. *International Journal of Curriculum Development and Learning Measurement*, *1*(2), 1–9. https://doi.org/10.4018/IJCDLM.2020070101

Camacho, L. F., & Leon Guerrero, A. E. (2022). Indigenous Student Experience in Higher Education: Implementation of Culturally Sensitive Support. In P. Pangelinan & T. McVey (Eds.), *Learning and Reconciliation Through Indigenous Education in Oceania* (pp. 254–266). IGI Global. https://doi.org/10.4018/978-1-7998-7736-3.ch016

Cannaday, J. (2017). The Masking Effect: Hidden Gifts and Disabilities of 2e Students. In P. Dickenson, P. Keough, & J. Courduff (Eds.), *Preparing Pre-Service Teachers for the Inclusive Classroom* (pp. 220–231). Hershey, PA: IGI Global. doi:10.4018/978-1-5225-1753-5.ch011

Cederquist, S., Fishman, B., & Teasley, S. D. (2022). What's Missing From the College Transcript?: How Employers Make Sense of Student Skills. In Y. Huang (Ed.), *Handbook of Research on Credential Innovations for Inclusive Pathways to Professions* (pp. 234–253). IGI Global. https://doi.org/10.4018/978-1-7998-3820-3.ch012

Cockrell, P., & Gibson, T. (2019). The Untold Stories of Black and Brown Student Experiences in Historically White Fraternities and Sororities. In P. Hoffman-Miller, M. James, & D. Hermond (Eds.), *African American Suburbanization and the Consequential Loss of Identity* (pp. 153–171). IGI Global. https://doi.org/10.4018/978-1-5225-7835-2.ch009

Cohen, M. (2022). Leveraging Content Creation to Boost Student Engagement. In T. Driscoll III, (Ed.), *Designing Effective Distance and Blended Learning Environments in K-12* (pp. 223–239). IGI Global. https://doi.org/10.4018/978-1-7998-6829-3.ch013

Contreras, E. C., & Contreras, I. I. (2018). Development of Communication Skills through Auditory Training Software in Special Education. In M. Khosrow-Pour, D.B.A. (Ed.), Encyclopedia of Information Science and Technology, Fourth Edition (pp. 2431-2441). Hershey, PA: IGI Global. doi:10.4018/978-1-5225-2255-3.ch212

Cooke, L., Schugar, J., Schugar, H., Penny, C., & Bruning, H. (2020). Can Everyone Code?: Preparing Teachers to Teach Computer Languages as a Literacy. In J. Mitchell & E. Vaughn (Eds.), *Participatory Literacy Practices for P-12 Classrooms in the Digital Age* (pp. 163–183). IGI Global. https://doi.org/10.4018/978-1-7998-0000-2.ch009

Cooley, D., & Whitten, E. (2017). Special Education Leadership and the Implementation of Response to Intervention. In F. Topor (Ed.), *Handbook of Research on Individualism and Identity in the Globalized Digital Age* (pp. 265–286). Hershey, PA: IGI Global. doi:10.4018/978-1-5225-0522-8.ch012

Cosner, S., Tozer, S., & Zavitkovsky, P. (2017). Enacting a Cycle of Inquiry Capstone Research Project in Doctoral-Level Leadership Preparation. In I. Management Association (Ed.), Educational Leadership and Administration: Concepts, Methodologies, Tools, and Applications (pp. 1460-1481). Hershey, PA: IGI Global. doi:10.4018/978-1-5225-1624-8.ch067

Crawford, C. M. (2018). Instructional Real World Community Engagement. In M. Khosrow-Pour, D.B.A. (Ed.), Encyclopedia of Information Science and Technology, Fourth Edition (pp. 1474-1486). Hershey, PA: IGI Global. doi:10.4018/978-1-5225-2255-3.ch127

Crosby-Cooper, T., & Pacis, D. (2017). Implementing Effective Student Support Teams. In P. Dickenson, P. Keough, & J. Courduff (Eds.), *Preparing Pre-Service Teachers for the Inclusive Classroom* (pp. 248–262). Hershey, PA: IGI Global. doi:10.4018/978-1-5225-1753-5.ch013

Related References

Curran, C. M., & Hawbaker, B. W. (2017). Cultivating Communities of Inclusive Practice: Professional Development for Educators – Research and Practice. In C. Curran & A. Petersen (Eds.), *Handbook of Research on Classroom Diversity and Inclusive Education Practice* (pp. 120–153). Hershey, PA: IGI Global. doi:10.4018/978-1-5225-2520-2.ch006

Dass, S., & Dabbagh, N. (2018). Faculty Adoption of 3D Avatar-Based Virtual World Learning Environments: An Exploratory Case Study. In I. Management Association (Ed.), Technology Adoption and Social Issues: Concepts, Methodologies, Tools, and Applications (pp. 1000-1033). Hershey, PA: IGI Global. https://doi.org/ doi:10.4018/978-1-5225-5201-7.ch045

Davison, A. M., & Scholl, K. G. (2017). Inclusive Recreation as Part of the IEP Process. In C. Curran & A. Petersen (Eds.), *Handbook of Research on Classroom Diversity and Inclusive Education Practice* (pp. 311–330). Hershey, PA: IGI Global. doi:10.4018/978-1-5225-2520-2.ch013

DeCoito, I. (2018). Addressing Digital Competencies, Curriculum Development, and Instructional Design in Science Teacher Education. In M. Khosrow-Pour, D.B.A. (Ed.), Encyclopedia of Information Science and Technology, Fourth Edition (pp. 1420-1431). Hershey, PA: IGI Global. https://doi.org/ doi:10.4018/978-1-5225-2255-3.ch122

DeCoito, I., & Richardson, T. (2017). Beyond Angry Birds™: Using Web-Based Tools to Engage Learners and Promote Inquiry in STEM Learning. In I. Levin & D. Tsybulsky (Eds.), *Digital Tools and Solutions for Inquiry-Based STEM Learning* (pp. 166–196). Hershey, PA: IGI Global. doi:10.4018/978-1-5225-2525-7.ch007

Delmas, P. M. (2017). Research-Based Leadership for Next-Generation Leaders. In R. Styron Jr & J. Styron (Eds.), *Comprehensive Problem-Solving and Skill Development for Next-Generation Leaders* (pp. 1–39). Hershey, PA: IGI Global. doi:10.4018/978-1-5225-1968-3.ch001

Demiray, U., & Ekren, G. (2018). Administrative-Related Evaluation for Distance Education Institutions in Turkey. In K. Buyuk, S. Kocdar, & A. Bozkurt (Eds.), *Administrative Leadership in Open and Distance Learning Programs* (pp. 263–288). Hershey, PA: IGI Global. doi:10.4018/978-1-5225-2645-2.ch011

Dickenson, P. (2017). What do we Know and Where Can We Grow?: Teachers Preparation for the Inclusive Classroom. In P. Dickenson, P. Keough, & J. Courduff (Eds.), *Preparing Pre-Service Teachers for the Inclusive Classroom* (pp. 1–22). Hershey, PA: IGI Global. doi:10.4018/978-1-5225-1753-5.ch001

Ding, Q., & Zhu, H. (2021). Flipping the Classroom in STEM Education. In J. Keengwe (Ed.), *Handbook of Research on Innovations in Non-Traditional Educational Practices* (pp. 155–173). IGI Global. https://doi.org/10.4018/978-1-7998-4360-3.ch008

Dixon, T., & Christison, M. (2021). Teaching English Grammar in a Hybrid Academic ESL Course: A Mixed Methods Study. In K. Kelch, P. Byun, S. Safavi, & S. Cervantes (Eds.), *CALL Theory Applications for Online TESOL Education* (pp. 229–251). IGI Global. https://doi.org/10.4018/978-1-7998-6609-1.ch010

Donne, V., & Hansen, M. (2017). Teachers' Use of Assistive Technologies in Education. In L. Tomei (Ed.), *Exploring the New Era of Technology-Infused Education* (pp. 86–101). Hershey, PA: IGI Global. doi:10.4018/978-1-5225-1709-2.ch006

Donne, V., & Hansen, M. A. (2018). Business and Technology Educators: Practices for Inclusion. In I. Management Association (Ed.), Business Education and Ethics: Concepts, Methodologies, Tools, and Applications (pp. 471-484). Hershey, PA: IGI Global. https://doi.org/ doi:10.4018/978-1-5225-3153-1.ch026

Dos Santos, L. M. (2022). Completing Student-Teaching Internships Online: Instructional Changes During the COVID-19 Pandemic. In M. Alaali (Ed.), *Assessing University Governance and Policies in Relation to the COVID-19 Pandemic* (pp. 106–127). IGI Global. https://doi.org/10.4018/978-1-7998-8279-4.ch007

Dreon, O., Shettel, J., & Bower, K. M. (2017). Preparing Next Generation Elementary Teachers for the Tools of Tomorrow. In M. Grassetti & S. Brookby (Eds.), *Advancing Next-Generation Teacher Education through Digital Tools and Applications* (pp. 143–159). Hershey, PA: IGI Global. doi:10.4018/978-1-5225-0965-3.ch008

Durak, H. Y., & Güyer, T. (2018). Design and Development of an Instructional Program for Teaching Programming Processes to Gifted Students Using Scratch. In J. Cannaday (Ed.), *Curriculum Development for Gifted Education Programs* (pp. 61–99). Hershey, PA: IGI Global. doi:10.4018/978-1-5225-3041-1.ch004

Egorkina, E., Ivanov, M., & Valyavskiy, A. Y. (2018). Students' Research Competence Formation of the Quality of Open and Distance Learning. In V. Mkrttchian & L. Belyanina (Eds.), *Handbook of Research on Students' Research Competence in Modern Educational Contexts* (pp. 364–384). Hershey, PA: IGI Global. doi:10.4018/978-1-5225-3485-3.ch019

Ekren, G., Karataş, S., & Demiray, U. (2017). Understanding of Leadership in Distance Education Management. In I. Management Association (Ed.), Educational Leadership and Administration: Concepts, Methodologies, Tools, and Applications (pp. 34-50). Hershey, PA: IGI Global. https://doi.org/ doi:10.4018/978-1-5225-1624-8.ch003

Elmore, W. M., Young, J. K., Harris, S., & Mason, D. (2017). The Relationship between Individual Student Attributes and Online Course Completion. In K. Shelton & K. Pedersen (Eds.), *Handbook of Research on Building, Growing, and Sustaining Quality E-Learning Programs* (pp. 151–173). Hershey, PA: IGI Global. doi:10.4018/978-1-5225-0877-9.ch008

Ercegovac, I. R., Alfirević, N., & Koludrović, M. (2017). School Principals' Communication and Co-Operation Assessment: The Croatian Experience. In I. Management Association (Ed.), Educational Leadership and Administration: Concepts, Methodologies, Tools, and Applications (pp. 1568-1589). Hershey, PA: IGI Global. https://doi.org/ doi:10.4018/978-1-5225-1624-8.ch072

Everhart, D., & Seymour, D. M. (2017). Challenges and Opportunities in the Currency of Higher Education. In K. Rasmussen, P. Northrup, & R. Colson (Eds.), *Handbook of Research on Competency-Based Education in University Settings* (pp. 41–65). Hershey, PA: IGI Global. doi:10.4018/978-1-5225-0932-5.ch003

Farmer, L. S. (2017). Managing Portable Technologies for Special Education. In V. Wang (Ed.), *Encyclopedia of Strategic Leadership and Management* (pp. 977–987). Hershey, PA: IGI Global. doi:10.4018/978-1-5225-1049-9.ch068

Related References

Farmer, L. S. (2018). Optimizing OERs for Optimal ICT Literacy in Higher Education. In J. Keengwe (Ed.), *Handbook of Research on Mobile Technology, Constructivism, and Meaningful Learning* (pp. 366–390). Hershey, PA: IGI Global. doi:10.4018/978-1-5225-3949-0.ch020

Ferguson, B. T. (2019). Supporting Affective Development of Children With Disabilities Through Moral Dilemmas. In S. Ikuta (Ed.), *Handmade Teaching Materials for Students With Disabilities* (pp. 253–275). IGI Global. doi:10.4018/978-1-5225-6240-5.ch011

Fındık, L. Y. (2017). Self-Assessment of Principals Based on Leadership in Complexity. In I. Management Association (Ed.), Educational Leadership and Administration: Concepts, Methodologies, Tools, and Applications (pp. 978-991). Hershey, PA: IGI Global. https://doi.org/ doi:10.4018/978-1-5225-1624-8.ch047

Flor, A. G., & Gonzalez-Flor, B. (2018). Dysfunctional Digital Demeanors: Tales From (and Policy Implications of) eLearning's Dark Side. In I. Management Association (Ed.), The Dark Web: Breakthroughs in Research and Practice (pp. 37-50). Hershey, PA: IGI Global. https://doi.org/ doi:10.4018/978-1-5225-3163-0.ch003

Floyd, K. K., & Shambaugh, N. (2017). Instructional Design for Simulations in Special Education Virtual Learning Spaces. In T. Kidd & L. Morris Jr., (Eds.), *Handbook of Research on Instructional Systems and Educational Technology* (pp. 202–215). Hershey, PA: IGI Global. doi:10.4018/978-1-5225-2399-4.ch018

Freeland, S. F. (2020). Community Schools: Improving Academic Achievement Through Meaningful Engagement. In R. Kronick (Ed.), *Emerging Perspectives on Community Schools and the Engaged University* (pp. 132–144). IGI Global. https://doi.org/10.4018/978-1-7998-0280-8.ch008

Ghanbarzadeh, R., & Ghapanchi, A. H. (2019). Applied Areas of Three Dimensional Virtual Worlds in Learning and Teaching: A Review of Higher Education. In I. Management Association (Ed.), *Virtual Reality in Education: Breakthroughs in Research and Practice* (pp. 172-192). IGI Global. https://doi.org/10.4018/978-1-5225-8179-6.ch008

Giovannini, J. M. (2017). Technology Integration in Preservice Teacher Education Programs: Research-based Recommendations. In M. Grassetti & S. Brookby (Eds.), *Advancing Next-Generation Teacher Education through Digital Tools and Applications* (pp. 82–102). Hershey, PA: IGI Global. doi:10.4018/978-1-5225-0965-3.ch005

Good, S., & Clarke, V. B. (2017). An Integral Analysis of One Urban School System's Efforts to Support Student-Centered Teaching. In J. Keengwe & G. Onchwari (Eds.), *Handbook of Research on Learner-Centered Pedagogy in Teacher Education and Professional Development* (pp. 45–68). Hershey, PA: IGI Global. doi:10.4018/978-1-5225-0892-2.ch003

Guetzoian, E. (2022). Gamification Strategies for Higher Education Student Worker Training. In C. Lane (Ed.), *Handbook of Research on Acquiring 21st Century Literacy Skills Through Game-Based Learning* (pp. 164–179). IGI Global. https://doi.org/10.4018/978-1-7998-7271-9.ch009

Hamidi, F., Owuor, P. M., Hynie, M., Baljko, M., & McGrath, S. (2017). Potentials of Digital Assistive Technology and Special Education in Kenya. In C. Ayo & V. Mbarika (Eds.), *Sustainable ICT Adoption and Integration for Socio-Economic Development* (pp. 125–151). Hershey, PA: IGI Global. doi:10.4018/978-1-5225-2565-3.ch006

Hamim, T., Benabbou, F., & Sael, N. (2022). Student Profile Modeling Using Boosting Algorithms. *International Journal of Web-Based Learning and Teaching Technologies*, 17(5), 1–13. https://doi.org/10.4018/IJWLTT.20220901.oa4

Henderson, L. K. (2017). Meltdown at Fukushima: Global Catastrophic Events, Visual Literacy, and Art Education. In R. Shin (Ed.), *Convergence of Contemporary Art, Visual Culture, and Global Civic Engagement* (pp. 80–99). Hershey, PA: IGI Global. doi:10.4018/978-1-5225-1665-1.ch005

Hudgins, T., & Holland, J. L. (2018). Digital Badges: Tracking Knowledge Acquisition Within an Innovation Framework. In I. Management Association (Ed.), Wearable Technologies: Concepts, Methodologies, Tools, and Applications (pp. 1118-1132). Hershey, PA: IGI Global. https://doi.org/ doi:10.4018/978-1-5225-5484-4.ch051

Hwang, R., Lin, H., Sun, J. C., & Wu, J. (2019). Improving Learning Achievement in Science Education for Elementary School Students via Blended Learning. *International Journal of Online Pedagogy and Course Design*, 9(2), 44–62. https://doi.org/10.4018/IJOPCD.2019040104

Jančec, L., & Vodopivec, J. L. (2019). The Implicit Pedagogy and the Hidden Curriculum in Postmodern Education. In J. Vodopivec, L. Jančec, & T. Štemberger (Eds.), *Implicit Pedagogy for Optimized Learning in Contemporary Education* (pp. 41–59). IGI Global. https://doi.org/10.4018/978-1-5225-5799-9.ch003

Janus, M., & Siddiqua, A. (2018). Challenges for Children With Special Health Needs at the Time of Transition to School. In I. Management Association (Ed.), Autism Spectrum Disorders: Breakthroughs in Research and Practice (pp. 339-371). Hershey, PA: IGI Global. doi:10.4018/978-1-5225-3827-1.ch018

Jesus, R. A. (2018). Screencasts and Learning Styles. In M. Khosrow-Pour, D.B.A. (Ed.), Encyclopedia of Information Science and Technology, Fourth Edition (pp. 1548-1558). Hershey, PA: IGI Global. doi:10.4018/978-1-5225-2255-3.ch134

John, G., Francis, N., & Santhakumar, A. B. (2022). Student Engagement: Past, Present, and Future. In S. Ramlall, T. Cross, & M. Love (Eds.), *Handbook of Research on Future of Work and Education: Implications for Curriculum Delivery and Work Design* (pp. 329–341). IGI Global. https://doi.org/10.4018/978-1-7998-8275-6.ch020

Karpinski, A. C., D'Agostino, J. V., Williams, A. K., Highland, S. A., & Mellott, J. A. (2018). The Relationship Between Online Formative Assessment and State Test Scores Using Multilevel Modeling. In M. Khosrow-Pour, D.B.A. (Ed.), Encyclopedia of Information Science and Technology, Fourth Edition (pp. 5183-5192). Hershey, PA: IGI Global. doi:10.4018/978-1-5225-2255-3.ch450

Kats, Y. (2017). Educational Leadership and Integrated Support for Students with Autism Spectrum Disorders. In I. Management Association (Ed.), Educational Leadership and Administration: Concepts, Methodologies, Tools, and Applications (pp. 101-114). Hershey, PA: IGI Global. https://doi.org/ doi:10.4018/978-1-5225-1624-8.ch007

Kaya, G., & Altun, A. (2018). Educational Ontology Development. In M. Khosrow-Pour, D.B.A. (Ed.), Encyclopedia of Information Science and Technology, Fourth Edition (pp. 1441-1450). Hershey, PA: IGI Global. doi:10.4018/978-1-5225-2255-3.ch124

Related References

Keough, P. D., & Pacis, D. (2017). Best Practices Implementing Special Education Curriculum and Common Core State Standards using UDL. In P. Dickenson, P. Keough, & J. Courduff (Eds.), *Preparing Pre-Service Teachers for the Inclusive Classroom* (pp. 107–123). Hershey, PA: IGI Global. doi:10.4018/978-1-5225-1753-5.ch006

Kilburn, M., Henckell, M., & Starrett, D. (2018). Factors Contributing to the Effectiveness of Online Students and Instructors. In M. Khosrow-Pour, D.B.A. (Ed.), Encyclopedia of Information Science and Technology, Fourth Edition (pp. 1451-1462). Hershey, PA: IGI Global. doi:10.4018/978-1-5225-2255-3.ch125

Koban Koç, D. (2021). Gender and Language: A Sociolinguistic Analysis of Second Language Writing. In E. Hancı-Azizoglu & N. Kavaklı (Eds.), *Futuristic and Linguistic Perspectives on Teaching Writing to Second Language Students* (pp. 161–177). IGI Global. https://doi.org/10.4018/978-1-7998-6508-7.ch010

Konecny, L. T. (2017). Hybrid, Online, and Flipped Classrooms in Health Science: Enhanced Learning Environments. In I. Management Association (Ed.), Flipped Instruction: Breakthroughs in Research and Practice (pp. 355-370). Hershey, PA: IGI Global. https://doi.org/ doi:10.4018/978-1-5225-1803-7.ch020

Kupietz, K. D. (2021). Gaming and Simulation in Public Education: Teaching Others to Help Themselves and Their Neighbors. In N. Drumhiller, T. Wilkin, & K. Srba (Eds.), *Simulation and Game-Based Learning in Emergency and Disaster Management* (pp. 41–62). IGI Global. https://doi.org/10.4018/978-1-7998-4087-9.ch003

Kwee, C. T. (2022). Assessing the International Student Enrolment Strategies in Australian Universities: A Case Study During the COVID-19 Pandemic. In M. Alaali (Ed.), *Assessing University Governance and Policies in Relation to the COVID-19 Pandemic* (pp. 162–188). IGI Global. https://doi.org/10.4018/978-1-7998-8279-4.ch010

Lauricella, S., & McArthur, F. A. (2022). Taking a Student-Centred Approach to Alternative Digital Credentials: Multiple Pathways Toward the Acquisition of Microcredentials. In D. Piedra (Ed.), *Innovations in the Design and Application of Alternative Digital Credentials* (pp. 57–69). IGI Global. https://doi.org/10.4018/978-1-7998-7697-7.ch003

Llamas, M. F. (2019). Intercultural Awareness in Teaching English for Early Childhood: A Film-Based Approach. In E. Domínguez Romero, J. Bobkina, & S. Stefanova (Eds.), *Teaching Literature and Language Through Multimodal Texts* (pp. 54–68). IGI Global. https://doi.org/10.4018/978-1-5225-5796-8.ch004

Lokhtina, I., & Kkese, E. T. (2022). Reflecting and Adapting to an Academic Workplace Before and After the Lockdown in Greek-Speaking Cyprus: Opportunities and Challenges. In A. Zhuplev & R. Koepp (Eds.), *Global Trends, Dynamics, and Imperatives for Strategic Development in Business Education in an Age of Disruption* (pp. 126–148). IGI Global. https://doi.org/10.4018/978-1-7998-7548-2.ch007

Lovell, K. L. (2017). Development and Evaluation of Neuroscience Computer-Based Modules for Medical Students: Instructional Design Principles and Effectiveness. In J. Stefaniak (Ed.), *Advancing Medical Education Through Strategic Instructional Design* (pp. 262–276). Hershey, PA: IGI Global. doi:10.4018/978-1-5225-2098-6.ch013

Maher, D. (2019). The Use of Course Management Systems in Pre-Service Teacher Education. In J. Keengwe (Ed.), *Handbook of Research on Blended Learning Pedagogies and Professional Development in Higher Education* (pp. 196–213). IGI Global. https://doi.org/10.4018/978-1-5225-5557-5.ch011

Makewa, L. N. (2019). Teacher Technology Competence Base. In L. Makewa, B. Ngussa, & J. Kuboja (Eds.), *Technology-Supported Teaching and Research Methods for Educators* (pp. 247–267). IGI Global. https://doi.org/10.4018/978-1-5225-5915-3.ch014

Mallett, C. A. (2022). School Resource (Police) Officers in Schools: Impact on Campus Safety, Student Discipline, and Learning. In G. Crews (Ed.), *Impact of School Shootings on Classroom Culture, Curriculum, and Learning* (pp. 53–70). IGI Global. https://doi.org/10.4018/978-1-7998-5200-1.ch004

Marinho, J. E., Freitas, I. R., Leão, I. B., Pacheco, L. O., Gonçalves, M. P., Castro, M. J., Silva, P. D., & Moreira, R. J. (2022). Project-Based Learning Application in Higher Education: Student Experiences and Perspectives. In A. Alves & N. van Hattum-Janssen (Eds.), *Training Engineering Students for Modern Technological Advancement* (pp. 146–164). IGI Global. https://doi.org/10.4018/978-1-7998-8816-1.ch007

McCleskey, J. A., & Melton, R. M. (2022). Rolling With the Flow: Online Faculty and Student Presence in a Post-COVID-19 World. In S. Ramlall, T. Cross, & M. Love (Eds.), *Handbook of Research on Future of Work and Education: Implications for Curriculum Delivery and Work Design* (pp. 307–328). IGI Global. https://doi.org/10.4018/978-1-7998-8275-6.ch019

McCormack, V. F., Stauffer, M., Fishley, K., Hohenbrink, J., Mascazine, J. R., & Zigler, T. (2018). Designing a Dual Licensure Path for Middle Childhood and Special Education Teacher Candidates. In D. Polly, M. Putman, T. Petty, & A. Good (Eds.), *Innovative Practices in Teacher Preparation and Graduate-Level Teacher Education Programs* (pp. 21–36). Hershey, PA: IGI Global. doi:10.4018/978-1-5225-3068-8.ch002

McDaniel, R. (2017). Strategic Leadership in Instructional Design: Applying the Principles of Instructional Design through the Lens of Strategic Leadership to Distance Education. In V. Wang (Ed.), *Encyclopedia of Strategic Leadership and Management* (pp. 1570–1584). Hershey, PA: IGI Global. doi:10.4018/978-1-5225-1049-9.ch109

McKinney, R. E., Halli-Tierney, A. D., Gold, A. E., Allen, R. S., & Carroll, D. G. (2022). Interprofessional Education: Using Standardized Cases in Face-to-Face and Remote Learning Settings. In C. Ford & K. Garza (Eds.), *Handbook of Research on Updating and Innovating Health Professions Education: Post-Pandemic Perspectives* (pp. 24–42). IGI Global. https://doi.org/10.4018/978-1-7998-7623-6.ch002

Meintjes, H. H. (2021). Learner Views of a Facebook Page as a Supportive Digital Pedagogical Tool at a Public South African School in a Grade 12 Business Studies Class. *International Journal of Smart Education and Urban Society*, 12(2), 32–45. https://doi.org/10.4018/IJSEUS.2021040104

Melero-García, F. (2022). Training Bilingual Interpreters in Healthcare Settings: Student Perceptions of Online Learning. In J. LeLoup & P. Swanson (Eds.), *Handbook of Research on Effective Online Language Teaching in a Disruptive Environment* (pp. 288–310). IGI Global. https://doi.org/10.4018/978-1-7998-7720-2.ch015

Related References

Meletiadou, E. (2022). The Use of Peer Assessment as an Inclusive Learning Strategy in Higher Education Institutions: Enhancing Student Writing Skills and Motivation. In E. Meletiadou (Ed.), *Handbook of Research on Policies and Practices for Assessing Inclusive Teaching and Learning* (pp. 1–26). IGI Global. https://doi.org/10.4018/978-1-7998-8579-5.ch001

Memon, R. N., Ahmad, R., & Salim, S. S. (2018). Critical Issues in Requirements Engineering Education. In I. Management Association (Ed.), Computer Systems and Software Engineering: Concepts, Methodologies, Tools, and Applications (pp. 1953-1976). Hershey, PA: IGI Global. doi:10.4018/978-1-5225-3923-0.ch081

Mendenhall, R. (2017). Western Governors University: CBE Innovator and National Model. In K. Rasmussen, P. Northrup, & R. Colson (Eds.), *Handbook of Research on Competency-Based Education in University Settings* (pp. 379–400). Hershey, PA: IGI Global. doi:10.4018/978-1-5225-0932-5.ch019

Mense, E. G., Griggs, D. M., & Shanks, J. N. (2018). School Leaders in a Time of Accountability and Data Use: Preparing Our Future School Leaders in Leadership Preparation Programs. In E. Mense & M. Crain-Dorough (Eds.), *Data Leadership for K-12 Schools in a Time of Accountability* (pp. 235–259). Hershey, PA: IGI Global. doi:10.4018/978-1-5225-3188-3.ch012

Mense, E. G., Griggs, D. M., & Shanks, J. N. (2018). School Leaders in a Time of Accountability and Data Use: Preparing Our Future School Leaders in Leadership Preparation Programs. In E. Mense & M. Crain-Dorough (Eds.), *Data Leadership for K-12 Schools in a Time of Accountability* (pp. 235–259). Hershey, PA: IGI Global. doi:10.4018/978-1-5225-3188-3.ch012

Mestry, R., & Naicker, S. R. (2017). Exploring Distributive Leadership in South African Public Primary Schools in the Soweto Region. In I. Management Association (Ed.), Educational Leadership and Administration: Concepts, Methodologies, Tools, and Applications (pp. 1041-1064). Hershey, PA: IGI Global. doi:10.4018/978-1-5225-1624-8.ch050

Monaghan, C. H., & Boboc, M. (2017). (Re) Defining Leadership in Higher Education in the U.S. In V. Wang (Ed.), *Encyclopedia of Strategic Leadership and Management* (pp. 567–579). Hershey, PA: IGI Global. doi:10.4018/978-1-5225-1049-9.ch040

Morall, M. B. (2021). Reimagining Mobile Phones: Multiple Literacies and Digital Media Compositions. In C. Moran (Eds.), *Affordances and Constraints of Mobile Phone Use in English Language Arts Classrooms* (pp. 41-53). IGI Global. https://doi.org/10.4018/978-1-7998-5805-8.ch003

Mthethwa, V. (2022). Student Governance and the Academic Minefield During COVID-19 Lockdown in South Africa. In M. Alaali (Ed.), *Assessing University Governance and Policies in Relation to the COVID-19 Pandemic* (pp. 255–276). IGI Global. https://doi.org/10.4018/978-1-7998-8279-4.ch015

Muthee, J. M., & Murungi, C. G. (2018). Relationship Among Intelligence, Achievement Motivation, Type of School, and Academic Performance of Kenyan Urban Primary School Pupils. In M. Khosrow-Pour, D.B.A. (Ed.), Encyclopedia of Information Science and Technology, Fourth Edition (pp. 1540-1547). Hershey, PA: IGI Global. https://doi.org/ doi:10.4018/978-1-5225-2255-3.ch133

Naranjo, J. (2018). Meeting the Need for Inclusive Educators Online: Teacher Education in Inclusive Special Education and Dual-Certification. In D. Polly, M. Putman, T. Petty, & A. Good (Eds.), *Innovative Practices in Teacher Preparation and Graduate-Level Teacher Education Programs* (pp. 106–122). Hershey, PA: IGI Global. doi:10.4018/978-1-5225-3068-8.ch007

Nkabinde, Z. P. (2017). Multiculturalism in Special Education: Perspectives of Minority Children in Urban Schools. In J. Keengwe (Ed.), *Handbook of Research on Promoting Cross-Cultural Competence and Social Justice in Teacher Education* (pp. 382–397). Hershey, PA: IGI Global. doi:10.4018/978-1-5225-0897-7.ch020

Nkabinde, Z. P. (2018). Online Instruction: Is the Quality the Same as Face-to-Face Instruction? In J. Keengwe (Ed.), *Handbook of Research on Digital Content, Mobile Learning, and Technology Integration Models in Teacher Education* (pp. 300–314). Hershey, PA: IGI Global. doi:10.4018/978-1-5225-2953-8.ch016

Nugroho, A., & Albusaidi, S. S. (2022). Internationalization of Higher Education: The Methodological Critiques on the Research Related to Study Overseas and International Experience. In H. Magd & S. Kunjumuhammed (Eds.), *Global Perspectives on Quality Assurance and Accreditation in Higher Education Institutions* (pp. 75–89). IGI Global. https://doi.org/10.4018/978-1-7998-8085-1.ch005

Nulty, Z., & West, S. G. (2022). Student Engagement and Supporting Students With Accommodations. In P. Bull & G. Patterson (Eds.), *Redefining Teacher Education and Teacher Preparation Programs in the Post-COVID-19 Era* (pp. 99–116). IGI Global. https://doi.org/10.4018/978-1-7998-8298-5.ch006

O'Connor, J. R. Jr, & Jackson, K. N. (2017). The Use of iPad® Devices and "Apps" for ASD Students in Special Education and Speech Therapy. In Y. Kats (Ed.), *Supporting the Education of Children with Autism Spectrum Disorders* (pp. 267–283). Hershey, PA: IGI Global. doi:10.4018/978-1-5225-0816-8.ch014

Okolie, U. C., & Yasin, A. M. (2017). TVET in Developing Nations and Human Development. In U. Okolie & A. Yasin (Eds.), *Technical Education and Vocational Training in Developing Nations* (pp. 1–25). Hershey, PA: IGI Global. doi:10.4018/978-1-5225-1811-2.ch001

Pack, A., & Barrett, A. (2021). A Review of Virtual Reality and English for Academic Purposes: Understanding Where to Start. *International Journal of Computer-Assisted Language Learning and Teaching*, *11*(1), 72–80. https://doi.org/10.4018/IJCALLT.2021010105

Pashollari, E. (2019). Building Sustainability Through Environmental Education: Education for Sustainable Development. In L. Wilson, & C. Stevenson (Eds.), *Building Sustainability Through Environmental Education* (pp. 72-88). IGI Global. https://doi.org/10.4018/978-1-5225-7727-0.ch004

Paulson, E. N. (2017). Adapting and Advocating for an Online EdD Program in Changing Times and "Sacred" Cultures. In I. Management Association (Ed.), *Educational Leadership and Administration: Concepts, Methodologies, Tools, and Applications* (pp. 1849-1876). Hershey, PA: IGI Global. https://doi.org/ doi:10.4018/978-1-5225-1624-8.ch085

Related References

Petersen, A. J., Elser, C. F., Al Nassir, M. N., Stakey, J., & Everson, K. (2017). The Year of Teaching Inclusively: Building an Elementary Classroom for All Students. In C. Curran & A. Petersen (Eds.), *Handbook of Research on Classroom Diversity and Inclusive Education Practice* (pp. 332–348). Hershey, PA: IGI Global. doi:10.4018/978-1-5225-2520-2.ch014

Pfannenstiel, K. H., & Sanders, J. (2017). Characteristics and Instructional Strategies for Students With Mathematical Difficulties: In the Inclusive Classroom. In C. Curran & A. Petersen (Eds.), *Handbook of Research on Classroom Diversity and Inclusive Education Practice* (pp. 250–281). Hershey, PA: IGI Global. doi:10.4018/978-1-5225-2520-2.ch011

Phan, A. N. (2022). Quality Assurance of Higher Education From the Glonacal Agency Heuristic: An Example From Vietnam. In H. Magd & S. Kunjumuhammed (Eds.), *Global Perspectives on Quality Assurance and Accreditation in Higher Education Institutions* (pp. 136–155). IGI Global. https://doi.org/10.4018/978-1-7998-8085-1.ch008

Preast, J. L., Bowman, N., & Rose, C. A. (2017). Creating Inclusive Classroom Communities Through Social and Emotional Learning to Reduce Social Marginalization Among Students. In C. Curran & A. Petersen (Eds.), *Handbook of Research on Classroom Diversity and Inclusive Education Practice* (pp. 183–200). Hershey, PA: IGI Global. doi:10.4018/978-1-5225-2520-2.ch008

Randolph, K. M., & Brady, M. P. (2018). Evolution of Covert Coaching as an Evidence-Based Practice in Professional Development and Preparation of Teachers. In V. Bryan, A. Musgrove, & J. Powers (Eds.), *Handbook of Research on Human Development in the Digital Age* (pp. 281–299). Hershey, PA: IGI Global. doi:10.4018/978-1-5225-2838-8.ch013

Rell, A. B., Puig, R. A., Roll, F., Valles, V., Espinoza, M., & Duque, A. L. (2017). Addressing Cultural Diversity and Global Competence: The Dual Language Framework. In L. Leavitt, S. Wisdom, & K. Leavitt (Eds.), *Cultural Awareness and Competency Development in Higher Education* (pp. 111–131). Hershey, PA: IGI Global. doi:10.4018/978-1-5225-2145-7.ch007

Richards, M., & Guzman, I. R. (2020). Academic Assessment of Critical Thinking in Distance Education Information Technology Programs. In I. Management Association (Ed.), *Learning and Performance Assessment: Concepts, Methodologies, Tools, and Applications* (pp. 1-19). IGI Global. https://doi.org/10.4018/978-1-7998-0420-8.ch001

Riel, J., Lawless, K. A., & Brown, S. W. (2017). Defining and Designing Responsive Online Professional Development (ROPD): A Framework to Support Curriculum Implementation. In T. Kidd & L. Morris Jr., (Eds.), *Handbook of Research on Instructional Systems and Educational Technology* (pp. 104–115). Hershey, PA: IGI Global. doi:10.4018/978-1-5225-2399-4.ch010

Roberts, C. (2017). Advancing Women Leaders in Academe: Creating a Culture of Inclusion. In S. Mukerji & P. Tripathi (Eds.), *Handbook of Research on Administration, Policy, and Leadership in Higher Education* (pp. 256–273). Hershey, PA: IGI Global. doi:10.4018/978-1-5225-0672-0.ch012

Rodgers, W. J., Kennedy, M. J., Alves, K. D., & Romig, J. E. (2017). A Multimedia Tool for Teacher Education and Professional Development. In C. Martin & D. Polly (Eds.), *Handbook of Research on Teacher Education and Professional Development* (pp. 285–296). Hershey, PA: IGI Global. doi:10.4018/978-1-5225-1067-3.ch015

Romanowski, M. H. (2017). Qatar's Educational Reform: Critical Issues Facing Principals. In I. Management Association (Ed.), Educational Leadership and Administration: Concepts, Methodologies, Tools, and Applications (pp. 1758-1773). Hershey, PA: IGI Global. https://doi.org/ doi:10.4018/978-1-5225-1624-8.ch080

Ruffin, T. R., Hawkins, D. P., & Lee, D. I. (2018). Increasing Student Engagement and Participation Through Course Methodology. In M. Khosrow-Pour, D.B.A. (Ed.), Encyclopedia of Information Science and Technology, Fourth Edition (pp. 1463-1473). Hershey, PA: IGI Global. doi:10.4018/978-1-5225-2255-3.ch126

Sabina, L. L., Curry, K. A., Harris, E. L., Krumm, B. L., & Vencill, V. (2017). Assessing the Performance of a Cohort-Based Model Using Domestic and International Practices. In I. Management Association (Ed.), Educational Leadership and Administration: Concepts, Methodologies, Tools, and Applications(pp. 913-929). Hershey, PA: IGI Global. https://doi.org/ doi:10.4018/978-1-5225-1624-8.ch044

Samkian, A., Pascarella, J., & Slayton, J. (2022). Towards an Anti-Racist, Culturally Responsive, and LGBTQ+ Inclusive Education: Developing Critically-Conscious Educational Leaders. In E. Cain-Sanschagrin, R. Filback, & J. Crawford (Eds.), *Cases on Academic Program Redesign for Greater Racial and Social Justice* (pp. 150–175). IGI Global. https://doi.org/10.4018/978-1-7998-8463-7.ch007

Santamaría, A. P., Webber, M., & Santamaría, L. J. (2017). Effective School Leadership for Māori Achievement: Building Capacity through Indigenous, National, and International Cross-Cultural Collaboration. In I. Management Association (Ed.), Educational Leadership and Administration: Concepts, Methodologies, Tools, and Applications (pp. 1547-1567). Hershey, PA: IGI Global. https://doi.org/ doi:10.4018/978-1-5225-1624-8.ch071

Santamaría, L. J. (2017). Culturally Responsive Educational Leadership in Cross-Cultural International Contexts. In I. Management Association (Ed.), Educational Leadership and Administration: Concepts, Methodologies, Tools, and Applications (pp. 1380-1400). Hershey, PA: IGI Global. https://doi.org/ doi:10.4018/978-1-5225-1624-8.ch064

Segredo, M. R., Cistone, P. J., & Reio, T. G. (2017). Relationships Between Emotional Intelligence, Leadership Style, and School Culture. *International Journal of Adult Vocational Education and Technology, 8*(3), 25–43. doi:10.4018/IJAVET.2017070103

Shalev, N. (2017). Empathy and Leadership From the Organizational Perspective. In Z. Nedelko & M. Brzozowski (Eds.), *Exploring the Influence of Personal Values and Cultures in the Workplace* (pp. 348–363). Hershey, PA: IGI Global. doi:10.4018/978-1-5225-2480-9.ch018

Siamak, M., Fathi, S., & Isfandyari-Moghaddam, A. (2018). Assessment and Measurement of Education Programs of Information Literacy. In R. Bhardwaj (Ed.), *Digitizing the Modern Library and the Transition From Print to Electronic* (pp. 164–192). Hershey, PA: IGI Global. doi:10.4018/978-1-5225-2119-8.ch007

Siu, K. W., & García, G. J. (2017). Disruptive Technologies and Education: Is There Any Disruption After All? In I. Management Association (Ed.), Educational Leadership and Administration: Concepts, Methodologies, Tools, and Applications (pp. 757-778). Hershey, PA: IGI Global. https://doi.org/ doi:10.4018/978-1-5225-1624-8.ch037

Related References

Slagter van Tryon, P. J. (2017). The Nurse Educator's Role in Designing Instruction and Instructional Strategies for Academic and Clinical Settings. In J. Stefaniak (Ed.), *Advancing Medical Education Through Strategic Instructional Design* (pp. 133–149). Hershey, PA: IGI Global. doi:10.4018/978-1-5225-2098-6.ch006

Slattery, C. A. (2018). Literacy Intervention and the Differentiated Plan of Instruction. In *Developing Effective Literacy Intervention Strategies: Emerging Research and Opportunities* (pp. 41–62). Hershey, PA: IGI Global. doi:10.4018/978-1-5225-5007-5.ch003

Smith, A. R. (2017). Ensuring Quality: The Faculty Role in Online Higher Education. In K. Shelton & K. Pedersen (Eds.), *Handbook of Research on Building, Growing, and Sustaining Quality E-Learning Programs* (pp. 210–231). Hershey, PA: IGI Global. doi:10.4018/978-1-5225-0877-9.ch011

Souders, T. M. (2017). Understanding Your Learner: Conducting a Learner Analysis. In J. Stefaniak (Ed.), *Advancing Medical Education Through Strategic Instructional Design* (pp. 1–29). Hershey, PA: IGI Global. doi:10.4018/978-1-5225-2098-6.ch001

Spring, K. J., Graham, C. R., & Ikahihifo, T. B. (2018). Learner Engagement in Blended Learning. In M. Khosrow-Pour, D.B.A. (Ed.), Encyclopedia of Information Science and Technology, Fourth Edition (pp. 1487-1498). Hershey, PA: IGI Global. doi:10.4018/978-1-5225-2255-3.ch128

Storey, V. A., Anthony, A. K., & Wahid, P. (2017). Gender-Based Leadership Barriers: Advancement of Female Faculty to Leadership Positions in Higher Education. In V. Wang (Ed.), *Encyclopedia of Strategic Leadership and Management* (pp. 244–258). Hershey, PA: IGI Global. doi:10.4018/978-1-5225-1049-9.ch018

Stottlemyer, D. (2018). Develop a Teaching Model Plan for a Differentiated Learning Approach. In *Differentiated Instructional Design for Multicultural Environments: Emerging Research and Opportunities* (pp. 106–130). Hershey, PA: IGI Global. doi:10.4018/978-1-5225-5106-5.ch005

Stottlemyer, D. (2018). Developing a Multicultural Environment. In *Differentiated Instructional Design for Multicultural Environments: Emerging Research and Opportunities* (pp. 1–27). Hershey, PA: IGI Global. doi:10.4018/978-1-5225-5106-5.ch001

Swagerty, T. (2022). Digital Access to Culturally Relevant Curricula: The Impact on the Native and Indigenous Student. In E. Reeves & C. McIntyre (Eds.), *Multidisciplinary Perspectives on Diversity and Equity in a Virtual World* (pp. 99–113). IGI Global. https://doi.org/10.4018/978-1-7998-8028-8.ch006

Swami, B. N., Gobona, T., & Tsimako, J. J. (2017). Academic Leadership: A Case Study of the University of Botswana. In N. Baporikar (Ed.), *Innovation and Shifting Perspectives in Management Education* (pp. 1–32). Hershey, PA: IGI Global. doi:10.4018/978-1-5225-1019-2.ch001

Swanson, K. W., & Collins, G. (2018). Designing Engaging Instruction for the Adult Learners. In M. Khosrow-Pour, D.B.A. (Ed.), Encyclopedia of Information Science and Technology, Fourth Edition (pp. 1432-1440). Hershey, PA: IGI Global. doi:10.4018/978-1-5225-2255-3.ch123

Swartz, B. A., Lynch, J. M., & Lynch, S. D. (2018). Embedding Elementary Teacher Education Coursework in Local Classrooms: Examples in Mathematics and Special Education. In D. Polly, M. Putman, T. Petty, & A. Good (Eds.), *Innovative Practices in Teacher Preparation and Graduate-Level Teacher Education Programs* (pp. 262–292). Hershey, PA: IGI Global. doi:10.4018/978-1-5225-3068-8.ch015

Taliadorou, N., & Pashiardis, P. (2017). Emotional Intelligence and Political Skill Really Matter in Educational Leadership. In I. Management Association (Ed.), Educational Leadership and Administration: Concepts, Methodologies, Tools, and Applications (pp. 1274-1303). Hershey, PA: IGI Global. https://doi.org/ doi:10.4018/978-1-5225-1624-8.ch060

Tandoh, K. A., & Ebe-Arthur, J. E. (2018). Effective Educational Leadership in the Digital Age: An Examination of Professional Qualities and Best Practices. In J. Keengwe (Ed.), *Handbook of Research on Digital Content, Mobile Learning, and Technology Integration Models in Teacher Education* (pp. 244–265). Hershey, PA: IGI Global. doi:10.4018/978-1-5225-2953-8.ch013

Tobin, M. T. (2018). Multimodal Literacy. In M. Khosrow-Pour, D.B.A. (Ed.), Encyclopedia of Information Science and Technology, Fourth Edition (pp. 1508-1516). Hershey, PA: IGI Global. doi:10.4018/978-1-5225-2255-3.ch130

Torres, K. M., Arrastia-Chisholm, M. C., & Tackett, S. (2019). A Phenomenological Study of Pre-Service Teachers' Perceptions of Completing ESOL Field Placements. *International Journal of Teacher Education and Professional Development*, 2(2), 85–101. https://doi.org/10.4018/IJTEPD.2019070106

Torres, M. C., Salamanca, Y. N., Cely, J. P., & Aguilar, J. L. (2020). All We Need is a Boost! Using Multimodal Tools and the Translanguaging Strategy: Strengthening Speaking in the EFL Classroom. *International Journal of Computer-Assisted Language Learning and Teaching*, 10(3), 28–47. doi:10.4018/IJCALLT.2020070103

Torres, M. L., & Ramos, V. J. (2018). Music Therapy: A Pedagogical Alternative for ASD and ID Students in Regular Classrooms. In P. Epler (Ed.), *Instructional Strategies in General Education and Putting the Individuals With Disabilities Act (IDEA) Into Practice* (pp. 222–244). Hershey, PA: IGI Global. doi:10.4018/978-1-5225-3111-1.ch008

Toulassi, B. (2017). Educational Administration and Leadership in Francophone Africa: 5 Dynamics to Change Education. In S. Mukerji & P. Tripathi (Eds.), *Handbook of Research on Administration, Policy, and Leadership in Higher Education* (pp. 20–45). Hershey, PA: IGI Global. doi:10.4018/978-1-5225-0672-0.ch002

Umair, S., & Sharif, M. M. (2018). Predicting Students Grades Using Artificial Neural Networks and Support Vector Machine. In M. Khosrow-Pour, D.B.A. (Ed.), Encyclopedia of Information Science and Technology, Fourth Edition (pp. 5169-5182). Hershey, PA: IGI Global. doi:10.4018/978-1-5225-2255-3.ch449

Vettraino, L., Castello, V., Guspini, M., & Guglielman, E. (2018). Self-Awareness and Motivation Contrasting ESL and NEET Using the SAVE System. In M. Khosrow-Pour, D.B.A. (Ed.), Encyclopedia of Information Science and Technology, Fourth Edition (pp. 1559-1568). Hershey, PA: IGI Global. doi:10.4018/978-1-5225-2255-3.ch135

Related References

Wiemelt, J. (2017). Critical Bilingual Leadership for Emergent Bilingual Students. In I. Management Association (Ed.), Educational Leadership and Administration: Concepts, Methodologies, Tools, and Applications (pp. 1606-1631). Hershey, PA: IGI Global. doi:10.4018/978-1-5225-1624-8.ch074

Wolf, F., Seyfarth, F. C., & Pflaum, E. (2018). Scalable Capacity-Building for Geographically Dispersed Learners: Designing the MOOC "Sustainable Energy in Small Island Developing States (SIDS)". In U. Pandey & V. Indrakanti (Eds.), *Open and Distance Learning Initiatives for Sustainable Development* (pp. 58–83). Hershey, PA: IGI Global. doi:10.4018/978-1-5225-2621-6.ch003

Woodley, X. M., Mucundanyi, G., & Lockard, M. (2017). Designing Counter-Narratives: Constructing Culturally Responsive Curriculum Online. *International Journal of Online Pedagogy and Course Design*, 7(1), 43–56. doi:10.4018/IJOPCD.2017010104

Yell, M. L., & Christle, C. A. (2017). The Foundation of Inclusion in Federal Legislation and Litigation. In C. Curran & A. Petersen (Eds.), *Handbook of Research on Classroom Diversity and Inclusive Education Practice* (pp. 27–52). Hershey, PA: IGI Global. doi:10.4018/978-1-5225-2520-2.ch002

Zinner, L. (2019). Fostering Academic Citizenship With a Shared Leadership Approach. In C. Zhu & M. Zayim-Kurtay (Eds.), *University Governance and Academic Leadership in the EU and China* (pp. 99–117). IGI Global. https://doi.org/10.4018/978-1-5225-7441-5.ch007

About the Contributors

Asli Lidice Gokturk-Saglam is working at University of South-Eastern Norway as a post-doc researcher. She holds a PhD in language teacher education. Her research interests include teacher education, educational technology, as well as assessment. She has been a teacher in EAP settings for more than 24 years.

Ece Sevgi-Sole holds a Ph.D. in Language Assessment from Yeditepe University. She has experience in teaching and testing academic writing, as well as training language teachers and running a university writing center. Currently, she is offering English language courses at University of Milan.

* * *

Imelda Bangun has worked with adult immigrants and refugees for twelve years as an educator and administrator. She has a Ph.D. in Technology in Education and Second Language Acquisition from the University of South Florida. She is currently an ESOL Professor and International Affairs Coordinator at Keiser University and adjunct faculty at Florida Southern College. Her research interests include e-learning, metacognition, motivation, and multiliteracy.

Sao Bui (Sao Thien Bui or Bùi Thiện Sao) works as a language test developer and researcher at the Center for Language Testing and Assessment, University of Languages and International Studies, Vietnam National University, Hanoi. She received her Master's degree in English Education from Korea University, Seoul, Korea. Her research interest includes language testing and assessment, reading comprehension, and learner differences.

Amy Burden is a TESOL and world languages educator and researcher with over 15 years of experience in language teaching and teacher training in higher education. She has teaching experiences in both the USA and The Philippines. She currently works as a multilingual multimodal test development manager for the Center for Applied Linguistics in Washington, DC, USA. Her research interests include integration of technology and language learning as well as gender and ethnicity representations in language learning materials and is the author of the forthcoming book At the Intersections of Gender and Ethnicity in English Language Learning Texts. She holds a Ph.D. in Applied Linguistics from the University of Memphis and a master's degree in Teaching Languages from The University of Southern Mississippi.

About the Contributors

Shree Deepa, an Associate Professor in the Centre for English Language Studies, University of Hyderabad has over 10 articles in various credible academic journals and 2 book chapters in the calendar year 2022. She has also edited a book volume in the same year and delivered more than 30 invited talks at various national and international forums. Her recent works are in the areas of Anthrogogy, inclusive English language classrooms and teacher education. She has completed one project with the British Council on Inclusivity and is currently working on an IoE project with the Sanskrit department on applying Indian Research Methodology to PhD dissertations submitted in India.

Geetha Durairajan has retired as a Professor from the English and Foreign Language University, Hyderabad, India. She is the editor of Dr. N S Prabhu's book, Perceptions of Language Pedagogy published in 2019. Her most recent research interests, publications, and projects are in the areas of anthrogogy and humane constructive language use. Her earlier publications were in the areas of multilingual education and language evaluation. She has taught and supervised several generations of ELT professionals in her 33 years of service, many of whom are now on the faculty of various universities in India and elsewhere. She has delivered many invited talks/ plenaries at national and international forums.

Simona Kalova joined the English language and literature department at the Faculty of Arts, Masaryk University in 2009, after pursuing a career as a language school teacher, and a freelance translator and interpreter. She is an assistant professor and teaches in the Program of Bachelor's Degree Studies. Simona is a teacher and coordinator in a skills-based Practical English course in the first year and also teaches a course focused on eliminating the interference of the mother tongue called Czenglish. She graduated from the Faculty of Arts, Masaryk University and holds an M.A. degree in English and Italian language and literature, and a Ph.D. in the Didactics of Foreign Language (2020). In her research, Simona focuses on aspects of learner language, the role of errors and questions of norm in English language teaching.

Ifigenia Karagkouni is specialized in Teaching Greek as L2. She works for the Ministry of Education, Lifelong Learning and Religious Affairs since 2019. Since 2020 she teaches in classes with children coming from vulnerable social groups. She also participates in Erasmus programs for the educational empowerment of refugee students. In the past she also worked as a teacher at the Association of Greek-Russian Friendship, Letters and Culture in Trikala. She is interested in the Refugee Education and Support Program as well as in the Teaching of Greek as L2 to vulnerable social groups.

Inanc Karagoz has recently received her Ph.D. degree in Technology in Education and Second Language Acquisition at the University of South Florida. She has teaching experience in EFL and ESL in Turkish and American higher education settings. Her research interests include digital social reading, reading engagement, and self-directed learning. Currently, she works as a teacher educator at Bartin University.

Toni Mäkipää works as a postdoctoral researcher in the Faculty of Educational Sciences at the University of Helsinki. His research interests include assessment, assessment literacy, teacher education, foreign language teaching, and self-regulated learning. Mäkipää is a teacher of English, Swedish, and French.

Linda Nepivodova works as a language exam specialist, test developer and teacher trainer at the Department of English and American Studies (Faculty of Arts) and at the Department of English Language and Literature (Faculty of Education) at Masaryk University. She holds a bachelor degree in English and Latin (2004), an M.A. in English language and literature, specialized in testing (2007) and a Ph.D. in Foreign Language Didactics (2018). She is CELTA and DELTA qualified and works as a freelance CELTA tutor. She mainly teaches in the MA teaching degree programmes and her research interests include testing and assessment, especially the comparison of different modes of test administration, error correction and second language acquisition.

Chi Nguyen is an English language teacher at VNU University of Languages and International Studies (ULIS-VNU). She has been involved in curriculum design projects and test item writing projects. She has also worked as a teacher trainer in the training programs for raters and test item writers. She obtained a PhD degree in English teaching methodology at ULIS-VNU. Her research interests include teacher professional development, testing and assessment, and teaching English to young learners.

Nguyen Thi Ngoc Quynh (also known as Quynh Thi Ngoc Nguyen or Quynh Nguyen) holds a PhD in Applied Linguistics from the University of Melbourne, Australia. She is the founding director of the Center for Testing and Assessment at the University of Languages and International Studies, Vietnam National University, Hanoi (ULIS-VNU). She is currently the Director of the Department of Research, Science and Innovation at ULIS-VNU. She is also the Co-President of the Asian Association for Language Assessment (AALA). She has participated as a key person in many national and international projects on education and assessment. She reviews for some journals on second language acquisition and teacher education, and has presented and published on second language education and assessment.

Thao Thi Phuong Nguyen is a lecturer and researcher at VNU University of Languages and International Studies. She earned a Master's degree in English Language Teaching from the University of Southampton, UK. She has participated in research projects on test development and examiner training. Her research interests include testing and assessment, teacher education, and professional development.

Yen Thi Quynh Nguyen (also known as Yen Nguyen) is the director of the Center for Language Testing and Assessment, the University of Languages and International Studies, Vietnam National University – Hanoi (ULIS-VNU). She holds an MA in Teaching English as a Second Language and a PhD in English Language Teacher Education. Her research interests include English linguistics, teaching methodology and language assessment.

Vicky Papachristou is an Assistant Professor of Linguistics at the Humanities Department of CITY College, University of York Europe Campus. She holds a BA in English Language and Literature from the Aristotle University of Thessaloniki, an MA in Phonetics from University College London (UK) and a PhD in Linguistics (Applied Phonetics) from the Aristotle University of Thessaloniki. She has been teaching courses in Phonetics and Phonology, Second/foreign Language Acquisition and Language Teaching Methodology both at an undergraduate and postgraduate level. She has been conducting and supervising research in the fields of Phonetics, pronunciation teaching, ELT and teachers' identity. She

About the Contributors

has presented and participated in a series of events (conferences, symposia, seminars) in Europe. She has also acted as a peer reviewer for academic journals in the field of Linguistics. She is currently the Vice Chair of TESOL Macedonia-Thrace, Northern Greece.

Gladys Quevedo-Camargo holds a PhD in Language Studies as well as the RSA/DELTA – Diploma in English Language Teaching to Adults. She works with English language teaching and teacher education at the Department of Foreign Languages and Translation and at the Applied Linguistics Post-Graduation Program at the University of Brasília (UnB), located in the capital of Brazil. She is co-founder and board member of LAALTA – Latin American Association for Language Testing and Assessment and a member of the BrazTesol Assessment Special Interest Group. She also coordinates the research group Language Academic Literacies in Higher Education - LALES. Her main areas of interest and research are language testing, classroom language assessment and language assessment literacy.

Thomais Rousoulioti holds a PhD in didactics, specialized in teaching and assessment of multilingual students, with emphasis on students of Greek as L2. She works as a Special Teaching Staff at the Department of Italian Language and Literature, Aristotle University of Thessaloniki, Greece (since 2017). She is a fellow Researcher at the Centre for the Greek Language in the division for the Support and Promotion of the Greek Language (since 2010). She is also a member of the Greek Applied Linguistics Association, of EALTA, ALTE and EnA OsloMet.

Maria-Araxi Sachpazian holds a BA in Education from the Aristotle University of Thessaloniki, a CEELT II and the Royal Society of Arts Diploma for Oversees Teachers of English (3 distinctions) from the University of Cambridge. Maria has been a practising English Language Teacher since 1992. She has worked in a variety of Foreign Language Schools. In 2005 she actively started training teachers for the QLS schools and went on to work for Publishing houses and later on for her own company. Since 2013 Maria is the owner and managing director of Input on Education (IoE) a company which specializes in educational management and academic support for foreign language schools. In 2016 Maria started Input for Teachers a branch of Input on Education which helps teachers build a strong portfolio and CV via training and provides teacher placement services. In her career, Maria Sachpazian has led many seminars and presentations for TESOL Macedonia-Thrace, PALSO NORTHERN GREECE (as well as many other PALSO organizations all over Greece), EUROPALSO, IATEFL, IATEFL Poland, IATEFL-BETA Bulgaria. She was the winner of the IATEFL Leadership and Management Special Interest Group scholarship for 2017 for her session entitled Cognitive distortions and the LTO Manager, which was presented in Glasgow in April 2017. Maria has been a member of TESOL MACEDONIA – THRACE, NORHTERN GREECE, since before she started teaching actively. She is the current chairperson of TESOL Macedonia-Thrace, Northern Greece and before that she had server on three different boards of TESOL MACEDONIA – THRACE, NORTHERN GREECE as Secretary General (1997-99, 1999-2001) and as Vice Chair (2005-2007). Maria has published teaching materials with McMillan, Burlington Books and Pearson Longman. She is currently an external teacher trainer for Oxford University Press.

Olga Safonkina is an Associate Professor at the Faculty of Foreign Languages, National Research Mordovia State University (Russia). She holds a BA in English Linguistics, MA in Social Studies, Central European University, and a PhD in Philosophy. She has been teaching courses in Second/foreign Language Acquisition, Testing and Assesment and Language Teaching Methodology at undergraduate level, Business English and Cross-Cultural Communication at postgraduate level. She has been conducting and supervising research. She has also been an item writer for National Test in English (Russia) and is affiliated with National Association of Teachers of English (NATE, Russia). Dr. Safonkina has experience in external quality assurance in the capacity of an institutional/program evaluation expert in Arts and Humanities. Also, she organizes, coordinates, and contributes to Erasmus+ projects including support in preparation of applications, project management, and project reporting.

Susan Sheehan is a Senior Lecturer in TESOL at the University of Huddersfield. She researches issues related to English language assessment and teacher education. She has presented on these subjects at various national and international conferences. Susan supervises doctoral candidates on topics related to assessment. She is the Course Leader for the BA TESOL course and also works with MA TESOL students.

Anna Soltyska is a member of academic staff at the Ruhr University in Bochum, Germany, and coordinates the English programme at the University Language Centre. Her current research interests include assessment literacy in post-COVID era, various aspects of assessment-related malpractice and the impact of AI on language learning, teaching and assessment in low- and high-stake contexts.

Thuy Thai is a PhD holder in language testing and assessment at School of Education and Professional Development, University of Huddersfield, the UK. Her main interests are speaking assessment, rater cognition, and classroom-based assessment.

Hien Tran Thi Thu is a lecturer-researcher at the University of Languages and International Studies, Vietnam National University, Hanoi. Her authored works are mainly in applied linguistics and language teaching. Her interests vary with ESP, advertising language and professional development. Recently, Hien has focused on CLIL, language testing and assessment.

Dina Tsagari is a Professor, Department of Primary and Secondary Teacher Education, Oslo Metropolitan University, Norway. Her research interests include language testing and assessment, LAL in particular, materials design and evaluation, differentiated instruction, multilingualism, distance education and learning difficulties. She coordinates research groups, e.g. CBLA SIG – EALTA, EnA OsloMet and is involved in EU-funded and other research projects.

Bruna Lourenção Zocaratto is a professor at the Federal Institute of Education, Science, and Technology in of Brasilia. She holds a Ph.D. in Education from the University of Brasilia and has recently completed her postdoctoral research in Applied Linguistics, which focused on the effects of online feedback on English language teachers in their education process. She writes and researches widely on issues of assessment of, for, and as learning, assessment literacy and English language teacher education, language assessors, and feedback. She is a member of the Language Academic Literacy in Higher Education (LALES) research group and the leader of the Assessment Literacy, Teacher Education, and Teaching Practice (LAFOPE) research group.

Index

A

Academic Integrity 22-25, 27, 33-38, 180, 196, 202
Academic Misconduct 21, 38, 207
Alternative Assessment 58, 60, 84, 97, 119, 121-123, 126, 129-131, 133-134, 136, 138, 151, 187, 195
Antiracist Assessment 119, 125, 132, 141
Asoe Inoue 119, 124, 136
Assessment Literacy 81, 94, 142-147, 155-158, 160, 162-163, 165, 167-169, 178-182, 184-186, 190, 192-193, 195-196, 198, 200-208
Assessment of Integrated Language Skills 208
Assessment Practice 69, 77, 126, 162, 164, 167, 177
Automated Writing Evaluation (AWE) 10, 19-20

C

Collaborative Learning 9, 18, 42, 115, 117, 160
Collaborative Reading 1, 5-6, 13, 18-19
Community of Practice 120, 144-145, 160, 169, 178
Computer-based Test 21, 27, 29, 33, 38
Continuous Professional Development 120, 160
Course Evaluation 142-144, 146-147, 152, 154, 156, 159-160
Covid-19 2, 21-22, 26, 36-37, 40-41, 44, 56-57, 59, 65, 80, 82-83, 88-89, 97, 99-101, 103-104, 137, 157, 159, 165-167, 170, 179-182, 185, 187-188, 191-192, 204, 206-207
Critical Thinking 1-3, 5-6, 8-9, 11, 14, 16, 18, 32, 65, 95, 119, 126-127, 132, 136, 144, 174

D

Digital Assessment 162-163, 167, 170, 175-176, 178, 202
Digital Classroom 39, 60, 175
Digital Storytelling 10-11, 14-15, 20
Distance Education 19, 37, 56, 60, 82-83, 94, 116, 142, 179

Dynamic Assessment 82-85, 94-98, 119, 123, 126-127, 129-130, 136-137, 139-140

E

E-learning 2, 8, 18, 56-57, 59, 83, 95, 130, 139, 142, 144, 146, 157-160
Electronic Village Online 145
Emergency Remote Assessment (ERA) 184, 188, 204, 208
Emergency Remote Teaching (ERT) 40-41, 56, 58-60, 65, 71, 167, 176, 178, 180, 182, 184-185, 187, 203-208
English for Academic Purposes (EAP) 1-2, 20, 188, 204
English Language Teaching 16, 39, 44, 57, 59-60, 115, 120
E-Portfolio 8, 39, 42-44, 46-48, 50-62
Experiential Learning 119-123, 125-141

F

Foreign Language 9, 18-19, 37, 39-40, 42-44, 53-56, 58-60, 69, 82, 95, 97, 109, 117, 121-122, 160, 165, 175, 182, 188, 190, 202, 206-207
Formative Assessment 1-3, 5-9, 11-14, 16-20, 39-43, 47-48, 52-57, 60-61, 66-69, 74-75, 77, 79-81, 104-105, 107, 139-140, 154-155, 179-181, 186, 188, 200-201, 208
Formative Reading Assessment 1, 3
Formative Writing Assessment 8, 14, 56

G

Group Dynamics 99-100, 106, 109-110, 114

L

Language Assessment 2, 15, 27, 35, 38, 54, 57, 78, 98, 114, 117, 122, 137-138, 140, 142-147, 150-

151, 153, 155-160, 162-164, 167-168, 170-171, 179-180, 182, 186, 188-189, 194-195, 203-208
Language Assessment Literacy 142-147, 156-157, 160, 163, 167-168, 179, 182, 186, 203-208
Language Assessors 64
Language Potentiality 99-101, 112-113, 115
Language Teacher Education 64, 77, 121

M

Mediation 82-91, 93-94, 96, 123, 140, 198
Metacognitive Reflection 124, 127, 132
More Knowledgeable Other 20

O

Online Assessment 3, 13-14, 36, 40-41, 44, 55-56, 60, 71, 102, 163-167, 170, 172, 177-178, 181, 184-185, 188, 193, 195-197, 200-203, 207-208
Online Assessment Tools 167
Online Course Evaluation 142, 146-147
Online EAP 1
Online Feedback 11, 17, 20, 64-79, 82, 167, 176
Online Learning 2, 7, 22, 40, 48, 54-55, 58, 62, 65, 72, 80, 116, 119, 122, 128, 135-137, 142-144, 152, 157-160, 163-166, 177, 180, 187-188, 205
Online Learning Platforms 142, 160
Online Portfolio 39
Online Quizzes 2-3, 12, 14, 40, 175
Oral 22-23, 26-27, 29-30, 32-36, 65, 71-72, 75-76, 117-118, 136, 149, 160, 164, 194, 196

P

Pandemic Pedagogy 187, 200
Participant Perspective 142, 146
Plurilingualism 99, 113
Pre-Service English Teachers 64, 72, 76
Proficiency Exam 22, 25, 27, 38

R

Remote Teaching 40-41, 56, 58-60, 65-66, 71, 81, 164-167, 176, 178, 180, 182, 184-185, 187-188, 190, 197, 200-208
Rubric Design 125-126, 129, 134-136

S

Scenario-Based Assessment 99-100, 104, 114-115, 117
Second Language 15-18, 20, 57, 60, 79, 82-83, 88, 94-96, 102, 111, 114, 116-117, 123, 140, 158, 166, 180-181, 204-206
Self-Learning 39-40, 43, 50, 53, 60
Self-Monitoring 40, 43, 47, 50, 52-53
Social Annotation 3-6, 13, 20
Summative Assessment 2, 8, 41, 103, 150, 208
Supervised Setting 21, 38

T

Teacher Education 15, 37, 64-66, 69-70, 77-78, 80, 113, 121, 137, 139-140, 142-143, 145, 154, 170, 185, 188-190, 200-202, 206-207
Teacher Professional Development 145, 202
Teacher's Intervention 85
Teaching Greek 82, 86
Teaching Methodology 54
Teaching of English 44, 53, 58
Telecollaboration 20, 138
Tertiary Education 21-22, 41, 95
TESOL 16, 36, 59, 115, 117, 124, 136, 138-140, 145, 181

U

Unsupervised Setting 21, 38

V

Virtual Context 68, 78, 81

Z

Zone of Proximal Development 3, 5, 15, 20, 84, 87, 94
Connectivism 39

Recommended Reference Books

IGI Global's reference books are available in three unique pricing formats:
Print Only, E-Book Only, or Print + E-Book.

Order direct through IGI Global's Online Bookstore at
www.igi-global.com or through your preferred provider.

Online Distance Learning Course Design and Multimedia in E-Learning
ISBN: 9781799897064
EISBN: 9781799897088
© 2022; 302 pp.
List Price: US$ 215

Global and Transformative Approaches Toward Linguistic Diversity
ISBN: 9781799889854
EISBN: 9781799889878
© 2022; 383 pp.
List Price: US$ 215

New Perspectives on Using Accreditation to Improve Higher Education
ISBN: 9781668451953
EISBN: 9781668451960
© 2022; 300 pp.
List Price: US$ 195

Impact of School Shootings on Classroom Culture, Curriculum, and Learning
ISBN: 9781799852001
EISBN: 9781799852018
© 2022; 355 pp.
List Price: US$ 215

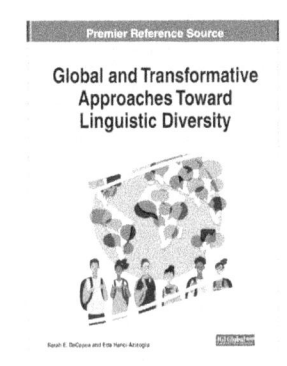

Modern Reading Practices and Collaboration Between Schools, Family, and Community
ISBN: 9781799897507
EISBN: 9781799897521
© 2022; 304 pp.
List Price: US$ 215

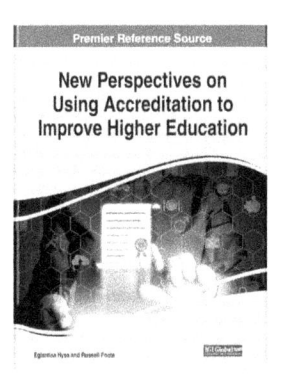

Designing Effective Distance and Blended Learning Environments in K-12
ISBN: 9781799868293
EISBN: 9781799868316
© 2022; 389 pp.
List Price: US$ 215

Do you want to stay current on the latest research trends, product announcements, news, and special offers?
Join IGI Global's mailing list to receive customized recommendations, exclusive discounts, and more.
Sign up at: **www.igi-global.com/newsletters**.

Publisher of Timely, Peer-Reviewed Inclusive Research Since 1988

IGI Global
PUBLISHER of TIMELY KNOWLEDGE

www.igi-global.com   Sign up at www.igi-global.com/newsletters   facebook.com/igiglobal   twitter.com/igiglobal   linkedin.com/igiglobal

Ensure Quality Research is Introduced to the Academic Community

Become an Evaluator for IGI Global Authored Book Projects

The overall success of an authored book project is dependent on quality and timely manuscript evaluations.

Applications and Inquiries may be sent to:
development@igi-global.com

Applicants must have a doctorate (or equivalent degree) as well as publishing, research, and reviewing experience. Authored Book Evaluators are appointed for one-year terms and are expected to complete at least three evaluations per term. Upon successful completion of this term, evaluators can be considered for an additional term.

If you have a colleague that may be interested in this opportunity, we encourage you to share this information with them.

Easily Identify, Acquire, and Utilize Published Peer-Reviewed Findings in Support of Your Current Research

IGI Global OnDemand

Purchase Individual IGI Global OnDemand Book Chapters and Journal Articles

For More Information:
www.igi-global.com/e-resources/ondemand/

Browse through 150,000+ Articles and Chapters!

Find specific research related to your current studies and projects that have been contributed by international researchers from prestigious institutions, including:

- Massachusetts Institute of Technology
- HARVARD UNIVERSITY
- COLUMBIA UNIVERSITY IN THE CITY OF NEW YORK
- Australian National University

- Accurate and Advanced Search
- Affordably Acquire Research
- Instantly Access Your Content
- Benefit from the InfoSci Platform Features

It really provides an excellent entry into the research literature of the field. It presents a manageable number of highly relevant sources on topics of interest to a wide range of researchers. The sources are scholarly, but also accessible to 'practitioners'.

- Ms. Lisa Stimatz, MLS, University of North Carolina at Chapel Hill, USA

Interested in Additional Savings?

Subscribe to
IGI Global OnDemand *Plus*

Learn More

Acquire content from over 128,000+ research-focused book chapters and 33,000+ scholarly journal articles for as low as US$ 5 per article/chapter (original retail price for an article/chapter: US$ 37.50).

7,300+ E-BOOKS.
ADVANCED RESEARCH.
INCLUSIVE & AFFORDABLE.

IGI Global e-Book Collection

- **Flexible Purchasing Options** (Perpetual, Subscription, EBA, etc.)
- Multi-Year Agreements with **No Price Increases** Guaranteed
- **No Additional Charge** for Multi-User Licensing
- No Maintenance, Hosting, or Archiving Fees
- Continually Enhanced & Innovated **Accessibility Compliance Features** (WCAG)

Handbook of Research on Digital Transformation, Industry Use Cases, and the Impact of Disruptive Technologies
ISBN: 9781799877127
EISBN: 9781799877141

Handbook of Research on New Investigations in Artificial Life, AI, and Machine Learning
ISBN: 9781799886860
EISBN: 9781799886877

Handbook of Research on Future of Work and Education
ISBN: 9781799882756
EISBN: 9781799882770

Research Anthology on Physical and Intellectual Disabilities in an Inclusive Society (4 Vols.)
ISBN: 9781668435427
EISBN: 9781668435434

Innovative Economic, Social, and Environmental Practices for Progressing Future Sustainability
ISBN: 9781799895909
EISBN: 9781799895923

Applied Guide for Event Study Research in Supply Chain Management
ISBN: 9781799889694
EISBN: 9781799889717

Mental Health and Wellness in Healthcare Workers
ISBN: 9781799888130
EISBN: 9781799888147

Clean Technologies and Sustainable Development in Civil Engineering
ISBN: 9781799898108
EISBN: 9781799898122

Request More Information, or Recommend the IGI Global e-Book Collection to Your Institution's Librarian

For More Information or to Request a Free Trial, Contact IGI Global's e-Collections Team: eresources@igi-global.com | 1-866-342-6657 ext. 100 | 717-533-8845 ext. 100

Are You Ready to Publish Your Research?

IGI Global
PUBLISHER of TIMELY KNOWLEDGE

IGI Global offers book authorship and editorship opportunities across 11 subject areas, including business, computer science, education, science and engineering, social sciences, and more!

Benefits of Publishing with IGI Global:

- Free one-on-one editorial and promotional support.
- Expedited publishing timelines that can take your book from start to finish in less than one (1) year.
- Choose from a variety of formats, including Edited and Authored References, Handbooks of Research, Encyclopedias, and Research Insights.
- Utilize IGI Global's eEditorial Discovery® submission system in support of conducting the submission and double-blind peer review process.
- IGI Global maintains a strict adherence to ethical practices due in part to our full membership with the Committee on Publication Ethics (COPE).
- Indexing potential in prestigious indices such as Scopus®, Web of Science™, PsycINFO®, and ERIC – Education Resources Information Center.
- Ability to connect your ORCID iD to your IGI Global publications.
- Earn honorariums and royalties on your full book publications as well as complimentary content and exclusive discounts.

Join Your Colleagues from Prestigious Institutions, Including:

- Australian National University
- Massachusetts Institute of Technology
- Johns Hopkins University
- Harvard University
- Tsinghua University
- Columbia University in the City of New York

Learn More at: www.igi-global.com/publish
or Contact IGI Global's Aquisitions Team at: acquisition@igi-global.com

Ingram Content Group UK Ltd.
Milton Keynes UK
UKHW030825180723
425342UK00012B/434